The Best American History Essays 2006

The Best American History Essays 2006

Edited by
Joyce Appleby for the
Organization of American Historians

THE BEST AMERICAN HISTORY ESSAYS 2006
© Edited by Joyce Appleby for the Organization of American Historians, 2006.

All rights reserved. No part of this book may be used or reproduced in any manner whatsoever without written permission except in the case of brief quotations embodied in critical articles or reviews.

First published in 2006 by
PALGRAVE MACMILLAN™
175 Fifth Avenue, New York, N.Y. 10010 and
Houndmills, Basingstoke, Hampshire, England RG21 6XS
Companies and representatives throughout the world.

PALGRAVE MACMILLAN is the global academic imprint of the Palgrave Macmillan division of St. Martin's Press, LLC and of Palgrave Macmillan Ltd.
Macmillan® is a registered trademark in the United States, United Kingdom and other countries. Palgrave is a registered trademark in the European Union and other countries.

ISBN-13: 978–1–4039–6840–1 (Hardcover)
ISBN-13: 978–1–4039–6852–4 (Paperback)
ISBN-10: 1–4039–6840–3 (alk. paper)
ISBN-10: 1–4039–6852–7 (pbk.)

Library of Congress Cataloging-in-Publication Data

The best American history essays of 2006 / edited by Joyce Appleby for the Organization of American Historians.
p. cm.
Includes bibliographical references and index.
ISBN 1–4039–6840–3 (alk. paper)—ISBN 1–4039–6852–7 (pbk.: alk. paper)
1. United States—History. 2. American essays. 3. United States—Historiography. I. Organization of American Historians.

E178.6.O15 2006
973—dc22 2005054649

A catalogue record for this book is available from the British Library.

Design by Newgen Imaging Systems (P) Ltd., Chennai, India.

First edition: April 2006

10 9 8 7 6 5 4 3 2 1

Printed in the United States of America.

Contents

List of Illustrations

Introduction

Joyce Appleby

In the last ten years, books about American history have had a strong readership, many ending up on the best-seller list. Especially popular have been studies of the founding era. One after the other, histories of the War for Independence and politics under the new U.S. Constitution have tumbled from the country's presses. The conflicts generated in the hothouse of George Washington's first administration have been refought in dozens of new publications. Biographies of the Founding Fathers have added to this avalanche of books. While unique in its success, David McCullough's *John Adams* sold two million copies, an indication of just how much the reading public has succumbed to Founders chic, a catchphrase for the phenomenal success of studies of the revolutionary period.

Echoes of the popularity of the founding era resound from the battlefields of the Civil War, the two world wars, and the war in Vietnam as well. For many general readers, presidents, wars, and high politics make for good reading. This interest in the nation's founding and the battles to preserve its integrity is estimable, but there's lots more that's fascinating about the American past.

This book brings to the public ten of the best articles in American history published between the summers of 2004 and 2005. President James Horton of the Organization of American Historians chose a group of scholars representing a breadth of fields to select the articles.[1] The volume itself aims to further the OAH's mission of promoting excellence in scholarship, teaching, and the presentation of American history and encouraging wide discussion of historical questions. In preparation for making the selection of articles for this volume, the nine-person committee canvassed over three-hundred learned and popular journals ranging from state historical magazines to specialized journals in topics like law, medicine, and agriculture to periodicals devoted to groups such as native Americans, women, and African Americans. Each member could nominate no more than four articles from those he or she had read, and the committee acted as a whole to winnow the group of contenders to ten.

A survey like this demonstrates the quite staggering amount of research, reflection, and interpretation of American history that goes on every year. Quite surprisingly, despite their different fields of expertise, committee members converged readily on the articles reprinted in this volume. No article had all the virtues that the committee sought in equal measure, but every one did possess the originality, clarity, coherence, accessibility, and excellence of thought and research the committee was looking for.

While introducing readers to fresh research about the past, these articles also showcase the different kinds of questions that today's historians are asking. Fresh investigations lead to different patches of the past and turn into evidence parts of that inert mass of material left over from past living. So while a good deal of historical writing revisits old scholarship, historians regularly discover surprising caches of records and remains from bygone years.

American history itself has a history which readers of this volume will find particularly interesting. Not only have new topics been introduced, but the backgrounds of the historians themselves have changed. During the nineteenth century studies of the country's past served as handmaidens in nation-building. History was supposed to be edifying; historians wrote to remind Americans, and especially schoolchildren, that the United States stood for something special. Always contrasting the United States with Europe, historians emphasized the country's fight against tyranny—multiple tyrannies, in fact—from an arrogant mother country, aristocratic traditions, and powerful European states that treated their male subjects as cannon fodder and the female ones as the producers of that fodder.

With the emphasis placed on the politics of achieving independence and maintaining the union, historians stayed pretty close to what Edmund Wilson labeled "patriotic gore." They wrote about Europeans struggling to maintain a toehold in the New World, the resistance movement that turned into a Revolution, the battles of the War for Independence, and debates over ratification of the U.S. Constitution. The country's population was less diverse then than now, and white, male scholars confined their attention to what their European ancestors had done. It made for a homogenized, national narrative.

The Civil War became the focus of histories in the closing decades of the century, but again it was the white northerners and their southern cousins who attracted most attention, even though the war ended with the abolition of slavery. American history celebrated the nation's successes and glorified its heroes—the presidents, senators, generals, and diplomats who had served the nation. Expansion into the West was viewed not as a war on the indigenous tribes, but rather as a fulfillment of a manifest destiny given to those states united along the Atlantic seaboard to create a continental nation "from sea to shining sea."

By the early twentieth century this patriotic way of viewing the United States became itself the object of political controversy. The scholars associated with the Progressive political movement—Charles Beard, Carl Becker, Fredrick Jackson Turner—redefined their subject. Moving beyond history as "past politics," they expanded the range of historical curiosity to include economic activities and relations between farmers and debtors, bankers and creditors, manufacturers and their employees as well as the diverse sections with their special interests. Business records, census reports, farmers' account books, and commercial newspapers became important sources of information.

Adding economic details to the political narrative of the nation meant recognizing conflict in daily life and not just in disputes over policy or about going to war. The Progressive historians made the dissidents themselves heroes in these ongoing domestic battles. Their avid chronicling of vested interests at play in politics reached out—in an irreverent gesture—to include the much admired Founding Fathers.

In *An Economic Interpretation of the United States Constitution*, Charles Beard argued that the Founding Fathers had been motivated more by their pocketbooks than their principles. In 1913 when the book was published, Beard enjoyed enormous, national popularity, so his book was something of a bombshell. While a later cohort of historians challenged his findings, historians at the time set off on a quest for the role that economic interests had played in the American past.

Two decades after World War II, scholarship took another, novel turn. The Russian success in launching Sputnik aroused the country to the seriousness of its rivalry with the Soviet Union. Higher education in the United States expanded quickly and dramatically. A new generation of historians emerged—most of them veterans encouraged by the GI Bill to pursue advanced degrees, many of them second- and third-generation immigrants or African Americans. Joined by women, these newly minted scholars invaded college history departments which had been the preserve of upper middle-class, male WASPs.

Reflecting the ethnic and racial diversity in the nation at large, these historians turned away from political and economic topics to study society itself. European academic influences had introduced a new kind of social history—fresh in scope, style, topics, methods, and questions. The nature of society—its integrative mechanisms, its systems for distributing power, authority, and respect, its ideological repertoire—furnished them with compelling questions. In taking up these themes, social historians left behind the older preoccupations with patriotism and Progressive politics. But there was an inevitably political component in their work, for they developed knowledge that could not easily fit into the imperative that the history of the United States be told as the history of the progress of the United States.

The computer facilitated these new social historians in their search for the details of the lives of ordinary Americans captured through the quantitative analysis of long-term data sets like the vital records kept by cities, counties, and the U.S. Bureau of the Census. Soon there was abundant research on slaves and not just slavery, women and not just the suffrage movement, immigrants and not just immigration, laborers and not just the union movement. Textbooks changed to include this new cast of characters—many of them unsung heroes—most of them undistinguished men and women whose lives gave texture and meaning to those of the long celebrated.

In the past score of years, the study of culture has engaged American historians. Drawing upon the theories of cultural anthropologists, historians are now fascinated by the way that the loose association of taboos, injunctions, tastes, and beliefs that we call culture influence behavior and characterize whole countries or—in a country like ours—distinguish groups within the nation. While culture involves deeply internalized assumptions, its communicative systems are social, sending out messages in dress, gesture, speech, spectacle, and architecture, while infusing all institutions with rituals. Because the study of cultural forms focuses upon details, cultural history has introduced microhistories which are necessarily truncated in time and scope because of the density of the topic, as distinguished from the macrohistory that takes a whole country through decades as a subject.

American historians when they think about their profession tend to reexamine the way that successive groups of scholars have written about the United States. The differences in approach, emphasis, perspective, and interpretation intrigue them. This interest often makes people who aren't historians nervous. The interpretive aspect of history writing disconcerts them, for they assume that somehow the past lingers on to force the hand of historians to write about it just as it happened.

Public opinion favors a view of the past as controlling historians, overwhelming them with incontrovertible evidence. The reverse is actually the case. Historians direct the conversation with the past. They ask the questions, often generated by contemporary concerns, but they are constrained by the evidence their questions take them to.

No one has a retrospective camera trained on the past. It's gone in a second and only becomes history when someone attempts to reconstruct that second. Even the memories, material traces, and written records that linger on after an event become evidence only when someone asks a question that leads him or her to them. It's hard to deal with the disappearance of the past because we know that things happened and that their consequences are going to affect subsequent events. The fact that only through further study can those consequences be determined becomes disquieting.

Large segments of the public are peculiarly resistant to the idea of historical revisions, even if based on new research. Turned into the pejorative "ism" of revisionism, new scholarship is often considered the result of arbitrary interpretive decisions rather than the normal follow-up to fresh findings. We never hear laments about revisionism in chemistry or economics. We expect those learned fields to be transformed over time with new investigations or new models of reality, but changes in a familiar historic narrative based on new research are often met with dismay.

Some parents become angry when they discover the addition of women, blacks, workers, or immigrants in their children's textbooks, particularly since their stories of struggles in the United States cast the country in a negative light.

Confronted with new interpretations of the American past, people tend to blurt out, "But aren't there historical facts?" Don't historians form their narrative accounts from facts and don't these facts stay the same from generation to generation, even though the authors themselves might change? Yes, there are historical facts, but they aren't very interesting, and they rarely tell us what we want to know about the past.

Carl Becker used Julius Caesar's crossing the Rubicon to make this point. That's a fact. Caesar did cross the Rubicon, but thousands of Romans walked through the stream called the Rubicon every day. Caesar's crossing only becomes interesting when it is connected with a broader interpretation of Roman politics. The Roman Senate ordered Caesar to disband his army. When he refused, crossing the Rubicon with his force, he changed the course of Roman history. Assessing the significance of Caesar's crossing makes the fact a memorable one.[2]

The remains of past living never speak for themselves. Others—historians, museum directors, or op-ed writers—must talk for them, sorting them out as they link them to causes and influences while judging their importance and relevance. And the facts that we care about are always attached to larger themes. Facts consist of established statements about the past like "George Washington was born on February 22nd." (Actually he was born on February 11th, but the date was pushed ahead 11 days after the Gregorian reform of the calendar in 1756.) What we want to know about Caesar and Washington has to do with their actions, their motives, what they thought they were doing, and their responses to the flow of events swirling around them, all information that comes laced with interpretations and analyses.

While these ruminations pertain to all history writing, the history of one's own country is even more complicated. Like all histories, national history springs from the human fascination with self-discovery, from persistent concerns about the nature of existence and the social matrix in which it takes places. But, with American national history, a relatively open-ended search about the past collides with the vigilant censors who see history as the cultivator of patriotic pride. Take the case of the National History Standards developed by professional historians in cooperation with history teachers in the schools. Their publication in 1994 prompted an outburst from many public figures who felt that the heroes of the American past were being shoved aside to make room for those previously excluded.

The brouhaha passed over quickly, leaving an awareness that historical knowledge, in the United States at least, has a psychological—even political—dimension that other subjects do not possess. The history we know is the history we learned in school. Changes in the story line brought in after that period in our lives disturb us. Because Americans are bound together by what they think the country has stood for in the past, challenges to a rosy view of the nation's history become controversial. In a backhanded way these responses to new historical scholarship point to the importance accorded to history. People want students to be able to remember the history that they were taught in school. Newspapers frequently run articles about how little young people know about the past. Has any reporter thought to investigate how much young people retain from their mathematics, literature, or physics classes? It's historical knowledge that counts because it is deemed essential to forming sound opinions, to behaving as responsible citizens, and to being ambassadors of goodwill for the United States.

The articles collected in this book exemplify many of the themes just talked about. The continuing importance of the founding era is reflected in Joseph Ellis's, "Inventing the Presidency" and Woody Holton's " 'Divide et impera': *Federalist 10* in a Larger Sphere." Historians sometimes bring a fresh understanding of a very old topic to the current reading public. Such is the case in Ellis's "Inventing the Presidency."[3] When George Washington was elected the first president under the U.S. Constitution in 1789 everything about the new government was undefined and the capital city itself temporary. Ellis deftly shows how Washington relied upon his experiences as proprietor of a large plantation and commander in chief of the Continental Army to govern the country. He established the presidential cabinet and held receptions to impress the federal officials and local elite in New York City. Both his dignity and his tendency to become irked by political wrangling set important precedents. The very adulation that Americans showered on Washington raised fears that his grandeur would overwhelm the simple forms most people felt most compatible with a republic.

After the draft Constitution was reported out of the Philadelphia convention in September 1787, Alexander Hamilton, John Jay, and James Madison put their heads together to plan a series of newspaper articles that would explain the intricacies of the new document to voters ready to elect delegates to state ratifying conventions. From the initial reception of *The Federalist Papers* published under the pseudonym of Publius, the tenth out of the total of 88 essays stood out because it presented a powerful explanation of why the new Constitution would preserve democracy while stabilizing the union of states. Historians, political scientists, judges, and law scholars have probed *Federalist 10* ever since.

In it, James Madison—often called the Father of the Constitution—maintained that "enlarging the sphere" in a federal nation would preserve democracy better than the existing confederation of sovereign states. Now 218 years later, Woody Holton offers a fresh interpretation of *Federalist 10*. Examining the debate then about the optimal size of electoral districts, he maintains that Madison and others feared popular enthusiasm for tax relief and sought to protect property and the eminent men who held lots of it. While traditional in its approach to subject and evidence, Holton's " 'Divide et Impera': *Federalist 10* in a Larger Sphere" confirms the importance of revisiting even the most written-about topics in our history.[4]

The nineteenth century is represented in this collection by Leslie A. Schwalm's " 'Overrun with Free Negroes': Emancipation and Wartime

Migration in the Upper Midwest" and Carl Osthaus's "The Work Ethic of Plain Folk: Labor and Religion in the Old South." Both excellent articles reveal the historian's truth that a sharply focused study can often throw the best light on a sweeping historical theory. A hundred years ago a German philosopher, Max Weber, wrote a provocative essay whose thesis is captured in its title, *The Protestant Ethic and the Spirit of Capitalism*. Until that time, scholars had focused on material factors in explaining the emergence of entrepreneurial economies in the late seventeenth century. Weber insisted that it took a new ethic to triumph over habitual mores and traditional modes of thought. Weber found it in the rise of Protestant churches with their bracing interpretation of Christianity. Applying Weber's theory to the United States, scholars would be more likely to look for these capitalist-promoting values in the northern states, but Osthaus has discovered their presence among the plain people of the South.[5]

Most scholars looking at the impact of the emancipation of slaves during the Civil War and after the passage of the Thirteenth Amendment have concentrated on the South and the border states. This is quite natural since slavery had been abolished in the North, state by state, at the end of the eighteenth century. By following the liberation of slaves into the Midwest, Leslie Schwalm in " 'Overrun with Free Negroes': Emancipation and Wartime Migration in the Upper Midwest" finds a mixed reception to freedmen and freedwomen.[6] There were resonances of the southern position that a biracial society without slavery was fraught with dangers while many in states like Illinois, Iowa, and Ohio worked to end discriminatory legislation and create openings for freedmen as citizens.

Danielle L. McGuire's " 'It was Like all of Us Had Been Raped': Sexual Violence, Community Mobilization, and the African American Freedom Struggle" explores the role that the rape of black women by southern white men played in the domination and subjection of African Americans, stretching from the centuries of slavery to the eve of the civil rights movement.[7] Using the successful prosecution of four white rapists by an all-white jury in Florida as a pivotal moment, McGuire explores the dramatic assertion by a succession of black women of their rights to personal autonomy. Treating rape like lynching and murder as a "tool of psychological and physical intimidation," she reveals its power as an animating force behind the civil rights movement.

Juxtaposing the Sun Belt with its bright suburbs against the Rust Belt with its sad remnants of vanishing industries, Eric Avila, in "Popular Culture in the Age of White Flight: Film Noir, Disneyland, and the Cold War (Sub)Urban Imaginary," traces the spatial transformation of American society in the decades after World War II.[8] By looking at popular forms of entertainment such as movies and theme parks as indicators of despair or optimism, he illuminates how attitudes and fears fused into powerful motives for moving out of the city. With fascinating detail, Avila confirms the historian's capacity to discover unexpected connections in the past.

The U.S. Supreme Court 1948 decision, *Shelly v. Kraemer* ruled that restrictive covenants written into real estate contracts to restrict the sale of houses to white buyers could not be enforced, but white homeowners continued to discriminate as Charlotte Brooks shows so well in "Sing Sheng vs. Southwood: Residential Integration in Cold War California."[9] After receiving threatening letters about his prospective purchase of a house in a white neighborhood, Sing Sheng, a Chinese American in San Francisco, called for an informal vote about his move among the homeowners in Southwood. He lost the vote, but the incident drew nationwide attention and positive expressions of support for Sing Sheng's quest for acceptance. Brooks embeds this story in the widest context possible, showing how American foreign policy initiatives in Asia nudged white Americans toward a more critical view of housing discrimination.

One of the most fascinating, taxing, and rewarding efforts historians undertake is tracking down elusive clues about historical figures. This is what Ralph Luker does in "Murder and Biblical Memory: The Legend of Vernon Johns." Johns was a legendary black preacher who preceded Martin Luther King, Jr. as pastor of the Dexter Avenue Baptist Church in Montgomery, Alabama.[10] He was also King's forerunner in the civil rights movement about to enflame the South in the 1960s. Johns had not been neglected in civil rights histories or biographies of King, but many of the tales told by people, including his family members and himself, proved inaccurate. An experienced scholar in African American history, Luker identified the telltale signs of fabrications, exaggerations, and composite stories. With great skill he takes the reader along with him as ferrets out the truth about Johns, his father, grandfathers—white and black—and the exploits that made him seem larger than life to his peers in the black ministry at midcentury.

While the nation's attention was focused on the brutal response to the Birmingham civil rights protesters in spring of 1963, demonstrations by black activists working with the Congress of Racial Equality and the National Association for the Advancement of Colored People in Philadelphia stirred the Kennedy and eventually, Nixon administrations to use executive authority to open up many all-white trades to blacks. Thomas Sugrue's "Affirmative Action from Below: Civil Rights, the Building Trades, and the Politics of Racial Equality in the Urban North, 1945–1969" takes exception to the orthodox view that affirmative action was a top-down expansion of the regulatory state. Digging, as historians often do, deeper down in the local records of the past, he finds a struggle over employment discrimination dating back to the Depression, with World War II accelerating the quest for both jobs and freedom.[11]

As many of the articles in this collection demonstrate, American historians have investigated with increasing comprehension and sophistication the nation's dramatic struggle to realize the ideals enunciated in the Declaration of Independence. Matthew D. Lassiter, in "The Suburban Origins of 'Color-Blind' Conservatism: Middle-Class Consciousness in the Charlotte Busing Crisis," charts the emergence of a white backlash to desegregation during the nation's first mandated busing in Charlotte, North Carolina.[12] His story is rich with the details of rhetorical appeals to the middle class goals of respectability and security, the powerful reasoning for equality in education, and the aggressive mobilization of both protagonists and opponents to gain the nation's assent.

A famous Dutch historian, Peter Geyl, described historians as "the guardians of the particular." The authors of these articles certainly conform to that rubric, but it would be a mistake to miss the forest for the trees. In every one of these essays, specific incidents are placed within a highly textured framework. Situations, styles, avenues of communication, cultural imperatives, national policies, and international considerations are all examined for their capacity to make the "micro" say something about the "macro." This is history writing at its best—ten slices of historical scholarship that will endure because of their excellence, while still telling us much about the scholarly concerns of the present.

Notes

Joyce Appleby, professor emerita, UCLA, has served as president of the Organization of American Historians and the American Historical Association. She is the author of several books on the Early Republic, including *Capitalism and a New Social Order: The Jeffersonian Vision of the 1790s, Liberalism and Republicanism in the Historical Imagination,* and *Inheriting the Revolution: The First Generations of Americans.*

1. Members of the committee were John Belohlavek, A.J. Badger, Flannery Burke, David Goldfield, M. Ruth Kelly, Jill Lepore, John Saillant, George Sanchez, and Gordon Wood.
2. Carl Lotus Becker, "What are Historical Facts," in *Detachment and the Writing of History* (Ithaca: Cornell University, 1955), 41–64.
3. *American Heritage* (October 2004): 43–53.
4. *William and Mary Quarterly*, 2nd Series, 62 (April 2005): 175–212.
5. *Journal of Southern History*, 70 (November 2004): 745–782.
6. Leslie A. Schwalm, " 'Overrun with Free Negroes': Emancipation and Wartime Migration in the Upper Midwest," *Civil War History*, 1 (June 2004): 145–174.
7. *Journal of American History*, 91 (December 2004): 906–931.
8. *Journal of Urban History*, 31 (November 2004): 3–22.
9. *Pacific Historical Review*, 73 (August 2004): 463–494.
10. *Virginia Magazine of History and Biography*, 112:4 (2005): 372–418.
11. *Journal of American History*, 91 (June 2004): 145–173.
12. *Journal of Urban History*, 30 (May 2004): 549–582.

Chapter 1

Inventing the Presidency

Joseph Ellis

From *American Heritage*

The Presidency

There were no primaries back then to select presidential candidates, no organized political parties, no orchestrated campaigns, not even any established election procedures. But it really didn't matter, because when the votes of that odd invention called the Electoral College were cast in February of 1789, George Washington had in effect won by acclamation. While no one could agree what kind of republican government the principles of the American Revolution required, all could agree that Washington embodied those principles more fully and fittingly than anyone else. His trip from Mount Vernon to the temporary capital in New York that April was a prolonged coronation ceremony: rose petals strewn in his path, choirs singing his praises to the tune of "God Save the King," and even a laurel wreath lowered onto his noble head. The inauguration was a more republican affair. Washington wore a simple suit of black velvet; and the ceremony itself had to be delayed for almost two weeks until a sufficient number of congressmen arrived. They were all, Washington included, making it up as they went along.

Looking back over two hundred years of the American Presidency, it seems safe to say that no one entered the office with more personal prestige than Washington, and only two Presidents—Abraham Lincoln and Franklin Roosevelt—faced comparable crises. The Civil War and the Great Depression, though now distant in time, remain more recent and raw in our collective memory than the American founding, so we find it easier to appreciate the achievements of Lincoln and Roosevelt. Washington's achievement must be recovered before it can be appreciated, which means that we must recognize that there was no such thing as a viable American nation when he took office as President, that the opening words of the Constitution ("We the people of the United States") expressed a fervent but fragile hope rather than a social reality. The roughly four million settlers spread along the coastline and streaming over the Alleghenies felt their primary allegiance—to the extent they felt any allegiance at all—to local, state, and regional authorities. No republican government had ever before exercised control over a population this diffuse or a land this large, and the prevailing assumption among the best-informed European observers was that, to paraphrase Lincoln's later formulation, a nation so conceived and so dedicated could not endure.

Presiding at the Presidency

Not much happened at the Executive level during the first year of Washington's Presidency, which was exactly the way he wanted it. His official correspondence was dominated by job applications from veterans of the war, former friends, and total strangers. They all received the same republican response—namely, that merit rather than favoritism must determine federal appointments. As for the President himself, it was not clear whether he was taking the helm or merely occupying the bridge. Rumors began to circulate that he regarded his role as primarily ceremonial and symbolic, that after a mere two years he intended to step down, having launched the American ship of state and contributed his personal prestige as ballast on its maiden voyage.

As it turned out, even ceremonial occasions raised troubling questions because no one knew how the symbolic centerpiece of a republic should behave or even what to call him. Vice President John Adams, trying to be helpful, ignited a fiery debate in the Senate by suggesting such regal titles as "His Elective Majesty" and "His Mightiness," which provoked a lethal combination of shock and laughter, as well as the observation that Adams himself should be called "His Rotundity." Eventually the Senate resolved on the most innocuous option available: The President of the United States should be called exactly that. Matters of social etiquette—how the President should interact with the public, where he should be accessible and where insulated—prompted multiple memorandums on the importance of what Alexander Hamilton called "a pretty high tone" that stopped short of secluding the President entirely. The solution was a weekly open house called the levee, part imperial court ceremony with choreographed bows and curtsies, part drop-in parlor social. The levee struck the proper middle note between courtly formality and republican simplicity, though at the expense of becoming a notoriously boring and wholly scripted occasion.

The very awkwardness of the levee fitted Washington's temperament nicely since he possessed a nearly preternatural ability to remain silent while everyone around him was squirming under the pressure to fill that silence with conversation. (Adams later claimed that this "gift of silence" was

Washington's greatest political asset, which Adams deeply envied because he lacked it altogether.) The formal etiquette of the levee and Washington's natural dignity (or was it aloofness?) combined to create a political atmosphere unimaginable in any modern-day national capital. In a year when the French Revolution broke out in violent spasms destined to reshape the entire political landscape of Europe, and the new Congress ratified a Bill of Rights that codified the most sweeping guarantee of individual freedoms ever enacted, no one at the levees expected Washington to comment on those events.

Even matters of etiquette and symbolism, however, could have constitutional consequences, as Washington learned in August of 1789. The treaty-making power of the President required that he seek "the Advice and Consent of the Senate." Washington initially interpreted the phrase to require his personal appearance in the Senate and the solicitation of senatorial opinion on specific treaty provisions in the mode of a large advisory council. But when he brought his proposals for treaties with several Southern Indian tribes to the Senate, the debate became a prolonged shouting match over questions of procedure. The longer the debate went on, the more irritated Washington became. Finally he declared, "This defeats every purpose of my coming here," and abruptly stalked out. From that time on, the phrase *advice and consent* meant something less than direct Executive solicitation of senatorial opinion, and the role of the Senate as an equal partner in the crafting of treaties came to be regarded as a violation of the separation-of-powers principle.

Though he never revisited the Senate, Washington did honor his pledge to visit all the states in the Union. In the fall of 1789 he set off on a tour of New England that carried him through 60 towns and hamlets. Everywhere he went, the residents turned out in droves to glimpse America's greatest hero parading past. And everywhere he went, New Englanders became Americans. Since Rhode Island had not yet ratified the Constitution, he skipped it, then made a separate trip the following summer to welcome the proudly independent latecomer into the new nation. During a visit to the Jewish synagogue in Newport he published an address on religious freedom that turned out to be the most uncompromising endorsement of the principle he ever made. (One must say "made" rather than "wrote" because there is considerable evidence that Thomas Jefferson wrote it.) Whatever sectional suspicions New Englanders might harbor toward that faraway thing called the federal government, when it appeared in their neighborhoods in the form of George Washington, they saluted, cheered, toasted, and embraced it as their own.

The Southern tour was a more grueling affair, covering nearly 2,000 miles during the spring of 1791. Instead of regarding it as a threat to his health, however, Washington described it as a tonic; the real risk, he believed, was the sedentary life of a deskbound President. The entourage of 11 horses included his white parade steed, Prescott, whom he mounted at the edge of each town in order to make an entrance that accorded with the heroic mythology already surrounding his military career. Prescott's hooves were painted and polished before each appearance, and Washington usually brought along his favorite greyhound, mischievously named Cornwallis, to add to the dramatic effect. Like a modern political candidate on the campaign trail, Washington made speeches at each stop that repeated the same platitudinous themes, linking the glory of the War for Independence with the latent glory of the newly established United States. The ladies of Charleston fluttered alongside their fans when Washington took the dance floor; Prescott and the four carriage horses held up despite the nearly impassable or even nonexistent roads; Cornwallis, however, wore out and was buried on the banks of the Savannah River in a brick vault with a marble tombstone that local residents maintained for decades as a memorial to his master's visit. In the end all the states south of the Potomac could say they had seen the palpable version of the flag, Washington himself.

During the Southern tour one of the earliest editorial criticisms of Washington's embodiment of authority appeared in the press. He was being treated at each stop like a canonized American saint, the editorial complained, or perhaps like a demi-god "perfumed by the incense of addresses." The complaint harked back to the primordial fear haunting all republics: "However highly we may consider the character of the Chief Magistrate of the Union, yet we cannot but think the fashionable mode of expressing our attachment . . . favors too much of Monarchy to be used by Republicans, or to be received with pleasure by the President of a Commonwealth."

Such doubts were rarely uttered publicly during the initial years of Washington's Presidency. But they lurked in the background, exposing how double-edged the political imperatives of the American Revolution had become. To secure the revolutionary legacy on the national level required a person who embodied national authority more visibly than any collective body like Congress could convey. Washington had committed himself to playing that role by accepting the Presidency. But at the core of the Revolutionary legacy lay a deep suspicion of any potent projection of political power by a "singular figure." And since the very idea of a republican Chief Executive was a novelty, there was no vocabulary for characterizing such a creature except the verbal tradition surrounding European courts and kings. By playing the part he believed history required, Washington made himself vulnerable to the most virulent apprehensions about monarchical power.

He could credibly claim to be the only person who had earned the right to be trusted with power. He could also argue, as he did to several friends throughout his first term, that no man was more eager for retirement, that he sincerely resented the obligations of his office as it spread a lengthening shadow of public responsibility over his dwindling days on earth. If critics wished to whisper behind his back that he looked too regal riding a white stallion with a leopard-skin cloth and gold-rimmed saddle so be it. He knew he would rather be at Mount Vernon. In the meantime he would play his assigned role as America's presiding presence: as so many toasts in his honor put it, "the man who unites all hearts."

The Great Delegator

Exercising Executive authority called for completely different talents than symbolizing it. Washington's administrative style had evolved through decades of experience as master of Mount Vernon and commander of the Continental Army. (In fact, he had fewer subordinates to supervise as President than he had had in those earlier jobs.) The Cabinet system he installed represented a civilian adaptation of his military staff, with Executive sessions of the Cabinet resembling the councils of war that had provided collective wisdom during crises. As Thomas Jefferson later described it, Washington made himself "the hub of the wheel," with routine business delegated to the department heads at the rim. It was a system that maximized Executive control while also creating essential distance from details. Its successful operation depended upon two skills that Washington had developed over his lengthy career: first, identifying and recruiting talented and ambitious young men, usually possessing formal education superior to his own, then trusting them with considerable responsibility and treating them as surrogate sons in his official family; second, knowing when to remain the hedgehog who keeps his distance and when to become the fox who dives into the details.

On the first score, as a judge of talent, Washington surrounded himself with the most intellectually sophisticated collection of statesmen in American history. His first recruit, James Madison, became his most trusted consultant on judicial and Executive appointments and his unofficial liaison with Congress. The precocious Virginian was then at the peak of his powers, having just completed a remarkable string of triumphs as the dominant force behind the nationalist agenda at the Constitutional Convention and the Virginia ratifying convention, as well as being co-author of *The Federalist Papers*. From his position in the House of Representatives he drafted the address welcoming Washington to the Presidency, then drafted Washington's response to it, making him a one-man shadow government. Soon after the inaugural ceremony he showed Washington his draft of 12 amendments to the Constitution, subsequently reduced to 10 and immortalized as the Bill of Rights. Washington approved the historic proposal without changing a word and trusted Madison to usher it through Congress with his customary proficiency.

One of Madison's early assignments was to persuade his reluctant friend from Monticello to serve as Secretary of State. Thomas Jefferson combined nearly spotless Revolutionary credentials with five years of diplomatic experience in Paris, all buoyed by a lyrical way with words and ideas most famously displayed in his draft of the Declaration of Independence.

Alexander Hamilton was the third member of this talented trinity and probably the brightest of the lot. While Madison and Jefferson had come up through the Virginia school of politics, which put a premium on an understated style that emphasized indirection and stealth, Hamilton had come out of nowhere (actually, impoverished origins in the Caribbean) to display a dashing, out-of-my-way style that imposed itself ostentatiously. As Washington's aide-de-camp during the war, he had occasionally shown himself to be a headstrong surrogate son, always searching for an independent command beyond Washington's shadow. But his loyalty to his mentor was unquestioned, and his affinity for the way he thought was unequaled. Moreover, throughout the 1780s Hamilton had been the chief advocate for fiscal reform as the essential prerequisite for an energetic national government, making him the obvious choice as Secretary of Treasury once Robert Morris had declined.

The inner circle was rounded out by three appointments of slightly lesser luster. Gen. Henry Knox, appointed Secretary of War, had served alongside Washington from Boston to Yorktown and had long since learned to subsume his own personality so thoroughly within his chief's that disagreements became virtually impossible. More than just a cipher, as some critics of Washington's policies later claimed, Knox joined Vice President Adams as a seasoned New England voice within the councils of power. John Jay, the new Chief Justice, added New York's most distinguished legal and political mind to the mix, and also extensive foreign policy experience. As the first Attorney General, Edmund Randolph lacked Jay's gravitas and Knox's experience, but his reputation for endless vacillation was offset by solid political connections within the Tidewater elite, reinforced by an impeccable bloodline. Washington's judgment of the assembled team was unequivocal. "I feel myself supported by able co-adjutors," he observed in June of 1790, "who harmonize extremely well together."

In three significant areas of domestic policy, each loaded with explosive political and constitutional implications, Washington chose to delegate nearly complete control to his "co-adjutors." Although his reasons for maintaining a discreet distance differed in each case, they all reflected his recognition that Executive power still lived under a monarchical cloud of suspicion and could be exercised only selectively. Much like his Fabian role during the war, when he learned to avoid an all-or-nothing battle with the British, choosing when to avoid conflict struck him as the essence of effective Executive leadership.

The first battle he evaded focused on the shape and powers of the federal courts. The Constitution offered even less guidance on the judiciary than it did on the Executive branch. Once again the studied ambiguity reflected apprehension about any projection of federal power that upset the compromise between state and federal sovereignty. Washington personally preferred a unified body of national law, regarding it as a crucial step in creating what the Constitution called "a more perfect union." In nominating Jay to head the Supreme Court, he argued that the federal judiciary "must be considered as the Key-Stone of our political fabric" since a coherent court system that tied the states and regions together with the ligaments of law would achieve more in the way of national unity than any other possible reform.

But that, of course, was also the reason it proved so controversial. The debate over the Judiciary Act of 1789 exposed the latent hostility toward any consolidated court system. The act created a six-member Supreme Court, 3 circuit courts, and 13 district courts but left questions of original or appellate jurisdiction intentionally blurred so as to conciliate the advocates of state sovereignty. Despite his private preferences, Washington deferred to the tradeoffs worked out in congressional committees, chiefly a committee chaired by Oliver Ellsworth of Connecticut, which designed a framework of overlapping authorities that was neither rational nor wholly national in scope. In subsequent decades John Marshall, Washington's most loyal and influential disciple, would move this ambiguous arrangement toward a more coherent version of national law. But throughout Washington's Presidency the one thing the Supreme Court could not be, or appear to be, was supreme, a political reality that Washington chose not to contest.

A second occasion for calculated Executive reticence occurred in February of 1790 when the forbidden subject of slavery came before Congress. Two Quaker petitions, one arguing for an immediate end to the slave trade, the other advocating the gradual abolition of slavery itself, provoked a bitter debate in the House. The petitions would almost surely have been consigned to legislative oblivion except for the signature of Benjamin Franklin on the second one, which transformed a beyond-the-pale protest into an unavoidable challenge to debate the moral compatibility of slavery with America's avowed Revolutionary principles. In what turned out to be his last public act, Franklin was investing his enormous prestige to force the first public discussion of the sectional differences over slavery at the national level. (The debates at the Constitutional Convention had occurred behind closed doors, and their records remained sealed.) If only in retrospect, the discussions in the House during the spring of 1790 represented the Revolutionary generation's final opportunity to place slavery on the road to ultimate extinction.

Washington shared Franklin's view of slavery as a moral and political anachronism. On three occasions during the 1780s he let it be known that he favored adopting some kind of gradual emancipation scheme and would give his personal support to such a scheme whenever it materialized. Warner Mifflin, one of the Quaker petitioners who knew of Washington's previous statements, obtained a private interview in order to plead that the President step forward in the manner of Franklin. As the only American with more prestige than Franklin, Washington could make the decisive difference in removing this one massive stain on the Revolutionary legacy, as well as on his own.

We can never know what might have happened if Washington had taken this advice. He listened politely to Mifflin's request but refused to commit himself, on the grounds that the matter was properly the province of Congress and "might come before me for official decision." He struck a more cynical tone in letters to friends back in Virginia: ". . . the introduction of the Quaker Memorial, rejecting slavery, was to be sure, not only an ill-judged piece of business, but occasioned a great waste of time." He endorsed Madison's deft management of the debate and behind-the-scenes maneuvering in the House, which voted to prohibit any further consideration of ending the slave trade until 1808, as the Constitution specified; more significantly, Madison managed to take slavery off the national agenda by making any legislation seeking to end it a state rather than federal prerogative. Washington expressed his satisfaction that the threatening subject "has at last been put to sleep, and will scarcely awake before the year 1808."

What strikes us as a poignant failure of moral leadership appeared to Washington as a prudent exercise of political judgment. There is no evidence that he struggled over the decision. Whatever his personal views on slavery may have been, his highest public priority was the creation of a unified American nation. The debates in the House only dramatized the intractable sectional differences he had witnessed from the chair at the Constitutional Convention. They reinforced his conviction that slavery was the one issue with the political potential to destroy the republican experiment in its infancy.

Finally, in the most dramatic delegation of all, Washington gave total responsibility for rescuing the debt-burdened American economy to his charismatic Secretary of the Treasury. Before Hamilton was appointed, in September of 1789, Washington requested financial records from the old confederation government and quickly discovered that he had inherited a messy mass of state, domestic, and foreign debt. The records were bedeviled by floating bond rates, complicated currency conversion tables, and guesswork revenue projections that, taken together, were an accountant's worst nightmare. After making a heroic effort of his own that merely confirmed his sense of futility, Washington handed the records and fiscal policy of the new nation to his former aide-de-camp, who turned out to be, among other things, a financial genius.

Hamilton buried himself in the numbers for three months, then emerged with a 40,000-word document titled *Report on Public Credit*. His calculations revealed that the total debt of the United States had reached the daunting (for then) size of $77.1 million, which he divided into three separate ledgers: foreign debt ($11.7 million), federal debt ($40.4 million), and state debt ($25 million). Several generations of historians and economists have analyzed the intricacies of Hamilton's *Report* and created a formidable body of scholarship on its technical complexities, but for our purposes it is sufficient to know that Hamilton's calculations were accurate and his strategy simple: Consolidate the messy columns of foreign and domestic debt into one central pile. He proposed funding the federal debt at par, assuming all the state debts, then creating a national bank to manage all the investments and payments at the federal level.

This made excellent economic sense, as the resultant improved credit rating of the United States in foreign banks and surging productivity in the commercial sector demonstrated. But it also proved to be a political bombshell that shook Congress for more than a year. For Hamilton had managed to create, almost single-handedly, an unambiguously national economic policy that presumed the sovereign power of the federal government. He had pursued a bolder course than the more cautious framers of the Judiciary Act had followed in designing the court system, leaving no doubt that control over fiscal policy would not be brokered to accommodate the states. All three ingredients in his plan—funding, assumption, and the bank—were vigorously contested in Congress, with Madison leading the opposition. The watchword of the critics was *consolidation*, an ideological cousin to *monarchy*.

Washington did not respond. Indeed, he played no public role at all in defending Hamilton's program during the fierce congressional debates. For his part, Hamilton never requested presidential advice or assistance, regarding control over his own bailiwick as his responsibility. A reader of their correspondence might plausibly conclude that the important topics of business were the staffing of lighthouses and the proper design of Coast Guard cutters to enforce customs collections. But no public statements were necessary, in part because Hamilton was a one-man army in defending his program, "a host unto himself," as Jefferson later called him, and by February of 1791 the last piece of the Hamiltonian scheme, the bank, had been passed by Congress and now only required the presidential signature.

But the bank proved to be the one controversial issue that Washington could not completely delegate to Hamilton. As a symbol it was every bit as threatening, as palpable an embodiment of federal power, as a sovereign Supreme Court. As part of a last-ditch campaign to scuttle the bank, the three Virginians within Washington's official family mobilized to attack it on constitutional grounds. Jefferson, Madison, and Randolph submitted separate briefs, all arguing that the power to create a corporation was nowhere specified by the Constitution and that the Tenth Amendment clearly stated that powers not granted to the federal government were retained by the states. Before rendering his own verdict, Washington sent the three negative opinions to Hamilton for rebuttal. His response, which exceeded 13,000 words, became a landmark in American legal history, arguing that the "necessary and proper" clause of the Constitution (Article 1, Section 8) granted implied powers to the federal government beyond the explicit powers specified in the document. Though there is some evidence that Washington was wavering before Hamilton delivered his opinion, it was not the brilliance of the opinion that persuaded him. Rather, it provided the legal rationale he needed to do what he had always wanted to do. For the truth was that Washington was just as much an economic nationalist as Hamilton, a fact that Hamilton's virtuoso leadership throughout the yearlong debate had conveniently obscured.

The Imperial Presidency

As both a symbolic political centerpiece and a deft delegator of responsibility, Washington managed to levitate above the political landscape. That was his preferred position, personally because it made his natural aloofness into an asset, politically because it removed the Presidency from the partisan battles on the ground. In three policy areas, however—the location of the national capital, foreign policy, and Indian affairs—he reverted to the kind of meticulous personal management he had pursued at Mount Vernon. What was called "the residence question" had its origins in a provision of the Constitution mandating Congress to establish a "seat of government" without specifying the location. By the spring of 1790 the debates in Congress had deteriorated into a comic parody on the gridlock theme. Sixteen different sites had been proposed, then rejected, as state and regional voting blocs mobilized against each alternative in order to preserve their own preferences. One frustrated congressman suggested that perhaps they should put the new capital on wheels and roll it from place to place. An equally frustrated newspaper editor observed that "since the usual custom is for the capital of new empires to be selected by the whim or caprice of a despot," and since Washington "had never given bad advice to his country," why not "let him point to a map and say 'here'?"

That is not quite how the Potomac site emerged victorious. Madison had been leading the fight in the House for a Potomac location, earning the nickname "Big Knife" for cutting deals to block the other alternatives. (One of Madison's most inspired arguments was that the geographic mid point of the nation on a north-south axis was not just the mouth of the Potomac, but Mount Vernon itself, a revelation of providential proportions.) Eventually a private bargain was struck over dinner at Jefferson's apartment, subsequently enshrined in lore as the most consequential dinner party in American history, where Hamilton agreed to deliver sufficient votes from several Northern states to clinch the Potomac location in return for Madison's pledge to permit passage of Hamilton's assumption bill. Actually, there were multiple behind-the-scenes bargaining sessions going on at the same time, but the notion that an apparently intractable political controversy could be resolved by a friendly conversation over port and cigars has always possessed an irresistible narrative charm. The story also conjured up the attractive picture of brotherly cooperation within his official family that Washington liked to encourage.

Soon after the Residence Act designating a Potomac location passed, in July of 1790, that newspaper editor's suggestion (give the whole messy question to Washington) became fully operative. Jefferson feared that the Potomac site would be sabotaged if the endless management details for developing a city from scratch were left to Congress. So he proposed a thoroughly imperial solution: Bypass Congress altogether by making all subsequent decisions about architects, managers, and construction schedules an Executive responsibility, "subject to the President's direction in every point."

And so they were. What became Washington, D.C., was aptly named, for while the project had many troops involved in its design and construction, it had only one supreme commander. He selected the specific site on the Potomac between Rock Creek and Goose Creek, while pretending to prefer a different location to hold down the purchase price for the lots. He appointed the commissioners, who reported directly to him rather than to Congress. He chose Pierre L'Enfant as chief architect, personally endorsing L'Enfant's plan for a huge tract encompassing nine and a half square miles and thereby rejecting Jefferson's preference for a small village that would gradually expand in favor of a massive area that would gradually fill up (figure 1.1). When L'Enfant's grandiose vision led to equivalently grandiose demands—he refused to take orders from the commissioners and responded to one stubborn owner of a key lot by blowing up his house—Washington fired him. He approved the sites for the presidential mansion and the Capitol as well as the architects who designed them. All in all, he treated the nascent national capital as a public version of his Mount Vernon plantation, right down to the supervision of the slave labor force that did much of the work.

It helped that the construction site was located near Mount Vernon, so he could make regular visits to monitor progress on his trips home from the capital in Philadelphia. It also helped that Jefferson and Madison could confer with him at the site on their trips back to Monticello and Montpelier. At a time when both Virginians were leading the opposition to Hamilton's financial program, their cooperation on this ongoing project served to bridge the widening chasm within the official family over the Hamiltonian vision of federal power. However therapeutic the cooperation, it belied a fundamental disagreement over the political implications of their mutual interests in the Federal City, as it was then called. For Jefferson and Madison regarded the Potomac location of the permanent capital as a guarantee of Virginia's abiding hegemony within the Union, as a form of geographic assurance, if you will, that the government would always speak with a Southern accent. Washington thought more expansively, envisioning the capital as a focusing device for national energies that would overcome regional jealousies, performing the same unifying function geographically that he performed symbolically. His personal hobbyhorse became a national university within the capital, where the brightest young men from all regions could congregate and share a common experience as Americans that helped to "rub off" their sectional habits and accents.

His hands-on approach toward foreign policy was only slightly less direct than his control of the Potomac project, and the basic principles underlying Washington's view of the national interest were present from the start. Most elementally, he was a thoroughgoing realist. Though he embraced republican ideals, he believed that the behavior of nations was driven not by ideals but by interests. This put him at odds ideologically and temperamentally with his Secretary of State, since Jefferson was one of the most eloquent spokesmen for the belief that American ideals *were* American interests. Jefferson's recent experience in Paris as a witness to the onset of the French Revolution had only confirmed his conviction that a global struggle on behalf of those ideals had just begun and that it had a moral claim on American support. Washington was pleased to receive the key to the Bastille from Lafayette; he also knew as well as or better than anyone else that the

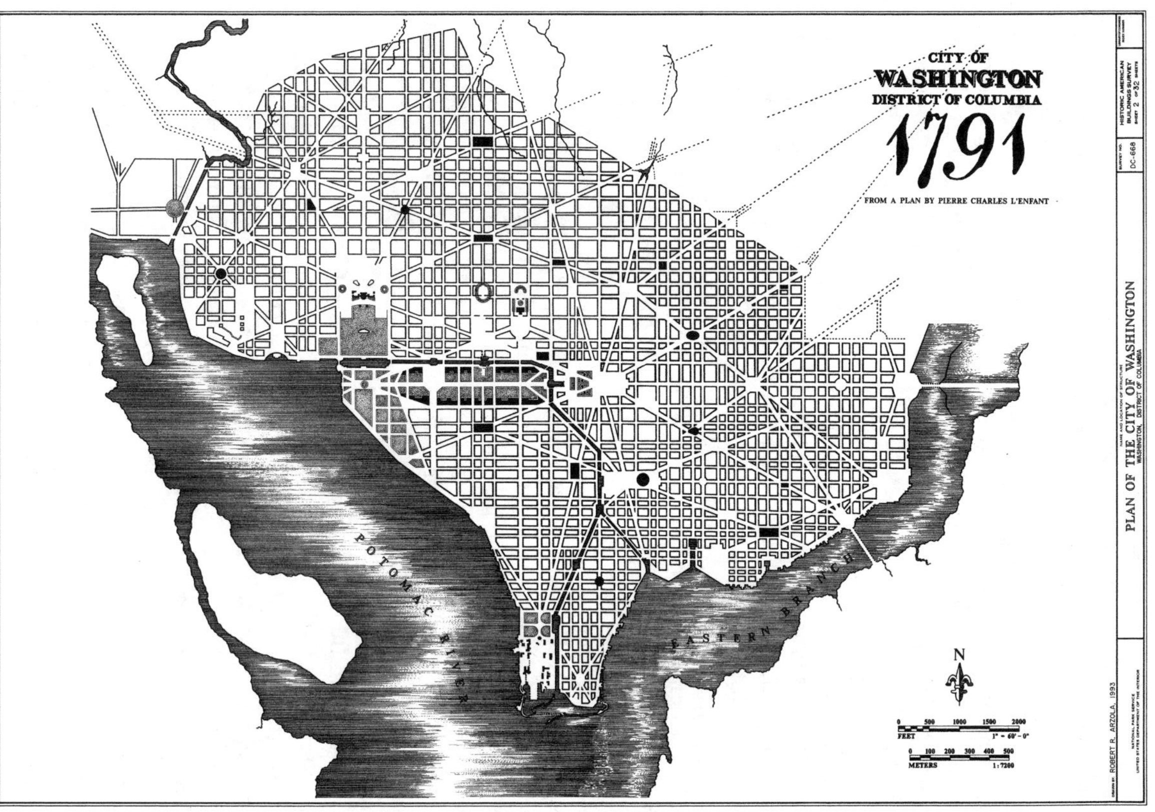

Figure 1.1 L'Enfant-McMillan Plan of Washington, DC.

Source: Historic American Buildings Survey, Library of Congress, Prints and Photograph Division.

victory over Great Britain would have been impossible without French economic and military assistance. But he was determined to prevent his warm memories of Rochambeau's soldiers and de Grasse's ships at Yorktown from influencing his judgment about the long-term interests of the United States.

Those interests, he was convinced, did not lie across the Atlantic but across the Alleghenies. The chief task, as Washington saw it, was to consolidate control of the North American continent east of the Mississippi. Although Jefferson had never been west of the Blue Ridge Mountains, he shared Washington's preference for Western vistas. (During his own Presidency Jefferson would do more than anyone to expand those vistas beyond the Mississippi to the Pacific.)

Tight presidential control over foreign policy was unavoidable at the start because Jefferson did not come on board until March of 1790. Washington immediately delegated all routine business to him but preserved his own private lines of communication on French developments, describing reports of escalating bloodshed he received from Paris "as if they were the events of another planet." His cautionary posture toward revolutionary France received reinforcement from Gouverneur Morris, a willfully eccentric and thoroughly irreverent American in Paris whom Washington cultivated as a correspondent. Morris described France's revolutionary leaders as "a Fleet at Anchor in the fog," and he dismissed as a hopelessly romantic illusion Jefferson's view that a Gallic version of 1776 was under way. The American Revolution, Morris observed, had been guided by experience and light, while the French were obsessed with experiment and lightning.

Washington's supervisory style, as well as his realistic foreign-policy convictions, was put on display when a potential crisis surfaced in the summer of 1790. A minor incident involving Great Britain and Spain in Nootka Sound (near modern-day Vancouver) prompted a major appraisal of American national interests. The British appeared poised to use the incident to launch an invasion from Canada down the Mississippi, to displace Spain as the dominant European power in the American West. This threatened to change the entire strategic chemistry on the continent and raised the daunting prospect of another war with Great Britain.

Washington convened his Cabinet in Executive session, thereby making clear for the first time that the Cabinet and not the more cumbersome Senate would be his advisory council on foreign policy. He solicited written opinions from all the major players, including Adams, Hamilton, Jay, Jefferson, and Knox. The crisis fizzled away when the British decided to back off, but during the deliberations two revealing facts became clearer, first that Washington was resolved to avoid war at any cost, convinced that the fragile American Republic was neither militarily nor economically capable of confronting the British leviathan at this time, and second that Hamilton's strategic assessment, not Jefferson's, was more closely aligned with his own, which turned out to be a preview of coming attractions.

Strictly speaking, the federal government's relations with the Native American tribes were also a foreign-policy matter. From the start, however, with Jefferson arriving late on the scene, Indian affairs came under the authority of the Secretary of War. As ominous as this might appear in retrospect, Knox took responsibility for negotiating the disputed terms of several treaties approved by the Confederation Congress. For both personal and policy reasons Washington wanted his own hand firmly on this particular tiller, and his intimate relationship with Knox assured a seamless coordination guided by his own judgment. He had been present at the start of the struggle for control of the American interior, and he regarded the final fate of the Indian inhabitants as an important piece of unfinished business that must not be allowed to end on a tragic note.

At the policy level, if America's future lay to the west, as Washington believed, it followed that the region between the Alleghenies and the Mississippi merited Executive attention more than the diplomatic doings in Europe. Knox estimated that about 76,000 Indians lived in the region, about 20,000 of them warriors, which meant that venerable tribal chiefs like Cornplanter and Joseph Brant deserved more cultivation as valuable allies than did heads of state across the Atlantic. At the personal level, Washington had experienced Indian power firsthand. As commander of the Virginia Regiment during the French and Indian War, he saw Native Americans not as exotic savages but as familiar and formidable adversaries fighting for their own independence, behaving pretty much as he would do in their place. Moreover, the letters the new President received from several tribal chiefs provided poignant testimony that they now regarded him as their personal protector. "Brother," wrote one Cherokee chief, "we give up to our white brothers all the land we could any how spare, and have but little left . . . and we hope you wont let any people take any more from us without our consent. We are neither Birds nor Fish; we can neither fly in the air nor live under water . . . . We are made by the same hand and in the same shape as yourselves."

Such pleas did not fall on deaf ears. Working closely with Knox, Washington devised a policy designed to create several sovereign Indian "homelands." He concurred when Knox insisted that "the independent tribes of indians ought to be considered as foreign nations, not as the subjects of any particular State." Treaties with these tribes ought to be regarded as binding contracts with the federal government, whose jurisdiction could not be compromised: "Indians being the prior occupants possess the right of the Soil . . . .To dispossess them . . . would be a gross violation of the fundamental Laws of Nature and of that distributive Justice which is the glory of a nation." A more coercive policy of outright confiscation, Washington believed, would constitute a moral failure that "would stain the character of the nation." He sought to avoid the outcome—Indian removal—that occurred more than 40 years later under Andrew Jackson. Instead, he envisioned multiple sanctuaries under tribal control that would be by passed by the surging wave of white settlers and whose occupants would gradually, over the course of the next century, become assimilated as full-fledged American citizens.

Attempting to make this vision a reality occupied more of Washington's time and energy than any other foreign or domestic issue during his first term. Success depended on finding leaders willing to negotiate yet powerful enough to impose a settlement on other tribes. Knox and Washington found a charismatic Creek chief of mixed blood named Alexander McGillivray, a literate man whose diplomatic skills and survival instincts made him the Indian version of Frances' Talleyrand, and in the summer of 1790 Washington hosted McGillivray and 26 chiefs for several weeks of official dinners, parades, and diplomatic ceremonies more lavish than any European delegation enjoyed. (McGillivray expected and received a personal bribe of $1,200 a year to offset the bribe the Spanish were already paying him not to negotiate with the Americans.) Washington and the chiefs locked arms in Indian style and invoked the Great Spirit, and then the chiefs made their marks on the Treaty of New York, redrawing the borders for a sovereign Creek Nation. Washington reinforced the terms of the treaty by issuing the Proclamation of 1790, an Executive Order forbidding private or state encroachments on all Indian lands guaranteed by treaty with the United States.

But the President soon found that it was one thing to proclaim and quite another to sustain. The Georgia legislature defied the proclamation by making a thoroughly corrupt bargain to sell more than 15 million acres on its western border to speculators calling themselves the Yazoo Companies, thereby rendering the Treaty of New York a worthless piece of paper. In the northern district above the Ohio, no equivalent to McGillivray could be found, mostly because the Six Nations, which Washington could remember as a potent force in the region, had been virtually destroyed in the War for Independence and could no longer exercise hegemony over the Ohio Valley tribes.

Washington was forced to approve a series of military expeditions into the Ohio Valley to put down uprisings by the Miamis, Wyandots, and Shawnees, even though he believed that the chief culprits were white vigilante groups determined to provoke hostilities. The Indian side of the story, he complained, would never make it into the history books: "They, poor wretches, have no press thro' which their grievances are related; and it is well known, that when one side only of a Story is heard, and often repeated, the human mind becomes impressed with it, insensibly." Worse still, the expedition commanded by Arthur St. Clair was virtually annihilated in the fall of 1791—reading St. Clair's battle orders is like watching Custer prepare for the Little Bighorn—thereby creating white martyrs and provoking congressional cries for reprisals in what had become an escalating cycle of violence that defied Washington's efforts at conciliation.

Eventually the President was forced to acknowledge that his vision of secure Indian sanctuaries could not be enforced. "I believe scarcely any thing short of a Chinese wall," he lamented, "will restrain Land jobbers and the encroachment of settlers upon the Indian country." Knox concurred, estimating that federal control on the frontier would require an arc of forts from Lake Erie to the Gulf of Mexico, garrisoned by no less than 50,000 troops. This was a logistical, economic, and political impossibility. Washington's vision of peaceful coexistence also required that federal jurisdiction over the states as the ultimate guarantor of all treaties be recognized as supreme, which helps explain why he was so passionate about the issue, but also why it could never happen. If a just accommodation with the Native American populations was the major preoccupation of his first term, it was also the singular failure.

By the spring of 1792, then, what Washington had imagined as a brief caretaker Presidency with mostly ceremonial functions had grown into a judicious but potent projection of Executive power. The Presidency so vaguely defined in the Constitution had congealed into a unique synthesis of symbolism and substance, its occupant the embodiment of that work in progress called the United States and the chief magistrate with supervisory responsibility for all domestic and foreign policy, in effect an elected king and prime minister rolled into one. There was a sense at the time, since confirmed by most historians of the Presidency, that no one else could have managed this political evolution so successfully, indeed that under anyone else the experiment with republican government would probably have failed at the start. Eventually the operation of the federal government under the Constitution would be described as "a machine that ran itself." At the outset, however, the now venerable checks and balances of the Constitution required a trusted leader who had internalized checks and balances sufficiently to understand both the need for Executive power and the limitations of its effectiveness. He made the Presidency a projection of himself.

Washington tried to step down after those first four years and, perhaps predictably, failed. His second term was increasingly full of rancor, with dramatic developments in Europe and mounting tensions between Jefferson and Hamilton within his Cabinet that together threatened to destroy all he had accomplished. But fierce though these conflicts were, they weren't powerful enough to destroy the foundation that Washington had built, and they haven't managed to yet.

This article has been adapted from His Excellency: George Washington, just published by Knopf. Joseph Ellis's previous book, Founding Brothers, *won the Pulitzer Prize.*

Chapter 2

"Divide et Impera": *Federalist 10* in a Wider Sphere

Woody Holton

From *The William and Mary Quarterly*

A month before publishing *Federalist 10*, James Madison sent his friend Thomas Jefferson a confidential summary of its thesis. "Divide et impera, the reprobated axiom of tyranny," Madison wrote, "is under certain qualifications, the only policy, by which a republic can be administered on just principles." Historians have shied away from the republican Madison's embrace of the strategy of divide and rule, which Americans of his era associated with that archetypical counselor to despots, Niccolò Machiavelli.[1] One way to make sense of Madison's statement is to place it in two insufficiently studied contexts: the discussion of the proper size of polities and legislative districts among his contemporaries and the contests over taxation and debt on which the dimensions debate was, to a large extent, based.

Most of the men who attended the Constitutional Convention in Philadelphia during the summer of 1787 joined Madison in the belief that transferring certain crucial duties from the thirteen states to a polity of continental proportions would solve one of their most vexing problems. As Douglass G. Adair pointed out in his 1943 doctoral dissertation, the framers ensured that the one popularly elected branch of the new national government, the House of Representatives, would be "carefully checked and balanced by a quasi-aristocratic (or plutocratic) senate, the electoral college, the presidential veto, and by judicial review." Some of the convention delegates proposed a battery of additional restraints on tyrannical majorities, including life terms for some elected officials, high property qualifications for voters (and still higher ones for officeholders), a congressional veto of state laws, and indirect election of the House of Representatives. These proposals put the framers in a quandary: how could they place the new government sufficiently beyond the reach of popular influence to ensure that it acted responsibly without making it so unresponsive to the popular will as to not only violate their highest ideals but also jeopardize ratification?[2]

The delegates' solution was to reject the most blatant restrictions on popular power in favor of subtler ones. For instance, the convention defeated Madison's inflammatory proposal to allow the national legislature to overturn state laws, but quietly gave that power to the federal courts. The framers also discovered that they could limit popular influence over the most crucial government functions, especially the levying of continental (federal) taxes and the regulation of debtor-creditor relations, simply by shifting them from the states, where the median population was two hundred fifty thousand souls, to a new national government that encompassed all 3.5 million Americans. Because congressional districts would encompass about ten times as many voters as the constituencies where state assemblymen were chosen, federal elections stood a much better chance of producing responsible officeholders.[3] Furthermore, after the Constitution shifted certain vital government duties to a polity that combined the territory of all thirteen states, grassroots efforts to pressure elected officials would rarely acquire that essential ingredient of political power: unity.

Yet not all categories of citizens would find unity equally elusive. Some interest groups—those the federal convention delegates and like-minded men considered the most virtuous—would outdo others at the art of coalescing. Well-to-do city dwellers (especially merchants), veteran officers, and investors in government bonds were much likelier than ordinary farmers to achieve the level of internal cooperation that was needed to exert influence on a government that embraced the combined territories of the thirteen states. Taking note of this disparity in organizing ability, the supporters of the Constitution affirmed that it would filter out unjust efforts to influence public officials but allow salutary influences to pass through.

Though scholarship on the debate over the size of the political sphere (meaning not only legislative districts but also the polity itself) tends to portray Madison as a pioneering soloist, his was actually only one voice in a choir.[4] By November 22, 1787, when *Federalist 10* appeared, a host of Madison's contemporaries had already discussed its primary theme: that the quality of legislative decisions depended in large measure on the sizes of election districts and of the polity itself. After the Constitution was ratified, each state had to decide whether its congressmen would be elected at large or in individual districts. In the ensuing legislative debates, advocates for the statewide election of congressmen argued that it would surpass district voting—just as congressional districts surpassed the much smaller constituencies where state legislators were chosen—at encouraging the election of responsible men. On the question of the optimal size of legislative districts, Madison was actually a relative moderate. Though he urged his colleagues at the Constitutional Convention to make congressional constituencies much larger than their state-level counterparts, Madison thought the districts the convention designed were twice as large as they ought to have been.

Other Americans did not want to enlarge the sphere of government at all, and many Americans' desire not to expand legislative districts or shift major civic responsibilities to a new national government led them to oppose the Constitution. The Anti-Federalists' critics accused them of simply parroting Baron Montesquieu's obsolete admonition that a large republic would quickly degenerate into despotism—a charge that even the Anti-Federalists' recent defenders do not deny. But then, according to the scholarly consensus, later generations of Americans discredited the Anti-Federalists' forebodings, and validated Madison's advocacy of large republics, by sustaining a national government that did not become tyrannical.[5] Actually, the Anti-Federalists (and later the advocates for electing congressmen in districts rather than statewide) also made several other arguments against extending the sphere that subsequent history has not yet refuted.

Scholars have had even less to say about the Americans of the revolutionary period who did not merely oppose enlarging the political sphere but tried to shrink it. In 1782 Pennsylvania millenarian Herman Husband published a pamphlet arguing that his state's legislative districts were too large.[6] Husband's essay reads like a mirror image of the case for extending the sphere that Federalists such as Madison would make five years later. Other Americans expressed their beliefs about the proper size of election districts not with advocacy but with action. They devised strategies for cutting excessively large legislative districts—the very ones Madison and many of his friends considered too small—down to size.

Why did so many Americans of the 1780s wish to enlarge or shrink the political sphere? Investigations of this question have been hampered by a narrow focus on one participant in the debate, Madison, and on the "literary cargo" his friend Jefferson sent him from France in 1785. Scholars have drawn attention to Madison's interest in religious toleration and to his reading of David Hume, Adam Smith, and other Europeans (see Historiographic Note, 212). Yet no other participant in the dimensions debate claimed his stance was influenced by a desire to expand or contract religious freedom, and even Madison believed the "most common and durable source of factions" was not religion but "the various and unequal distribution of property" (10.7).[7] The motive that Madison and other Americans who debated the relative merits of large and small polities and districts repeatedly mentioned was the desire to modify the state governments' approach to two critical issues: taxation and debt. Almost without exception the admirers of large polities and districts wanted the states to crack down on delinquent debtors and taxpayers, whereas Americans who wished to shrink the sphere of government or maintain its current size were advocates for debt and tax relief.[8]

Focusing on participants in the dimensions debate other than Madison, examining not only their ideologies but also the specific legislative outcomes they sought, and taking into account their widespread expectation that wealthy Americans would surpass their countrymen at achieving unity can shed light on the framers' motivations, on the ways in which ordinary

Americans influenced the creation of the Constitution, on the scholarly tendency to transform the framers' stands on hotly contested issues into indisputable facts, and even on modern questions of democratic governance.

At the end of *Common Sense*, which appeared in January 1776, Thomas Paine argued that, upon declaring independence, the thirteen colonies should amalgamate into a single continental government. Paine thus became the first American of his era to argue that his brand of radically democratic republicanism could thrive in a government that spanned the entire nation. Also the last. Even before the ratification of the Articles of Confederation in 1781, men such as Alexander Hamilton, who in 1785 affirmed his preference for legislators whose "principles are not of the *levelling kind*," began trying to shift some of the most crucial governmental responsibilities from the states to the federal government to put them beyond the reach of popular pressure.[9]

Often the dispute over whether policy decisions were best made at the state or federal level was accompanied by a debate over how many voters to put in each legislative district, with Americans who wished to reduce grassroots influence over public officials favoring large legislative districts, whereas more populist writers and speakers wanted small ones. In 1782 Benjamin Gale, a Killingworth, Connecticut, physician and businessman, published a pamphlet celebrating the fact that the upper house of the Connecticut legislature was elected statewide. Anticipating some of the assertions James Madison would make in *Federalist 10* five years later, Gale argued that because the council of assistants represented many more constituents than the lower house, whose members were chosen by the towns, it had legislated more wisely and justly. Unlike members of the lower house, who frequently fell victim to some "popular whim," incumbent councilors were almost never defeated, because it was "not so easy to *electerize* the whole State with the spirit of party, faction and intrigue, as the narrow compass of a town." Gale's reasons for preferring large legislative districts were not only philosophical but also practical. He believed the agrarian majority in the Connecticut House of Representatives had oppressed the state's mercantile minority by saddling commercial men with a disproportionate share of the tax burden. Had it not been for the wise restraining influence of the council, he contended, the lower house would have yielded even more often to "popular freaks and commotions."[10]

In the same year Gale rejoiced that Connecticut councilors were elected statewide, Herman Husband published his pamphlet declaring Pennsylvania's legislative districts too large. Unlike men such as Gale and Madison, Husband wanted ordinary voters' influence in elections increased, not diminished. Toward that end he wrote that assembly districts should not be expanded but contracted.

The sheer size of the Pennsylvania legislative constituencies, which spanned entire counties and were among the most populous in the nation, kept farmers and artisans out of the state assembly, Husband believed. A "County is too large a Bound," he declared, and there are only "a few

Men in a County who are generally known throughout the whole of it." These prominent men who had the best chance of getting elected were "generally the most unsuitable, they being chiefly Tavern-keepers, Merchants, &c. in the County Towns, with the Officers, Lawyers, &c." Husband proposed the creation of new county legislatures, each comprising representatives from every town in the county, which would, in turn, choose the state representatives. Farmers and artisans would easily win election to the county legislatures, and once there they could send one of their own to the state assembly. Another problem with large districts, in his view, was that constituents had little contact with their representatives and were unable "to call them to any Account." County legislatures would not only increase the percentage of less wealthy candidates who made it to the statehouse but also help farmers and artisans acquire the confidence they needed to seek higher office in the first place. As long as their representatives were chosen countywide, Husband argued, ordinary men would be "apt to conceive of ourselves [as] too insignificant to represent the County." The county legislature would "prove as a School to train up and learn Men of the best Sense and Principles the Nature of all publick Business, and give them Utterance to speak to the same."[11]

Like Gale, Husband believed the size of the districts that sent men to a legislature helped determine what sort of policies came out of it. He implied that Pennsylvania assemblymen would not have allowed creditors to demand gold and silver (as opposed to paper money) from their debtors if they had been chosen in smaller districts. The Pennsylvania constitution of 1776, which provided for no governor or senate, was probably, for its time, the most democratic government charter on earth. And yet in Husband's view, until the size of the election districts was reduced, it would not be democratic enough.

One of the principal sources for Husband's political vision was the prophet Ezekiel, whose narrative blueprint for the temple to be built in Jerusalem was founded on the principle of gradation. When the elements used to construct a building are lined up in order of size, Husband believed, the size should increase from one element to the next at an exactly constant rate. After all, the dimensions of the parts of the human body build gradually and constantly from the smallest measurement—the distance between two knuckles—all the way to the largest, the person's height (figures 2.1 and 2.2). By the same token, the United States should not consist simply of the rulers and the ruled but of a series of layers ascending gradually, pyramid style, from the citizenry through the county legislatures to the state assemblies and to Congress. The key element the United States lacked was the county legislature. "Our Want of the proper Use of those lesser Joints in the Body-politick," Husband wrote, "is as though we wanted our Finger-joints in our Bodies natural; without which we could not carry on the finer Parts of mechanick Work."[12]

In New England the members of the lower houses of state assemblies were, unlike their Pennsylvania counterparts, chosen by the towns. Except

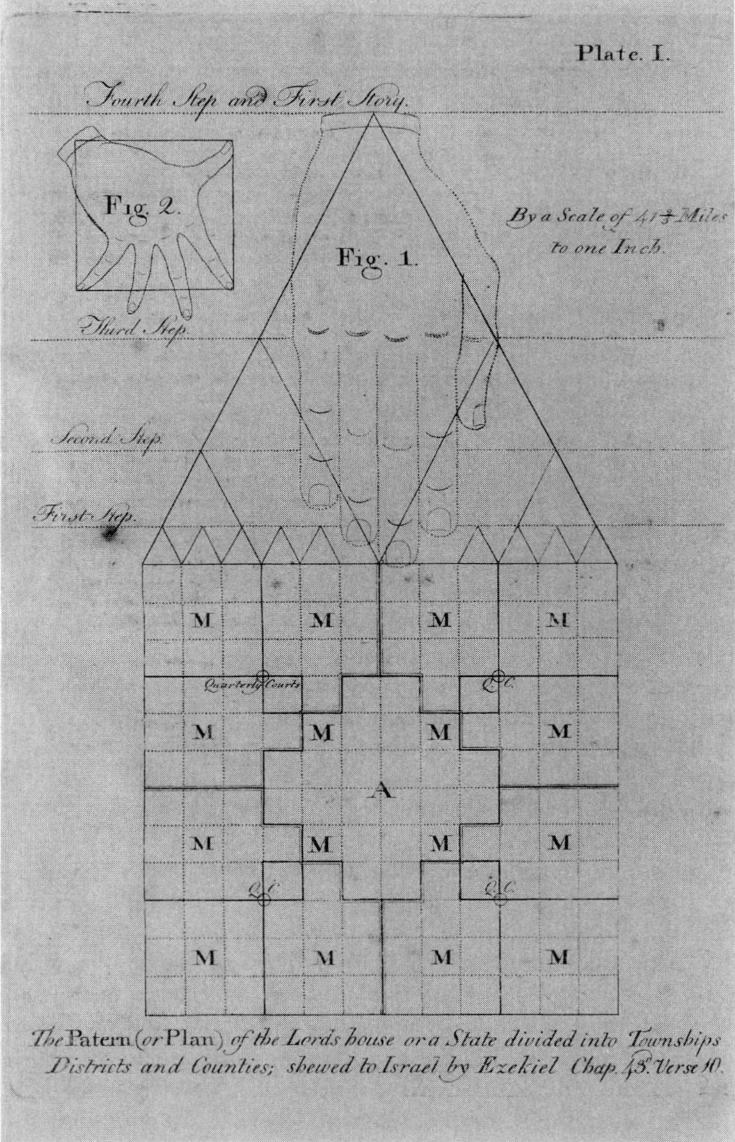

Figure 2.1 Herman Husband, *A Dialogue between an Assembly-Man and a Convention-Man, on the Subject of the State Constitution of Pennsylvania . . .* (Philadelphia, 1790), between pages 8 and 9. Herman Husband believed truly representative government requires several layers of representation between the individual and the national government. He insisted that there be no variation in the increment by which the size of each element of the government surpassed the size of the next-smallest element. He found inspiration for this proportionality in Ezekiel 43:10 (which reads, in the King James version, "Thou son of man, shew the house to the house of Isreal, that they may be ashamed of their iniquities: and let them measure the pattern") and in the proportions in the human body. Here Husband compares a state to a human hand.

Source: The Historical Society of Pennsylvania.

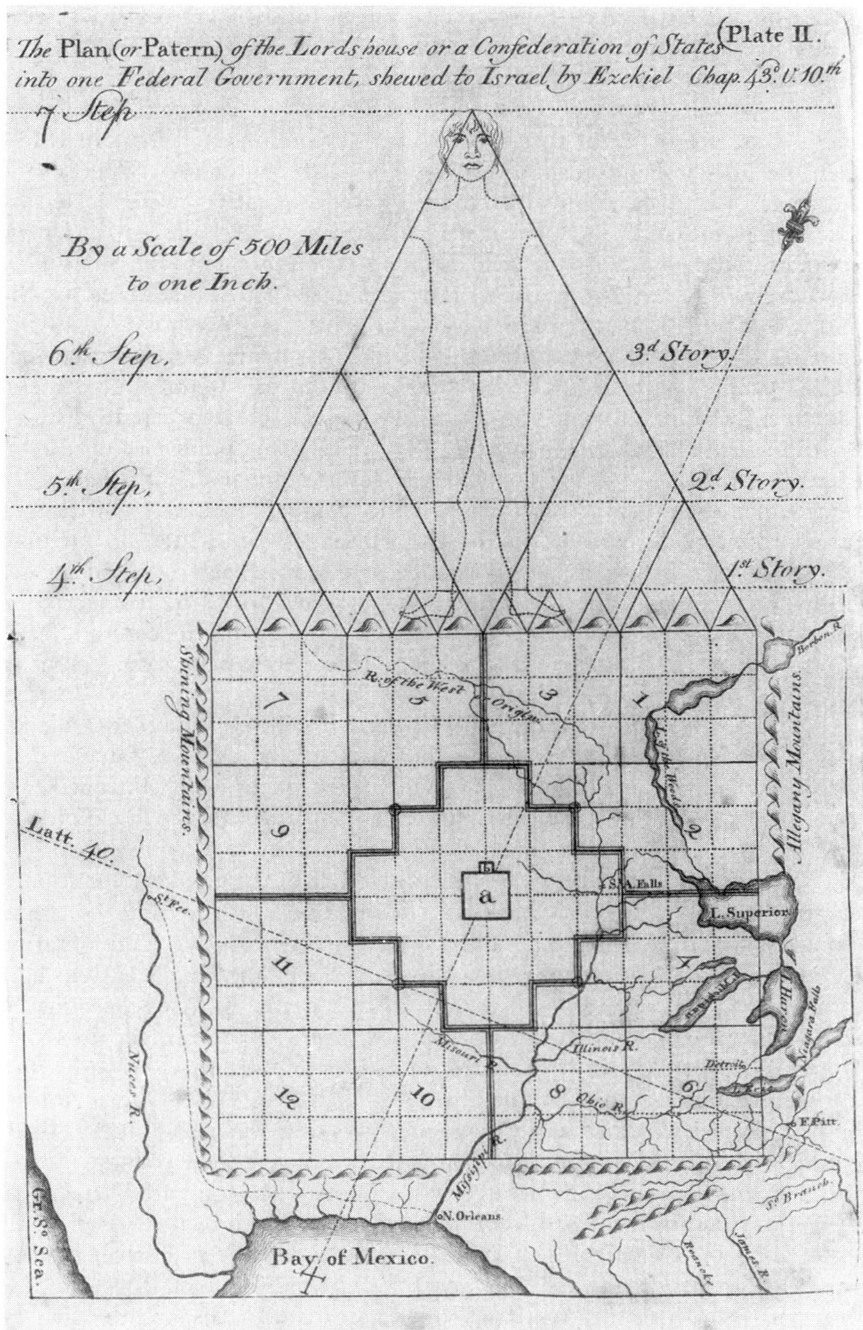

Figure 2.2 Herman Husband, *A Dialogue between an Assembly-Man and a Convention-Man, on the Subject of the State Constitution of Pennsylvania . . .* (Philadelphia, 1790), between pages 8 and 9. Herman Husband used a map of North America and a diagram of a human body to demonstrate his belief that the various layers of representative government in the United States should exhibit the same proportionality as the human body.

Source: The Historical Society of Pennsylvania.

in the largest cities, they represented so few constituents that they were personally acquainted with most of them. New England's upper houses were another matter. In Rhode Island, as in Connecticut, councilors were elected statewide. Massachusetts and New Hampshire elected their senators in districts, yet many of these constituencies contained even more voters than the outsize Pennsylvania districts Husband denounced. Whereas the members of the Massachusetts House of Representatives were elected by town meetings and could be instructed, senators were chosen by entire counties. Many farmers believed the senate's immunity to accountability helped explain the harsh fiscal and monetary policies adopted in the mid-1780s, and many participants in Shays's Rebellion (1786–87) demanded that the senate be abolished. Some of the same Massachusetts citizens, recognizing that they were unlikely ever to obtain a unicameral assembly, sought informal means of cutting the bloated senate districts down to size. During the spring of 1787, newspapers published the names of senate candidates who seemed likely to support tax and debt relief. At the same time, several town meetings in Suffolk and Worcester counties proposed countywide conventions to choose senate candidates. In October 1786 an antitax newspaper essayist suggested that in each county delegates from every town should convene twice a year: "once to instruct their Senators, and once, at the close of the General Court, to examine their conduct, that they might be able to judge whether they are safe persons to be trusted in [the] future."[13]

Relief advocates in southern New England faced the even taller challenge of defeating members of an upper house that was elected statewide. In October 1776 an anonymous Connecticut newspaper essayist argued that voters' inability to become personally acquainted with council candidates left the system "too much expos'd to the intreagues of designing men." In 1783, a year after Gale celebrated the immunity of the Connecticut council to voter revolt, councilors blocked a lower house proposal to condemn Congress's plan to give five million dollars' worth of "Commutation Certificates" to Continental army officers. In September angry citizens held a convention that agreed on a slate of council candidates. An essayist quoted some of these malcontents saying "openly, [that] if they can get rid of the Upper House of Assembly they can do as they please. First, however they are attempting to change the members." In the fall of 1787, Oliver Wolcott Sr. learned of another set of citizens' meetings that was also aimed at overcoming the difficulty of replacing councilors who were elected statewide. He told his son that a group of Litchfield County "Malcontent[s]" had held "Meetings before the last Election, to consider of Grievances and to fix upon good men" to represent them. A list of allegedly profarmer council candidates was drawn up, one man "was sent off with this into the Northern Parts of this County," and another was dispatched "to the Southward." Yet in the end this attempt to unite advocates for tax and debt relief behind a slate of council candidates proved "less Successful" than a similar effort the previous spring.[14]

Just to the east, a campaign to overcome the excessive size of election districts was much more successful. By 1786 Rhode Island farmers feared they were in imminent danger of losing their property, at a fraction of its real value, to tax collectors and private creditors. Most agreed that the reason for the recession was an acute shortage of gold and silver coin and that the solution was to expand the money supply. Even as Madison was coming to see paper money as the single greatest threat to the property rights on which American freedom was founded, these Rhode Islanders, and thousands of other Americans such as Husband, became convinced that the only way they could preserve their property from unjust seizure was to elect a new assembly that would emit currency. Fearing Rhode Island's conservative council would block their proposal, paper money advocates gathered in East Greenwich in mid-February and settled on a slate of proemission council candidates. The list was printed and distributed under the heading "To Relieve the Distressed." In the April 1786 elections, more than half the nominees were elected. The Rhode Island paper money advocates' electoral victory was the high-water mark for efforts to use political organizing to overcome the excessive size of legislative districts. By organizing on a statewide basis, paper money advocates showed that they understood the point Madison would make in the early 1790s: "a general intercommunication of sentiments & ideas among the body of the people, as a free press, compact situation, good roads, interior commerce &c. is equivalent to a contraction of the orbit within wch. the Govt. is to act." Yet this effort succeeded only in Rhode Island, which was not only the smallest state but also less populous, even, than most of the Pennsylvania legislative districts Husband denounced.[15]

Even as numerous advocates for tax and debt relief blamed their failures in the state assemblies on the excessive size of election districts, their opponents articulated the antithetical position that state assemblymen had granted debtors and taxpayers too much respite because they were too beholden to them. In their eyes relief not only cheated bondholders and private creditors but also damaged the economy. The Constitutional Convention delegates' fear that the new national government might also become too sensitive to popular pressure was the primary reason they guaranteed that no law would take permanent effect without the approval of the president, the Supreme Court justices, and the members of the Senate—none of whom would be selected directly by the voters.[16]

Several convention delegates did not even want to give voters free rein in filling the House of Representatives. Elbridge Gerry of Massachusetts confessed that his republicanism had been chastened by the "excess of democracy" and the "levilling spirit" in the thirteen American republics. In his own home state, "County Conventions had declared a wish for a *depreciating* paper" currency. Gerry proposed that the voters in each congressional district elect a slate of candidates from which their state legislature would then choose their congressman for them. General Charles Cotesworth Pinckney of South Carolina proposed to exclude the voters from the process altogether, leaving selection of the powerful new Congress right where it had been under the Articles of Confederation: in the hands of the state legislatures. Pinckney told his fellow delegates a "majority of the people in S. Carolina" had been "notoriously for paper money as a legal tender" for debts. Yet the assembly had voted to give creditors the option of refusing the paper money that it approved in October 1785, and state legislators would similarly manage to resist demands that they send politicians who supported measures such as paper money to Congress.[17]

Other delegates in Philadelphia thought the House of Representatives should be popularly elected. If the convention proposed a new government in which the voters were not allowed to fill even one branch, the Constitution would stand little chance of being ratified. Delegates who supported the direct election of congressmen lacked none of their opponents' determination to prevent the adoption of legislation they considered irresponsible; they were simply proposing a different route to the same destination. Writing George Washington on the eve of the Constitutional Convention, James Madison advocated shifting certain key responsibilities, especially control over the money supply, from the state to the federal level. "There has not been any moment since the peace at which the representatives of the union would have given an assent to paper money or any other measure of a kindred nature," he wrote. George Mason agreed. Republics suffer from the constant "danger of the majority oppressing the minority," he said, and "The Gen[era]l Government of itself will cure these" ills.[18]

As Madison pointed out, the Constitution would "extend the sphere" of government in two distinct ways: some of the states' most crucial powers would be shifted to a new government that spanned the entire continent, and congressmen would represent districts that were roughly ten times larger than their state-level counterparts (10.20; 57.15). If "the Election is made by the Peop. in large Districts there will be no Danger of Demagogues" being elected, Madison told the convention. Decades after the Constitution was adopted, Madison would recall being confident that "large districts" would be "manifestly favorable to the election of persons" with a "probable attachment to the rights of property." Other framers agreed. "There is no danger of improper elections if made by *large* districts," James Wilson affirmed. "Bad elections proceed from the smallness of the districts which give an opportunity to bad men to intrigue themselves into office."[19]

As Madison noted many years later, one reason larger districts are less likely to elect demagogues is that they diminish the influence of "personal solicitations." Much of the eloquent candidate's advantage would pass to the contender who had already been prominent before he declared his candidacy. During the Virginia ratification debate, an anonymous author compared the electoral prospects of Washington and Patrick Henry (neither of whom he named) in large and small districts. In a sly reference to Henry's brief military career, he wrote, "a few marches and retreats about Williamsburg at the beginning of the war, the taking a tory or two by surprise at their own houses by night, together with a popular eloquence, will be sufficient recommendations, both military and civil," to elect someone to the governorship of a state. Yet for a candidate to win the presidency of the vast new nation the framers had proposed in Philadelphia, "A general"—the double entendre was probably intentional—"reputation throughout the continent, both military and political, will be necessary," he quipped.[20]

Why did delegates want to enhance the prospects of candidates with extensive prior reputations? One reason Madison gave was that "in free Governments, merit and notoriety of character are rarely separated." To a generation that considered the quest for fame one of the noblest of human pursuits, it seemed logical that the most virtuous characters would tend to become the best known. Another reason delegates wished to favor the more famous candidate is that they correlated fame with the possession of a large amount of property. Granted, Indian captives and itinerant preachers (to name only two cases) sometimes acquired fame without amassing wealth, yet most well-known Americans were also well-to-do. Once "the sphere of election is enlarged," Pinckney explained to his colleagues in the South Carolina legislature in January 1788, the wealthier candidate with his more extensive reputation and wider sphere of influence (especially his network of customers, debtors, partners, employees, tenants, and suppliers) would start with a tremendous advantage over his rival, the "little demagogue of a petty parish or county," who "probably would not be known."[21] Thus the authors of the Constitution agreed with Husband that large election districts tend to elect wealthy men, the only difference being that they celebrated what he bemoaned.

The framers' desire to tilt elections in favor of wealthy candidates should not simply be ascribed to the fact that most of them were well-to-do. They genuinely believed that property purchased virtue. Whereas "people in general are too ignorant to manage affairs which require great reading and an extensive knowledge of foreign nations," as Noah Webster told readers of the *Connecticut Courant* on November 20, 1786, affluent officeholders were much likelier to have acquired the "extensive information" that men such as William Plumer considered "requisite to form the statesman." They also had more leisure time and, perhaps most crucially, sufficient economic independence to place them beyond the reach of bribery or intimidation. Furthermore, as Madison pointed out years later, the wealthy representative was likely to exhibit a healthy "attachment to the rights of property" for the simple reason that he himself owned so much of it.[22]

Constitutional Convention delegates who wished to allow the voters to choose members of Congress pointed out that allowing state legislatures to appoint congressmen would put this choice in the hands of legislators who were themselves elected in relatively small districts: the very men whose unjust and unwise relief policies had made the convention necessary. Mason "was persuaded there was a better chance for proper elections by the people, if divided into large districts, than by the State Legislatures." Contending that in some states where assemblymen had emitted currency most of the voting public actually opposed it, Mason asked his convention colleagues if they really wanted to allow legislators who favored "paper money or any other Bad measure" to fill Congress with the friends of "these favorite measures."[23]

Many federal convention delegates were so confident that large districts would do a better job of ensuring the election of virtuous officeholders that they wanted to allow the voters to choose United States senators—a right they did not actually obtain until 1913. When, on the floor of the Philadelphia convention, Gerry argued the ultimately successful position that "the commercial & monied interest wd. be more secure in the hands of the State Legislatures, than of the people at large," Wilson replied that state legislators were the very ones who had "sacrificed the commercial to the landed interest." Wilson preferred "election by the people in large districts." Madison argued that state assemblymen were the last people the convention should call on for help in preventing the election of senators who supported debt and tax relief. "The great evils complained of were that the State Legislatures run into schemes of paper money &c, whenever solicited by the people," Madison reminded his fellow delegates. Letting the assemblies choose senators, far from "checking a like propensity in the National Legislature, may be expected to promote it," he said. The two most vocal delegates at the Constitutional Convention, Madison and Gouverneur Morris, even supported, at least in theory, a reform Americans still have not achieved: popular election of the president. Why? Because the "little combinations" and "momentary lies" that sometimes determined elections "within a narrow sphere" would carry little weight in a vote taking place across "so great an extent of country," Morris believed.[24]

In addition to increasing the likelihood that wealthy, responsible men would seek and gain elective office, enlarging election districts would make it easier for them, once elected, to retain their posts. Congressional incumbents' relatively safe seats would embolden them to reject irresponsible legislation. At the Constitutional Convention, several delegates endorsed Morris's view that unless senators were "chosen *for life*," they would not be "completely independent." The convention mandated life terms for only one category of federal officials: judges (and even they could be impeached). Yet by enlarging election districts, the Constitution gave members of the House of Representatives a dose, albeit a considerably smaller one, of the same protection. During the ratification struggle, Webster echoed a theme from the essay published in 1782 by fellow Connecticut native Gale. Webster pointed out that in Connecticut, as well as in Maryland where senators were picked statewide by electors who had been chosen by the voters, members of the upper house almost never had to worry about being defeated. They had no one "to fear or to oblige." Given their manner of election, Webster said, it was no surprise that the Connecticut councilors and Maryland senators had "prevented the most rash and iniquitous measures" from being adopted. In Maryland a "rage for paper money, bordering on madness," swept through the state and led the House of

Delegates to approve an emission. Yet the senate thwarted the plan. Morris's expectation that enlarging legislative districts would protect incumbents helps explain why he had no qualms about allowing the voters to choose the president. Presidents would generally serve for life, Morris predicted, since the "extent of the Country would secure his reelection agst the factions & discontents of particular States."[25]

Precisely how large should congressional districts be? Madison wanted to peg the membership of the First Congress at 130, which would give the average representative fifteen to twenty thousand constituents. Since Congress would be assuming some of the most important duties of the state legislatures, which had a combined total of about two thousand members, Madison's proposal to limit the number of congressmen to 130 was radical indeed. Yet it seems moderate compared with the number of seats the convention eventually decided to create in the First Congress: sixty-five, which made it smaller than most of the state legislatures. Given that most historians associate Madison with the idea of enlarging election districts, it is somewhat jarring to discover that he considered the districts the convention created twice as large as they should be, and that his proposal to double the membership of the House of Representatives was identical to one that would be offered a year later by Melancton Smith, a leading Anti-Federalist. Madison reminded his colleagues that legislation would not need sixty-five votes to pass, just a majority of the congressmen present. "A *majority of a Quorum of 65* members, was too small a number to represent the whole inhabitants of the U. States," Madison declared. "They would not possess enough of the confidence of the people, and wd. be too sparsely taken from the people, to bring with them all the local information which would be frequently wanted."[26]

Popular influence on legislation would be reduced not only by enlarging election districts but also by shifting authority over matters such as debtor-creditor legislation and continental taxation (which were arguably the two most important topics legislators confronted in peacetime) from the thirteen individual states to a new national polity that embraced all of them. Even as the staggering of Senate terms prevented voters from replacing a majority of the senators at the same time, the sheer size of the polity would make it very difficult for an angry populace to pull off an electoral sweep of the House of Representatives. By throwing so many heterogeneous groups into a single polity, the framers made it much harder for any effort at influencing the government to attract a majority of the populace. Though, as numerous scholars have shown, the most forceful articulation of this belief was *Federalist 10*, many of James Madison's contemporaries shared it.[27]

Madison and other friends of the Constitution affirmed that relief proposals and other bad ideas tended to spread among the people like "wild fire" or an "epidemic malady."[28] In hopes of preventing the blaze or contagion from spreading to federal officeholders, the framers surrounded them with a set of concentric barriers. In a nation of continental proportions, unlike in any one of the thirteen states, a majority of the electorate would seldom experience the same grievance—or concur in a single remedy. Charles Cotesworth Pinckney assured the South Carolina ratifying convention that in a large republic, it would "not easily be in the power of factious and designing men to infect the whole people." Suppose, for instance, that the bulk of the populace opposed redeeming Revolutionary War bonds (which had been bought up by speculators at bargain prices) in gold and silver at face value. They would still disagree about whether to redeem the bonds at market value, with paper money, or in some other way. "As the States will not concur at the same time in their unjust & oppressive plans," George Mason told the federal convention, "the general Govt. will be able to check & defeat them."[29]

Even if most Americans were to support some particular piece of legislation, the transfer of vital government functions from the state to the national level would make it harder for them to communicate with each other. "[I]n small societies," Pinckney told the South Carolina ratifying convention, "the people are easily assembled and inflamed." Pinckney believed it was no coincidence that paper money supporters achieved their aims in Rhode Island, "the most contracted society in the union." In neighboring Massachusetts, "where the sphere was enlarged, similar attempts have been rendered abortive," he noted. This salutary effect would be multiplied once control over matters such as paper money had been turned over to a government that embraced the even more "extensive territory" of the United States, since the sheer "number of its citizens will not permit them all to be assembled at one time, and in one place." Once deprived of the ability to hold meetings, Pinckney predicted, the "multitude will be less imperious."[30] Pinckney had a point. If Congress had had control of the money supply in 1786, the paper money advocates who assembled in East Greenwich, Rhode Island, that February would have had to target federal, not state, incumbents, and they almost certainly would not have defeated a majority of them.

Citizens seeking to exert collective pressure on their legislators could, of course, do so without actually assembling, yet the shift of power from the state to the national level would inhibit other forms of communication as well. In *Federalist 60*, which appeared on February 23, 1788, Alexander Hamilton predicted that critics of national legislation would rarely be able to form "a concert of views, in any partial scheme of elections" (60.3). One reason Gouverneur Morris was willing to allow voters to choose the president directly was that, though even "little combinations" could dominate elections "within a narrow sphere," voters would not be able to coalesce in "so great an extent of country" as the United States.[31]

The best-known champion of the large polity was, of course, Madison. The "father of the Constitution" told his convention colleagues that by uniting Americans under one political roof, the new national charter would "divide the community into so great a number of interests & parties, that . . . they may not be apt to unite in the pursuit" of any particular goal. Even if a majority of Americans agreed to support a particular proposal—say, the emission of a million dollars' worth of paper money—it would be difficult for them to organize to pressure Congress, since, in a polity as large as the United States, they would still be divided by sectional, ethnic, and religious differences. The manner in which Madison expressed his thesis in *Federalist 63* was strange but telling; he declared that the Constitution would protect citizens from "the danger of combining" (63.8). Madison's October 24, 1787, letter to Jefferson was even pithier, for it was there that he announced the strategy of divide and rule.[32]

It is unfortunate that historians have steered away from Madison's explosive phrase. Throughout the 1780s Americans who tried to organize campaigns in favor of relief legislation had discovered again and again just how hard it was to "act unaformly" over an extensive territory. Madison had made the same discovery, and it became one of his principal motives for shifting power from the state to the national level. Seldom would a majority of United States citizens share the same grievance. Even when they did, citizens would rarely be able "to discover their own strength" (10.20), much less "act in concert."[33]

Would the new national government be equally impervious to every sort of grassroots pressure? Several Constitutional Convention delegates were sure that it would not, since some clusters of like-minded Americans would outdo others at achieving unity. Gouverneur Morris told his fellow delegates, "the schemes of the Rich will be favored by the extent of the Country. The people in such distant parts can not communicate & act in concert" and would be at a disadvantage compared with "those who have more Knowledge & intercourse" with each other.[34]

In case any of the convention delegates doubted Morris's claim that the rich would still be able to act in concert even after some of the state governments' most important duties had been transferred to a government that spanned all thirteen states, Elbridge Gerry supplied an illustration. On May 10, 1783, Continental army officers had formed the Society of the Cincinnati, partly with the intention of making sure Congress and the states came through with their promised bonuses. Gerry did not want to leave the election of the president to the voters because groups such as the Cincinnati would be able to sway elections using their superior capability of "acting in Concert."[35]

Gerry's fellow delegates did not have to look far for proof of his point. Indeed, as they had gathered at the Pennsylvania statehouse in May 1787, another national convention, the triennial meeting of the Cincinnati, was adjourning just down the street. It was no coincidence that the federal convention and the Cincinnati met in the same city during the same month. Though the president of the officers' group, George Washington, decided not to attend its triennial meeting, he set it for the week before the opening of the federal convention in the expectation, which proved correct, that some of the federal convention delegates would also attend the Cincinnati meeting.[36]

Bondholders also recognized the value of collective action. Former Continental army surgeon William Eustis believed that by "holding a correspondence" with each other, veteran officers could achieve sufficient unity to "promote their *pecuniary* interests," especially their goal of "rendering their securities more valuable." Officers formed several organizations, in fact, and they proved especially adept at obtaining congressional title, on highly favorable terms, to Indian land. Other bondholders also organized. "There are paper speculators dispersed over every part of the United States," Boston merchant George Flint told the firm of Constable Rucker and Company on December 17, 1785. "They keep up a constant & accurate communication. The information flies from one to another in every direction like an electrical shock."[37]

The bondholders' ability to bring concerted pressure to bear on Congress was not shared by ordinary citizens. When Morris told the federal convention that ordinary Americans would be entirely unable to "communicate & act in concert," he exaggerated their rural isolation, since myriad interactions connected ordinary farm families with their neighbors and even the wider Atlantic world.[38] Their social webs, however, were not nearly as extensive as those of wealthier Americans. This liability became clear in the mid-1780s when far-flung advocates for tax and debt relief tried to form statewide organizations.

Activists were not naive about the impediments to unity, and they tried in often remarkable ways to overcome them. Sometimes relief advocates in different parts of a state would make a point of adopting identical proposals. Others tried to establish committees of correspondence. On several occasions relief advocates seeking strength through uniformity tried to harness the power of the printed word. In January 1786, as Massachusetts farmers were beginning to demand debt and tax relief, an anonymous newspaper essayist urged that town instructions to representatives "be inserted in the publick prints, that there may be concurrence and uniformity." In 1784 Thomas Tudor Tucker wrote a pamphlet urging his fellow South Carolinians to instruct their representatives to vote for a convention to revise the state constitution. Recognizing that "measures that might happen, in some particulars, to be contradictory, would be apt to defeat the main intention," Tucker drew up a "uniform plan" and published it in hopes that all the instructing jurisdictions would copy it verbatim.[39]

One of the most intriguing efforts to use print to harmonize relief proposals occurred in New Hampshire, where it must have seemed to paper money advocates that their opponents in the legislature had adopted a deliberate strategy of divide and rule. In asking participants in special town meetings to vote on its very modest paper money proposal, the assembly did not challenge them to take it or leave it (as the Constitutional Convention would do less than a year later), instead inviting them to propose amendments or alternatives. A month later a newspaper writer lamented that supporters of paper money had divided themselves among "so many different plans for funding and giving it a circulation." Another essayist tried to heal the divisions among the currency advocates by urging all the town meetings to copy the bold proposal he described in a handbill. Though at least one town, Stratham, followed the handbill proposal quite closely, most did not. In January 1787 the legislature counted the returns and announced, to no one's surprise, that, though two-thirds of the towns had voted in favor of some sort of paper money, none of the specific plans had obtained anything close to a majority. It declined to print any paper.[40]

Few of the other efforts to unite relief advocates behind a single proposal fared any better than the New Hampshire handbill. Like its counterpart to the north, the Massachusetts legislature, which held a special session in the fall of 1786 to respond to Shays's Rebellion, was able to reject the most radical relief proposals as "inconsistent with each other."[41] Relief advocates seeking the power of unity would face even greater obstacles if control over the money supply, continental taxation, and other vital matters passed to a national government. Their opponents would, too, but the gap between the two groups' ability to exert collective pressure on elected officials was expected to widen.

The framers apparently expected a similar disparity to result from the expansion of legislative districts. In the new congressional districts, no cluster of voters with similar interests would find coalescing behind a single candidate as easy as it had been in the much smaller constituencies where state legislators were chosen. Yet some interests were expected to do better than others at surmounting this new obstacle. Shortly after the Constitution was ratified, James Madison cautioned Kentuckians who were preparing to write a state constitution that even if they were to mandate that senators be elected statewide, as he recommended, they should still carve the state into districts and require candidates to live in the districts they hoped to represent. Otherwise, he warned, the residents of the "large towns" could "easily unite their votes" behind slates of senate candidates made up primarily of their fellow urbanites.[42] Though Madison's residency requirement would stop city dwellers from filling every seat in the senate, it would not prevent them from coalescing behind the most prourban candidate in each district. That advantage was an inherent consequence of statewide elections, and it was one that would accrue to any other group that did a better job than its rivals at overcoming the obstacles presented by large election districts.

This problem was also apparent to Herman Husband. In his 1782 pamphlet, Husband contended that the framers of the state constitutions had deliberately established large legislative districts with no intermediaries between legislators and their constituents because they knew that in this system, "the Body of the Governors" would be able to "combine," whereas "the Body of the Governed" was "cut off from the Benefit of the Circulation of Life and Knowledge, and so become dead and ignorant." Like the framers' preference for wealthy officeholders, their decision to create a government that was more amenable to pressure from above than to pressure from below should not be ascribed to simple favoritism toward their own class. For the most part, the authors of the Constitution, as well as its numerous supporters in every state, appear to have sincerely believed that men such as merchants and bondholders were more likely than farmers and artisans to support legislation, especially in the areas of taxation and the money supply, that promoted the common good.[43]

In addition to yielding all these electoral and legislative benefits, shifting control of certain key policies from the states to a new national government was also expected to help stop the wave of agrarian uprisings that had swept over the United States in the 1780s. "When the citizens are confined within a narrow compass, as was the case of Sparta, Rome, &c. it is within the power of a factious demagogue to scatter sedition and discontent, instantaneously, thro' every part of the State," John Stevens Jr. declared in a November 1787 essay. "Republics, limited to a small territory, ever have been, and, from the nature of man, ever will be, liable to be torn to pieces by faction." Stevens applied this lesson of ancient history to the American context: "Had the commotion, which Shays excited in Massachusetts, happened in a state of *small territory*, what would have been the probable consequences?" he asked. "Before the people had recovered from their madness, perhaps all would have been lost." As eager as the framers were to place obstacles in the path of future rebels, some of the Constitution's strongest supporters recognized that they might someday regret doing so. They warned that by enlarging their polity sufficiently to prevent would-be rebels from uniting, Americans would be endangering their own ability to resist tyranny. In a January 1787 newspaper essay, Benjamin Rush reminded his readers that the Abbé Raynal had claimed "Sweden lost her liberties . . . because her citizens were so scattered, that they had no means of acting in concert with each other." Similarly, in his October 24, 1787, letter to Thomas Jefferson touting large republics, Madison warned against constructing "too extensive a one," where "a defensive concert may be rendered too difficult against the oppression of those entrusted with the administration."[44]

Since most accounts of the struggle over the ratification of the Constitution focus on a single aspect of the Anti-Federalists' case against an American republic of continental proportions—their fear that it would degenerate into tyranny—the Constitution's critics have acquired reputations as poor prophets.[45] Yet the other, overlooked aspects of the Anti-Federalists' case may actually have a much better chance of standing up to modern scrutiny.

Many critics denounced the very features of the Constitution its supporters most enthusiastically celebrated. Anticipating by three months Alexander Hamilton's contention that the Constitution would prevent "a concert of views, in any partial scheme of elections" (60.3), an Anti-Federalist observed in October 1787 that if the Constitution were adopted, "The people in Georgia and New-Hampshire would not know one another's mind, and therefore could not act in concert to enable them to effect a general change of representatives." Readers may recall seeing the claim that voters could not act in concert previously: James Madison had used it in his federal convention speech touting the benefits of the extended sphere.[46]

The most common critique of the idea of extending the sphere of government focused on the immensity of the new congressional districts, which Anti-Federalists feared would block the flow of information from the constituent to the representative and vice versa. Once members of Congress were "chosen within large circles," a Massachusetts essayist feared, "they will be unknown to a very considerable part of their constituents, and their constituents will be not less unknown to them."[47]

In making the case that large election districts would prevent representatives from gathering sufficient information about their constituents, Anti-Federalist writers and speakers drew on the notion, popularized by Adam Smith in his 1759 *Theory of Moral Sentiments*, that all humans are "naturally sympathetic" with other people's sorrows, joys, and needs—but that they "feel . . . little for another, with whom they have no particular connexion." Since a representative with tens of thousands of constituents "can never be well informed as to the circumstances of the people," the "Federal Farmer" warned, he cannot "sympathize with them" either. Ironically, the ratifying convention delegate who drew most heavily on the notion of sympathy was George Mason, who had urged his colleagues at the Philadelphia convention to shift some of the states' power to a national polity with outsize legislative districts. The convention's omission of a Bill of Rights and other crucial safeguards led Mason to reject its final product, and in speech after speech at the Virginia convention, he used "fellow-feeling" to describe the vital bond between constituent and representative that the Constitution would sever.[48]

As alarming as the sheer number of constituents in every congressional district was to Anti-Federalist writers, it was not their paramount concern. An even greater threat lurked in the widespread expectation that the men elected in these large, new federal legislative districts would far surpass their constituents in wealth. If only "*eight* men should represent the people of this Commonwealth," John Quincy Adams of Massachusetts warned a cousin in December 1787, "they will infallibly be chosen from the aristocratic part of the community." In Connecticut the argument that the Constitution would ensure the election of wealthy men who could not understand the problems of ordinary Americans was made, surprisingly enough, by Benjamin Gale, the man who had praised the electoral invulnerability that Connecticut councilors received by being elected statewide. There were to be so few congressmen that they would assuredly all be "of the higher class of people who know but little of the poverty, straits, and difficulties of the middling and lower class of men," Gale said. The widespread fear that a wealthy legislator could not properly represent poor and middling voters was informed by the notion of fellow feeling. "In order for one man properly to represent another," an Anti-Federalist declared, "he must feel like him, which he cannot do if he is not situated like him." Whether rich, poor, or middling, legislators felt "an involuntary bias towards those of their own rank," he wrote.[49]

At the Constitutional Convention, Madison had expressed similar doubt about the ability of officeholders to sympathize with members of social classes other than their own. "The man who is possessed of wealth, who lolls on his sofa or rolls in his carriage," he had said on June 26, "cannot judge of the wants or feelings of the day laborer." Madison was apparently even more concerned about the corollary inability of the laborer to empathize with the needs of the man in the carriage; the point of his speech was to warn that the nation's poor majority might someday demand that officeholders confiscate and redistribute the property of the rich. The only way "to protect the minority of the opulent against the majority," he said, would be to give United States senators extremely long terms.[50] During the ratification debate, Madison stifled his doubts about the limits of sympathy, indeed expressing confidence that the representative's "interest" and "ambition" would ensure his "fidelity and sympathy with the great mass of the people" (57.14; 35.5–11).

Most historians have ignored what was arguably the Anti-Federalists' most intriguing case against outsize legislative districts. Like several federal convention delegates, numerous opponents of the Constitution predicted that well-to-do Americans would prove more capable than farmers and artisans at augmenting their influence in congressional elections by coordinating their efforts. "The great easily form associations," Melancton Smith told the New York ratifying convention on June 21, 1788, but "the poor and middling class form them with difficulty." The framers had, in fact, exacerbated this disparity by not requiring runoffs in congressional elections where no candidate obtained a majority, Smith said. He and other Anti-Federalists worried that in large districts, holding plurality elections (in which the victory simply went to the candidate with the most votes) would tilt the balance of political power in favor of those segments of the population that were best able to concentrate their votes on a single candidate. "If the elections be by plurality," Smith declared, "the natural aristocracy" could "easily unite their interests." By contrast, "the common people will divide, and their divisions will be promoted by the others."[51]

Anti-Federalists pointed out that the framers had also decided not to carve the states into single-member congressional districts. If a state legislature, or, what seemed more likely, Congress, decided that congressmen should be elected statewide, *Federal Farmer* cautioned, "the people who live scattered in the inland towns" would disperse their votes among a wide variety of profarmer candidates. By contrast, in, say, a state entitled to five congressmen, a "few men in a city, in any order or profession, may unite and place any five men they please highest among those that may be voted for." In Massachusetts a newspaper writer named Cornelius expressed a similar fear: "The citizens in the seaport towns are numerous; they live compact; their interests are one; there is a constant connection and intercourse between them," he noted. Thus Massachusetts merchants and their followers would be able to "centre their votes where they please": namely, on the same eight candidates. Farmers, on the other hand, would be entirely unable "to concert uniform plans for carrying elections of this kind." Farmers, unlike city people, "are scattered far and wide; they have but little intercourse and connection with each other." *Federal Farmer* even claimed that in one unspecified district that annually elected six state legislators by plurality, a faction of "men of some influence" had recently managed "to divide and distract the voters in general," and thereby stack the district's entire assembly delegation with their nominees. After distributing their slate to their friends, the men had circulated several additional lists of nominees among other citizens who then divided their votes among the various lists. Though some of the group's nominees "were very disagreeable to a large majority of the electors," all had won, he said. Even James Madison conceded that after the Constitution placed ordinary citizens in an "extended situation," preventing them from "combining," they would be vulnerable to manipulation resulting from "the combined industry of interested men" (63.8).[52]

After the Constitution was ratified, several states did in fact decree that their congressmen would be elected at large. Advocates for statewide voting believed it would ensure the election of the most able men; their opponents maintained that unless congressmen were chosen in districts, they and their constituents would know too little about each other. Back in 1782 Herman Husband had argued against the countywide election of Pennsylvania assemblymen, since only the wealthiest men in any county were "generally known throughout the whole of" it. To illustrate his point, Husband had taken it to what he considered a ridiculous extreme, pointing out that "this Defect would be still more easily seen and felt by all if we were to vote for a few Men in a whole State to sit in Congress." In November 1788 the Pennsylvania assembly decided that the state's first members of the newly created United States House of Representatives would be chosen using the very system Husband had conjured up as an extreme example of unrepresentative government. The statewide election of congressmen favored candidates from the area around Philadelphia, and westerners took the lead in contending that it was, as Husband put it in 1789, "far from being satisfactory, for the bounds are too large for the common people to act in." Public pressure forced the legislature to adopt the district method for all subsequent elections, but Husband warned that even in states where congressmen were chosen "in separate districts," federal constituencies were so large that the state legislatures "might as well have empowered the officers and wealthy men to have held those elections without mocking the public and the body of freemen."[53]

Connecticut also initially opted to elect its congressional delegation statewide, and when some residents proposed to switch to single-member districts, William Beers denounced the idea in a 1791 pamphlet that calls to mind Madison's October 1787 letter to Thomas Jefferson. "It would hardly appear beneficial to carry into the government the irregular passions, caprices and fanciful wishes of the people," Beers wrote. When you "enlarge the acting body," he explained, "you augment the force of the wise, the uninfluenced and steady, and you divide and waste the strength of the opposite party." The following year another anonymous Connecticut writer, probably Windham lawyer, assemblyman, and future Federalist congressman

Zephaniah Swift, defended district voting. Connecticut was divided into two mutually antagonistic classes, Swift said. "Creditors are naturally rich, and debtors poor: the former are usually few, the latter many," he wrote. "The terms few, rich, rulers, creditors, imply inequality of condition, and numbers. These persons naturally form a class in society distinct from the opposite class, of the many, the ruled, the poor, the debtors." Swift described the effect of at-large voting on this divided society using the English translation of the Latin phrase with which Madison had privately summarized *Federalist 10*. "The wide dispersion of the freemen in this state, with their consequent incapacity of acting in concert in these elections, appears to have been considered as recommending this mode by being advantageous to the cause of government," Swift wrote. " 'Divide and rule' is a favourite maxim of despotism."[54]

Like many Americans of the previous decade, Swift linked the size of the political sphere to economic policy. He suggested that if Connecticut's congressmen had not been elected statewide, their increased sensitivity to public opinion might have prevented them from supporting the unpopular federal Excise Act of 1791 (which was destined to provoke the Whiskey Rebellion two years later). Since wealthy people imported most of their alcoholic beverages, wrote Swift (with some exaggeration), the 1791 "duty on domestic spirits is a tax on the poor, rather than the rich, whose wealth and consequent rank in life forbid the use of them."[55] Noting that many congressmen owned government bonds or shares in the Bank of the United States, Swift hinted that they might favor their fellow stockholders at the expense of taxpayers, unless states such as Connecticut made their congressional delegations more susceptible to popular pressure by electing them in single-member districts.

In other states, too, nearly everyone agreed that congressmen elected statewide would be less dependent on the voters. An anonymous Marylander warned that single-member congressional districts would tilt elections in favor of politicians who would "not be too proud to court what are generally called the *poor folks*, shake them by the hand, ask them for their vote and interest, and . . . treat them to a can of grog, and . . . join heartily in abusing what are called the *great people*." Like the Anti-Federalists, advocates for single-member districts argued that enlarging districts sapped the representatives' ability to empathize with their constituents. By contrast Beers spoke for other supporters of at-large voting when he ridiculed the notion that "sympathy and fellow feeling" were "essential in a representative." "[S]hall a man be distitute of property in order to sympathize with the indigent?" he asked. If "a man of virtue and benevolence is acquainted with the wants and feelings of his constituents, he must sympathize with them of course," Beers concluded. During the ratification debate, Madison had argued that congressmen could adequately represent constituents unlike themselves because it would be in their interest to do so. For Beers virtue would induce congressmen to pity their constituents. What Beers and Madison had in common was the conviction that the congressman and his constituents need have nothing in common: no bond of empathy.[56]

Some opponents of statewide congressional districts revived a claim that had been made by several Constitutional Convention delegates and numerous Anti-Federalists: that large congressional constituencies would thwart some attempts at organized political action more effectively than others. Swift noted that as the number of citizens sharing a particular interest increased, it became harder and harder for them to "act in concert." He contended that those whose "skill, wealth and connections, can most easily overcome these difficulties can the most easily effect their own particular wishes; and thus those persons possess the most liberty and power." William Findley told his colleagues in the Pennsylvania legislature, "while three fourths of the state are divided among five or six sets of men . . . the other one fourth may carry the election by acting in concert, and holding a correspondence with each other."[57]

Though numerous Americans of the founding era disputed the framers' contention that officeholders should be made less responsive, there was broad consensus about how it could be done. Almost everyone thought accountability decreased as the population of legislative districts grew. Numerous advocates for increasing and decreasing legislators' amenability to public pressure also concurred in the belief that large election districts were more likely than small ones to elect, and then reelect, wealthy candidates. Yet another point on which the adversaries generally converged was that the more people a nation contains, the harder it is for citizens seeking policy change to unite. Indeed, nine of the authors and speakers quoted in this article used the same word, "concert," to describe what large polities inhibit. (James Madison used "concert" four times in *Federalist 10* alone [10.12–13, 20–21].)

Despite all these agreements about what one historian has called "the politics of size," extending the sphere was a much subtler way to reduce popular influence on government than many of the other devices that had been proposed at the Constitutional Convention. The notion that the republican form of government works best in a large area, which has been called America's single greatest contribution to political theory, might never have been developed if the authors of the Constitution had not feared that dissipating grassroots influence on government using some more blatant tactic, such as electing the House of Representatives indirectly, would provoke a public outcry. *Federal Farmer* acknowledged with dismay that in statewide plurality elections "men of elevated classes in the community" benefit from "silent operations, which are not immediately perceived by the people in general." Zephaniah Swift was paying a rueful compliment to his opponents' ingenuity when he noted that Connecticut's statewide congressional elections were "calculated to induce the freemen to imagine themselves at liberty, while they are thus destined to be allured or driven round as if impounded, being at the same time told that nothing confines them, although they have not the powers of escape." Once the expansion of legislative districts had penned freemen behind this invisible fence, Swift warned, fewer and fewer of them would turn out to vote. Herman Husband believed the process of inducing apathy had already begun with the first federal election. He claimed that anyone who examined the voting lists for Pennsylvania's at-large congressional election of 1788 would "find few who voted." Indeed, Husband wrote, "in many districts [precincts] the people never opened any election."[58]

Husband and his contemporaries could not foresee the potential of party politics and modern transportation and communication to effectively shrink congressional districts. Nonetheless, it would be unwise to assume that participants in modern debates over the proper size of polities and legislative districts have nothing to learn from early Americans. For instance, are Americans correct in viewing the 1913 constitutional amendment mandating the popular election of senators as a giant step toward true democracy? A politician elected statewide may actually be less beholden to the voters than one who is chosen by state legislators representing small districts. Moreover, no eighteenth-century observer would be surprised to find more millionaires in the United States Senate than in the House of Representatives (for which only the tiny, single-member states hold statewide elections), and more in Congress than in state legislatures.

If the documents that survive from the 1780s and 1790s reveal a great deal about how Americans proposed to increase or decrease popular influence on public officials, they also offer hints about why. Madison opened his best-known argument for shifting some of the states' power to a continental polity with a description of the problem he hoped to solve. "Those who hold, and those who are without property, have ever formed distinct interests in society," he wrote. "Those who are creditors, and those who are debtors, fall under a like discrimination" (10.7).[59] Madison believed the size of legislative districts and of the polity itself helped determine whether a particular government would favor the "monied interest" (bondholders and private creditors), the "landed interest" (farmers and plantation owners), or any of the other "different classes" (10.7).

Almost every member of what Madison called the moneyed interest avidly endorsed the Constitution, and the new Congress gave them no reason to regret their choice. In September 1789 a group of federal bondholders living in Philadelphia asked the House of Representatives to devise a way to raise the market value of their greatly depreciated securities. Five months later Congressman Madison, who had had second thoughts about bond speculators' virtue, proposed an alternative: Congress should force the current holders of the bonds to share the benefits of its funding bill with the original owners, including Continental army veterans. Opponents of Madison's proposal demanded why, if this matter was so important to the soldiers, they had sent Congress "no petitions or remonstrances" of their own. Madison replied that the veterans "were so dispersed, that their interests and efforts could not be brought together," but that "the case of the purchasing holders was very different."[60]

Indeed it was. During the battle over funding, bondholders regularly corresponded with their counterparts in other states. As Congress debated the topic at Federal Hall in New York City, "the galleries were unusually crowded" with a "numerous body of citizens." Historians have long wondered what had made Madison and the other Constitutional Convention delegates so confident that extending the sphere of government would stymie irresponsible factions without also neutralizing virtuous ones.[61] The answer may lie in the framers' belief that the very qualities that made some Americans more virtuous than others—their wealth, education, and frequent dealings with like-minded individuals in other states—would also ensure that they were better organizers. The Federalists' opponents—the Anti-Federalists, the advocates for single-member congressional constituencies, and the Americans who thought even the state legislative districts were too large—agreed that shifting certain core governmental duties to national legislators would thwart some grassroots organizing efforts more effectively than others. All they denied was that the pernicious influences were the ones that would be filtered out.

Historiographic Note

For the influence of Hume on Madison, see Ralph L. Ketcham, "Notes on James Madison's Sources for the Tenth Federalist Paper," *Midwest Journal of Political Science* 1, no. 1 (May 1957): 23–24; Douglass Adair, " 'That Politics May Be Reduced to a Science': David Hume, James Madison, and the Tenth Federalist," in Colbourn, *Fame and the Founding Fathers*, 132–51; Wills, *Explaining America*; Morton White, *Philosophy, The Federalist, and the Constitution* (New York, 1987); Mark G. Spencer, "Hume and Madison on Faction," *William and Mary Quarterly (hereafter WMQ)* 59, no. 4 (October 2002): 873–86.

For claims that Madison was more influenced by others than by Hume, see Epstein, *Political Theory of The Federalist*, 101–2; Morgan, *Huntington Library Quarterly* 49: 95–112; Morgan, *Inventing the People*, 268; Samuel Fleischacker, "Adam Smith's Reception among the American Founders, 1776–1790," *WMQ* 59, no. 4 (October 2002): 897–924; Colleen A. Sheehan, "Madison and the French Enlightenment: The Authority of Public Opinion," *WMQ* 59, no. 4 (October 2002): 925–56.

On Madison's passion for religious freedom, see Banning, *Sacred Fire of Liberty*, 131, 207; Banning, "The Practicable Sphere of a Republic: James Madison, the Constitutional Convention, and the Emergence of Revolutionary Federalism," in *Beyond Confederation: Origins of the Constitution and American National Identity*, ed. Richard Beeman, Stephen Botein, and Edward C. Carter II (Chapel Hill, N.C., 1987), 183; Fleischacker, *WMQ* 59: 907–13; Jack N. Rakove, "A Nation Still Learning What Madison Knew," *New York Times*, Mar. 11, 2001; Spencer, *WMQ* 59: 886–95; Conniff, *Political Theory* 8: 387, 395, 397–98.

For framers' elitism, see Robert A. Dahl, *A Preface to Democratic Theory* (Chicago, 1956), chap. 1; Hanna Fenichel Pitkin, *The Concept of Representation* (Berkeley, Calif., 1967), 196; Wood, *Creation of the American Republic*, 507, 610; Paul F. Bourke, "The Pluralist Reading of James Madison's Tenth *Federalist*," *Perspectives in American History* 9 (1975): 269–95; Epstein, *Political Theory of The Federalist*, 107–8; Martin Diamond, *As Far as Republican Principles Will Admit*, ed. William A. Schambra (Washington, D.C., 1992).

For scholarship denouncing Constitution historians' narrow focus on abstract philosophy, see Rakove, *James Madison*, 50; Banning, *Sacred Fire of Liberty*, 204; Brown, *Redeeming the Republic*.

Notes

Woody Holton is associate professor in the History Department, University of Richmond. He wishes to thank Alex Bushel, Robert A. Gross, Travis Hardy, Adrienne Huckabee, Michael A. McDonnell, Gretchen Ferris Schoel, Rebecca M. Shewman, Peter H. Wood, Alfred F. Young, and anonymous readers for the William and Mary Quarterly, as well as the American Antiquarian Society, the Boston Early American History Seminar (especially Christine Desan, Pauline Maier, Kent Newmyer, and Lisa Wilson), the John Carter Brown Library, the Connecticut Historical Society, the Fall Line Early American Society (especially Doug Winiarski), the Massachusetts Historical Society (especially Peter Drummey, Margaret A. Hogan, Megan Milford, Cherylinne Pina, and Conrad E. Wright), the Massachusetts State Archives, the National Endowment for the Humanities, the Newberry Library (especially Sara Austin), the New England Regional Fellowship Consortium, the New Hampshire Historical Society, the New Hampshire State Archives, the University of Richmond History Department (especially Deborah Govoruhk and Hugh West), and the Virginia Foundation for the Humanities.

1. James Madison to Thomas Jefferson, Oct. 24, 1787, in Robert A. Rutland et al., eds., *The Papers of James Madison* (Chicago, 1977), 10: 214. For attributions of "divide et impera" to Machiavelli, see William Watson, *A Decacordon of Ten Quodlibeticall Questions Concerning Religion and State . . .* (1602; repr., Ilkley, England, 1974), 69; Richard Overton with William Walwyn, "A remonstrance of many thousand citizens . . . ," July 7, 1646, on http://www.constitution.org/lev/ eng_lev_04.htm; Robert Beverley, *The History and Present State of Virginia*, ed. Louis B. Wright (1705; repr., Chapel Hill, N.C., 1947), 106; Jonathan Swift, "On the Irish Bishops" (1731), in *The Poems of Jonathan Swift*, ed. William Ernst Browning (London, 1910), 2: 246; Henry Knox, "Plan for the General Arrangement of the Militia," Mar. 28, 1786, in North Callahan, *Henry Knox, General Washington's General* (New York, 1958), 239; E. Cobham Brewer, *Dictionary of Phrase and Fable . . .* ([1870]; repr., New York [1881?]), 231; "Ab nihilo—Citations latines" (http://www.abnihilo.com).
2. Douglass G. Adair, *The Intellectual Origins of Jeffersonian Democracy: Republicanism, the Class Struggle, and the Virtuous Farmer*, ed. Mark E. Yellin (Lanham, Md., 2000), 124; J. Allen Smith, *The Spirit of American Government: A Study of the Constitution, Its Origin, Influence and Relation to Democracy* (New York, 1907), chaps. 3–6; Gordon S. Wood, *The Creation of the American Republic, 1776–1787* (Chapel Hill, N.C., 1969); Daniel W. Howe, "The Political Psychology of The Federalist," *William and Mary Quarterly*, 3d ser., 44, no. 3 (July 1987): 493; Robert A. Dahl, *How Democratic Is the American Constitution?* (New Haven, Conn., 2001), 11–12.
3. Alfred F. Young, "Conservatives, the Constitution, and the 'Spirit of Accommodation,' " in *How Democratic Is the Constitution?*, ed. Robert A. Goldwin and William A. Schambra (Washington, D.C., 1980), 117–47; Bernard Bailyn, *To Begin the World Anew: The Genius and Ambiguities of the American Founders* (New York, 2003), 122–23.
4. For exceptions to this narrow focus on Madison, see Rosemarie Zagarri, *The Politics of Size: Representation in the United States, 1776–1850* (Ithaca, N.Y., 1987); Larry D. Kramer, "Madison's Audience," *Harvard Law Review* 112, no. 3 (January 1999): 611–79.

5. Cecelia M. Kenyon, "Men of Little Faith: The Anti-Federalists on the Nature of Representative Government," *WMQ* 12, no. 1 (January 1955): 12–13, 39 (though Kenyon ultimately dismissed the Anti-Federalists' ideas as "obsolete," she also showed very clearly that the American critique of large legislative districts went far beyond Montesquieu's); Kenyon, ed., *The Antifederalists* (Indianapolis, Ind., 1966), xxxix–xlii; Robert J. Morgan, "Madison's Theory of Representation in the Tenth *Federalist*," *Journal of Politics* 36, no. 4 (November 1974): 870; Charles F. Hobson, "The Negative on State Laws: James Madison, the Constitution, and the Crisis of Republican Government," *WMQ* 36, no. 2 (April 1979): 220; Murray Dry, "Anti-Federalism in *The Federalist*: A Founding Dialogue on the Constitution, Republican Government, and Federalism," in *Saving the Revolution*: The Federalist Papers *and the American Founding*, ed. Charles R. Kesler (New York, 1987), 41; Stanley Elkins and Eric McKitrick, *The Age of Federalism* (New York, 1993), 83, 87; Kramer, *Harvard Law Review* 112: 664; Saul Cornell, *The Other Founders: Anti-Federalism and the Dissenting Tradition in America, 1788–1828* (Chapel Hill, N.C., 1999), 58.
6. [Herman Husband], *Proposals to Amend and Perfect the Policy of the Government of the United States of America; or, The Fulfilling of the Prophecies in the Latter Days . . .* (Philadelphia, 1782), 3–4. Attribution of *Proposal to Amend and Perfect* to Husband is from Mark H. Jones, "Herman Husband: Millenarian, Carolina Regulator, and Whiskey Rebel" (Ph.D. diss., Northern Illinois University, 1982), 272–79.
7. I use the edition of *The Federalist* edited by Jacob E. Cooke (Middletown, Conn., 1961), and cite it by essay number and paragraph.
8. James Madison, June 26, 1787, in Max Farrand, ed., *The Records of the Federal Convention of 1787* (New Haven, Conn., 1911), 1: 431; Charles A. Beard, *An Economic Interpretation of the Constitution of the United States* (New York, 1913), chap. 6. For taxation and debt, see Woody Holton, "'From the Labours of Others': The War Bonds Controversy and the Origins of the Constitution in New England," *WMQ* 61, no. 2 (April 2004): 271–316.
9. Thomas Paine, *Common Sense*, in *The Complete Writings of Thomas Paine*, ed., Philip S. Foner (New York, 1945), 1: 28–29; Alexander Hamilton to Robert Livingston, Apr. 25, 1785, in Harold C. Syrett et al., eds., *The Papers of Alexander Hamilton* (New York, 1962), 3: 609; Charles Royster, *Light-Horse Harry Lee and the Legacy of the American Revolution* (New York, 1981), 89; E. James Ferguson, *The Power of the Purse* (Chapel Hill, N.C., 1961), 337; Ferguson, "The Nationalists of 1781–1783 and the Economic Interpretation of the Constitution," *Journal of American History* 56, no. 2 (September 1969): 242; Merrill Jensen, *The Articles of Confederation: An Interpretation of the Social-Constitutional History of the American Revolution, 1774–1781* (Madison, Wis., 1940), esp. 239–45.
10. [Benjamin Gale], "A Friend to his Country" *Brief, Decent, but Free Remarks, and Observations, on Several Laws Passed by the Honorable Legislature of the State of Connecticut, Since the year 1775* (Hartford, Conn., 1782), 32–33; Timothy Dwight, *Travels in New England and New York*, ed. Barbara Miller Solomon (Cambridge, Mass., 1969), 1: 188–90.
11. Husband, *Proposals to Amend and Perfect*, 3–4, 10, 8; [Zephaniah Swift], *The Security of the Rights of Citizens in the State of Connecticut Considered* (Hartford, Conn., 1792), 47n; Edmund S. Morgan, *Inventing the People: The Rise of Popular Sovereignty in England and America* (New York, 1988), 247.
12. Husband, *Proposals to Amend and Perfect*, 15.
13. Boston dateline, *State Gazette of* (Charleston) *South Carolina*, Oct. 19, 1786; Boston dateline (Boston) *Massachusetts Centinel*, July 29, 1786; "Camillus," *Maryland Journal and Baltimore Advertiser*, Apr. 13, 1787 (reprinted from the

[Boston] Independent Chronicle); Stoughton, Massachusetts, town meeting, circular letter, Jan. 29, 1787 (Portsmouth) *New Hampshire Spy*, Feb. 16, 1787 (reprinted from the Mass. Centinel).

Anonymous essay, news item, *Worcester Magazine* 2, no. 51: 628, 637; Edward Davis, "Election," Mar. 28, 1787, Lunenburg town committee to Athol selectmen, Mar. 7, 1787, Athol selectmen to Lunenburg town committee, Mar. 15, 1787, ibid., 2, no. 52 (all in unpaginated special section); Harvard town meeting and dissident freemen's "Protest," Mar. 19, 1787, ibid., 3, no. 1: 10–11; "A Freeman," ibid., 2, no. 28: 337.

"Locke," "To the free Electors of Massachusetts," (Worcester) *Massachusetts Spy*, May 8, 1788 (reprinted from the [Boston] *Ind. Chron.*); Roger H. Brown, *Redeeming the Republic: Federalists, Taxation, and the Origins of the Constitution* (Baltimore, 1993), 119; Jackson Turner Main, *Political Parties before the Constitution* (Chapel Hill, N.C., 1973), 117.

14. On statewide elections, see "A. B.," (New Haven) *Connecticut Journal*, Oct. 23, 1776; Jackson Turner Main, *The Upper House in Revolutionary America, 1763–1788* (Madison, Wis., 1967), 180–82. For commutation certificates, see Stephen Reed Grossbart, "The Revolutionary Transition: Politics, Religion, and Economy in Eastern Connecticut, 1765–1800" (Ph.D. diss., University of Michigan, 1989), 210, 225; Ferguson, *Power of the Purse*, 188. On the citizen convention, see "An Address to the Discontented People of America," (Bennington) *Vermont Gazette, or Freemen's Depository*, Sept. 11, 1783 (reprinted from the [Hartford] *Connecticut Courant*); Christopher Collier, *Roger Sherman's Connecticut: Yankee Politics and the American Revolution* (Middletown, Conn., 1971), 215; Richard Buel Jr., *Dear Liberty: Connecticut's Mobilization for the Revolutionary War* (Middletown, Conn., 1980), 307–9; Richard J. Purcell, *Connecticut in Transition, 1775–1818* (Washington, D.C., 1918), 192–202.

Oliver Wolcott Sr. to Oliver Wolcott Jr., Sept. 24, 1787 (typescript), in Merrill Jensen et al., eds., *The Documentary History of the Ratification of the Constitution* (Madison, Wis., 1981), microfilm supplement, CN: item 19, 110–11; "An Intercepted Letter," *Conn. Courant*, Oct. 23, 1786 (reprinted from the *New-Haven Gazette*). For a New Jersey effort to nominate candidates, see "A Friend to New Jersey," (Elizabethtown) *New-Jersey Journal and Political Intelligencer*, Aug. 29, 1787 (reprinted from a Philadelphia newspaper).

15. Brown, *Redeeming the Republic*, 86–93; James Madison, "Influence of the Size of a Nation on Government," [1791–92?], in Rutland et al., *Papers of James Madison*, 14: 159; Colleen A. Sheehan, "The Politics of Public Opinion: James Madison's 'Notes on Government,' " *WMQ* 49, no. 4 (October 1992): 615; "One of the People," (Philadelphia) *Pennsylvania Gazette*, Oct. 17, 1787.
16. Wood, *Creation of the American Republic*; Brown, *Redeeming the Republic*; Morgan, *Inventing the People*, 245–62; W. Paul Adams, "Republicanism in Political Rhetoric before 1776," *Political Science Quarterly* 85, no. 3 (September 1970): 397–421; Smith, *Spirit of American Government*, chaps. 3–6; Dahl, *How Democratic?*; Young, "Conservatives"; Daniel Lazare, *The Frozen Republic: How the Constitution Is Paralyzing Democracy* (New York, 1996); Woody Holton, "Did the Constitution Save the Economy?" *Journal of American History* 92, no. 2 (September 2005): 442–469.
17. Elbridge Gerry, May 31, June 7, 1787, Charles Cotesworth Pinckney, June 6, 1787, John Rutledge, June 21, 1787, in Farrand, *RFC*, 1: 48, 155, 137, 365.
18. James Wilson, May 31, 1787, James Madison, May 31, 1787, George Mason, June 4, 1787, John Dickinson, June 6, 1787, Madison, June 6, 1787, Mason, Aug. 13, 1787, in Farrand, *RFC*, 1: 57, 49, 101, 143, 134, 2: 273; Young, "Conservatives," 130–38; Dahl, *How Democratic?*, 11–12; Madison to George Washington, Apr. 16,

1787, Madison to Thomas Jefferson, Oct. 24, 1787, in Rutland et al., *Papers of James Madison*, 9: 384, 10: 212; Morgan, *Inventing the People*, 268–69.

19. James Madison, May 31, 1787 ["James Madison: Note to His Speech on the Right of Suffrage"], ca. 1821, James Wilson, June 6, 1787, in Farrand, *RFC*, 1: 56, 3: 454, 1: 133 [emphasis in original]; Madison, "Remarks on Mr Jeffersons Draught of a Constitution," 1788, in Julian P. Boyd et al., eds., *The Papers of Thomas Jefferson* (Princeton, N.J., 1950), 6: 309; [Alexander Contee Hanson], "Aristides." *Remarks on the Proposed Plan of a Federal Government* (Annapolis, Md., 1788), "An American Citizen," Philadelphia *Independent Gazetteer*, Sept. 29, 1787, in Jensen et al., *DHRC*, 15: 525, 13: 272. My thanks to John Leonard for the Hanson reference.
20. "Madison: Note to His Speech," in Farrand, *RFC*, 3: 454; "The State Soldier II," Va. Ind. Chron., Feb. 6, 1788, in Jensen et al., *DHRC*, 8: 348; Jay Fliegelman, *Declaring Independence: Jefferson, Natural Language, and the Culture of Performance* (Stanford, Calif., 1993); Sandra M. Gustafson, *Eloquence Is Power: Oratory and Performance in Early America* (Chapel Hill, N.C., 2000).
21. Madison, "Remarks on Mr Jeffersons Draught," in Boyd et al., *Papers of Thomas Jefferson*, 6: 309. On the pursuit of fame, see James Conniff, "The Enlightenment and American Political Thought: A Study of the Origins of Madison's *Federalist Number 10*," *Political Theory* 8, no. 3 (August 1980): 386–87; Douglass Adair, "Fame and the Founding Fathers," in *Fame and the Founding Fathers: Essays by Douglass Adair*, ed. Trevor Colbourn (1974; repr., Indianapolis, Ind., 1998), 3–36. Charles Cotesworth Pinckney, speech in the South Carolina House of Representatives, Jan. 18, 1788, in Jonathan Elliot, ed., *The Debates in the Several State Conventions on the Adoption of the Federal Constitution . . .* (Washington, D.C., 1836), 4: 302. Moreover, "the best men in the country," many of whom had refused state assembly seats, would "consent to serve" in Congress (3.8; 53.9); Garry Wills, *Explaining America: The Federalist* (Garden City, N.Y., 1981), 227, 251.
22. For attribution of the *Conn. Courant* article to Noah Webster, see Jensen et al., *DHRC*, 13: 169n. William Plumer to Samuel Plumer Jr., June 6, June 9, June 17, 1786, William Plumer to John Hale, Aug. 13, 1786, in "Letters of William Plumer, 1786–1787," *Publications of the Colonial Society of Massachusetts, Volume 11, Transactions 1906–7* (Boston, 1910): 385–87; "Madison: Note to His Speech," in Farrand, *RFC*, 3: 454.
23. George Mason, June 6, 1787, in Farrand, *RFC*, 1: 134, 142.
24. Elbridge Gerry, June 7, 1787, James Wilson, June 7, 1787, James Madison, June 7, 1787, John Dickinson, June 7, 1787, Gouverneur Morris, July 19, 1787, Madison, July 19, 1787, in Farrand, RFC, 1: 152–55, 2: 54, 56–57. The belief that the state legislatures, not the people, should choose senators united admirers of the state assemblies (most of whom came from small states) with delegates who feared the people (Jack N. Rakove, *James Madison and the Creation of the American Republic* [Glenview, Ill., 1990], 57–63). The latter fear seems to have been the greater one for at least three delegates from large states—Gerry of Massachusetts and the two Charles Pinckneys of South Carolina—all of whom supported election by the legislatures. Morris and Madison are described as the two most vocal delegates in Catherine Drinker Bowen, *Miracle at Philadelphia: The Story of the Constitutional Convention, May to September 1787* (Boston, 1966), 42.
25. Gouverneur Morris, July 2, 1787, Alexander Hamilton, June 18, 1787, Morris, July 19, 1787, in Farrand, *RFC*, 1: 517, 291, 2: 54; "A Citizen of America" [Noah Webster], "An Examination into the Leading Principles of the Federal Constitution," Oct. 17, 1787, in Bernard Bailyn, ed., *The Debate on the Constitution: Federalist and Antifederalist Speeches, Articles, and Letters During the Struggle over Ratification* (New York, 1993), 1: 133, 140n.

26. John Williams, June 21, 1788, Melancton Smith, June 20, 1788, in Elliot, *Debates in the State Conventions*, 2: 242, 229–30; Edmund S. Morgan, "Safety in Numbers: Madison, Hume, and the Tenth *Federalist*," *Huntington Library Quarterly* 49, no. 2 (Spring 1986): 106; James Madison, July 10, 1787, in Farrand, *RFC*, 1: 568; "Federal Farmer," *An Additional Number of Letters from the Federal Farmer to the Republican; Leading to a Fair Examination of the System of Government Proposed by the Late Convention . . .* (New York, 1788), in Jensen et al., *DHRC*, 17: 291.
27. For scholars who believe Madison relied more heavily on the large polity than the large legislative district, see Albert Furtwangler, *The Authority of Publius: A Reading of the* Federalist *Papers* (Ithaca, N.Y., 1984), 116; David F. Epstein, *The Political Theory of* The Federalist (Chicago, 1984), 109; Lance Banning, *The Sacred Fire of Liberty: James Madison and the Founding of the Federal Republic* (Ithaca, N.Y., 1995), 208–9, 469 n. 52; Alan Gibson, "Impartial Representation and the Extended Republic: Towards a Comprehensive and Balanced Reading of the Tenth *Federalist* Paper," *History of Political Thought* 12, no. 2 (Summer 1991): 270, 282–304. For scholars who reverse that prioritization, see Wood, *Creation of the American Republic*; Kramer, *Harvard Law Review* 112; Morgan, *Journal of Politics* 36; Wills, *Explaining America*.
28. One of Madison's fears was that "factious leaders may kindle a flame" (10.22). For others' fears of bad ideas spreading like "wild fire," see Alexander Hamilton, June 18, 1787, in Farrand, *RFC*, 1: 289; George Washington to David Stuart, Dec. 6, 1786, in W. W. Abbot and Dorothy Twohig, eds., *The Papers of George Washington*, Confederation Series (Charlottesville, Va., 1995), 4: 446.

    For comparisons between bad ideas and contagions, see James Madison to Thomas Jefferson, Aug. 12, 1786, in Rutland et al., *Papers of James Madison*, 9: 95 ("epidemic malady"); Madison, July 25, 1787, "Madison: Note to His Speech," in Farrand, *RFC*, 2: 110, 3: 454; Cooke, *Federalist*, 65, 425; Madison, in Drew R. McCoy, *The Last of the Fathers: James Madison and the Republican Legacy* (Cambridge, 1989), 65; "The Petition of the Committee of Public Creditors of the City and Liberties of Philadelphia," *Pa. Gaz.*, Dec. 15, 1784; Elizabeth-Town dateline, *N.-J. Journal and Polit. Intell.*, Oct. 4, 1786; "Camillus," *Worcester Mag.* 3, no. 1: 3; Newport dateline, *Va. Ind. Chron.*, June 20, 1787; "Extract of a Letter from South-Kingstown, July 4," *Providence Gazette and Country Journal*, July 14, 1787.
29. Charles Cotesworth Pinckney, May 14, 1788, in Bailyn, *Debate on the Constitution*, 2: 586; George Mason, Aug. 13, 1787, "Madison: Note to His Speech," in Farrand, *RFC*, 2: 273–74, 3: 454.
30. Charles Cotesworth Pinckney, May 14, 1788, in Bailyn, *Debate on the Constitution*, 2: 586; Wills, *Explaining America*, 205.
31. Gouverneur Morris, July 19, 1787, in Farrand, *RFC*, 2: 54.
32. McCoy, *Last of the Fathers*, 73 ("Father of the Constitution"); James Madison, June 6, 1787, in Farrand, *RFC*, 1: 136; Cooke, *Federalist*, 63–64. On obstacles to organizing, see Adair, *Intellectual Origins*, 123; Owen S. Ireland, *Religion, Ethnicity, and Politics: Ratifying the Constitution in Pennsylvania* (University Park, Pa., 1995). My thanks to Loren Young for his insight on this point. James Madison to Thomas Jefferson, Oct. 24, 1787, in Rutland et al., *Papers of James Madison*, 10: 214.
33. [William Whiting], "Some Remarks on the Conduct of the Inhabitants of the Commonwealth of Massachusetts in Interupting the Siting *[sic]* of the Judicial Courts in Several Counties in That State . . . ," in Stephen T. Riley, ed., "Dr. William Whiting and Shays' Rebellion," *Proceedings of the American Antiquarian Society* 66, pt. 2 (October 1956): 153–54; James Madison, June 6, June 7, 1787, in Farrand, *RFC*, 1: 136, 152; Madison, "Vices of the Political System of the U. States," [Apr.–June 1787], in Rutland et al., *Papers of James Madison*, 9: 356–57; Adair,

Intellectual Origins, 123. Cherishing at once a republican belief in the importance of electing virtuous statesmen and a liberal realization that most people were not at all virtuous, the framers hoped to force selfish constituents to choose virtuous representatives (Wood, *Creation of the American Republic*, 475; John M. Murrin, "Fundamental Values, the Founding Fathers, and the Constitution," in *To Form a More Perfect Union: The Critical Ideas of the Constitution*, ed. Herman Belz, Ronald Hoffman, and Peter J. Albert [Charlottesville, Va., 1992], 30–31; Joyce Appleby, "The American Heritage: The Heirs and the Disinherited," *Journal of American History* 74, no. 3 [December 1987]: 803; Gibson, *History of Political Thought* 12: 302–4).

34. Gouverneur Morris, July 2, 1787, in Farrand, *RFC*, 1: 514.
35. Elbridge Gerry, July 25, 1787, in Farrand, *RFC*, 2: 114.
36. Elbridge Gerry, July 25, 1787, George Mason, July 26, 1787, in Farrand, *RFC*, 2: 114, 119; Minor Myers Jr., *Liberty without Anarchy: A History of the Society of the Cincinnati* (Charlottesville, Va., 1983), x, 96.
37. W[illiam] Eustis to Henry Knox, Feb. 3, 1785, Henry Knox Papers (microfilm), box 17, item 165, Massachusetts Historical Society, Boston; Elbridge Gerry to Rufus King, Mar. 28, 1785, in Charles R. King, ed., *The Life and Correspondence of Rufus King, Comprising His Letters, Private and Official, His Public Documents, and His Speeches* (1894; repr., New York, 1971), 1: 83; Sidney Kaplan, "Veteran Officers and Politics in Massachusetts, 1783–1787," *WMQ* 9, no. 1 (January 1952): 29–57; George Flint, in Ferguson, *Power of the Purse*, 254; Noah Webster, "A Private Citizen" *Attention! or, New Thoughts on a Serious Subject, Being an Enquiry into the Excise Laws of Connecticut* . . . (Hartford, Conn., 1789), 17; Forrest McDonald, *Alexander Hamilton: A Biography* (New York, 1979), 44; McDonald, *E Pluribus Unum: The Formation of the American Republic, 1776–1790* (Boston, 1965), 34; Alfred F. Young, *The Democratic Republicans of New York: The Origins, 1763–1797* (Chapel Hill, N.C., 1967), 76.
38. Gouverneur Morris, July 2, 1787, in Farrand, *RFC*, 1: 514; Laurel Thatcher Ulrich, *A Midwife's Tale: The Life of Martha Ballard, Based on Her Diary, 1785–1812* (New York, 1990), 91.
39. "An Old Republican II," "Strictures upon County Conventions in General, and Upon the Late Meeting Holden at Hatfield in Particular . . . ," (Springfield, Mass.) *Hampshire Herald*, Sept. 12, 1786; Worcester Co. convention, proceedings, Sept. 26–28, 1786, *Worcester Mag.* 2, no. 27: 318; "Address to the Inhabitants of the County of Worcester," ibid., 2, no. 28: 335–36; George Richards Minot, *The History of the Insurrections, in Massachusetts, in the Year MDCCLXXXVI, and the Rebellion Consequent Thereon* (Worcester, Mass., 1788), 54; Whiting, "Some Remarks,"153–54; "Plain Reason," *Va. Ind. Chron.*, Aug. 29, 1787; Bezaleel Howard, in Richard D. Brown, "Shays's Rebellion and Its Aftermath: A View from Springfield, Massachusetts, 1787," *WMQ* 40, no. 4 (October 1983): 602; "Publick Faith," *Mass. Centinel*, Feb. 8, 1786 (reprinted from the *Hampshire Herald*, Jan. 31, 1786); "Philodemus" [Thomas Tudor Tucker], *Conciliatory Hints, Attempting, By a Fair State of Matters, To Remove Party-Prejudices* . . . *And Proposing a Convention* . . . (Charleston, S.C., 1784), 29.
40. "Disculpus," (Portsmouth) *New Hampshire Mercury*, Oct. 18, 1786; "Thoughts on Paper Money," ibid., Nov. 8, 1786; Stratham town meeting (Nov. 27, 1786), Stratham Town Records, 2: 27, New Hampshire State Library, Concord. A legislative committee counted the number of citizens who had voted for and against paper money in the various town meetings and declared that it had lost by one vote (Jere R. Daniell, *Experiment in Republicanism: New Hampshire Politics and the American Revolution, 1741–1794* [Cambridge, Mass., 1970], 198–99; John H.

Flannagan Jr., "Trying Times: Economic Depression in New Hampshire, 1781–1789" [Ph.D. diss., Georgetown University, 1972], chap. 5; Lynn Warren Turner, *The Ninth State: New Hampshire's Formative Years* [Chapel Hill, N.C., 1983], 52, 56).

41. Minot, *History of the Insurrections*, 68; Massachusetts House of Representatives proceedings, *Worcester Mag.* 2, no. 30: 362 (reprinted from the [Boston] *Ind. Chron.*, Oct. 19, 1786); "Address to the People," ibid., 2, no. 37: 444; Samuel A. Otis to Theodore Sedgwick, Sept. 8, 1787, in Sedgwick Papers 1, Massachusetts Historical Society, Boston.
42. Madison, "Remarks on Mr Jeffersons Draught," in Boyd et al., *Papers of Thomas Jefferson*, 6: 309.
43. Husband, *Proposals to Amend and Perfect*, 8; Holton, *JAH* 42.
44. "Americanus I" [John Stevens Jr.] (New York) *Daily Advertiser*, Nov. 2, 1787, in Bailyn, *Debate on the Constitution*, 1: 229–30; Benjamin Rush, "Harrington," *Pa. Gaz.*, May 30, 1787; Benjamin Rush, *American Museum*, January 1787, in Jensen et al., *DHRC*, 13: 118, 48; James Madison to Thomas Jefferson, Oct. 24, 1787; Madison, "Consolidation," *National Gazette*, Dec. 5, 1791, in Rutland et al., *Papers of James Madison*, 10: 214, 14: 138; Sheehan, *WMQ* 49: 614; Banning, *Sacred Fire of Liberty*, chaps. 7, 11.
45. "Brutus I," *New York Journal*, Oct. 18, 1787, in Jensen et al., *DHRC*, 13: 417. For scholarship on Anti-Federalists, see Kenyon, *WMQ* 12; Banning, *Sacred Fire of Liberty*, 204; Zagarri, *Politics of Size*, 86, 93–94.
46. "Brutus I," *N.Y. Journal*, Oct. 18, 1787, in Jensen et al., *DHRC*, 13: 420; James Madison, June 7, 1787, in Farrand, *RFC*, 1: 152.
47. "Cornelius," (Springfield, Mass.) *Hampshire Chronicle*, Dec. 18, 1787, in Jensen et al., *DHRC*, 4: 412; Zagarri, *Politics of Size*, 91–93.

    On constituents not knowing enough about representatives, see "John De Witt III," American Herald, Nov. 5, 1787, in Jensen et al., *DHRC*, 4: 197; George Athan Billias, *Elbridge Gerry: Founding Father and Republican Statesman* (New York, 1976), 163; Norman K. Risjord, *Chesapeake Politics, 1781–1800* (New York, 1978), 278–79.

    On representatives not knowing enough about constituents, see George Mason, "Objections to the Constitution of Government Formed by the Convention," Oct. 7, 1787, "Brutus I," *N.Y. Journal*, Oct. 18, 1787, "John De Witt III," *American Herald*, Nov. 5, 1787, "Centinel I" [Samuel Bryan], *Phil. Ind. Gaz.*, Oct. 5, 1787, in Jensen et al., *DHRC*, 13: 348, 420, 4: 197, 13: 335.
48. Adam Smith, *The Theory of Moral Sentiments*, ed. D. D. Raphael and A. L. Macfie (1759; repr., Oxford, England, 1976), 86, 90; Francis Hutcheson, in Garry Wills, *Inventing America: Jefferson's Declaration of Independence* (Garden City, N.Y., 1978), 287; "Federal Farmer," *Additional Number of Letters*, in Jensen et al., *DHRC*, 17: 281; William Symmes, speech in Massachusetts ratifying convention, Jan. 22, 1788, in Herbert J. Storing, ed., *The Complete Anti-Federalist* (Chicago, 1981), 4: 63; Samuel Chase ["Notes of Speeches Delivered to the Maryland Ratifying Convention"], April 1788, ibid., 5: 90; Zagarri, *Politics of Size*, 91.

    George Mason, June 4, June 11, June 16, 1788, Patrick Henry, June 12, 1788, Edmund Randolph, June 6, June 17, 1788, George Nicholas, June 14, 1788, in Elliot, *Debates in the State Conventions*, 3: 30–31, 34, 262, 264, 426, 327, 123, 470, 393; Mason, June 6, 1787, in Farrand, *RFC*, 1: 133–34.
49. John Quincy Adams to William Cranch, Dec. 8, 1787, "O," *American Herald*, Feb. 4, 1788, "Federal Farmer," *Observations Leading to a Fair Examination of the System of Government Proposed by the Late Convention . . .* (New York, 1787), "Brutus III," *N.Y. Journal*, Nov. 15, 1787, in Jensen et al., *DHRC*, 4: 401, 5: 855, 14: 31,

123; Melancton Smith, June 21, 1788, in Elliot, *Debates in the State Conventions*, 2: 246; Rawlins Lowndes, speech in the South Carolina House of Representatives, Jan. 16, 1788, in Bailyn, *Debate on the Constitution*, 2: 22.

Benjamin Gale, Nov. 12, 1787, in Jensen et al., *DHRC*, 3: 423. Scholars such as Kenyon (*WMQ* 12) believe the Federalists' assessment of a representative's virtue hinged on his willingness to sacrifice the narrow interests of his region. Though that was often the case, numerous opponents as well as supporters of the Constitution worried more about finding officeholders who would not be too biased in favor of their own social class.

"O," *American Herald*, Feb. 4, 1788, "Brutus III," *N.Y. Journal*, Nov. 15, 1787, in Jensen et al., *DHRC*, 5: 855, 14: 123; Samuel Chase ["Notes of Speeches Delivered to the Maryland Ratifying Convention"], April 1788, in Storing, *Complete Anti-Federalist*, 5: 90; Melancton Smith, June 21, 1788, in Elliot, *Debates in the State Conventions*, 2: 247–48; Wood, *Creation of the American Republic*, 490; Zagarri, *Politics of Size*, 92.

50. James Madison, May 31, June 26, 1787, "Madison: Note to His Speech," in Farrand, *RFC*, 1: 50, 431, 3: 451.
51. Melancton Smith, June 21, 1788, in Elliot, *Debates in the State Conventions*, 2: 246; "Federal Farmer," *Additional Number of Letters*, in Jensen et al., *DHRC*, 17: 280.

    For proposals to hold runoffs, see Jeremiah Hill to George Thatcher, Sept. 25, 1788, "A Real Farmer," *Hampshire Chron.*, Nov. 5, 1788, in Merrill Jensen et al., eds., *The Documentary History of the First Federal Elections, 1788–1790* (Madison, Wis., 1976), 1: 462–63, 471–72; "Federal Farmer," *Additional Number of Letters*, in Jensen et al., *DHRC*, 17: 313–14.
52. "Federal Farmer," *Additional Number of Letters*, in Jensen et al., *DHRC*, 17: 312. "Brutus," who may have been Melancton Smith, warned that if congressmen were elected statewide, "the natural aristocracy of the country" would be able to "concenter all their force in every part of the state into one point, and by acting together, will most generally carry their election." "Federal Farmer," *Observations Leading to a Fair Examination*, "Brutus III," *N.Y. Journal*, Nov. 15, 1787, "Cornelius," *Hampshire Chron.*, Dec. 18, 1787, in Jensen et al., *DHRC* 13: 411n, 14: 31, 122–23, 4: 414; Kenyon, *WMQ* 12: 12–13, 40; Dry, "Anti-Federalism in *The Federalist*," 49; William B. Allen, "Federal Representation: The Design of the Thirty-Fifth *Federalist Paper*," *Publius* 6, no. 3 (Summer 1976): 67.
53. Zagarri, *Politics of Size*, 105–18; Husband, *Proposals to Amend and Perfect*, 3–4; "Lycurgus III" [Herman Husband], *XIV Sermons on the Characters of Jacob's Fourteen Sons* (Philadelphia, 1789), 29. For attribution of *XIV Sermons* to Husband, see Jones, "Herman Husband," 310.
54. "A Citizen of Connecticut" [William Beers], *An Address to the Legislature and People of the State of Connecticut, On the Subject of Dividing the State into Districts for the Election of Representatives in Congress* (New Haven, Conn., 1791), 17, 18, 29, 35–36; Swift, *Security of the Rights*, 22, 75, 87; "Publius Secundus Americanus," *Daily Advertiser*, Nov. 10, 1788, in Jensen et al., *History of the First Federal Elections*, 3: 210–11.
55. Swift, *Security of the Rights*, 92.
56. (Baltimore) *Maryland Journal*, Nov. 14, 1788, anonymous essay, *Daily Advertiser*, Nov. 7, 1788, in Jensen et al., *History of the First Federal Elections*, 2: 125, 3: 209–10; Beers, *Address to the Legislature*, 31. Men's positions in the debate over how to elect congressmen reflected not only their political philosophies but also their beliefs about which method was likely to favor their own party (Benjamin Rush to Jeremy Belknap, Oct. 7, 1788, "The Belknap Papers," part 3, *Collections of the Massachusetts Historical Society*, 6th ser., 4 [1891]: 418–19; Zagarri, *Politics of Size*, 113–18).

57. Swift, *Security of the Rights*, 75; William Findley, speech in Pennsylvania assembly, Sept. 24, 1788, "A Real Farmer," *Hampshire Chron.*, Nov. 5, 1788, in Jensen et al., *History of the First Federal Elections*, 1: 287, 471; *State Gazette*, and (Trenton) *New-Jersey Advertiser*, Mar. 13, 1798, in Zagarri, *Politics of Size*, 111.
58. Zagarri, *Politics of Size*; Donald S. Lutz, *Popular Consent and Popular Control: Whig Political Theory in the Early State Constitutions* (Baton Rouge, La., 1980), xiv; "Federal Farmer," *Observations Leading to a Fair Examination*, in Jensen et al., *DHRC*, 14: 31; Swift, *Security of the Rights*, 83–85; Husband, *XIV Sermons*, 29.
59. James Madison, June 26, 1787, in Farrand, *RFC*, 1: 431; Beard, *Economic Interpretation*, chap. 6 ("The Constitution as an Economic Document"). Douglass Adair ("The Tenth Federalist Revisited," in Colbourn, *Fame and the Founding Fathers*, 106–31) and Banning (*Sacred Fire of Liberty*, 205) reject this contention that property was the fundamental divide.
60. For bondholders' support for the Constitution and windfalls from the funding act, see Samuel P. Savage to George Thatcher, Feb. 17, 1788, in Jensen et al., *DHRC*, 7: 1704–5; Alexander Hamilton, "The Defence of the Funding System," [July 1795], in Syrett et al., *Papers of Alexander Hamilton*, 19: 5; Beard, *Economic Interpretation*; McDonald, *E Pluribus Unum*, 34; Ferguson, *Power of the Purse*, 340–41; Young, *Democratic Republicans of New York*, 75; Leonard L. Richards, *Shays's Rebellion: The American Revolution's Final Battle* (Philadelphia, 2002), 156–59; Robert A. McGuire and Robert L. Ohsfeldt, "Economic Interests and the American Constitution: A Quantitative Rehabilitation of Charles A. Beard," *Journal of Economic History* 44, no. 2 (June 1984): 509–19; Robert A. McGuire, *To Form a More Perfect Union: A New Economic Interpretation of the United States Constitution* (Oxford, Eng., 2003).

    For bondholders' request, see "The Memorial and Petition of the Public Creditors . . . of Pennsylvania . . . ," Aug. 21, 1789 (presented Aug. 28, 1789), in *Annals of Congress*, 1st Cong., 1st sess., 822–25.

    On original bond recipients' failure to petition Congress, see Elias Boudinot, speech in House of Representatives, Feb. 17, 1790, in *Annals of Congress*, 1st Cong., 2nd sess., 1297; James Madison, speech in House of Representatives, Feb. 18, 1790, in Rutland et al., *Papers of James Madison*, 13: 52.
61. Theodore Sedgwick, speech in House of Representatives, Jan. 28, 1790, and editor's footnote, in *Annals of Congress*, 1st Cong., 2nd sess., 1135, 1135n; Sam[uel] Breck to John Brown, Dec. 30, 1790, Brown Papers, John Carter Brown Library, Providence, R.I.; Joseph Barrell to Samuel Webb, Jan. 31, 1790, in Worthington Chauncey Ford, ed., *Correspondence and Journals of Samuel Blachley Webb* (New York, 1894), 3: 150. On thwarting bad factions but not good ones, see James MacGregor Burns, *The Deadlock of Democracy: Four-Party Politics in America* (Englewood Cliffs, N.J., 1963), 21–22; Gibson, *History of Political Thought* 12: 289–91; John Zvesper, "The Madisonian Systems," *Western Political Quarterly* 37, no. 2 (June 1984): 244.

Chapter 3

"Overrun with Free Negroes": Emancipation and Wartime Migration in the Upper Midwest

Leslie A. Schwalm

From *Civil War History*

In March 1863 a Union officer wrote to his hometown newspaper inquiring, "Are there any contrabands wanted in Iowa City, or its vicinity for help this spring? If so, please let me hear from you. I could send a large number to Iowa, if they were wanted, as there are many brought up the river at this time . . . ." Writing from St. Louis, he noted that many of the former slaves gathered there "prefer going to Iowa [more] than any other place." But back in Iowa, some of his neighbors had organized a public meeting to oppose "all schemes . . . to fill our schools and domestic circle with the African race" because of their belief that recently emancipated African Americans, "unaccustomed to our climate, unskilled in our mode of agriculture, undisciplined in habits, and unfit for society," would "destroy the dignity of white labor" in Johnson County. That Iowans were not all of one mind about the arrival of emancipated slaves was further evidenced in the tone of newspaper coverage when former slaves were brought to a nearby Mississippi River town. As sarcastically noted in the local paper, potential employers were not difficult to find: "When the negroes arrived, there was a great fluttering . . . for the best 'take.' Philanthropy ran very high indeed—provided the services of a good stout negro could be obtained for his victuals and clothes. Visions of retired gentlemen and gentlewomen, with black servants to attend their every want and wish, overcame some . . . [who] felt as though 'it were the happiest day of their lives.' "[1] White Midwesterners disagreed on the implications of the arrival of newly freed African Americans; but whether or not they welcomed former slaves as a new labor source or feared workplace competition, whether or not they participated in philanthropic work on behalf of former slaves or were suspicious of the motives of those who did, white Midwesterners agreed on one thing: that the consequences of emancipation extended well beyond the slaveholding South.

Scholars have focused the study of African American emancipation on the policies debated in the nation's capital and the progression of slavery's destruction in the Confederate South and the slaveholding Border States, but the varied and conflicting midwestern responses to wartime emancipation and black migration suggest that the implications and consequences of emancipation were also confronted outside the South. While a small if vocal minority of Northern white people pressed for an end to slavery at the outset of the war, many more opposed abolition and feared its consequences. From the Connecticut soldier who reacted to emancipation celebrations in Beaufort, South Carolina, by threatening to kill any former slave who tried to "get in on" him, to the Iowan who complained of former slaves "crowding" whites aside on local city sidewalks, many Northern whites feared that severing the bonds of slavery would bring unwelcome changes to the "place" of African Americans—and, by implication, to that of whites—in a postemancipation nation.[2]

By the eve of the Civil War, public debate over the place of African Americans in the nation had a long history, expressed most cynically by the colonization and emigration movements whose advocates asserted that white supremacy left no opening for black political and civic equality in the United States.[3] During the war these debates became more urgent as the Northern public contemplated slavery's destruction. As Harriet Beecher Stowe observed early in the war, "Many well-meaning people can form no idea of immediate emancipation but one full of dangers and horrors. They imagine the blacks free from every restraint of law, roaming abroad a terror and nuisance to the land." In 1862 *Harper's Weekly* condemned those fears as petty and unchristian but joined Stowe in acknowledging their strength and persistence, noting the nation's inability to "tolerate negroes, except as slaves. We can't bear them. We don't want them in our houses. We won't meet them in public assemblages, or concede to them any rights whatever, except the bare right of living and working for us, sometimes for wages, generally without." Sharply aware of the prevalence of such sentiments among Northern and Border State white people, Congress and the president brought colonization proposals forward with nearly every discussion of emancipation.[4] The war's emancipationist direction raised the unanswered question: what would be the social, political, and geographic destiny of African Americans in the aftermath of slavery's destruction?

As readers and writers, legislators and city council members, farmers and dockhands, workers and employers, Northern men and women responded to this question with a public debate over the possible outcomes of emancipation. Among them, most Northern blacks rejected the prospect of colonization and embraced the hope that emancipation would lead to full political and civic equality. That hope was not without foundation; besides the real and symbolic importance of emancipation and black enlistment, legislative advancements had been made. During the war reformers eroded discriminatory laws in Iowa, Illinois, California, and Ohio and successfully challenged streetcar segregation in New York and Washington, D.C. Still, advocates for racial equality knew that more would be needed to end the "mockery of freedom" that Northern blacks endured with the "pain, the penalties, the soul-cutting degradations" of their circumscribed citizenship.[5] State laws, public support, and generations of practice fortified legal and customary discrimination against any easy incursion, yet the war seemed poised to threaten this status quo. From Washington, D.C., to Canada West, white people anxiously predicted that emancipation would be followed by an unwelcome migration of African Americans into the North.[6]

During the course of the war the debates over "place" within a racially stratified society became yoked to a debate over "location," as slavery's wartime collapse led to the migration and relocation of former slaves out of the South. In 1862 and 1863 these debates were joined by threats and violence with attacks on black workers in Chicago, Cincinnati, and Boston; on African American communities in Massachusetts, Connecticut, New York, and New Jersey; on black bystanders during the New York City and Detroit draft riots; and on newly arriving black migrants in midwestern river towns from New Albany, Indiana, to St. Paul, Minnesota. White violence against black people was the most extreme manifestation of the wartime politics of race and place.[7]

The Upper Midwest shared in this larger national conflict. Among many Midwesterners, the idea of emancipating and aiding former slaves who intended to stay in the South was viewed as a humanitarian matter. But when former slaves—by their own volition or with the help of others—made their way north, emancipation became a critical and vigorously debated matter of public policy. Revealing a deep-seated belief in a racially ordered society, many midwestern whites assumed that any possibility of black gains in the region would impinge upon white status and citizenship. For Midwesterners whose understanding of white supremacy had been premised on the right and ability to exclude first Indian people and then African Americans from the region, the physical mobility of former slaves suggested an unwelcome change in racial boundaries and practices in a postslavery nation.

Several studies of the Northern home front take up the topic of emancipation's meaning, but most are southward gazing, viewing slavery and its destruction as primarily Southern phenomena. A surprisingly scant scholarship has attempted to understand emancipation's meaning and impact in the North.[8] An important exception is *Free but Not Equal*, V. Jacque Voegeli's 1967 landmark study of wartime black migration to the Midwest. Path breaking for its illumination of Midwestern racism and its assessment of the migration's centrality to Northern debates over the meaning of the war, Voegeli's study largely concerns the influence of those debates on electoral politics. He left for other scholars the task of unearthing the experience of the migrants themselves, the informal politics of race, and the ramifications of migration outside the Midwest and after 1863. The experience of wartime migrants has almost completely eluded the attention of scholars. Without an understanding of the actual dynamics and experience of wartime migration, as well as the concomitant creation of a public politics of race in wartime America, scholars will continue to underestimate the national meaning and consequences of emancipation.[9]

This essay explores the wartime confrontation of residents of the upper Mississippi Valley—Wisconsin, Minnesota, and Iowa—with the meaning of emancipation in their Northern homes and communities, specifically through their encounters with black mobility. While Northern encounters with black migrants produced striking and often similar developments in other regions, especially the Ohio Valley and along the eastern Atlantic corridor, the response to emancipation and migration in the Upper Midwest is especially instructive about the wartime politics of race.

The Upper Midwest may seem an unlikely setting for an intense and far-reaching debate about the place of African Americans in the postemancipation nation. Midwesterners had a long history of concern over the prerogatives of whiteness, but it was primarily in relation to the Indian population against which white settlers constructed themselves as the bearers of civilization and progress. The region was closely tied to the South by many of its Southern-born settlers, by the need for markets for Midwestern grain and livestock, and by the Mississippi River itself. Yet the Upper Midwest was culturally and politically predicated on the antislavery article of the Northwest Ordinance, the idealization of free labor, and a critique of Southern slaveholding for the limits it placed on the economic and political opportunities of Southern yeomen. The region drew migrants from the upland South, southern New England, and the mid-Atlantic states as well as from Germany, Ireland, and Scandinavia; yet despite its white ethnic diversity, its black population was very small before the war.

When the wartime destruction of Southern slavery became linked with the possibility, and then the reality, of black migration into the region, residents of the northernmost reaches of the upper Mississippi Valley quickly realized that wartime emancipation had meaning beyond the borders of the slaveholding South. On the farms, in the churches and shops, and on the streets and levees of Midwestern cities the arrival of newly emancipated slaves fueled political debate, infiltrated political rhetoric, and informed popular politics—especially the politics of workplace segregation. Their arrival also became a lightning rod for regional debates about the causes and consequences of the war, the proper function of the Federal government, the meaning of masculinity in households seemingly turned upside down by wartime mobilization, as well as the implications of black freedom and citizenship. To expand our understanding of the meanings and implications of emancipation outside the slaveholding South, this essay first considers the events that framed the Upper Midwest's encounter with emancipation—especially the patterns of wartime black migration to the region—and then explores how and why this wartime migration provoked a battle over the multiple meanings of emancipation in the nation's Midwest.

The midwestern experience of slavery's destruction was shaped by the confluence of regional history, national developments, and the geography of the river valley that linked Iowa, Wisconsin, and Minnesota with the South. Prior to the Civil War, vigorous white Midwestern opposition to the western extension of slavery was an expression of the idealization of free labor but also an assertion of disdain toward people of African descent. Racism and antagonism toward African Americans had come to the region in the habits and culture of its earliest white settlers from both North and South, whether those settlers were accustomed to the fact of Southern slavery or what Joanne Pope Melish refers to as the fiction of a "historically free, white New England."[10] While foreign-born Midwesterners occupied a range of positions in their cultural and political viewpoints on slavery and black equality, even those most likely to support antislavery measures were cautious of nativist impulses within the Republican party. And even with strong pockets of abolitionist sentiment and open resistance to the recapture of fugitive slaves, Midwestern territorial and state governments legislated white supremacy with the overwhelming support of their constituents. They circumscribed black freedom by disfranchisement, prohibiting blacks from testifying against whites in court or serving in state militias, segregating schools, and prohibiting interracial marriage. In Iowa, for example, territorial legislatures, the first constitutional convention, and antebellum legislative assemblies concurred with this pattern of white supremacy, rendering the state constitution a social compact to which African Americans were not party. Legislation first limited (1839) and then barred (1851) black settlement in Iowa, and residents in both Minnesota and Wisconsin petitioned lawmakers before and during the war to pass similar legislation. Though lax in their enforcement, these laws nonetheless placed black Midwesterners in the perpetually vulnerable position of knowing that their freedom was not assured.[11]

A hidden history of slavery not only attenuated black freedom in the antebellum Midwest but also contributed to the substance of white supremacy. In the northern Mississippi Valley slave owners hid the real status of their chattel, claimed fictional residences in the South, or simply disregarded Federal prohibitions against slavery in free territories.[12] Miners, fur traders, farmers, territorial officials, and army officers stationed in the region owned and employed slave labor. Nonetheless, to enslaved people in the South the Upper Midwest offered the promise of freedom. In the decades before the war, their flight into the region points to the contrast they saw between Southern slavery and even the circumscribed black freedom of the Midwest.[13]

The migration of former slaves to the Midwest during the Civil War was a flight toward freedom as well as an escape from the violence and chaos of war. The numbers of wartime migrants, however, are difficult to assess. Although all three states conducted an 1865 census, in each instance it was enumerated prior to the return of black soldiers and the family members who accompanied them to the South. Wisconsin's census survives only in fragments. Even with this undercounting, the rate of increase for Minnesota and Iowa in the growth of the black population between 1860 and 1865 was significant: 158 percent in Minnesota (from 259 to 411) and 337 percent in Iowa (1,069 to 3,608).[14] Between 1860 and 1870 the Federal census reports an overall net increase of 6,135 African Americans for all three states, from 1,171 to 5,762 in Wisconsin, 259 to 759 in Minnesota, and 1,069 to 5,762 in Iowa, a net increase of 80 percent, 193 percent, and 439 percent, respectively.[15]

Although the Federal census does not allow us to distinguish between wartime and postwar migration, it does indicate that the seeming racial homogeneity of the midwestern experience was disrupted, particularly at the county and township level. Slightly less than half (45) of Iowa's counties reporting in the 1860 census had no blacks in 1860. By 1870 only 15 of those counties (16 percent) had no black inhabitants, while 64 Iowa townships gained black residents. This meant that in 1860 almost 47,000 white Iowans lived in townships that in the next ten years went from having no black residents to having 10 or more. In Wisconsin the wartime movement of African Americans into small towns often occurred en masse, as local religious leaders answered the call to provide Northern homes and employers for black refugees. Between the fall of 1862 and the spring of 1863, 40 or 50 African Americans were brought at one time to Beaver Dam, 75 to Fond du Lac, and 25 to Trenton. Racine, a larger city, received 150 black migrants at one time.[16] In Minnesota Mississippi River steamboats in government service brought the largest number of former slaves, including about 30 on the *War Eagle* in the fall of 1862 and 125 on the *Northerner* and 233 on the *Davenport* in May 1863. These refugees from slavery settled largely in the St. Paul, Minneapolis, and St. Anthony area as well as in southeastern counties bordering the Mississippi and Minnesota Rivers.[17] Whether we look to the region's rural counties or its cities, the number of African Americans newly arrived from Southern slavery increased during the war—sometimes overnight. This had a major impact on the region.

"Migration" is a generic term that can obscure significant differences in wartime black mobility, differences that shaped the experience of migration as well as responses to it. African Americans who fled slavery in the Mississippi River Valley pursued one of three distinct paths to the Upper Midwest. All three paths involved autonomous decision making and action on the part of enslaved people, but the first can best be characterized as self-liberation by flight, in which the entire migration process was directed by enslaved people themselves. The second path involved arrangements made by white soldiers and officers from Midwestern states to transport fugitive slaves north to family and friends. The third path consisted of the organized relocation of large numbers of fugitive slaves ("contrabands") to Northern employers under the auspices of military authority or with the assistance of freedmen's aid societies and other interested civilians.

The first path to freedom—self-liberation by flight—had a long antebellum history but was prompted more immediately by the proximity of Union forces and the chaos of war. Within the Mississippi Valley, opportunities for flight increased dramatically in the spring and summer of 1862, as Union forces occupied middle and west Tennessee, northern Alabama, portions of Arkansas and northern Mississippi, and southern Louisiana. By the end of 1862 the flow of slaves to Union lines grew so large that the army established a string of contraband camps throughout the valley. As the Union gained control of the Mississippi River and the heart of the valley's plantation economy in the summer of 1863, emancipation, the enlistment of slave men, and the employment of all others on abandoned plantations brought freedom to thousands of slaves.[18]

In Missouri, an important gateway to the Upper Midwest for fugitive slaves, a different set of circumstances prevailed. Reluctant to alienate loyal slave states, the Lincoln administration offered significant protections to Missouri's Unionist slave holders, including the exclusion of Missouri from the provisions of the Emancipation Proclamation.[19] Black enlistment opened up new opportunities for Missouri slave men in the fall of 1863, but slave women and children accompanying men to recruiting stations were turned away or, even worse, returned to the custody of loyal slave owners who responded violently and vengefully to the erosion of their authority. In fear for their lives and in pursuit of their freedom, thousands of enslaved women and children fled west to Kansas, east across the Mississippi to Illinois, or north to St. Louis, Iowa, and beyond. They fled on foot, with stolen horses or wagons, by steamboat and train, individually, in family groups, and, as slavery came to the brink of collapse, by the tens and hundreds.[20]

Wartime flight was dangerous for slaves anywhere in the Mississippi Valley. Missouri closely enforced state laws barring common carriers from transporting slaves without their owners' permission, and it was not uncommon for slave owners to pursue fugitives well into Iowa or Illinois.[21] Confederate troops and guerrilla warfare also made escape particularly difficult. Iowa soldiers captured by Confederate forces in Marks Mills, Arkansas, witnessed the massacre of half of the 300 unarmed contrabands who had joined with a Union supply train to "get from bondage." Confederate troops could not be restrained "from vengeance on the negros," whose bodies "were piled in great heaps about the wagons, tangled brushwood, and upon the muddied and trampled road."[22] These dangers reflect the tremendous difficulties set in motion by military policies that often left enslaved women and children to fend for themselves.

A second avenue for wartime black migration opened up when midwestern soldiers and officers returned home with black servants or made arrangements to relocate individual fugitives or small families to farms and households in need of additional labor, most typically with a soldier's own family or one in his home community. Soldiers' wives were not always enthusiastic about their husbands' plans, however, as Mary Ann Graham Rogers of Tama, Iowa, related when her spouse announced that he might bring a fugitive slave boy home. "I wondered what I would do with another boy and he a black one," she wrote. "There was not a colored person in our town or ever had been that I knew of".[23] Because military policy required the exclusion of fugitive slaves from army camps (especially in Missouri) and protected the property rights of loyal slave owners, it was not unusual for fugitives to be refused safe harbor in army encampments.[24] But enforcement of that policy weakened as soldiers became unwilling to participate directly in the return to bondage of men and women whose labor had eased the harshness of camp life.[25] For Midwestern soldiers uncomfortable with official policy and sharply aware of the labor shortage affecting their families and home communities, sending fugitive slaves north offered an alternative solution.

The fugitives' perspective on this opportunity is harder to document. While gaining a safer harbor from the threat of reenslavement, African Americans who went north left spouses, family, and friends behind; were wholly dependent on the trustworthiness of their benefactors; and faced long, risky journeys to unknown locations where they would live with white strangers for an indeterminate length of time. Elizabeth Estell, a fugitive from Missouri slavery, was sent by steamboat, train, and stage coach to Cleveland, Minnesota, by the white officer commanding her husband's company. Restless throughout her stay in rural Minnesota, Estell missed her husband and the two children she left behind. Perhaps the cooking, sewing, laundry, cleaning, and farm chores that she was expected to perform for a family of four were harder or more tedious than she had expected or the isolation more stark or the lack of a firm arrangement concerning her wages too disappointing for her to appreciate the lessons in reading and writing and the occasional sleigh ride she received in exchange for her labor. Certainly her experience was not unique among the hundreds, perhaps thousands, of African American adults and children who came to the rural Midwest under similar circumstances.[26]

There is good reason to be skeptical about the quality of life and the extent of freedom enjoyed by these isolated refugees. Some newly arrived black people discovered a presumption among local whites (and potential employers) that a former slave's Northern benefactor held a claim to their labor, as was the case for a young former slave from Tennessee who was brought to Des Moines, Iowa, by Governor Kirkwood. The youth wanted to leave his situation with Kirkwood, but local businessmen refused to come between him and his powerful employer. Other former slaves found themselves stranded without any formal arrangement for wages or living quarters. In Fairfield, Iowa, for example, a soldier was charged with illegally bringing a slave boy, James Robinson, home with him from the service and using him as a slave. Refugees who became sick and unable to work were sometimes abandoned to local charity. In October 1862 an unnamed man brought to Keokuk, Iowa, by Col. John W. Rankin was left at the Lee County poor house when he became ill. Other former slaves were threatened with return to the South should their work or behavior not meet expectations.[27] Not the least of their worries was the threat posed by Iowa's law against the migration of free blacks into the state, as well as the racism supporting such laws, as expressed by a vocal minority in Minnesota and Wisconsin.[28]

The third path of wartime black migration, the relocation of groups of former slaves to the Upper Midwest, was conducted by both civilians and the military. Beginning in the summer of 1862, large numbers of fugitive slaves behind army lines were increasingly viewed by Union commanders and soldiers as "a burden and an encumbrance to the army and the cause," largely because of the numbers of women and children among them.[29] One remedy adopted by military authorities was the transportation of hundreds of women and children from army camps throughout the Mississippi Valley to contraband camps at Cairo, Illinois, or St. Louis and then to Northern employers who sought replacements for enlisted white workers.[30]

The organized relocation of fugitive slaves to the upper Mississippi Valley was first attempted in September 1862 when 700 slaves, mostly women and children who had been sent to the contraband camp at Cairo, were transported north to potential employers at government expense.[31] Officers in the field welcomed the opportunity to relieve their camps of fugitive slaves. Minnesotan Lucius Hubbard, writing from northern Alabama in September 1862, noted, "I am constantly besieged by men, women and children, who apply for 'protection,' and facilities for leaving the country . . . . I was sorely puzzled to know what to do with them." The following month he described sending 500 former slaves north. "They flocked into my camp in great crowds, and I shipped them as fast as I could get transportation. They are in a free state by this time."[32] But if relocation temporarily eased the pressure on Union officers, it met strong opposition on the home front from white Midwesterners who feared that Federal authorities would unleash a flood of black migration. Concerns about relocation and black labor competition reverberated loudly during the 1862 elections; Democrats across the Midwest successfully used the threat of black migration to gain white working-class support for their candidates. Midwestern Republicans complained that Democratic victories were carried by the threat of a black tide flowing up the Mississippi River that would throw white men out of work or cut their wages to 25 cents a day. Even the strongest Republican response fell back on familiar racist rhetoric; Iowa's oldest Republican newspaper insisted that African Americans were of such inferior ability and intelligence that they could never compete with white workers.[33]

During the summer of 1862, white hostility toward blacks erupted into riots in Toledo, Cincinnati, Chicago, and Peoria. By mid-October, fearing that relocating former slaves into the Upper Midwest would provoke the same response, and undermine support for Republican candidates in the upcoming election, the secretary of war brought organized relocation to an abrupt but temporary halt. After the election, the program was quickly resurrected, and former slaves were once more transported north.[34]

Although military authorities, under pressure from the Lincoln administration, looked to black enlistment and the employment of contrabands on abandoned plantations in the South to absorb some of the refugees and assuage Northern anxiety about the migration, organized relocation continued. Many of the army chaplains in charge of contraband camps used their association with denominational and freedmen's aid societies to assist in the relocation of large numbers of former slaves to Northern employers.[35] With or without military involvement, the link between emancipation and black migration became a point of considerable political debate in the Midwest, across the North, out East, and in the halls of Congress. Not only did it shape the 1862 elections, but it also shaped debate later in the war about the nation's responsibilities toward freed slaves.[36]

From the threat of a "black tide heading up the Mississippi," to the portrayal of African Americans "coming in vast herds to the fair prairies of the North West," the caricatures of black migration that appeared in the regional Democratic press drew their exaggerated imagery from the Midwestern landscape, dehumanizing black migrants and likening them to the cattle and hogs driven to Mississippi Valley market towns. Even more exaggerated were the portrayals of migration's consequences, including threats that jobs left vacant by soldiers would be "filled by lazy, shiftless negroes" and that the dependents of white working men would be forced onto the same economic and social level as black people, "until the white man conscious of the outrage inflicted upon him, would rise up and throw off the incubus."[37]

These dire predictions have largely been treated by scholars as opportunistic, partisan efforts to rally Democratic votes in the upcoming elections. There is no question that the rhetoric of black migration was deployed by peace Democrats, Copperheads, and conservative Republicans to attack and derail the emancipationist Radical Republican proposals. But the "sound and fury" over emancipation and migration that we tend to label as midwestern Copperheadism was not just a discursive political device to use against the Lincoln administration, as some scholars have suggested. It also represented a complex and multidimensional public politics of race, whose exaggerations and escalated racial anxieties attest to the war's challenges to racial thought and practice in the Upper Midwest. Never limited to political campaigns or party schemes, this politics of race quickly found wide expression in mass meetings, household and private correspondence, and discourse on farms and levees.[38]

The Midwest's encounter with emancipation was compounded by national developments. The Democratic party's success in focusing resistance to relocation tapped not only into Midwestern racism but also into growing apprehension about the changing role of the Federal government. The preliminary Emancipation Proclamation was but one of a series of developments that led Midwesterners to associate the Republican party with an increasingly centralized, powerful Federal government whose policies were affecting daily life in unprecedented and unwelcome ways.[39] Steady inflation had already brought home the cost of war, and some Midwesterners saw Federal aid to fugitive slaves as depriving more worthy citizens of financial support. Civilians and soldiers alike ruminated on the expense of Federal aid to the contrabands. "$62,000 of your money taken . . . to keep in idleness a lot of vagrant negroes," reported one Minnesota newspaper about the cost of providing for contrabands for five months at Fort Monroe in Virginia. In Wisconsin, the *Manitowoc Pilot* complained that the expense of relocation was shouldered by the public treasury, while the cost of supporting the freed people once they had arrived would be shouldered by local white residents. "Meanwhile, the white laborer . . . through out the north, has to pay about double for everything . . . everything must go 'up,' 'up,' if we white men must be compelled thus to feed, clothe, nurse, and take care of the millions of lazy contrabands, which the abolitionists threaten to loose upon us."[40]

It was not only the cost of Federal aid that excited Midwestern criticism but also the symbolic meaning of the unprecedented expenditure of human and financial resources on behalf of African Americans. While Midwestern votes helped elect Lincoln to the presidency, few white Midwesterners disagreed with Stephen Douglas's insistence that the nation was "founded on the white basis." The editor of one Wisconsin newspaper, reporting on Lincoln's December 1862 address to Congress, complained that "the President is troubled with 'nigger on the brain.' The message commences with 'nigger,' and ends with 'nigger,'—not a word for the benefit of the white people of the country."[41] Public and private discussions of black migration and employment also revealed a growing resentment that the increasingly powerful Federal government was failing to safeguard what current scholarship would call the political and psychological wages of whiteness. That failure was viewed as part of the erosion of the racially determined economic and political privilege that many white Midwesterners believed lay at the core of the republic.[42] In the Midwest comparisons between the Federal government's conduct toward the Sioux, former slaves, and white citizens caused some to believe that the government was failing to act in the best interest of white citizens and even demonstrated preferential treatment toward nonwhites.

The failure of Federal Indian policy during the Civil War compounded midwestern criticism of the Federal government's wartime priorities and policies. In August 1862, Dakota warriors killed about 500 white settlers and militiamen in an uprising fueled by the malfeasance of Federal Indian agents and white settlers' disregard for Indian treaty rights. In the panic that followed, thousands of white Midwesterners fled their homes, and alarm spread quickly throughout the region. As far away as central and eastern Wisconsin, rumors of imminent attack heightened anti-Indian racism, prompting hysteria and panicked flight.[43] From the perspective of many white Midwesterners, the Federal response to the Minnesota uprising was characterized by inadequate relief for white victims, slow and ineffective military retaliation, and the ultimate insult of Lincoln's officer of clemency to all but thirty-eight of the 307 Dakota and *Métis* who were sentenced to execution by a military commission.

Carrying out this sentence—the largest mass execution in American history—did little to assuage Midwestern anger. The racial identity of Midwestern whites was defined by their claim to have "civilized" the Midwest by conquering, containing, and displacing Indian people, a process enabled and mediated by Federal, territorial, and state authorities.[44] In that light, the Federal government's failure to divert manpower and resources to a more immediate and brutal military campaign against the Indians was viewed as a deep betrayal. That sense of betrayal was sharpened by belief that even while white Midwesterners' needs were ignored, large sums of public money were being spent by Congress and the military to support fugitive slaves in the South. As one editor noted, "The just demands and unquestioned rights of Minnesota have no chance in this Congress. Suffering from the horrors of an unparalleled Indian massacre, the fault or not of the very powers from whom she seeks redress, she comes to Congress with her country devastated, her women ravished—murdered a thousand times over—her suckling children hanging crucified to her door posts, her men lying on the plains and in the ditches, the victims of infernal fiends, and implores assistance–redress. The answer is, Wait. 'Four millions of Southern slaves must have their freedom . . . .' Little is expected of this Congress but the eternal discussion of the nigger question."[45]

Further aggravating Minnesotans' dim view of the Republican administration during this time of crisis was the army's transportation of more than 100 contrabands to St. Paul, ostensibly to support the military expedition against the Dakota. More than half of those transported were women and children, who were viewed by local whites as a burden, not a help, during the crisis. "Women and pickaninnies will not render material assistance in driving mule teams over the plains," complained the editor of the *St. Paul Pioneer Press*. Not surprisingly, this group of former slaves found their arrival physically resisted by St. Paul policemen and Irish gangs on the levees.[46]

Influenced by both national and regional developments in their responses to emancipation and relocation, Midwestern whites also read an erosion of their status and prerogatives into the most disparate of wartime circumstances. Ignoring the struggle by African Americans for the right to enlist, some Midwestern whites complained that until late 1863, white families shouldered the burden of military service while black families did not. Some argued that pension board authorities subjected the widows of black veterans to less rigorous rules than white widows. When Senator Charles Sumner described a Union soldier's act of kindness toward a slave girl as "the most touching" act of the war, he was met with furious Midwestern criticism for making a symbol of a black child rather than highlighting the wartime sacrifices of white women. Others argued that the loss of family farms to mortgage companies drew little sympathy, because only white families were affected; had those farmers been black, they argued, a host of philanthropists would be offering their aid. St. Louis shoemakers posed the question asked by many Midwesterners: "Have we no eye for the relief of anybody but negroes? Are we not just as much entitled to freedom as the negro?"[47]

Military service took a toll on white Midwestern families as their husbands and sons experienced particularly high mortality rates in the Western Theater of war, and working-class households were hard hit by the absence of wage earners and farm hands. Their suffering led to resentment that white soldiers were seemingly slighted to the advantage of fugitive slaves and free blacks.[48] As one Minnesota soldier noted, "I am as much in favor of abolishing slavery as anybody . . . but since I have been in the Army and seen them better treated than White Men . . . I lost all my love for the colored Gentlemen."[49] A Wisconsin newspaper complained that white soldiers, their families in want and themselves suffering without food or clothing, "must stand aside" while the government attended to former slaves. Contrabands were reportedly given better rations than white soldiers in the South. Rumors spread that white soldiers were arrested for using the most commonplace derogatory language toward former slaves, while black people were free to insult white soldiers. White men in uniform were reported to have been barred from public events that admitted African Americans. On the home front rumors circulated about "the pernicious workings of the 'Freedom Policy,' " in which "hundreds on hundreds of the hated negroes . . . flock to the stations on rail roads running north, claiming protection and transportation to the exclusion of sick soldiers, and army stores." Asked one Iowa editor, "What next will the colored people get from our long heeled despots superior to that which they dole out to white people?"[50]

Fear of how emancipation and the migration of former slaves into the Upper Midwest would alter Midwestern life frequently focused on workplace issues. As Jacqueline Jones notes in her study of race and American labor, "Jobs are never just jobs; they are social markers of great real and symbolic value".[51] How fragile were the ideas and practices that protected white privilege in the Midwestern workplace, which kept most black workers out of all but the most menial of work and perpetuated the notion that independence and dependence were raced? Despite pretensions of racial solidarity, white employers could not be counted on to maintain an exclusively white workplace. Both before and after the Federal government relocated contrabands to Northern employers, some employers experimented with using former slaves to replace enlisted workers or as replacements for striking workers.[52] "White" jobs were disappearing. One southeastern Iowa newspaper editor insisted that "a white drayman can scarcely live; neither can a blacksmith, plasterer, nor many other tradesmen, to say nothing of common laborers" because of competition from black workers. In July 1864, the *Keokuk (Iowa) Constitution* decried the practice of "would be loyal merchants" who fired white men and hired "female shades to do their work at such reduced prices, that, considering the present rates for the commodities it would be impossible for any man of a family to keep his head above water." "Why not," asked one Iowa editor, "while the bones of your sons are bleaching on the southern plains, allow the accursed source of all our trouble to come here and enjoy the business your sons are deprived of, and compete with the poor laborers of your State?" Again, a feeling of betrayal by the Federal government further added to white concerns: "White men and women in want of employment, are advised to black themselves with burnt cork, rubbed with lard, and make immediate application to the Government . . . Ebony is all the go now, and who would not prefer a black skin to an empty stomach?"[53]

Concerns about losing jobs and, by extension, economic and political independence went far beyond the exchange of partisan editorials. Black workers and their white employers became the targets of mass meetings, protests, threats, and occasional violent attacks. White men gathered in Wapello and Johnson Counties to "resist the introduction of free negroes into Iowa; first by lawful means, and when that fails, we will drive them, together with such whites as may be engaged in bringing them in, out of the State or afford them 'hospitable graves.' " This being the Midwest, the protests and attacks included farmers—the largest source of employment in the region. In northeastern Page County, farmers who had employed "some colored girls . . . in their houses . . . were soon notified, by a man in their neighborhood . . . that they must send those 'niggers' back, or they would be burnt out." Similar threats were made against an Appanoose County, Iowa, farmer who hired former slaves. A Muscatine County farmer employing a contraband boy was visited by twenty local residents who hoped, "by threats of personal violence," to "convince him of his error."[54] Even the chaplains who aided in the relocation process were sometimes awakened by nighttime attackers. For example, the Reverend J. B. Rogers, superintendent of contraband at Corinth, Mississippi, and then at the Cairo, Illinois, contraband camp, escorted seventy-five people to his home in Fond du Lac, Wisconsin, so that local farmers might employ them. He was subsequently the target of late-night vandalism. "Don't I know," recalled one of the contrabands who had been a small child at the time and slept in Rogers's house that night, "how they threw a rock through the window of his house?"[55]

The intensity and occasional violence of these protests can be explained by white Midwesterners' deep investment in a segregated economy and the social meaning of white labor. Yet their fear of replacement by black workers is difficult to reconcile with the widely acknowledged labor shortage affecting the region. The war not only increased demand for midwestern agricultural products but also significantly reduced the agricultural workforce through enlistments.[56] "No whites can be gotten," insisted labor-hungry farmers; blacks were the "last resort" of employers desperate for workers. When shiploads of contrabands disembarked at Mississippi River towns, they were often outnumbered by the employers who anxiously awaited them.[57] Furthermore, hundreds—if not thousands—of contrabands were relocated to labor-deprived farms and households throughout the

Midwest—and not by the Federal government but by Midwestern soldiers and officers as a help to their own struggling families.[58]

Competing claims among native-born, immigrant, and ethnic Americans to the prerogatives of whiteness also played an underlying role in shaping the Midwestern response to emancipation and wartime black migration. Native-born employers, who responded to strikes or labor shortages by hiring black workers, seemed to deny Irish and working-class immigrants the right to claim the privilege of an all-white workplace.[59] The tenuous hold of unskilled Irish workers on white entitlements in the Midwest was revealed in reports that blamed Irish workers for the most vigorous opposition to black relocation.[60] From St. Paul came comparisons of the "low Irish" with newly arrived African Americans: "The contrast between the two classes as they came in contact was decidedly in favor of the contrabands, and the Irish appreciated it by expressing fear of competition." Local newspapers announced that the Irish had good reason to fear competition from the more pliable contraband laborers.[61]

For all the outrage men expressed over the erosion of white workingmen's rights in the face of emancipation and relocation, it would be easy to overlook the likelihood that the majority of relocated and migrating contrabands were women and children and that their employers were very often white women.[62] Many Midwestern women were eager to employ former slave women as household and farm workers during the war, despite the expressed intention of white men to defend the domestic circle from "the African race." White women also took an active role in encouraging and arranging for the transportation of former slaves north. White women who were sympathetic toward the plight of slaves, or who were simply desperate for domestic and farm help, responded eagerly when authorities invited Northerners to make applications for contraband laborers. Several women also contacted Annie Wittenmyer, the Midwest's preeminent wartime relief organizer, hoping that her extensive contacts in the South could help them obtain black workers. They wrote detailed solicitations, very specifically listing their preferences. "If a *good* servant could be had I would take her even with a child—rather than not get one," wrote one woman from Bentonsport, Iowa. Another requested a "woman from 18 to 40—capable of general housework. Should she have a boy—or brother from 12 to 16—and even a young child—we will take them all." She continued, "There are quite a number here that would be glad to get them [women]—for servants," and she needed help "oh so much—and what we get here is so poor." A number of families in and around Vinton, Iowa, also hoped to get contrabands, both for field hands and house servants. Many others made arrangements with missionaries and ministers working in contraband camps as well as with their male kin enlisted and stationed in the Mississippi Valley. One Minnesota soldier's parents wrote him, "You know just what we want—a servant that is *neat honest & active*. I earnestly hope you will find a 'darkey woman' suited to your mind and ship her forthwith for Red Wing." With so many Midwestern women struggling to keep households and farms afloat, the opportunity to hire contraband women was a welcome development. In fact, as such arrangements met with success, friends and neighbors quickly followed suit. One Minnesota family noted that the success of their own arrangements "had given house wives all around the wench fever."[63]

Although the wartime debate over emancipation's impact on white privilege in the workplace focused on occupations dominated by men, the dynamic meanings of race and free labor were also played out in Midwestern households. The employment of newly freed black women as domestics and farm workers introduced new and complicated dynamics into employment relations between servants and the women who hired them. In St. Paul, white servants were viewed by some potential employers as less "respectable" than black servants, leading to an increased demand for contraband workers. Whether native born or immigrant, white women employed in households rejected the prospect of working alongside black women. Louisa Johnson, a Swedish employee in a Minnesota household, was described by her employer as having "a fear that she and a darkey would be identified as help or that she would be set aside for the ebony article." Residents of MacGregor, Iowa, angry that local white women welcomed the arrival of former slave women in the town, "advised the Norwegian, German and Irish girls to emigrate to the region of the Rocky Mountains and thus make room for the new order of things."[64] Yet families seeking to employ household and farm labor turned to former slaves in part because white farm and household workers took advantage of the wartime labor shortage to pursue more advantageous positions, especially during harvests, when they could demand higher wages.

Native-born whites seem to have harbored some resentment at their abandonment by immigrant workers seeking better opportunities, suggesting that the turn to black workers was part of the larger struggle over the meaning of ethnicity in the Midwest. For example, a farmer in Elm Grove, Wisconsin, "talked of sending for a 'contraband' to fill the place of the transitory Swedes." Another man from the same town complained that "the prices for labor are so high and the day labor is more independent than the employer." And in Red Wing, Minnesota, Orrin Densmore complained when immigrant day workers gave notice of their intent to "go into the country through harvest for higher wages."[65]

It is also important to question whether the "wench fever" that swept Midwestern communities reflected a perceived change in the status of white women who employed black, rather than white, household laborers. Until the Civil War, black employment in Midwestern households had been limited to an elite group of whites—Southerners vacationing along southern Minnesota's lakes who brought their slaves with them, former Southerners who brought slaves with them when migrating to the Midwest, and army officers stationed at Midwestern posts who hired or purchased slaves as household servants. Perhaps the ability to employ African American women as laborers imparted a new aura of status and respectability to Midwestern white women.

Whether the employment of black workers offered a welcome remedy to wartime labor shortages, a solution to unreliable immigrant workers, or an opportunity to boost one's status, white women who sought to employ newly arrived African Americans in their households often faced their strongest opposition from white men. In meetings, rallies, and the ongoing editorial dialogue over the threat posed by black migration, white men repeatedly asserted their right and intent to defend the racial purity of the white household and the family it sheltered. "While our brothers, sons and neighbors are doing battle in our country's cause, and enduring the hardships of the battlefield, we will keep their homes unspotted by the black race," asserted men in Johnson County, Iowa, and elsewhere. "On account of the respect and affection we have for our wives, sisters, and daughters, we will resist all schemes . . . to fill our schools and domestic circle with the African race."[66]

It is not clear whether these public assertions by men ready to defend hearth and home against the "threat" posed by African American women were directed at other white men or at white women who were obviously eager to find household workers. But there is little doubt that the war had already eroded masculine authority in the domestic sphere. More than half of Iowa's white men of military age were enlisted or drafted during the war, leaving many Midwestern farms and households bereft of husbands, fathers, and elder sons who now found themselves receiving orders rather than giving them.[67] The wartime economy may have benefited some, but many men found their ability to support their families seriously impaired by inflation, the loss of Southern markets for their produce, and the loss of labor at critical moments. Compounding these developments, many Midwestern white women were taking on unprecedented responsibilities in both public and private settings. With their men away, women became the arbiters of loyalty and patriotism, as they defined and monitored the obligations of their congregations and communities on behalf of the soldier and the Union cause.[68] While many men publicly endorsed the patriotism of Midwestern women, we must wonder whether men welcomed all of the changes war brought to gender relations within their own households and also whether white men's strident insistence on defending their households was in part an effort to shore up their own political authority by reclaiming the ability and the right to dictate domestic affairs. After all, men who insisted on defending their families against the new migrants also implied their ability to do so. That a defense of their authority could be framed in racialized terms—defending the racial purity of their households—suggests how intimately masculine authority and racial prerogative were linked.

The ideas white Midwesterners held about race and place in their society became explicit in the public dialogue that accompanied wartime black migration. Male or female, former slaves were often derided as impertinent and disrespectful to whites, eager to challenge the public rituals of racial domination and subordination, and anxious to challenge the boundaries of white privilege. Newly arrived former slave women were caricatured as styling themselves too good for menial household labor, having been falsely imbued with the notion that better things awaited them in their new Midwestern homes.[69] Black men and women alike were portrayed as "impudent and fresh" in their behavior toward white people. Whites, in turn, claimed to suffer "many and gross outrages at the hands of these fugitives from the South" who refused to yield on city sidewalks, refused to doff their hats when spoken to, and refused to remain silent when treated in a disrespectful or demeaning manner.[70] If whites' accounts of frequent insult are suspect for their one-sidedness, they nonetheless confirm what many Midwesterners had feared about the uncontainable consequences of emancipation and relocation: former slaves were rejecting the notion that the destruction of slavery alone constituted the fullest extent of freedom. In so doing, white Midwesterners believed, freed people threatened the very foundations of white privilege in the region.

The wartime conflict over black mobility demonstrated how closely white Midwesterners linked the stability of their own local racial hierarchies with Southern slavery. Until the war the exclusion of all but a few African Americans from the Midwest—one of the region's characteristic features—had been accomplished by legislation and, indirectly, by slavery's containment of almost 90 percent of the nation's black population in the South.[71] When slavery's wartime collapse led to the northward migration of African Americans, Midwestern whites perceived an unprecedented challenge to the practices and ideas that sustained white supremacy in their region.

As Midwestern whites struggled to defend what they felt were the entitlements accorded them by race—from jobs, farm ownership, and the political and economic independence they afforded to a segregated workplace, control over public spaces, and exclusive claims to citizenship—they revealed how deeply white privilege saturated daily life in the region. At the same time, the response to black migration also suggests how contingent Midwestern white supremacy was on white mutuality, which was demonstrated when white men mobilized in political meetings, at informal gatherings, and in threatening visitations to wayward neighbors. Such collective action sought to repair the social fabric of white supremacy and to reinforce the public authority of white men, an authority that had been challenged not only by the threat of black mobility but also by the war's disruption of households and male authority within them. Finally, the debate over race and place also revealed that out of the war came new exigencies that competed with antebellum practices in influencing Midwestern beliefs and behavior. During the war the need to unburden the army of its civilian encumbrance, the imperative to bring in harvests when labor was scarce, and the ability to protect independence and perhaps profit through the exploitation of vulnerable workers challenged the region's history of black exclusion. In order to meet these demands, white Midwesterners had to develop more elastic responses to the relocation of former slaves and their employment in the Upper Midwest. The white men and women who aided in the relocation of former slaves to the North and those who employed former slaves in their homes, on their farms, and in their businesses had not necessarily abandoned their own race-based prerogatives. Instead, they tried to reconcile the unprecedented events of the war with an ideology that required new practices. Farm wives and merchants who welcomed the opportunity to employ African Americans could accommodate their presumptions of racial superiority by treating their new employees as servile workers.

Ultimately, the proximity of African Americans proved less of a threat to racial hierarchies than many Midwesterners might have expected. As a result, emancipation and black migration set the stage for a much longer battle over "place" and citizenship. Nonetheless, the wartime struggle over the implications of emancipation represent a pivotal moment in the history of Midwestern black political and social life. Wartime events not only increased the size of black communities in the Upper Midwest but, perhaps more importantly, mobilized black Midwesterners to mount a public defense of their race and a claim to citizenship that gained momentum with the enlistment of black men, the mobilization of black women to support black soldiers, and postwar demands for citizenship and equal protection under the law. For black Midwesterners, the wartime conflicts over emancipation's consequences launched an unprecedented era of regional activism and organizing. Former slaves like Moses Mosely, who came to Iowa during the war, were glad to take their new freedom "in the rough," but they were also determined to "make the best of it we can." After the war they pressed for full citizenship not only through the franchise and the law but also by contending with the public and private politics of race that continued to prevail in midwestern households, farms, and streets through the end of the nineteenth century.[72]

Notes

Leslie A. Schwalm is associate professor at the University of Iowa. She is the author of *A Hard Fight for We: Women's Transition from Slavery to Freedom in South Carolina* (1997), which won the Willie Lee Rose book prize. Her current project "Emancipation's Diaspora," explores the ways in which the destruction of slavery became a national phenomenon, by investigating the meaning, impact, and public memory of emancipation among white and African American midwesterners.

1. *Iowa City Republican*, Apr. 1, 8, 1863; *Muscatine (Iowa) Courier*, Oct. 2, 1862.
2. Nina Silber and Mary Beth Sievens, eds., *Yankee Correspondence: Civil War Letters between New England Soldiers and the Home Front* (Charlottesville: Univ. Press of Virginia, 1996), 74; *Keokuk (Iowa) Daily Constitution*, Sept. 15, 1862.
3. Floyd J. Miller, *The Search for a Black Nationality: Black Emigration and Colonization 1783–1863* (Urbana: Univ. of Illinois Press, 1975); David W. Blight, *Frederick Douglass' Civil War: Keeping Faith in Jubilee* (Baton Rouge: Louisiana State Univ. Press, 1989).
4. *Independent* (New York), Aug. 21, 1862; *Harper's Weekly*, Apr. 5, 19, June 28, Sept. 6, 1862. On the Lincoln administration's advocacy for colonization, see Blight, *Frederick Douglass' Civil War*, 134–47.
5. Robert Hamilton, quoted in *Weekly Anglo-African* (New York), Sept. 26, 1863. See also Phillip Shaw Paludan, *"A People's Contest": The Union and the Civil War,*

1861–1865 (New York: Harper & Row, 1988), 220–21; and James M. McPherson, *The Struggle for Equality: Abolitionists and the Negro in the Civil War and Reconstruction* (Princeton: Princeton Univ. Press, 1964), 235–37.

6. Ira Berlin, Wayne Durrill, Steven F. Miller, Leslie S. Rowland, and Leslie Schwalm, " 'To Canvass the Nation': The War for Union Becomes a War for Freedom," *Prologue* 20, no. 4 (1988): 235–36; Jane Rhodes, *Mary Ann Shadd Cary: The Black Press and Protest in the Nineteenth Century* (Bloomington: Univ. of Indiana Press, 1988), 151.
7. Iver Bernstein, *The New York City Draft Riots: Their Significance for American Society and Politics in the Age of the Civil War* (New York: Oxford Univ. Press, 1990); Jacqueline Jones, *American Work: Four Centuries of Black and White Labor* (New York: W. W. Norton, 1998), 290–92; Emma Lou Thornbrough, *The Negro in Indiana before 1900: A Study of a Minority* (1957; reprint, Bloomington: Indiana Univ. Press, 1993), 185–92; V. Jacque Voegeli, *Free but Not Equal: The Midwest and the Negro during the Civil War* (Chicago: Univ. of Chicago Press, 1967), 34–35; and Williston H. Lofton, "Northern Labor and the Negro during the Civil War," Journal of Negro History 34 (July 1949): 251–73.
8. On white abolitionists and wartime race relations in the North, see McPherson, *The Struggle for Equality*, and George M. Frederickson, *The Inner Civil War: Northern Intellectuals and the Crisis of The Union* (New York: Harper & Row, 1965). On the varied racial attitudes of Northern white soldiers, see Joseph T. Glatthaar, *Forged in Battle: The Civil War Alliance of Black Soldiers and White Officers* (New York: Free Press, 1990); and James M. McPherson, *For Cause and Comrades: Why Men Fought in the Civil War* (New York: Oxford Univ. Press, 1997).
9. See Voegeli, *Free but Not Equal* and his recent, Eastern-focused article, "A Rejected Alternative: Union Policy and the Relocation of Southern 'Contrabands' at the Dawn of Emancipation," *Journal of Southern History* 69, no. 4 (Nov. 2003): 765–90. Two exceptions are Carol Faulkner's study of the freedmen's aid movement, "The Hard Heart of the Nation: Gender, Race, and Dependency in the Freedmen's Aid Movement" (Ph.D. diss., Binghamton, State University of New York, 1998), which pays particular attention to the experiences of Reconstruction-era black migrants in the northeast and their criticism of relocation arrangements that splintered families or placed them in exploitative situations; and Michael Johnson's "Out of Egypt: The Migration of Former Slaves to the Midwest during the 1860s in Comparative Perspective," in *Crossing Boundaries: Comparative History of Black People in Diaspora*, ed. Darlene Clark Hine and Jacqueline McLeod (Bloomington: Indiana Univ. Press, 1999), 223–45, which utilizes census data to trace patterns of household composition, wealth, property ownership, and occupational status of the migrant population in 1870.
10. Joanne Pope Melish, *Disowning Slavery: Gradual Emancipation and "Race" in New England, 1780–1860* (Ithaca: Cornell Univ. Press, 1998), xv. Many assessments of the popular politics of race in the Midwest have been premised on the assumption that pro-slavery and anti-black values were the product of white migration from the South. Melish exposes the active workings of racism in the creation of a fictional New England free of its history of slavery and distant from the production of a racist state during the process of gradual emancipation.
11. Michael J. McManus, *Political Abolitionism in Wisconsin, 1840–1861* (Kent, Ohio: Kent State Univ. Press, 1998), 34–35; Gary Libman, "Minnesota and the Struggle for Black Suffrage, 1849–1870, A Study in Party Motivation" (Ph.D. diss., University of Minnesota, 1972), 11–14; Earl Spangler, *The Negro in Minnesota* (Minneapolis: T. S. Denison, 1961), 27, 34–35, 44; Robert R. Dykstra, *Bright Radical Star: Black Freedom and White Supremacy on the Hawkeye Frontier* (Ames: Iowa State Univ.

Press, 1997), 108–13; *St. Paul Daily Press*, Feb. 10, 1863; State of Wisconsin, *Journal of the Senate, 1863 Annual Session* (Madison: S. D. Carpenter, 1863), 633–37; and *Journal of the Assembly of the State of Wisconsin, 1863 Annual Session* (Madison: S. D. Carpenter, 1863), 287, 529–31.

12. On slaves in the antebellum Midwest, see John Carl Parish, *John Chambers* (Iowa City: State Historical Society of Iowa, 1909), 113, 118, 122, 125, 139, 226, 240; Edward Stiles, *Recollections and Sketches of Notable Lawyers and Public Men of Early Iowa* (Des Moines: Homestead, 1916), 10, 14; Herbert M. Hoke, "Negroes in Iowa: Evidence of Negroes Here in the Early Days," May 7, 1940, MsC295, Federal Writers Project, Iowa, University of Iowa Special Collections, Iowa City; George Frazee, "The Iowa Fugitive Slave Case," *Annals of Iowa* (Apr. 1899): 118–37; "A Slave Owner in Iowa," The Palimpsest 22 (Nov. 1941): 344–45; Olive Cole Smith, *Mt. Pleasant Recalls Some of the Happenings of Her First Hundred Years* (1942; reprint, Mt. Pleasant, Iowa: n.p., 1967), 15–16; *Davenport (Iowa) Gazette*, Aug. 5, 1865 (noting a district court suit by a former slave woman held by her owners to uncompensated labor for thirteen years while a resident of Iowa); Nathan Isabell Diary, June 8, 1848, D8 Folder 1, Iowa State Historical Society, Iowa City (hereafter ISHS); *History of Johnson County, Iowa* (Iowa City: n.p., 1882), 463; Charles Ray Aurner, *Leading Events in Johnson County Iowa History* (Cedar Rapids: Western Historical Press, 1912), 463–64; Jack Hardin Gillihan, Memoir and Clippings, n.p., Nodaway Valley Museum Underground Railway Binder, and BH 128, Nodaway Valley Museum Black History Binder, both in Nodaway Valley Museum, Clarinda, Iowa; Hiram F. Stevens, *History of the Bench and Bar of Minnesota* (Minneapolis: Legal Publishing and Engraving Company, 1904), 1:30–36; Zachary Cooper, *Black Settlers in Rural Wisconsin* (Madison: Wisconsin State Historical Society, 1977), 3–4; and John Nelson Davidson, *Negro Slavery in Wisconsin and the Underground Railroad* (Milwaukee: Parkman Club Publications, 1897). On slaves held by U.S. Army officers, see Lea Vander Velde and Sandhya Subramanian, "Mrs. Dred Scott," *Yale Law Journal* 106 (Dec.–Jan.1997): 1033–122.
13. Dykstra, *Bright Radical Star*, 90–99; unidentified clipping, n.p., Nodaway Valley Museum Underground Railway Binder; unidentified clipping, BH128, Nodway Valley museum Black History Binder; *Burlington (Iowa) Hawk-Eye*, May 11, 1900.
14. *Annual Report of the Secretary of State to the Legislature of Minnesota* (St. Paul: Frederick Driscoll, State Printer, 1866); John T. Hull, 1836–1880: *Census of Iowa for 1880* (Des Moines: F. M. Mills, State Printer, 1883).
15. In comparison, the highest net increase in the nation occurred in Nevada (693 percent), from 45 to 357. In contrast, New York saw an increase of only 6 percent, Pennsylvania of 15 percent, Massachusetts of 45 percent, and Ohio of 72 percent. See the 1860 and 1870 censuses, University of Virginia Geospatial and Statistical Center, *United States Historical Census DATA Browser*, online, 1998, University of Virginia. Available: http:fisher.lib.virginia.edu//census, Oct. 12, 1999.
16. *Manitowoc (Wisc.) Pilot*, Apr. 17, 1963; *Fond du Lac (Wisc.) Reporter*, Oct. 25, 1862; *The History of Dodge County, Wisconsin* (Chicago: Western Historical Company, 1880), 711–12; Sister Mary Demetria Meyer, "The Germans in Wisconsin and the Civil War" (M.A. thesis, Catholic University, 1937), 36.
17. *Minneapolis Spokesman*, Mar. 14, 1958; "History, Pilgrim Baptist Church, The First Negro Church in St. Paul," Minnesota Historical Society, St. Paul (hereafter MHS); *St. Paul Pioneer*, May 6, 15, 1863; *St. Paul Daily Press*, June 16, 1863.
18. Louis S. Gerteis, *From Contraband to Freedman: Federal Policy toward Southern Blacks 1861–1865* (Westport, Conn.: Greenwood Press, 1973), 119–81; Ira Berlin et al., eds., *The Destruction of Slavery*, ser. 1, vol. 1 of *Freedom: A Documentary History of Emancipation, 1861–1867* (New York: Cambridge Univ. Press, 1985),

1–56, 249–69, 395–412; Ira Berlin et al., eds., *The Wartime Genesis of Free Labor: The Lower South*, ser. 1, vol. 3 of *Freedom: A Documentary History of Emancipation, 1861–1867* (New York: Cambridge Univ. Press, 1990), 1–83, 621–50; and Ira Berlin et al., eds., *The Wartime Genesis of Free Labor: The Upper South*, ser. 1, vol. 2 of *Freedom: A Documentary History of Emancipation, 1861–1867* (New York: Cambridge Univ. Press, 1993), 551–64.

19. Although the legislature moved in 1863 to delay the end of Missouri slavery until 1870, Missouri ratified the Thirteenth Amendment in January1865. See William E. Parrish, *Turbulent Partnership: Missouri and the Union, 1861–1865* (Columbia: Univ. of Missouri Press, 1963), 130–48, 201.
20. Quintard Taylor, *In Search of the Racial Frontier: African Americans in the American West, 1528–1990* (New York: W. W. Norton,1998), 95–99; testimony of Dr. George Park, May 21, 1881, testimony of Eveline Pace, Mar. 4, 1879, and testimony of Mathilda Henderson, Mar. 5, 1879, in pension claim of George C. Young, XC 133472, Civil War Pension Files, Record Group 15, National Archives and Records Administration, Washington, D.C. (hereafter NARA); Berlin et al., eds., *The Wartime Genesis of Free Labor: The Upper South*, 555–56; Jacob G. Forman, *The Western Sanitary Commission: A Sketch* (St. Louis: Mississippi Valley Sanitary Fair, 1864), 133–34; *The Annual Report of the Freedmen's Relief Society of St. Louis, Missouri for 1863 (St. Louis Missouri Democrat*, 1864); Samuael Sawyer to Brigadier General Rentiss, Mar. 16, 1863, and Lucien Eaton to Major General Schofield, May 30, 1863, both in series 2593, Letters Received, 1861–1867, Department of the Missouri, Record Group 393 Pt. I, NARA.
21. On the pursuit of fugitive slaves into Iowa during the war, see Rev. J. Cross to Rev. S. S. Jocelyn, Sept. 9, 1863, American Missionary Association Letters (Iowa), ISHS, Iowa City. On the recapture of a group of slave women and children heading for southern Iowa, see the *St. Louis Missouri Democrat*, Nov. 8, 1863.
22. A. F. Sperry, *History of the 33rd Iowa Infantry Volunteer Regiment 1863–6*, ed. Gregory J. W. Urwin and Cathy Kunzinger Urwin (1866; reprint, Fayetteville: Univ. of Arkansas Press, 1999), 293n2.
23. M. A. Rogers, "An Iowa Woman in Wartime, Part II," *Annals of Iowa* 35 (Spring 1961): 614. For retrospective accounts, see the *Milwaukee Journal*, Apr. 19, 1981; *Mukwonago (Wisc.) Chief*, Nov. 14, 1984; and *Stevens Point (Wisc.) Journal*, May 22, 1975. See also T. W. Newson, *Pen Pictures of St. Paul, Minnesota and Biographical Sketches of Old Settlers* (St. Paul: privately published, 1886), 396; Abram L. Harris, *The Negro Population in Minneapolis: A Study of Race Relations* (Minneapolis: Urban League and Phyllis Wheatley Settlement House, 1926), 6; *St. Peter (Minn.) Tribune*, Aug. 30, 1865; *Minneapolis Spokesman*, May 27, 1949; and the *New Ulm (Minn.?) Review*, Apr. 21, 1915. For the most comprehensive overview of the widely varying policies of commanders in the Mississippi Valley, see Berlin et al., eds., *The Destruction of Slavery*, 249–69. Midwestern regiments served largely, although not exclusively, in the Western Theater of war. Most of the fugitive slaves with whom they made arrangements were from the Mississippi Valley, but those white soldiers who served in the East also sent former slaves to their midwestern homes. See William Cohen, *At Freedom's Edge: Black Mobility and the Southern White Quest for Racial Control, 1861–1915* (Baton Rouge: Louisiana State Univ. Press, 1991), 92.
24. For a discussion of the policy and its enforcement, see Berlin et al., eds., *The Destruction of Slavery*, 398–401, 404–10; and the *Burlington (Iowa) Hawk-Eye*, Sept. 18, 1862.
25. For an example of a Minnesota soldier refusing to return slaves, see Berlin et al., eds., *The Destruction of Slavery*, 467–68. See also Maj. George E. Waring, Jr. to Acting

Major General Asboth, Dec. 19, 1861, *The War of the Rebellion: A Compilation of the Official Records of the Union and Confederate Armies*, 128 vols. (Washington, D.C.: GPO, 1880–1901), ser. 1, vol. 3:451–51. On soldiers' appreciation for the labor of fugitive slaves in their camps, see the *Burlington Hawk-Eye*, Dec. 18, 1862, and Judson Wade to "My Dear Mother," Feb. 26, 1863, Judson Wade Papers, box 1, P1922, MHS; and Thomas Montgomery to "Parents and Brother," Mar. 23, 1864, Thomas Montgomery Papers, MHS. On the employment of contraband women in army camps, see Jonathan Ricketts to Peter Mowrer, Sept. 1, 1862, Ellen Mowrer Miller Collection, Iowa Women's Archives, University of Iowa, Iowa City.

26. On Elizabeth Estell, see Thomas Montgomery to Mother, May 27, June 14, Aug. 22, 31, Oct. 12, 27, Nov. 27, 1864, Jan. 1, 14, 1864 [1865], June 11 [1865], Jan. 16, May 29, Dec. 5, 1866; Thomas Montgomery to Parents and Brothers, Oct. 22, 1864, Sept. 5, 1866; Thomas Montgomery to Charles, Oct. 26, Dec. 17, 1864, Feb. 21, 1865, Mar. 29, 1866; and Thomas Montgomery to Father, Mar. 22, 1865, Feb. 23, 1866; all in Thomas Montgomery Papers, MHS.
27. *Keokuk Constitution*, Feb. 13, 1863; *Fairfield (Iowa) Ledger*, June 26, 1862; *Keokuk Constitution*, Oct. 20 and Oct. 21, 1862. For other cases of exploitation, see the *Burlington Hawk-Eye*, Feb. 6, 1863; *Muscatine Journal*, Nov. 14, 1863; and the *Davenport Daily Democrat and News*, Feb. 2, Apr. 25, May 26, 1863.
28. Iowa's law was only sporadically enforced and was subsequently found to be unconstitutional. In 1863 several hundred petitioners requested a similar law in Wisconsin, and an unknown number petitioned Minnesota as well. See Dykstra, *Bright Radical Star*,198–200; Spangler, *The Negro in Minnesota*, 44; State of Wisconsin, *Journal of the Senate, Annual Session 1863* (Madison: S. D. Carpenter, 1863), 633–37; State of Wisconsin, *Journal of the Assembly of the State of Wisconsin, Annual Session 1863* (Madison: S. D. Carpenter, 1863), 286–87, 529.
29. On the army's response to the numbers of fugitive slaves gathering behind Union lines, see Maj. Gen. B. M. Prentiss to Maj. Gen. J. Schofield, Helena, Ark., June 16, 1863, ser. 2593, Letters Received, Dept. Of the Missouri, Record Group 393 Pt. I, NARA.
30. Both Cairo (later replaced by a camp on Island No. 10) and St. Louis were recipients of contraband slaves forwarded by military authorities from places further south. See, for example, the testimony of Ellen Reed, Dec.10, 1896, in pension file of Cassius Reed, WC 41146, Civil War Pension Files, Record Group 15, NARA. For an early outline of the relocation program, see S. A. Duke to Major General Curtis, Mar. 9, 1863, ser. 2593, Letters Received, Dept. of the Missouri, Record Group 393, Pt. I, NARA.
31. The number is reported in the *Burlington Hawk-Eye*, Sept. 1, 1862. Large numbers of contrabands similarly gathered at Helena, Arkansas, Jackson, Tennessee, and Corinth, Mississippi, in September 1862, placing additional pressure on General Grant and Secretary of War Stanton to authorize their relocation to Northern employers. See Berlin et al., eds., *The Wartime Genesis of Free Labor: The Upper South*, 27–29, 665–70.
32. Lucius Hubbard to "My Dear Aunt Mary," Sept. 8, Oct. 13, 1862, Lucius F. Hubbard and Family Papers, AH875, MHS.
33. *Burlington Hawk-Eye*, Oct. 10, 1862.
34. Voegeli, *Free but Not Equal*, 13–20, 34–35, 60–63; Berlin et al., eds., *The Wartime Genesis of Free Labor: The Upper South*, 28–29.
35. Rev. J. B. Rogers, *War Pictures: Experiences and Observations of a Chaplain in the U.S. Army* (Chicago: Church & Goodman, 1863), 125–27, 132. Rogers, chaplain of the 14th Wisconsin Volunteers, served as superintendent of the camp at Cairo from the fall of 1862 until April 1863. For further accounts of organized relocation, see

Missouri Democrat, Mar. 20, 1863; *Keokuk Constitution*, Oct. 5, 9, 10, 20, 21, 23, 25, 1862; *Keokuk Daily Gate City*, Aug. 20, Oct. 29, 1862, Apr. 1, 1863; *Iowa City Republican*, Apr. 1, 1863; Voegeli, *Free but Not Equal*, 89–90; Forman, *The Western Sanitary Commission*, 133–34; Berlin et al., eds., *The Wartime Genesis of Free Labor: The Upper South*, 566, 598, 615; and Samuel Sawyer to Brigadier General Rentiss, Mar. 16, 1863, Samuel Sayer to Major General Curtis, Apr. 20, 1863, and Chaplain H. D. Fischer [5th Kansas Vols.] to Major General Schofield, June 22, 1863, all in Series 2593, Letters Received, Dept. of the Missouri, Record Group 393 Pt. I, NARA.

36. In 1864 the Senate's debates over the Freedmen's Bureau bill revealed the continuing influence of Northern opposition to organized relocation. Disagreement erupted over whether the Bureau would be given authority to operate in Border States, and an amendment was proposed that directed the bureau commissioner to correspond with Northern governors about the possibility of relocating freed people to their states (a hostile amendment intended to sink the bill entirely). Supporters of the latter amendment insisted that Republican resistance to relocation revealed the hypocrisy of the party's emancipationist rhetoric. *Congressional Globe*, 38th Cong., 1st sess., June 28, 1864, 2933–34, 3328–36.
37. *Muscatine Courier*, Oct. 2, 13, 1862.
38. This conceptualization of wartime politics follows Jean Baker's study of the nineteenth-century Democratic party. Jean H. Baker, *Affairs of Party: The Political Culture of Northern Democrats in the Mid-Nineteenth Century* (Ithaca: Cornell Univ. Press, 1983). See also Mary Ryan, *Civic Wars: Democracy and Public Life in the American City during the Nineteenth Century* (Berkeley: Univ. of California Press, 1997); Joanne Pope Melish, "Of Politics and Publics," *Radical History Review* 709 (Winter 2001): 157–67; and Alice Fahs, *The Imagined Civil War: Popular Literature of the North & South, 1861–1865* (Chapel Hill: Univ. of North Carolina Press, 2001).
39. On the association of the Republican party with an increasingly large, centralized, and powerful state, see Richard Franklin Bensel, *Yankee Leviathan: The Origins of Central State Authority in America, 1859–1877* (New York: Cambridge Univ. Press, 1990), 236, 423; and David Montgomery, *Beyond Equality: Labor and the Radical Republicans, 1862–1872* (Urbana: Univ. of Illinois Press, 1981), 102.
40. *Mankato (Minn.) Semi-Weekly Record*, Apr. 23, 1862; *Manitowoc Pilot*, Apr. 17, 1863, Dec. 5, 1862. See also James J. Robertson Jr., "Such is War: The Letters of an Orderly in the 7th Iowa Infantry," unidentified clipping, Civil War Files No. 1 Musser Public Library, Muscatine, Iowa; and the *St. Paul Pioneer Press*, Jan. 31, 1863.
41. Stephen Douglas, quoted in Leon F. Litwack, *North of Slavery: The Negro in the Free States, 1790–1860* (Chicago: Univ. of Chicago Press, 1965), 268–69; *Manitowoc Pilot*, Dec. 12, 1862. In the Jan. 30, 1863, issue, the same editor complained that "while our volunteers are yet unpaid and their families suffering actual want, the public money is to be further wasted on the liberation of a class whom we shall have to feed afterwards."
42. For example, Florence Chapman of Indianola, Iowa, reported the attitude among many in her town that the entire purpose of the war was to elevate the negro and degrade the white man. Florence Chapman to Philo Chapman, Apr. 25, 1863, Chapman Papers, 1855–1866, ISHS, Iowa City. On white privilege, see David R. Roediger, *The Wages of Whiteness: Race and the Making of the American Working Class* (New York: Verso, 1999); and Matthew Frye Jacobson, *Whiteness of a Different Color: European Immigrants and the Alchemy of Race* (New York: Cambridge Univ. Press, 1998), 13–31, 204–5.
43. For a substantive treatment of the events leading up to and following the August 1862 Dakota uprising, see Gary Clayton Anderson, *Kinsmen of Another*

Kind: Dakota-White Relations in the Upper Mississippi Valley, 1650–1862 (Lincoln: Univ. of Nebraska Press,1984), 203–80; Alvin M. Josephy, *The Civil War in the American West* (New York: Alfred A. Knopf, 1991), 95–154; Francis Paul Prucha, *The Great Father: The United States Government and the American Indians* (Lincoln: Univ. of Nebraska Press, 1984), 437–47; and Richard N. Current, *The History of Wisconsin*, Vol. 2: *The Civil War Era,1848–1873* (Madison: n.p., 1976), 319–24. In addition to some 40,000 Minnesotans who fled into Wisconsin, panic also struck such towns as Manitowoc, Menomonie, Superior City, Sheboygan, Milwaukee, and Wauwatosa, among others. See Kerry A. Trask, *Fire Within: A Civil War Narrative from Wisconsin* (Kent, Ohio: Kent State Univ. Press, 1995), 132–340; *Manitowoc Herald*, Apr. 4, 1862; Senator Edward Salomon's message to the Wisconsin Senate and Assembly, reprinted in the *Manitowoc Herald*, Sept. 18, 1862; and Milo M. Quaife, "The Panic of 1862 in Wisconsin," *Wisconsin Magazine of History* 4 (Dec. 1920): 166–95.

44. The centrality of relations with Indian people in the creation of a midwestern "white" consciousness is discussed by Susan E. Gray in "Stories Written in the Blood: Race and Midwestern History," in *The American Midwest*, ed. Andrew R. L. Cayton and Susan E. Gray (Bloomington: Indiana Univ. Press, 2001), 123–39; and Bruce M. White, "The Power of Whiteness, or, The Life and Times of Joseph Rolette Jr.," *Making Minnesota Territory, 1849–1858, Special Issue of Minnesota History*, ed. Anne R. Kaplan and Marilyn Ziebarth (1999): 26–.
45. The contrast between white-Indian histories in the Upper Midwest, where Indian populations persisted at midcentury, and the history of displacement in the Lower Midwest, is noted by Andrew R. L. Cayton and Susan E. Gray in "The Story of the Midwest: An Introduction," in *The American Midwest*, ed. Cayton and Gray, 14–15. *St. Paul Pioneer Press*, Feb. 10, 1863.
46. *St. Paul Daily Press*, June 6, 1863; *St. Paul Pioneer Press*, May 6, June 6, 1863.
47. *Iowa City Republican*, July 1, 1863; *Fairfield Ledger*, Mar. 19, 1863; Berlin et al., eds., *The Black Military Experience*, ser. 2, vol. 1 of *Freedom: A Documentary History of Emancipation, 1861–1867* (New York: Cambridge Univ. Press, 1985), 85; *Mankato Semi-Weekly Record*, Apr. 23, 1862; *St. Paul Pioneer Press*, Dec. 21, 1862, Feb. 10, 1863; *Iowa Washington Democrat*, Aug. 23, 1864; *St. Paul Pioneer & Democrat*, Oct. 1, 1862; *Mankato Semi-Weekly Record*, June 21, 1862; *Missouri Democrat*, Apr. 14, 1864.
48. The predominantly rural western soldiers suffered a higher rate of mortality from disease than did their more urban eastern counterparts, although the latter suffered higher rates of battle deaths. See James M. McPherson, *Battle Cry of Freedom: The Civil War Era* (New York: Oxford Univ. Press, 1988), 471–72; McPherson, *Ordeal by Fire: The Civil War and Reconstruction* (New York: McGraw-Hill, 2001), 516; Robert R. Dykstra, *Radical Republicans in the North: State Politics during Reconstruction* (Baltimore: Johns Hopkins Univ. Press, 1976), 171–72.
49. Quoted in George Bodnia, "The Racial and Political Attitudes of Minnesota Soldiers during the Civil War" (M.A. thesis, University of Minnesota, 1974), 77–78.
50. *Manitowoc Pilot*, Feb. 13, 1863; *St. Paul Pioneer Press*, Dec. 21, 1862; *Oskaloosa (Iowa) Times*, Mar. 5, 1863; *Keokuk Constitution*, Oct. 8, Feb. 12, 1863; Florence Chapman to Philo Chapman, Feb. 1, 1863, Chapman Papers, ISHS; and *Iowa Washington Democrat*, Aug. 23, 1864.
51. Jones, *American Work*, 13.
52. For examples of employers hiring black labor (either in the Midwest or recruited from St. Louis) see Peter H. Jaynes, ed., *Highlights of Henry County, Iowa History 1833–1976* (Burlington: Doran & Ward Lithographing Co., 1976), 41–42.
53. *Keokuk Constitution*, Sept. 5, 1862, July 15, 1864; *St. Paul Pioneer Press*, Mar. 26, 1863; *Fairfield Ledger*, Dec. 4, 1862.

54. *Fairfield Ledger*, Apr. 28, 1863; *Iowa City Republican*, Apr. 8, 1863, May 6, 1863; J. Cross to Rev. S. S. Jocelyn, June 4, 1863, American Missionary Association Papers, ISHS; Burlington *Hawk-Eye*, Sept. 28, 1863, April 6, 1864; *Muscatine Journal*, Aug. 1, 1863; *St. Paul Daily Press*, June 16, 1863. See also the *St. Paul Pioneer Press*, Jan. 4, May 7, 1863; *St. Paul Daily Press*, May 6, 15, 16, 1863; *Burlington Hawk-Eye*, Sept. 28, 1863; and *Fond du Lac Commonwealth Reporter*, Oct 13, 1933.
55. Mrs. Francis Harris Shirley recalled the attack in a 1933 interview. *Fond du Lac Commonwealth Reporter*, Oct. 13, 1933. On Rogers, see Berlin et al., eds., *The Wartime Genesis of Free Labor: The Lower South*, 667–70; and Rev. J. B. Rogers, *War Pictures*.
56. On the wartime agricultural economy, see chapter 7 of Paludan, "*A People's Contest*"; and Hubert H. Wubben, *Civil War Iowa and the Copperhead Movement* (Ames: Iowa State Univ. Press, 1981), 134–36. On midwestern urban economies, see Russell Lee Johnson, "An Army for Industrialization: The Civil War and the Formation of Urban-Industrial Society in a Northern City" (Ph.D. diss., University of Iowa, 1996).
57. *Keokuk Daily Gate City*, Oct. 29, 1862, March 25, 1863; *St. Paul Pioneer Press*, March 26, 1863.
58. On the involvement of midwestern soldiers in the relocation of former slaves, see John L. Mathews to Sister, Aug. 14, 1863, John L. Mathews Papers, ISHS, Iowa City; Spangler, *The Negro in Minnesota*, 48–49; Lucius F. Hubbard to Aunt Mary, Sept. 8, Oct. 13, 1862, Lucius F. Hubbard and Family Papers, MHS; Orrin Densmore to Daniel Densmore, Mar. 24, 1864, Densmore Family Papers, MHS; Current, *The History of Wisconsin* 2: 390–91; *Burlington Hawk-Eye*, Feb. 10, Mar. 17, 1864; *Keokuk Constitution*, Oct. 20, 1862; *Iowa City Republican*, Apr. 1, 1863; *Fairfield Ledger*, June 26, 1862; *Iowa State Register*, June 13, 1863; *Fond du Lac Weekly Commonwealth*, Oct. 22, 1862; A. T. Glaze, *Incidents and Anecdotes of Early Days and History of Business in the City and County of Fond du Lac* (Fond du Lac: P. B. Haber Print Co., 1905); *Delevan Enterprise*, Feb. 13, 1986; *Milwaukee Journal*, Apr. 19, 1981; *Racine Journal*, Feb. 22, 1922.
59. On wartime labor unrest in Midwestern town and cities, see Wubben, *Civil War Iowa*, 137–38, 151–52. On ethnicity and race, see Jacobson, *Whiteness of a Different Color*, 15–55; Noel Ignatiev, *How the Irish Became White* (New York: Routledge, 1995); Roediger, *The Wages of Whiteness*, 144–56, 167–76; June Drenning Holmquist, ed., *They Chose Minnesota: A Survey of the State's Ethnic Groups* (St. Paul: Minnesota Historical Society Press, 1981), 130–52; and Jones, *American Work*, 270–72, 281–92.
60. *Christian Recorder*, Dec. 6, 1862. Native-born ambivalence about the racial identity of Irish immigrants was expressed in the manuscript census, where Iowa census takers recorded Irish as "mulatto." See, for example, the 1856 manuscript census for Davenport, Scott County, Iowa, p. 27; and the 1869 manuscript census for 1st Ward, Keokuk, Lee County, p. 22.
61. For attacks by Irish workers on black workers, see *Mankato Semi-Weekly Record*, June 14, 1862; *Burlington Hawk-Eye*, Apr. 6, 1864; Johnson, "An Army for Industrialization," 343; and Wubben, *Civil War Iowa*, 158. For attacks on contrabands arriving St. Paul, see *St. Paul Daily Press*, May 15, 16, June 6, 1863.
62. Considerable evidence suggests that during the war the population of Southern black migrants in the Midwest consisted largely of women and children. Men were readily employed and then enlisted by military authorities in the South. In contrast, women and children were gathered at contraband camps from which they were then relocated North. While former slave men also made their way to the Upper Midwest,

many of these men later returned south in the uniform of the Union army. Midwestern newspapers commented frequently on the composition of the groups of former slaves being sent north, often noting a majority of women and children. See, for example, *Iowa State Register*, Sept. 24, 1862; *Fairfield Ledger*, Oct. 30, 1862; *Keokuk Constitution*, Feb. 13, 1963; *St. Paul Daily Press*, May 27, 1863; and *Burlington Hawk-Eye*, Dec. 18, 1863.

63. William W. Sandford to Annie Wittenmyer, n.d., unknown to Annie Wittenmyer, Oct. 27, 1862, and Mrs. John Shane to Annie Wittenmyer, Oct. 27, Dec. 8, 1862, Mar. 20, 1863, all in Annie Wittenmyer Papers, ISHS, Des Moines; Orrin Densmore to Benjamin Densmore, Aug. 20, 1864, and Orrin Densmore Jr. To Daniel Densmore, Oct. 27, 1864, Densmore Family Papers, MHS.

64. *St. Paul Daily Press*, May 17, 1863; Orrin Densmore to Daniel Densmore, Apr. 28, 1864, Densmore Family Papers, MHS; Wubben, *Civil War Iowa*, 132–33.

65. Orrin Densmore to Benjamin Densmore, June 11, 1863; Norman Densmore to Daniel Densmore, Jan. 15, 1864; and Orrin Densmore to Daniel Densmore, July 10, 1864; all in Densmore Family Papers, MHS.

66. *Iowa City Republican*, Apr. 8, 1863; *Des Moines Daily State Register*, Jan. 31, 1863. R. E. Robinson, discovering two black children paying in a farmyard in Monroe County, Iowa—where the wartime black population increased from two to twenty-six—pulled up his wagon and offered passing farmers taking produce to market an agitated, impromptu address on "the evil consequences resulting from the emancipation of the black race," including "a premonition of the debasement and ultimate coalescence of the two races." Frank Kickenlooper, *An Illustrated History of Monroe County, Iowa* (Albia, Iowa, n.p. 1896), 183.

67. A. F. Sperry, *History of the 33rd Iowa Infantry Volunteer Regiment, 1863–6*, xxv–xxvi.

68. On Northern white women's wartime activism, see Elizabeth D. Leonad, *Yankee Women: Gender Battles in the Civil War* (New York: W. W. Norton, 1994); Mary Elizabeth Massey, *Women in the Civil War* (Lincoln, Neb.: Univ. of Kansas Press, 1994); Fahs, *The Imagined Civil War*; and Catherine Clinton and Nina Silber, eds., *Divided Houses: Gender and the Civil War* (New York: Oxford Univ. Press, 1992).

69. *St. Paul Pioneer Press*, June 7, 28, 1863.

70. According to white observers, blacks acted in the South like they knew "their place" in white society, but "a few weeks or months in the North entirely ruins" them. See, for example, *Fairfield Ledger*, Aug. 7, 1862.

71. In 1860 of the 4,441,830 African Americans in the United States, 226,152 (5 percent) resided in the North; 3,953,760 slaves resided in the South (89 percent), as did 261,918 free blacks. See Joe William Trotter Jr., *The African American Experience* (Boston: Houghton-Mifflin, 2001), A–23.

72. Moses Mosely, *The Colored Man of America as a Slave and a Citizen of the United States* (Mt. Pleasant, Iowa: Journal Co. Printers, 1884), 7. On postbellum challenges to segregation, see *Coger v. North West Union Packet Co.*, 37 Iowa 145 (1873); Robert D. Marshall, "Mount Pleasant: 'The Athens of Iowa,' 1865–1875" (M.A. thesis, University of Iowa, 1963), 51; *Clark v. Board of Directors*, 24 Iowa 266 (1868); *Dove v. The Independent School District of the City of Keokuk*, 40 Iowa 518 (1875). On Keokuk firefighters and their defense of segregation, see Fay Emma Harris, "A Frontier Community: The Economic, Social, and Political Development of Keokuk, Iowa, from 1820 to 1866" (Ph.D. diss., University of Iowa, 1965), 389. See also William D. Green, "Race and Segregatio in St. Paul's Public Schools, 1846–1869," *Minnesota History* 55 (Winter 1996–97): 138–49; Leslie H. Fishel Jr., "The North and the Negro, 1865–1900: A Study in Race Discrimination" (Ph.D. diss., Harvard University, 1953), 238–40; and Dykstra, *Bright Radical Star*, 229.

Chapter 4

The Work Ethic of the Plain Folk: Labor and Religion in the Old South

Carl R. Osthaus

From *The Journal of Southern History*

Faced with the prospect of imminent departure to serve in the Confederate army, North Carolina farmer John Fletcher Flintoff instructed his family on life and faith in his diary[1] entry of March 10, 1864: "I desire that you live on the *premises* I leave you and work the land to make your support—Rember my Father was a poor man—He was not able to leave his children anything to start upon the journey of life but I leave you 217 acres of land, 7 negroes, 3 good horses, 6 head of cattle 15 hogs and wagons, house & kitchen well furnished, plantation tools, etc.—a years supply of everything—I exhort you to be industrious, kind, persevering, thoughtful, economical, love and serve God and good to each other." Fortunately, the forty-year-old Flintoff saw only local service, survived the war, and lived into the new century, all the while living as he preached, by hard work and through love of family and God. As the postwar years passed, his estate grew, revealing, he believed, God's favor in his ability to work for his children and their families and help them through their "journey of life."

Flintoff knew hard, manual labor as a young farmhand, as a struggling farm owner, and even as an elderly patriarch content with his fields, barns, and work stock. In reflections in his diary, especially on the anniversary of his birth, he recalled his early struggles in North Carolina and Mississippi, when he worked for wages or managed relatives' farms and plantations. Fondly did he hope that laboring for others would not be the lot of his children. As a poor boy, faith sustained him. He later urged his children to be religious and join the church when young, as he did by becoming a Methodist at age ten. Believing that education bolstered faith and opened opportunities, he attended Centenary College in Jackson, Mississippi, for two years. Back in North Carolina in 1850, he married Mary Pleasant of

Caswell County and began to acquire slaves and livestock. Four years later at age thirty-one, having toiled long and hard, saved, purchased slaves, and borrowed heavily, he bought a farm and house of his own. Working beside his slaves, he performed all of the tasks necessary on a small piedmont farm: he raised corn, wheat, and oats; grew fodder for his animals; primed, topped, wormed, and harvested substantial tobacco crops; hewed logs and built houses, barns, wagons, and outbuildings; hauled logs and tobacco; and in winter made shoes for the family. And he prospered. "I want to try to make money to pay my debts. I work hard to do this with my heart raised up to God to his blessing," he recorded in 1856. Postwar labor adjustments proved difficult; in his view free blacks would not work honestly or steadily for wages, while whites faced the rigors of excessive work from dawn to dark. He resented idleness, even when found in his dearly beloved wife, whom he feared lived too much the life of a lady. In 1890 Flintoff boasted of a good year's work for his age and in 1891 recorded that "I am at work now in the field with the hoe 9 to 10 hours per day and am very thankful I am as well as I am and humbly trust in God for the future."[2]

Flintoff's life, steeped in faith and focused on hard, manual labor of the sort performed by slaves, reflected not one iota of the dictum that southerners derogated manual labor because it was, in the common idiom of the day, "nigger work." Flintoff was not a planter, and he was not rich; neither was he representative of the southern rural masses since his achievements in accumulating slaves and property and passing his wealth to his children were substantial. His work ethic, however, was shared by the masses of rural plain folk from whom he had emerged—those who worked with their hands and performed field labor even though some of them also benefited from ownership of a small number of slaves. Flintoff knew hard work and believed it honorable. On the one hand, his work was not menial labor. That was drudgery performed for another or directed by another, for which the worker received minimal benefit and profited but little in the long run—work typically performed by slaves. Manual labor performed at one's own behest and for the benefit of one's own family, on the other hand, was admirable. Mucking out one's barn, surely among the least pleasant farm tasks, was part of honorable work, given the right circumstances. Honorable work enabled Flintoff and his peers to attain that secure, independent existence that was the minimal goal of all. Logically a slave society might be expected to diverge significantly from Max Weber's Protestant ethic and reject outright many of Benjamin Franklin's precepts, but at the heart of the antebellum southern fanner, respect for hard work, independence, and the ability to provide for one's own were core values. Antebellum southern spokesmen might celebrate the leisured lifestyle of a planter elite and proclaim the virtues of an aristocratic existence even as Yankees and a few southerners denounced lazy white "trash," but farmers who earned their red necks honestly by steady labor, in season and out, understood the value and rewards of daily toil. Plain-folk endorsement of hard work, part of plain-folk honor, created a discordant note that was at best ill suited to those who championed a distinctly non-Yankee South dedicated to gracious living. An examination of the labor of the plain folk and their attitudes and values, however, reveals that John Flintoff's work ethic was shared by the southern masses. Many of these attitudes resonated deep into the elite by the late antebellum period.

While the omega of historical insight into the work ethic has not been reached, the alpha originated with Max Weber in *The Protestant Ethic and the Spirit of Capitalism*, the famous essay that inaugurated a one-hundred-year debate (or hopelessly futile academic squabble) over the spirit of capitalism and the nexus of capitalism and religion. Weber's Protestant ethic emphasized the moral obligation to work to glorify God and the methodical use of every God-given moment of time. God called everyone to productive labor—to a world of hard, unending, physical or mental work—and the greatest of sins was idleness. Because the result of labor might be wealth and consequent idleness, asceticism became a way of life—an asceticism that rejected leisure and the spontaneous enjoyment of life.[3] While critics of Weber's thesis have dominated the scholarly melee, one recent authority maintains that "it is just as difficult to demolish Weber's thesis as it is to substantiate it."[4] Despite partisan contention, the thesis has influenced scholarly thinking as well as popular conceptions concerning the relationship of economic progress, the valuation of work, and religious faith. Weber's idea has been used to buttress historical images of Yankee drive and southern sloth. Although Weber intended his analysis as an objective evaluation and not as an admiring moral judgment, many antebellum Americans (and some scholars since) attached their own positive value to the key traits that Weber identified as forming the Protestant ethic.

Weber and subsequent writers located the strongest bastion of the Protestant ethic in Puritan New England and Quaker Pennsylvania, but few had anything positive to say about the moral value of work in the land of cotton and slaves. Historian Edmund S. Morgan, however, voices a dissenting view, arguing that the Puritan ethic—that cluster of values, ideas, and attitudes advanced by Weber—influenced all Americans by the time of the Revolution. Nevertheless, Morgan emphasizes "the evil effect of slavery on the industry and frugality of both master and slave . . . ." Among southerners, he holds, slavery "eroded the honor accorded work . . . ."[5] But did the plain folk, whom Morgan does not discuss, suffer from the stigma on work supposedly inherent in a slave society? Both Rhys Isaac and Christine Leigh Heyrman suggest that yeomen developed immunity to slavery's presumed debilitating effect, stressing the influence of the First Great Awakening in fostering a more Weber-like attitude in the South. Conversion to an evangelical faith encouraged, even sanctified, a simple life richer in spiritual than material rewards and thus challenged if not transformed the hedonistic lifestyle of the planter leadership.[6]

Although the intensity of religiosity in early New England and the concept of work as God's calling declined as the country embraced secularization in the age of Jackson, the Second Great Awakening in both the

North and South rekindled earlier faith. Simultaneously, a market revolution encouraged dedication to work and economic advancement. Many people lived with both a secular ethic and an ethic attuned to faith; sometimes an individual's work ethic had a reinforcing religious dimension, though at other times it did not, leaving a Weberian ethic without asceticism. According to Daniel T. Rodgers, a work ethic remained "the core of the moral life," finding its strongest affirmation among the Protestant bourgeoisie. It was "the distinctive credo of preindustrial capitalism" entrenched in "artisans' shops, farms, and countinghouses." Rodgers identifies four ingredients in the mid-nineteenth-century work ethic: "the doctrine of usefulness"; "an intense, nervous fear of idleness" (both of which were "legacies of the Reformation"); "the dream of success"; and "a faith in work as a creative act." The South, Rodgers discovers, was considered a deviant society. When the dignity of labor emerged as a distinctive feature of northern politics and culture, Republican leaders and other middle-class spokesmen savaged the South for its perversion of values, poverty and degradation of the masses, and general economic backwardness. Abolitionist criticism and Republican rhetoric best encapsulated the southern ethic: "shiftlessness and exploitation were the rule." The South reflected "a nightmarish inversion of Northern work values, where idlers ruled and laborers stood in chains."[7]

In 1967 David Bertelson's *The Lazy South* pronounced judgment upon the South's work ethic. Bertelson argues that southerners' penchant for leisure and idleness was caused by what he labels the doctrine of "allurement," not by the traditional suspects of slavery, climate, disease, or parasites. The virgin lands of the earliest southern colonies attracted Englishmen with the allure of fortunes to be made in the international tobacco trade. When the Old World's demand for tobacco met the opportunity abounding in the new lands, unrestricted freedom to enrich oneself resulted in fortunes for many and created a rigid adherence to individualism with a consequent lack of community spirit that boded poorly for socially useful labor. Thus southerners were attentive to self-interest, not the common good; the inducement to work came not from within but from the promise of material reward. Virginians, Marylanders, and later South Carolinians and other southerners busily set about exploiting natural resources and labor and expanding farms and plantations; the end of labor was personal wealth and leisure, not salvation, godly community, or local or regional economic development.[8]

C. Vann Woodward joined this discussion in 1968, arguing for the existence of a distinct southern ethic within a Puritan world. Woodward's southern ethic deviates from the concepts of Weber or maxims of Franklin and scores high on leisure or laziness, depending on whether one opts for "an attractive" or "an unattractive countenance" of the mythical "Janus-faced" South. With his typically telling and witty commentary on the relevant literature, especially the work of Bertelson and Morgan, Woodward offers several hypotheses in explanation of the southern leisure-laziness ethic but attributes special salience to the impact of slavery.

Evidence of southern distinctiveness, in this instance leisure-laziness, was everywhere: "Where there is so much smoke—whether the superficial stereotypes of the Leisure-Laziness sort, or the bulky literature of lamentation, denial, or celebration that runs back to the seventeenth century, or the analytical monographs of the present day—there must be fire."[9]

For most historians who have analyzed agriculture, labor conditions, and slavery in the Old South, the existence of a flawed work ethic—if there was a work ethic at all—is axiomatic. Some stress the leisured aspects of the South, others the lazy aspects. To Eugene D. Genovese, writing in 1965, a dominant planter elite, commanding politics and setting the tone for social life, fastened aspirations to luxury and ease upon the Old South. Even aggressive, nouveau southwestern planters, the southern Yankees, reflected merely a time lapse and not a strong work ethic; these hardworking farmers, planters to be, were only a generation removed from refinement and aristocratic graces. Genovese concludes that slavery inevitably produced feelings of contempt for all labor and especially menial labor—labor performed for another.[10]

Leisure and laziness surface in extreme form in the works of historian Grady McWhiney, who argues that planters and plain folk alike, as descendants of Celts notoriously unburdened by a work ethic, avoided steady labor—rigorously, constantly, and conscientiously. McWhiney agrees with one visitor to the South who concluded that the word *haste* was not in the southern vocabulary. Careless, unhurried farmers and herdsmen lived lavishly upon the abundance of field and forest and the labor of an ample supply of bondpeople; but McWhiney's special interpretation emphasizes how inherited cultural traits—rather than slavery, climate, disease, or parasites—explain attitudes and values that the masses considered rational and superior.

> Being lazy to Celts and Southerners did not mean being indolent, shiftless, slothful, and worthless; it meant being free from work, having spare time to do as they pleased, being at liberty, and enjoying their leisure. When a Celt or a Southerner said that he was being lazy he was not reproaching himself but merely describing his state of comfort. He suffered no guilt when he spent his time pleasantly—hunting, fishing, dancing, drinking, gambling, fighting, or just loafing and talking.[11]

To outsiders, an unambitious plain folk lived in squalor, but to the white rural masses, enjoying an easy living from livestock that roamed in the woods and a sufficiency of fish and game, there was no pressing need to labor as long as they possessed an abundance of tobacco, liquor, and food.

The views of Genovese, McWhiney, and many others might appropriately be called the conventional historical wisdom of the 1970s and 1980s, despite the earlier, somewhat-novel view of Frank L. Owsley and his students, who emphasized steady labor and seriousness of purpose among the plain folk.[12] Much of the conventional wisdom stressed the hegemony of the planter class and popular images of gentlemen and refined ladies. Nevertheless, yeomen and community studies in the 1980s and 1990s eroded the so-called Big House interpretation of the South and enormously expanded our understanding of the values and attitudes of the plain folk. Instead of seeing them as "no account folk," lazy hellions, a miserable underclass lacking an ethic of work and success, or the willing dupes or deferential underlings of planters, we have an image of a sturdy, industrious, self-sufficient folk, tough, proud, and fiercely independent. In fact, the republican independence of the plain folk, a desire to control their own destiny and scorn of being controlled, plays a pivotal role in every study of yeoman communities.[13] The accumulation of a certain level of wealth provided the basis of independence, but the primary goal was acquisition of respectability achieved through personal independence and family self-sufficiency, often augmented by status within a religious community. Plain-folk farmers exhibited a typically American faith in upward mobility—that hard work paid over time and that it was not unreasonable to expect an increase in wealth as one approached middle age. Farming was both an honorable occupation, worthy in and of itself, and an opportunity for advancement that drew many middle-class and lower-middle-class farmers, men on the make, to the piney-woods frontier.[14] Work, if not an end in itself, surely was the means to republican independence and self-sufficiency and was the major daily activity of yeomen and their wives. It was not a degrading sign of slave-like status but rather a means of differentiating themselves from slaves by achieving and maintaining independence.

This last point has not been fully appreciated because of popular misconceptions about the lazy South, the *idée fixed* that white society scorned manual labor as "nigger work," and a lack of consensus among the historians conducting community studies. Some in the latter group continue to stress the importance of leisure-time activities, especially hunting, drinking, and fighting. In a fine study of North Carolina's "common whites," Bill Cecil-Fronsman argues that given a choice of work or leisure, North Carolina piedmont farmers came down on the side of leisure; they did what work they had to do, then stopped.[15] Whether the findings of community studies of the 1980s and 1990s (which stress yeoman independence and work) will supplant the conventional wisdom of a leisured-lazy South has yet to be determined.

Clearly, the antebellum South had a troubled approach to labor and its value and exhibited no single, unified, socially approved work ethic. Dissonance is palpable. Many planters and their wives endorsed and honored values of diligence and thrift in their everyday routines, and even those who professed to value some degree of leisure did not want to be considered lazy. As in the American middle class as a whole, they were raised on maxims of work and thrift inculcated by parents, ministers, schoolmasters, editors, essayists, and other authority figures. Nevertheless, the region's population undoubtedly included wealthy southerners who seldom performed physical labor because of the work of overseers, drivers, and slaves. The fact is that a considerable number of primary sources apparently document a lazy South. The lamentations of southern agricultural editors, who forged a prescriptive literature for planters, emphasized the lack of active and scientific farm management and the incompetence and neglect of overseers. Antebellum travel literature, replete with the exaggerated likes and dislikes of outsiders who expected to encounter the exotic, contributed to stereotypical images of laziness. For example, the most famous Old South tourist, the strongly antislavery Frederick Law Olmsted, argued that slavery destroyed the capacity to work and that the slovenly, careless work of slaves set the southern standard.[16] Perhaps most important, attacks by abolitionists and Republicans, who denounced the brutalized slave drudgery that damaged all ranks and aspects of southern society, were answered by proslavery partisans and southern apologists, who glorified a superior way of life embodied by gentlemanly Cavaliers. The antebellum sectional conflict was perfect for shaping powerful mythologies of a southern way that diverged from Yankee norms. One marvels that Woodward would stress smoke over fire.

The purpose of this essay is to reaffirm the centrality of work and its importance in the antebellum South. Most southerners experienced the harsh reality of endless physical labor, especially slaves and plain-folk families. They knew hard work. Attitudes toward work and the esteem placed upon steady labor with one's hands provided a fault line that challenged southern unity, dividing a small but articulate and influential part of the planter elite from self-working farmers and their families—those who knew, accepted, and lived by the toils of field and household labor. Work was an essential part of plain-folk identity; here was the core of southern life.

The yeomen of the South never celebrated the mythical leisure ethic of the Old South because they were too busy working to put food on the table, maintain their homes, and structure lives that would guarantee independence and respectability. This yeomanry, the plain folk of the Old South, varied enormously in wealth and status. Some possessed only a few acres of land while others had several hundred. Though most owned no slaves or just a small number, a few grew prosperous from the labor of as many as ten or more. Whether they eked out a bare subsistence on a few acres in the piedmont or piney-woods wiregrass or accumulated land and a handful of slaves in the South Carolina Lowcountry and aspired to join the elite, the lowest common denominator among plain-folk men was that they performed agricultural field labor for all or a significant portion of the year. They were self-working farmers.[17] To be sure, upwardly mobile, slave-owning farmers performed less field work while shouldering additional supervisory tasks, but their callused hands were all too familiar with plows, hoes, axes, shovels, pitchforks, and saws. Long hours of manual labor under the hot southern sun—plowing, hoeing, weeding, picking, ditching, clearing land, and chopping wood—became the common burden of the plain folk and the subject of loud lamentations and complaints or proud boasts of toughness and achievement.[18] While not always blessed, manual labor was one of the ties that bound many southern males.

Honorable work and respect for independence blurred class lines. White men and women who owned but a few slaves labored beside their bondmen and bondwomen, experiencing the lot of the field workers and domestic help—sore hands and backs, sweat-stained vision, and a nighttime weariness that sometimes precluded sleep. Even most planters, who as boys had worked with plows and hoes, walked the fields and actively supervised a labor force engaged in work they had once performed. Those in the slave-owning class who escaped the burdens of manual labor or active management—indeed they might aspire all of their lives to employ more slaves and better overseers—could not forget their origins or the fact that successful farming was the source of their profits. Perhaps the vaunted white southern unity of the antebellum period rested upon the farmers' world of work as well as a dedication to slavery and maintenance of the racial status quo.

Most rural southerners inhabited a world of work, not leisure and play. Of the more than sixteen hundred Tennessee Civil War veterans who were questioned via mail by historians in the 1910s and 1920s, slightly over 80 percent emphasized that hard work was the common lot of the plain folk.[19] These Tennessee veterans, largely of the yeoman class, gave responses in writing to precise questions about the amount of work and leisure in rural Tennessee life, the kinds of labor their parents performed, the value and honor accorded physical labor, and the accuracy of historians' portrayal of a lazy South. Although some might belittle the significance of their testimony given the passage of years and the veterans' tendencies toward nostalgia and self-praise, several yeomen diaries, the memoirs and autobiographies of antebellum rural ministers, and the varied sources dealing with the lives of antebellum farmwives support the veterans' memories. Unfortunately, the diarists and autobiographers have also drawn criticism as reliable sources because, it is said, they are few in number and unrepresentative of the non-literate yeomanry. While it is good to be cautious regarding sources, it is not helpful to be hastily and unfairly dismissive. The diary-keeping farmers and autobiographers performed the same work as the Tennessee veterans, and the values exhibited by the former reflect the spirit of the age, finding confirmation in the prescriptive literature of the era, the piety and morality of southern evangelicals, and yes, the voices of the Tennessee veterans. In the end, the varied sources left by the plain folk tell a common story: endless, exhausting work was a way of life for non-elite southerners, a people who accepted hard labor, rejected leisure and aristocratic values, and discovered self-esteem and reputation in their work-related accomplishments and independence.

The vast majority of yeoman farmers across the South—whether in the Lowcountry, piedmont, backcountry, or frontier—were masters of many tasks. Survival and independence, to say nothing of material progress, depended on expertise in the varied duties of homestead farming and skillful employment of family labor as much as on soil conditions and crop prices. Success for farm families began with their household economy—planting, tending, and harvesting crops; feeding and clothing themselves;

clearing forests and grubbing stumps for farmland; cutting down trees for building materials and firewood for cooking and heating; constructing homes, barns, and outbuildings; and raising animals for power, meat, and hides. Much of what they produced they immediately consumed, thus census takers would find little record of a substantial part of their labor.[20] If farmers successfully marketed a small money crop or had the good fortune to sell an excess of corn or garden produce in the local town to earn money for hardware or luxury items, they faced the temptation of expanding their cash-crop activities. Eventually they might buy more and produce less of what they consumed.[21]

The seven-year diary of Joseph B. Lightsey, who in 1847 at age sixteen began work as a full hand on his father John's 150-acre farm in southeastern Mississippi, details the work life of a yeoman farmer—the varied tasks, diverse crop mix, and the plodding dedication to dreary labor.[22] Joseph received $10 a month and the use of five to six acres, on which he raised cotton and produce for the local market by working for himself on Saturday mornings and weekday mornings before breakfast. Because of the poor health of their father, Joseph and his brother, working alongside eight adult slaves, composed the labor force that typically worked one hundred acres in corn, twenty-five in cotton, five in potatoes, eight or nine in rice, and one in peanuts. The family also grew oats, wheat, rye, a small amount of sugar cane, peas, cucumbers, watermelons, and other garden produce. Each day Joseph recorded his work. Plowing, planting and replanting after torrential rains, hoeing and weeding, and picking corn and cotton consumed a major portion of his year, but other crops and farm duties required many days as well. Everything had to be hauled; days were spent carting corn to the local mill or market or hauling timber, firewood, or manure. Fields had to be ditched and cleared, logs rolled, and brush burned. Lightsey cut firewood and timber and split rails to make fences. Typically he spent three or more weeks in late July and early August pulling fodder.[23] By age twenty-two Lightsey was a skilled and accomplished farmer, but his diary reveals that he was something of a jack-of-all-trades. He helped build a house and chimney, cover a roof, and dig a well; he repaired guns and knives, fixed a floodgate and a gate, and repaired farm implements in a blacksmith's shop; and he built pens to catch small game and worked sporadically over a period of three years making a fish pond.[24]

Lightsey's diary offers little evidence of idleness except for an infrequent admission of "knocking about today."[25] Inclement weather or sickness might keep him from his six full days of labor per week, but there were times when he worked in the rain or with a slight fever. Otherwise, only a rare trip to town for a circus, a murder trial, or a barbecue and election frolic took him from his labors. On one occasion, he recorded a community corn-shucking at night after a full day's work, and increasingly he satisfied his passion for the hunt by hunting at night. Mostly, however, daily life for him meant field labor, as typical diary entries indicate: "I dug potatoes all day long," "I hoed cotton again today all . . . day long," "I ploughed again all day long," "I pulled fodder all day," and "I dropped corn again all day long."[26]

For most southern farmers, life amounted to unrelenting toil. To be sure, field work slowed temporarily in late summer or early fall when crops were laid by and normally came to a halt when it rained, although outdoor labor was then usually replaced by household tasks. Work rhythms responded to the slow pace of valuable draft animals that needed to be watered and rested. Indeed, plowing mules, horses, and oxen probably received more rest than the men who trudged behind them. Nevertheless, daily work, even if delayed by rain or at a pace less than feverish, was unending. The hours were long—from daybreak to dark, and sometimes beyond. For Tennessee veterans William Denier Hardin and William Sidney Hartsfield, labor from dawn to late at night seemed a normal activity; for South Carolina yeoman James Sloan, who owned land valued at $1,000 but no slaves, night work was occasional but unavoidable. William E. Orr, whose father farmed about 130 acres near Ohita, Arkansas, recalled how his mother would take "us kids" at night to the new ground and "spred down an old quilt for us to play or sleep on while she burned the big brush piles while my father cut timber and made poplar & oak rails." "Honesty industry and frugality with plenty of sticktooativeness never fails," he concluded.[27] Basil Armstrong Thomasson, a poor, non-slave-owning farmer in the North Carolina piedmont, even worked on the day of his wedding. "Clear and hot," he recorded in his diary. "Bound oats till 10 o'clock, then put on my Sunday [best?] and went over to Mr. Bell's and got married!"[28]

Everyone worked, the young and the old. In early-nineteenth-century rural America, children were economic assets, and many an aging farmer boasted of the tender years when he plowed his first furrows. "I was in the field dropping corn when I shed my first two teeth April before I was six in November," recalled Jeptha Marion Fuston, the son of a non-slaveholding farmer and blacksmith. It was not uncommon for young boys to become plow hands at eight, nine, or ten years of age and to begin working as full field hands in their early teens. The fact that school terms were irregular, being built around periods of peak labor, proved to be a signal indication of the importance of labor over all else. Girls rivaled boys in assuming adult tasks at an early age; they were simultaneously apprentices to their mothers and full work hands in sewing, washing, cooking, gardening, and all the myriad and unending tasks of running a homestead. Entry into adulthood was associated with participation in the household economy.[29]

Children of substantial slaveholders frequently performed field labor, either because additional hands were always needed or because actual labor was the best instruction for future farm management. Many parents insisted that the virtue of hard work was a lesson all should learn. T. J. Howard, the son of a farmer who owned ten slaves and two thousand acres, boasted how his father "was opposed to idleness and trained his boys to work and the necessity for it. We were taught and required to do every kind of farm work the slaves did and consider it an honor in stead of disgrace."[30]

Work did not cease with old age but only with sickness and infirmity. William C. Anderson, who had farmed and worked in a hotel in the South Carolina piedmont, expressed annoyance at being a consumer rather than a producer, and at age seventy-six he sought full-time employment. James Sloan worked into his eighties. For William Woodall, a poor farmer in Halifax County, North Carolina, work served as therapy for a troubled soul and mind. To his brother he confessed that "difficulties and trials" had harassed him almost to distraction and madness "but for my close application to hard work." Yet what was good for his mind had a debilitating effect on his physical health, for later that year he reported that his hard work and exposure to the sun had laid him low with "Neuralgea, Dyspepsia and all their horrid consequences."[31]

Yeomen, of course, did not work every God-given moment of their lives, but aside from church attendance, most respectable social or quasi-recreational activities were work-centered. Hunting and fishing, a genuine pleasure to most, provided food for the table. Self-working farmers and their wives joined neighbors and kin in house- and barn-raising, corn-shucking, rail-splitting, log-rolling, wheat-threshing, and quilting.[32] The grandson of one of the South's famous preachers recalled that amusements of the 1820s and 1830s were conducted with an eye to something useful: "The young people had their cotton-pickings, and at these there would be a good deal of mirth and gayety, but a large quantity of cotton picked also. At the quiltings they would have a lively time, chatting, joking, and courting: but there was a pretty quilt to show when all was over. House-raising and log-rolling involved so much hard work, that one would think they could not have been regarded as holidays, but they were nevertheless."[33]

Although self-working farmers were the most public and visible half of a plain-folk culture that emphasized hard work, women played a vital role in the success of yeoman establishments. Unfortunately, not everyone has understood this point, then or now. A few farmers apparently placed a premium upon field work to the detriment of inside work, trivializing work within the house. Several of the farmers' accounts cited herein elaborately record the activities of outdoor work and the products of fields, orchards, and pastures but neglect the activity of the household.[34] Nevertheless, it is easy to argue that women worked as hard as, if not harder than, men. The daily drudgery of maintaining a large family that owned no slaves meant that farmwives, aided by their children, labored full-time as cooks, cleaning women, washerwomen, gardeners, and essential hands for raising poultry and running a small dairy and perhaps a household manufacturing concern. In addition they carried, gave birth to, and cared for children. With good reason, a few sons saw the labor of their mothers as slave-like. Their work was the same, and their pay (shelter, clothing, and food to maintain their health) was the same. Their labor, however, was willingly performed, for they worked in their own houses and for their own children and husbands and took pride in tidy kitchens, bountiful gardens, fancy preserves, and warm and attractive quilts.[35]

Few labor-saving devices eased their toil; they toted heavy pots, skillets, and water buckets and sweated over wood-burning stoves and fireplaces to prepare meals, make bread and biscuits, preserve food for winter consumption, and heat water for laundry. "The kitchen was the nerve center for farm activity," asserts historian Claudia Bushman. "Workers prepared meals there; dishes and preserves, candles and containers, pots and supplies of all kinds filled the shelves. The women compounded medicines, tried out tallow, made candles and soap, and washed dishes in this stressful and crowded atmosphere."[36] Washday was grueling; women worked outdoors, often in extreme heat or cold, spending hours "soaping, boiling, beating, and hand rubbing until the clothes became reasonably clean."[37] Women made and repaired clothes by spinning, weaving, knitting, and sewing flax, wool, or cotton. Seventy-seven-year-old Tennessee veteran William C. Dillihay recalled that his "mother did her washing and cooking as well as other household duties including weaving coverlids and clothes for the family. Such work as she did would be a cu[r]iosity to women today. I sleep under two of her coverlids that was woven by her 65 years ago."[38] Many women even worked in the fields when necessity dictated the use of additional hands, and when husbands became incapacitated or died, women became full-time field workers. Zachary Taylor Dyer, a poor farmer from Giles County, Tennessee, after the death of his father learned about the world of work from his mother, who taught him "to plow, hoe, to spin, knit, weave, sew, milk, cook, wash, fill quills, make-up bead [bed] and anything that came to hand and I can do it now thank God for such a mother."[39] Women also sold garden produce, eggs, milk, clothing, quilts, fancy sewing, and other items produced at home, and the proceeds from their expertise, diligence, and frugality might amount to the most sizable portion of a farmer's cash income. The independence of frontier and upcountry yeomen, in part, reflected dependence on wives and children, a conclusion also reached by Stephanie McCurry for the yeomen of the supposedly aristocratic South Carolina Lowcountry.[40]

With sweaty brows and dirty hands, southern farmwives were admired as paragons of industry. "Hard work to the end" epitomized "a female life well lived," as is illustrated by a Mrs. Henry Boughton of Virginia, mother of nine. Without slaves or servants, Mrs. Boughton did the cooking, washing, milking, sewing, and mending for her entire family and also took in weaving and sewing to increase the family's income. Often in delicate health, she eventually "succumbed to breast cancer after suffering for four or five years." Virginia planter Bernard Walker "greatly respected this" industrious and energetic person, whom he praised as a woman of enormous worth and integrity despite her position "in the lower walks of life."[41] Agricultural newspapers applauded plain-folk mothers and wives for well-kept homes, kitchens, and gardens, praised their decorum and manners, and heralded their efficient work, which stood in distinct contrast to the uselessness of fashionable ladies.[42] The Baltimore *American Farmer* even argued that "women were 'more happily circumstanced' than men because 'the important and fatiguing advocations *[sic]* of men necessarily impose seasons of inactivity . . . .' Women, on the other hand, need never cease their labors; while visiting or 'resting' they could do their practical sewing."[43] One Tennessee veteran in particular captured the image of the farmwife ideal: "Mother was very industrious," he fondly remembered. "Clothed her family by work. Spun and wove cloth, carded her own wool. Knit all the socks and stockings worn by the family. I never seen my mother sit down and be idle and do nothing. Always had work in her hand. I had the best mother."[44] Given the contributions of farmwives (and also children, who were apprentice farmers or homemakers), it may be that historian Eugene D. Genovese's rule about slave labor, that "all hands" must "be occupied at all times," is as appropriate for slaveless yeoman households as for the slaves on plantations.[45]

Because the middle and upper-middle classes in nineteenth-century America knew household chores to be exhausting, those who could afford domestic help, in both the North and South, seldom skimped on hiring or owning extra hands to ease women's domestic burdens. In the South, with some notable exceptions, yeoman families with a small number of slaves assigned a slave or two to the most onerous household tasks. Often working side by side with their slaves, these farmwives experienced firsthand some of the drudgery of domestic slavery.[46] Fortunate as they were to have domestic help, it arrived encumbered with the task of slave supervision, which was then added to their own demanding physical chores.

In the world of the plain folk, a woman's reputation rested on a well-kept home and steady production of ample clothing and food. For men, the hard work of daily life—even more than the no-holds-barred, eye-gouging fight or the drunken frolic celebrated by many southern historians—established a man's reputation and tested his virility, toughness, and independence.[47] Neighbors were judged by their industry: farmers won recognition for steady work, the earliest crops, the largest yields, or the straightest furrows while farmwives received praise for well-kept kitchens, productive gardens, and accomplishments in sewing.[48] It has become something of a cliché that southern yeomen, whether solidly middle class or poor, joined the South's circle of honor because they were free and white in a slave society, but much more was involved in establishing reputation and status. To be free was one thing. However, enjoying the full benefits of freedom required independence, and that necessitated work. The external world of honor—status and reputation—was derived from struggles to achieve and maintain independence, but honor was also matched by an internal world of values—the farmers' self-esteem—that was predicated upon survival and triumph in a world of unrelenting toil that tested a man's skills, steadiness, and toughness and a woman's stoic regard for faith, production, and labor and sacrifices for family.

"[W]e were working people," proclaimed T. L. Johnson; "A working man stood as high in the commun[i]ty as any body." The Tennessee veterans believed that honest workers were "the bone and seneou [sinew]" of the country and that honest toil—"respectable and honorable"—was essential "to good citizenship." Being a willing worker "was a mark of distinction";

a man who worked industriously stood high in his neighborhood society. "[I]t was the hard enerjetic *[sic]* people was the respected ones," pronounced Joe C. Brooks, a poor farm boy from McNairy County, Tennessee.[49] William Anderson Wilson, the son of a slaveless farmer and mechanic, boasted, "I worked on the farm and did every kind of work . . . and never [k]new what idleness was and can say the same for my three brothers and all the rest of the family—can all so say that the man or woman boy or girl who did not do their part was a rare exception."[50] Many Tennessee veterans stated emphatically that they worked as hard as slaves and labored beside them in the fields as well. George A. Rice, from Decatur County, even implied a certain rough equality of condition among whites and blacks when he wrote of his early life:

> Plowed oxens and horses, also hoed, and during summer months hauled barral staves 16 miles with 4 yoke cattle on Linch . . . wagon 4 trips a week . . . . Father taught school and worked on farm, seeing after us boys and nigars slaves. Mother cooked on fire place used pot racks, scilits kettle etc and spone and weaved cloth to make all of everyday clothing also cut and made our cloths . . . . [W]e all worked as hard as our slaves and give the same to eat we got[.]

John H. O'Neal and Peter Donnell recorded similar experiences. "My father had 7 boys 6 of them older than myself," and "We all went to the field, same as the Negroes . . . ." "I worked . . . with the darkes—plowed howed mowed—cut wheat oats split rales don anything the darkes don."[51]

The diary of Basil Armstrong Thomasson provides a fine example of the way in which one yeoman developed a strong self-concept and a prescription for a happy life from years of hard labor. A young farmer working sixty improved acres in Iredell County in the western piedmont of North Carolina, Thomasson each day recorded accomplishments in field, barn, and orchard and not infrequently affirmed his prescription for a successful life. Although poor—his farm and livestock were valued at only $200 in the 1860 census, and there were periods when food was in short supply—Thomasson was a Ben Franklin- and Bible-quoting farmer who waxed poetic about the benefits of home sweet home and the delights of farming. All work was honorable, he believed; all must work who wished to be happy. He advised his fellow man to be "industrious, honest and frugal"; "Make a good, and proper use of your time, reader, if you wish to be 'healthy, wealthy and wise.' " Six days a week he labored hard, but Sunday was a day of rest for the soul and improvement for the mind. He rejected idle chat, lived frugally, and avoided borrowing because it threatened his independence, and he criticized the use of liquor, tobacco, and coffee but indulged in the purchase of books and agricultural newspapers for self-improvement.[52]

Thomasson usually rose before dawn and attended diligently to the varied tasks confronting a self-working farmer. "Ploughing is hard work," he admitted, but he lived by the motto that if something was worth doing, it was worth doing well. On occasion his need for cash forced him to experiment with other occupations, such as clerking, school-teaching, and carriage-making, but he always returned to farming as the occupation that best offered secure returns.

> I fear tho' that trade would not pay as well as farming. Dr. Ben. Franklin said, "Keep thy shop and thy shop will keep thee." The bible says, "He that tilleth his land shall have plenty of bread." Now I believe I had rather risk the Bible and the farm; tho' the man who keeps his shop *may* live well, but the man [who] tills the soil will be certain to have bread to eat.[53]

Thomasson scorned leisure and luxury, and as historian Paul D. Escott concludes, he appears to have been more like the conscience-driven, self-regulating Yankee than the honor-seeking, self-regarding southerner depicted by Bertram Wyatt-Brown in *Southern Honor*.[54] In all economic decisions, Thomasson "sought independence, respectability, and progress rather than the values of aristocracy," and his self-sufficiency enabled him to avoid entanglement in the vagaries of the cash-based market economy. Still, like other yeomen he could never achieve complete independence since a shortage of labor and cash necessitated swapping work with family and friends to secure additional hands for essential farm tasks such as harvesting, log-rolling, and erecting barns and outbuildings. Here Thomasson amassed significant moral capital; a reputation for steady and efficient labor was a vital, marketable commodity. Although other yeomen seldom kept diaries, Thomasson was unusual only in his rigid notions regarding liquor, coffee, and tobacco; his dedication to labor and independence, concern for his work reputation, and avoidance of idleness echoed among the southern plain folk.[55]

The pride in work resonating throughout plain-folk society did not exist in the abstract, for it was coupled with a belief in upward mobility as the product of industry and economy. Here was a very practical reason for daily labor. Most Tennessee veterans believed that the hardworking, industrious poor could save to insure a competence, perhaps to buy a farm, a business, or a slave or two.[56] W. A. Duncan, the son of a non-slaveholding farmer owning but fifty acres, readily affirmed how poor folks, if they were good workers and managers, could purchase a small farm or go into business even if they started with nothing.[57] Of course, mobility might not always be upward, but Tennessee's veterans and farmers expressed faith in their society and its rewards. W. J. Tucker of Maury County, a farmer and veteran whose father had owned no slaves but could claim solid, middle-class status, reflected how "It dos seem that the rich boy in many cases would loose and became poor, while the poor boy had become rich. Many cases in my knowing that way. The hustler gets these[.]"[58]

In the same breath that common whites praised the virtue of hard work, they used contemptuous, pillorying terms for those who shirked honest toil and a full day's labor, labeling them worthless, mean, trashy, or trifling. "A man who did not work was not considered much account," said Edwin M. Gardner. "[I]t was a bad county for fops," declared George W. Samuel, while Thomas M. Patterson noted that a lazy person sometimes slipped into his community but did not last long, moving on to Arkansas to hunt and fish. Isaac Nelson Rainey emphasized that "The loafer, rich or poor, was despised."[59] Drones, vagabonds, bums, deadbeats, deadheads, nobodies, damned rapscallions, and baser specimens of the community were some of the other unflattering terms applied to the able-bodied who did not work. Folks expressed strong views on this subject: "if a man didnt work neither should he eat"; the few that would not work were "not respected and hated by rich and poor"; and "a man that did not work either with his hands or his head was not regarded as a man atall."[60]

Many Tennessee veterans took umbrage at the myth of southern laziness, especially when reminded in the questionnaires that "certain historians" believed white farmers avoided heavy field labor. "[H]istorians are verry rong when they say whi[t]e men would not work," declared J. L. Walton, while R. T. Mockbee accused such historians of ignorance or willful falsification. A farmer and tanner from Rhea County, Edward Gannaway labeled "certain historians" either "natural born" fools or likely candidates for the penitentiary "for malicious lying." Mississippi-born Gentry Richard McGee, whose parents owned an eighty-acre farm and six slaves, recalled how he and all of his acquaintances did all of the usual farmwork. "The historians who say Southern white men did not work before the Civil War belong to the Annanias Club," he concluded.[61]

When plain folk admitted idleness in their communities, they most often had in mind a small minority of disreputable, poor people or a few rich planters and their kin, sometimes described as effete fops or dandies. An essayist in the Jonesborough *Tennessee Farmer* cast scorn upon "a wandering tribe of work-haters," serious pests to any community, who roved about under the pretense of getting jobs, but it was the job of eating, not work, they sought.[62] It is noteworthy that Tennessee veterans seldom mentioned the South's stereotypical white trash, but when they did, their scorn was stinging. A few veterans attributed the South's reputation for laziness to these worthless, "whiskey drinking degenerates" and thugs, the wild and reckless few who would not work. These low-down people had no status; they had sunk so low that slaves would not associate with them, and it was the slaves, white farmers insisted, who were most likely to call them poor white trash.[63] The verdict was inescapable, concluded a Tennessee veteran from a modest home that had known its share of both hard work and foxhunting: the white trash brought "opp[ro]brium upon themselves by being too lazy to work and too thriftless to save."[64] Fortunately, trashy whites were few, perhaps one in twenty, ventured G. W. Park, son of a modest farmer who owned no slaves.[65] Moreover, hardworking farmers, slaveholders and slaveless alike, saw idleness (and the poverty stemming from it) as an individual flaw, a failure of character, and not a stigma of class or an unfortunate result of slavery or slave competition.

Tennessee veterans more often located the South's idle people among the wealthy rather than at the lower end of the social scale. A few poor farmers, perhaps out of envy, claimed with considerable extravagance that slave owners enjoyed leisurely lives because poor folk, whites and blacks, did all of the work of their communities. Drones in the planter class spent their time in hunting, fishing, and riding around the country.[66] A writer in the Jonesborough *Tennessee Farmer* contrasted the honest industry of the farmer with the activities of an elite of brainless dandies, useless females, and social butterflies.[67] Even a working planter directing his slaves might be criticized. A classic incident from Hinds County, Mississippi, in the 1830s reveals the resentment directed toward planters who failed to soil their hands or work up a sweat while slaves and whites did hard field work. In this incident, the father of Susan Dabney Smedes, a wealthy planter who had moved there from Virginia, came to the aid of a neighbor by loaning twenty slaves to help clear a grassy field. The farmer showed little appreciation for this neighborly kindness, complaining that "if Colonel Dabney had taken hold of a plough and worked by his side he would have been glad to have his help, but to see him sitting up on his horse with his gloves on directing his Negroes how to work was not to his taste."[68] The farmer was angry because of the colonel's refusal to join him as an equal and no doubt resented the implied superiority in the planter's distancing himself from the farmer, especially when the planter's instructions to his slaves might by implication be aimed at the farmer himself. Such feigned superiority (consciously adopted or otherwise) could easily offend working people while simultaneously affirming and justifying the self-esteem of those with callused hands, red necks, and sturdy backs.

Although idleness among large slaveholders—most of them active managers who had once worked in the fields and who currently worked their own sons—was not the rule, wherever it surfaced it was denounced in no uncertain terms. Perhaps 2 percent were idle, estimated Joel L. Henry, but they were fools if they did not believe honest toil was respectable. A few rich men's idle sons, labeled "worthless curs" by William Grant, did not amount to much. "Some persons never worked," reported Thomas Jefferson Howard, but "they became vagabonds and died in misery and want" following the war.[69]

Much harder to bear than the simple knowledge of idleness among some of the wealthy was the occasional hint that idle slaveholders and rich folk derogated the hard work of the yeomen. Contrary views about the nobility and significance of labor—especially on the part of the wealthy—surfaced infrequently among Tennessee veterans, a situation understandable in a democratic society of isolated communities in which large landowners and slaveholders wanted and needed the votes, popular acclaim, and economic support of the masses. The wealthy who disparaged honest toil, asserted Zachary Taylor Dyer, had more "money than brains." R. H. Mosley, the son of a non-slaveholding farmer in Williamson County, Tennessee, and one of the few who revealed considerable resentment of wealthy slave owners whom he claimed did nothing, accused the rich of viewing farming as a "low" calling and referring to poorer folks as clodhoppers.[70] Perhaps a bit more common among the elite was the attitude that while manual labor was not in itself disreputable, it was a sign that the person who spent a lifetime in field work "lacked brains, education, or money."[71] Still, this view was not expressed often.

In general, most plain folk recognized the important contributions and labor of slave owners and others who might do little actual physical work. Those who earned an honest living through farm management, mental labor, or community service as doctors, lawyers, or preachers were held in high esteem. Idleness was the culprit, and it drew strong condemnation. When wealthy, slaveholding planters revealed themselves as busy, productive, and knowledgeable about crops, draft animals, farm implements, fertilizer, and the myriad difficulties of running a farm, the plain folk could easily accord honor and respect to active farm management.

In light of the esteem associated with hard work, a sense of guilt sometimes troubled those self-working farmers who failed their communities as paragons of diligence. One example of a self-working farmer, John Osbourn (or Osbourne), stands in distinct contrast to Lightsey, Thomasson, the Tennessee veterans, and the others cited here because he would just as soon go on a drinking spree as complete a day's work. Osbourne typically labored alongside a small number of slaves on his three North Carolina farms, but in numerous diary entries, he confessed to drinking too much and gadding about and indicated his intention to reform. Rather than pride in his frolics, he showed a sense of guilt and clearly understood his duty and what would win respect.[72] Similarly, the Reverend William E. Hatcher recalled the acute embarrassment and pain that his childhood stubbornness and renunciation of dirt farming caused his father, "a stalwart old farmer" who worked a small plantation with a few slaves and primitive equipment. The hardworking father, who could foresee none of his offspring's future success in the pulpit, believed his young son was "grievously and unpardonably lazy." What was God's purpose in creating a son so devoted to idleness? With a sorrowful mien, Hatcher's father reached his conclusion—that God created him "to starve, as a warning for all idle boys that may come on later."[73]

Unending physical labor structured the lives of plain-folk families most of their waking hours, but for many the world of work was inseparable from a religious faith that supported, justified, and commended daily toil. When Richard Enos Sherrill, a Tennessee veteran and the son of a modestly affluent slaveholder, recalled his youth, he boasted of working "on the farm did all kinds of work plowed hoed any thing come to hand all the neighbors in our neighborhood did all kind of farm work[.]" Was honest toil respected? "[Y]es, it was," he responded, "we lived in a Christian . . . community 2 miles from Old 'Mt. Carmel Church' widley known strickly Blue Stocking Presbyterian."[74] What Sherrill alluded to—the connection between labor and evangelical faith—the Reverend Watkins of the "Old Pine Farm," a South Carolina country minister who served four rural congregations while farming three hundred acres, made explicit: "Faithfulness to secular engagements is a part of religion, and in observing this we render an acceptable service to God . . . . one may serve God in his field, his storehouse, or his workshop."[75] In Georgia's Cherokee territory in the 1830s, Zillah Haynie Brandon also affirmed the role of faith in everyday toil. Brandon cheerfully endured struggles and hardships because she felt sustained by Him who "from the heights of heaven" "stooped to listen to my complaints and number my tears." In her memoirs she confided, "My health seemed entirely impa[i]red, yet I was compelled from unavoidable circumstances to perform from year to year, that amount of labor sufficient for three able hands, in order to maintain a character, as Christian and mother to which I felt I was justly entitled."[76]

The spirit of Wesley, Calvin, and Luther survived in the antebellum South, and yeoman farmers, as ministers, deacons, and elders, along with farmwives, who outnumbered men in church membership, testified to the links among hard, steady labor in field and household, evangelical faith, and a belief in a simple way of life joined to a gospel of work. Such lives were highly esteemed—in fact, sometimes praised as almost saint-like. For example, eighty-one-year-old David Shires Myers Bodenhamer, originally of Giles County, Tennessee, lauded the self-sacrificing qualities of his tireless mother, who rose early and worked "willingly and diligently with her own hands." The thirty-first chapter of Proverbs, which he loosely quoted, captured her essential nature: "She layeth her hands to the distaff and her hands hold the spindle . . . the hum of industry [is] in her home and in the kitchen garden, poultry yard and cow lot there is busy work . . . . The Sabbath is kept sacred . . . the Bible is first in her home . . . . Her children rise up and call her blessed."[77] In describing Republican culture in the North, Eric Foner noted that "the moral qualities which would ensure success in one's calling—honesty, frugality, diligence, punctuality, and sobriety—became religious obligations." Such words would be applicable below, as well as above, the Mason-Dixon line.[78]

It had not always been so, not in the colonial world of the gentleman planter; but by the late eighteenth century, the dissenting churches of upstart Baptists, Methodists, and Presbyterians challenged the dominance of the established Anglican and elite culture. The ascetic, church-based social and religious lifestyle of many plain-folk communities clashed with an aggressive, worldly, hedonistic culture of honor stereotypically associated with the planter elite. Unfortunately, popular images of a violent South and enduring myths of moonlight, magnolias, and mint juleps reveal that too much attention has been directed toward the power, prerogatives, and pleasures of stereotypical planters. Among the more-numerous plain folk of the antebellum period and even within the ranks of the planters, an evangelical lifestyle influenced daily activity, although it never vanquished the extremes of male excesses on the dueling grounds or in the gaming pits, barrooms, and brothels. Evangelicals, who had begun as dissenters, modified many of their pristine practices and values to enter the mainstream by the 1830s, with the result that most people lived under the sway of religion, regardless of whether they attended church or participated in church activities.[79]

Although it may be true that only one-fifth to one-third of all antebellum southerners were church members, mostly Baptist, Methodist, and Presbyterian, congregations were two-to-four-times larger than the actual number of church members. In certain areas of the South, evangelicalism had spread to a majority of households.[80] "To a remarkable degree," concludes John B. Boles, "evangelical religion shaped the mentalité of antebellum southerners, rich and poor, slaveholder and nonslaveholder. By 1830 the 'Solid South' was more a religious than a political reality."[81] Even in Lowcountry South Carolina, the bastion of southern wealth and class-consciousness, evangelical churches, which were essentially yeoman institutions, set the tone of society.[82]

Ministers were revered community leaders called to serve in the rural South more often because of their faith and personal characteristics than their education or theological training. Although the level of education steadily improved among the clergy, itinerant, poorly trained lay preachers, especially among Baptists and Methodists, often filled rural pulpits on a rotating schedule of Sundays as they traveled from one isolated crossroads church to another. As late as 1860, lay preachers outnumbered ordained preachers among Virginia Methodists.[83]

Whether lay preachers or ordained ministers, most rural preachers relied upon outside work, at least in part, to support themselves and their families since congregations were poor and salaries inadequate or even non-existent.[84] In frontier regions of the South, it would not be unusual for farmer-preachers to do the heaviest of farm labor and to hunt and fish for food.[85] In lieu of a salary, many ministers received free-will offerings, usually an amount as uncertain as it was inadequate, but some backcountry evangelical congregations and ministers believed in principle that preaching the Lord's word should not require financial remuneration of any sort. The experience of Reuben Davis's father, a farmer-preacher of limited means with only a pioneer's rudimentary education, provides a case in point. A well-respected Baptist minister, he busied himself "during the week . . . with ordinary farm labor" and would never accept compensation for services to the church. Such, he considered, was "serving the Lord for hire."[86]

Highly respected bi-vocational ministers displayed strong faith and strong character, setting examples of proper deportment and the ennobling discipline of work. For such preachers, work was both necessary and honorable. One minister, whose "heart was set on" the work of the church, still "considered his duty to his family paramount, remembering that the sacred volume placed those who did not provide for their families lower than the infidel himself."[87] The Reverend Watkins titled his autobiography *The Old Pine Farm* because he labored there diligently, raising corn and livestock to support his family and secure the means to tend to his four congregations. Although his house was essentially two log pens and two backroom sheds, with a passage through the center and a piazza in front (an architectural style common among the plain folk), he boasted that its neatness, cleanliness, and furnishings "marked the refined taste of the preacher and his family." The operation of his farm, he believed, was "conducted in a manner creditable to" his industry and good judgment.[88] The Reverend William Capers, a future Methodist bishop, also expressed pride in his achievements in field and pulpit. The son of a Lowcountry planter, he came to know the hardships and struggles of a circuit-riding minister after his father's sudden death left him without an inheritance or financial security. Later, with a family to support, he secured a church and then turned to the task of earning an income.

> The house ready for occupancy, I became too much interested in the field to be only a manager, and betook myself to the plough; which having done, I must prosecute it diligently for example's sake . . . . I had never done an hour's work in a field in my life when I began to do this; and was there ever a severer exercise for one who never held a plough before? At first, I ploughed all day, and at night had fever; then I ploughed all day, and had no fever; and after some few weeks, I had rather plough than not; so that I have never been able to pity a ploughman since. Every thing kept in good condition about me, and in the fall of the year there were provisions enough made for the year ensuing, and pigs and poultry a plenty, in view of the expected large family I was to have.[89]

Unlike Capers, the Reverend Richard Hooker Wilmer, the future Episcopal bishop of Alabama, experienced the rigors of farm life at an early age as the chief provider for his widowed stepmother and his siblings. Later, as pastor of rural parishes in Virginia in the 1840s and 1850s, he would work in garden and field before undertaking pastoral duties—perhaps a ten-mile journey to pray with a parishioner. On occasion he might squeeze in an hour or two of reading or study before "refreshing slumber." When his woodpile was depleted, he would hitch up his own team to go after wood and on numerous occasions acted as his own teamster in bringing supplies from Richmond. A minister's chopping and hauling wood and carting goods from town—work typical of slaves and servants—caused a certain amount of consternation among a congregation that saw the Lord's servant as a gentleman of refinement. His parishioners' concern, however, never resulted in increased pastoral support. Ignoring their somewhat-delicate sensibilities, Wilmer accepted their lack of support with equanimity because he found physical work invigorating and idleness burdensome. In 1850, when illness kept him from his calling in pulpit and field, he wrote: "I have been oppressed with the intolerable burden of having nothing to do—the most engrossing and slavish life that it has ever fallen to my lot to experience."[90]

John Frederick Mallet, a North Carolina farmer-preacher and colporteur, shared Wilmer's horror of idleness, viewing it as a falling away from God. After the death of his wife, Mallet despaired of his ability to work, suffering a lethargy that may have been due to depression, but he interpreted his ineffectualness as an inability to follow God's way, remarking, "Done nothing to day—warm and pleasant why do I live from God—Oh Lord deliver me from my own wicked heart of unbelief & sin." And the next day he lamented that although the weather was warm and pleasant and he had sown some seeds, he had "done but little else—yet I love God & will trust him for all."[91]

Ministers, elders, and deacons exhibited enormous concern for economic affairs and the daily toils of church members. Numerous sermons, essays, and clerical admonitions depicting the dangers of both idleness and mammonism and endorsing the ennobling discipline of labor reveal that the evangelicals' concern with the practical aspects of daily life was part of their traditional obsession with fundamental questions of sin and personal wrongdoing and the hope for God's forgiveness and salvation. A Methodist "Class-Book" in 1833, for example, pronounced idleness "incompatible with the spirit of true devotion," while a writer in the Baptist-affiliated Washington (Ga.) *Christian Index* contended that leisure and relaxation afforded by riches constituted the type of idleness that debased the soul.[92] An editor in the Richmond *Religious Herald*, a leading Virginia Baptist periodical, argued: "Idle amusements, idle conversation, and whatever will affect our communion with God, are inconsistent with our Christian profession."[93] Several of the well-known published sermons of one of the South's famous Presbyterian minister-theologians, the Reverend Thomas Smyth, warned of the evils of indolence and pronounced labor a blessing, not a curse. "The worker . . . is the true noble," he argued, and industry the most effective way to achieve respectable standing and success in life's pursuits. Smyth preached that "God Himself" exhibited to man "a sublime example of working six days . . . in the creation of the world" before He rested and that throughout the Bible, industry, diligence, and exertion appeared "in terms of strong commendation." "The law of labour is therefore to be regarded as a divine law; so that in working with our hands, or in any other way, the thing that is good, we are fulfilling the appointment of the Creator."[94]

In addition to the dangers of idleness, southern evangelicals warned of the perils of mammonism, even to the extent of denouncing wealth or at least the sinful ways in which it was often acquired or used. The affluent were linked to wicked indolence and soul-destroying worldliness; they were tempted to spend their way to damnation or could be driven from God by desires for fashionable dress, luxuries, or dangerous amusements.[95] An essayist in the Jonesborough *Tennessee Farmer* warned against the temptations of wealth and fame that could transform lawful occupations and honorable pursuits into the worship of Mammon and a rejection of the claims of one's Creator upon a higher calling.[96] Basil Thomasson, in reflections on a sermon he had just read, revealed an extreme fear of materialism, concluding that it was "very dangerous to be rich, or even to desire riches. We should not 'lay up' for ourselves 'treasures upon earth,' but 'having food and raiment' we should 'be therewith content.' "[97] Similarly, Daniel Cobb, who saw himself as one of God's poor despite his steadily increasing wealth, deplored wealth as dangerous, "the rival of God in the heart."[98] Articles in the Washington (Ga.) *Christian Index* emphasized that true wealth was found in a spiritual state and not in money, and while encouraging the training of youth in industry, the writers warned against the tendency to stress money-making.[99] The sins of greed and materialism loomed so prominently in clergymen's sermons that, according to Kenneth Moore Startup, most clerics feared that a "deadly spirit of avarice, covetousness, and materialism" might overwhelm Christian spirituality.[100]

Southern evangelicals placed their hope in the plain folk—the hardworking, worthy poor and middle class who were viewed as rich in faith and its rewards but lacking in luxuries and long-term security. When the Reverend William E. Hatcher, perhaps the best known of the Virginia Baptist ministers, confessed that mixing with the godly poor always enriched him, he stood as one with a Protestant faith that had always exhibited a tendency to link poverty to true spirituality. Other ministers such as Richard Furman, perhaps the South's leading Baptist minister, even emphasized the blessings of poverty—a poverty that required the masses "to remember their maker and to live circumspectly in consideration of their dependence upon God's merciful provision of their daily needs."[101] While celebrating the worthy poor, ministers readily lapsed into condemnations of the extremes of southern society—trashy whites who lived without morals or labor, women lost to the world of fashion, and effeminate dandies whose soft, white hands proclaimed that they were less than real men. Whereas idleness at either end of the economic spectrum bred negative results, rustic labor would produce spiritual and physical health; order, economy, and peace were to be found on the yeoman's farm.[102]

Believing that the church should mold all parts of individual and community existence, evangelicals expected the gospel to improve every aspect of life that it touched—spiritual, moral, intellectual, and material.[103] Especially in towns and cities, evangelicals led the fight for temperance, improved education, penal reform, and other progressive causes; evangelical communities everywhere emphasized self-improvement, self-discipline, sober-mindedness, and hard work.[104] Work was a calling expected of a Christian, for it also produced intangible benefits of humility, patience, moderation, diligence, integrity, self-sufficiency, self-esteem, and self-control and delayed gratification.[105] Practitioners of such a faith, no matter how poor, were not nobodies; they deserved respect. The word *respectable*, argues Donald G. Mathews in his seminal work *Religion in the Old South*, "came to mean 'pious' or 'moral,' rather than 'capable of eliciting respect by reason of social rank'; and *vulgar* came to mean 'impious' or 'immoral,' rather than indicating commonness or 'low social rank.' " The hardworking, progressive, and spiritually motivated evangelicals—the respectable folk of the South—were, in Mathews's words, "moving not only through space (to better farms) and time (to a better status) but also through eternity, that is, to a community" that replaced the traditional, pleasure-seeking "ethic with a new one."[106] That new ethic, even in a slave society, reflected the moral imperative to work.

Although evangelical Protestantism did not completely overcome the male culture of honor analyzed by Bertram Wyatt-Brown in *Southern Honor*, evangelicalism was nevertheless a powerful, cohesive force in many plain-folk communities. Some men might still consider churchgoing unmanly, and intemperance, personal violence, and the sporting life of the so-called hell-of-a-fellow might continue to torment evangelical communities. But for the southern yeomanry, evangelical religion was a vital element sustaining a culture of faith, work, and commitment to independence and respectability. It appears that self-working southerners functioned within either a culture of secular honor or a culture of religious honor, or both. Together the two cultures incorporate most of the diverse characteristics ascribed to the southern plain folk: stoicism in the face of adversity, toughness in personal confrontation, piety and asceticism, a high regard for white supremacy, and, above all, pride in independence. Hard work was a core value in each culture, which suggests that a culture of secular honor and a culture of religious honor need not be mutually exclusive. In fact, many a churchgoing, God-fearing farmer never refused a drink or permitted a personal insult.[107] He might pray hard, or he might play hard, or he might do some of both; but like all of the plain folk who shared in a culture of honor, secular or religious, he worked hard. Reuben Davis spoke for his friends and neighbors and most of the South's plain folk when he penned his memoirs:

> It was to the moral fibre of these pioneers that we chiefly owe the wonderful success they achieved. I wish to state this very strongly because I am aware that, upon this subject, much injustice has been done us, both at home and abroad. Our first settlers have too often been characterized as a set of ruffians and desperadoes, whose courage degenerated into ferocity, and whose freedom was license and debauchery. The Mississippian has been caricatured into a swaggering rowdy, always drinking whiskey and flourishing revolvers and bowieknives. It is true that many of them drank hard, swore freely, and were utterly reckless of consequences when their passions were aroused. But it is equally true that the great body of the settlers were sober, industrious men, who met hardships and toil with patient courage, and whose hands were as ready to extend help as they were to resist violence and oppression.[108]

As this essay contends, the southern common folk harbored a work ethic suggestive of Benjamin Franklin's Poor Richard or Max Weber's theories. All work was not ennobling, a part of one's offering to God or one's duty to society. Drudge-work had little value in the South. Self-working farmers and their families rejected servile work or any work under the direction of someone else. Manual labor was the province of free citizens of the republic; menial labor was the work of slaves and was barren of purpose, nobility, and meaning. Coerced labor was not redemptive or ennobling. Yeoman husbands and wives (and their children) worked with their hands, performing the same tasks as slaves, but it made all the difference in the world that white farmers and homemakers were free and independent citizens, working for themselves and their families and immune to the orders and the disdain of anyone who presumed to be their superior. The yeomanry would not bear any sign of humiliation. As landowning, independent farmers, many southern whites insulated themselves from degraded status. To be white but landless and dependent bore a stigma, but it could be offset by exhibiting a reputation for respectable work and a strong moral and religious character and/or by asserting one's toughness and demanding mannerly treatment from one's superiors. The small class of southern whites who labored as mechanics expected and received respectful treatment and status because of their skills and accomplishments; many owned property in the form of slaves or a shop and tools and not infrequently employed others to labor for them, which enhanced their respectability. Common laborers suffered from the burden of diminished respect. In southern cities, where ordinary workers needed to find employers and to satisfy bosses, blacks and the Irish, not native-born whites, supplied unskilled labor.[109]

In antebellum America, many elite planters and proslavery ideologues joined with abolitionists to emphasize the supposed laziness of slaves, the former attributing that alleged laziness to a natural indolence and inferiority and the latter blaming the lack of positive incentive. Tennessee veterans, mostly self-working farmers and/or sons of self-working farmers, voiced little criticism of slaves' work habits and did not indulge in accusations of slaves' laziness, perhaps because they knew all about the travails of working people, which is to say the common experiences of blacks and whites in field, kitchen, and dairy. Tennessee veteran Theodric E. Lipscomb, who labored by the side of slaves in Maury County, revealed his respect for slaves' diligence when he proudly boasted that no slave could gain a round on him.[110] John Russell Dance, whose wealthy father put him to work to learn all about farming, boasted how he plowed and worked with the hoe, and he recalled that "Some of my hardest work as a boy was trying to beat the fastest negro cotton picker."[111] The conditions and results of the yeomen's labor, the privileges of whiteness, the yeomen's status as voters or potential voters, and courteous treatment by wealthy planters, politicians, and most authority figures—but not their work per se—made their standing superior to that of any slave. The freedom and independence of the southern yeomanry bolstered their self-esteem and guaranteed their position in the circle of southern honor.

An understanding of the southern plain-folk work ethic in the antebellum era makes clearer many later developments. The "New South" rhetoric endorsing the seriousness of work and the need for a new ethic was aimed at that portion of the elite who, even as plantation managers, never subscribed to a work ethic. Ordinary folks needed no such message. Those farmers and their families who moved into the mills and mill villages were exchanging one form of hard labor for another, but the greatest change was in their loss of independence and their altered conditions of work. The Populist momentum of the 1890s reflected outrage at the increasingly dismal returns from farm labor and threats to the security of those who had always labored to protect their independence and birthright as white southerners. And finally, because the labor performed by freedmen, now potential competitors for land and the yeoman's cherished independence, was still the same as that of many whites, the yeoman's sense of superiority needed the support of increased racial distance of both psychological and physical sorts.

This essay does not claim that southerners marched in lockstep with stereotypically driven, acquisitive Yankees or that a putative Protestant work ethic dripped like Spanish moss in the Lowcountry, but neither was the Old South essentially a land of leisured gentlemen, slothful, fun-loving, good old boys, or common folk who shunned field and household work as demeaning and un-remunerative. The plain folk of the Old South saw themselves as an honorable people, worthy of praise as the salt of the earth, a dependable people upon whom the republic rested. The evidence presented here suggests several explanations for the vast majority's acceptance and even admiration of hard work in a slave society. The plain folk often had no alternative to working hard; steady labor, often in the most trying circumstances, was not necessarily a conscious choice since field work and household labor had always been their lot. In short, they were raised to work. Furthermore, most took pride in their accomplishments and ability to maintain their families and keep decent homes, and most saw in steady labor the promise of upward mobility and success. Their evangelical faith sustained them, even commanded and commended them, as it embraced serious-minded individuals intent upon creating faith-based communities that scorned idleness and were dedicated to God's way. Eighty-year-old Tennessee veteran T. W. Walthall presented all of these reasons and more as he reviewed his life and pronounced it good. His testimony represents the finest traditions and successes of the South's self-working farmers, driven by faith-oriented and secular values. He deserves the last word.

> I have farmed the most of the time. I cept store 3 years. I have worked hard all of my life and still plow now. I enjoy it and believe it has perlong my life. I droped [adopted] the rule after I came home not to do aney thing that would hurt me phically. I do not use tobaco nor whiskey. I never drank of of thease soft drink in my life I never went to see a base ball game in my life. I never gambled in my life. I have ben Justice of the peace 34 yearss and hold some [same] today, have been school commishonr 30 odd years. I have done lots of work for good road. I maried prety and a good woman we had nothing to begin with we went to work have made a home and enough to keep the wolf from our door. [R]aised 7 children all living and doing well, all members of Baptist church.[112]

Notes

Mr. Osthaus is a professor and chair of the department of history at Oakland University. The author would like to thank his wife, Wendy B. Osthaus, for her research assistance, and Cara Shelly for her humorous and insightful comments during the draft stages of this article.

1. John F. Flintoff Diary, March 10, 1864, p. 16 (Private Collections, North Carolina State Archives, Office of Archives and History, Raleigh), microfilm typescript.
2. *Ibid.*, June 6, 1856, p. 10 (first quotation); August 18, 1876, p. 20; October 1, 1889, p. 21; June 1, 1891, p. 28 (second quotation); and various entries from 1850 to 1900, pp. 7–43.
3. Max Weber, *The Protestant Ethic and the Spirit of Capitalism*, trans. Talcott Parsons (London, 1930), 156–59, 166–67, 172–79.

4. Alastair Hamilton, "Max Weber's Protestant Ethic and the Spirit of Capitalism," in Stephen Turner, ed., *The Cambridge Companion to Weber* (Cambridge, Eng., 2000), 169.
5. Edmund S. Morgan, "The Puritan Ethic and the American Revolution," *William and Mary Quarterly*, 3rd ser., 24 (January 1967), 3–7, 22–24 (first quotation on p. 23; second quotation on p. 24). To Morgan, Thomas Jefferson offered a prime example of the Puritan ethic of the South; "a more methodically industrious man never lived." See *ibid.*, 7.
6. Rhys Isaac, *The Transformation of Virginia, 1740–1790* (Chapel Hill, 1982), chap. 8; Christine Leigh Heyrman, *Southern Cross: The Beginnings of the Bible Belt* (New York, 1997), 3–27.
7. Daniel T. Rodgers, *The Work Ethic in Industrial America, 1850–1920* (Chicago, 1974), xi (first three quotations), 8–17 (fourth through eighth quotations on p. 12), 31 (final two quotations); Eric Foner, *Free Soil, Free Labor, Free Men: The Ideology of the Republican Party before the Civil War* (New York, 1970), 11, 46.
8. David Bertelson, *The Lazy South* (New York, 1967), viii, 10 (quotation), 58–59, 65–67, 90, 96–97, 216.
9. C. Vann Woodward, "The Southern Ethic in a Puritan World," in *American Counterpoint: Slavery and Racism in the North-South Dialogue* (Boston, 1971), 13–46 (first three quotations on p. 13; fourth quotation on pp. 25–26).
10. Eugene D. Genovese, *The Political Economy of Slavery* (New York, 1965), 48.
11. Grady McWhiney, *Cracker Culture: Celtic Ways in the Old South* (Tuscaloosa, 1988), 44, 45, 72, 76, 78–79 (quotation). See also Forrest McDonald and Grady McWhiney, "The South From Self-Sufficiency to Peonage: An Interpretation," *American Historical Review*, 85 (December 1980), 1095–118. Grady McWhiney and Forrest McDonald assessed North-South labor time and found the South lacking—lazy, to be specific. Their method of employing gross output and crop yields from the census and comparing them with estimated times necessary to produce standard yields is open to challenge. Such crop-time methods underestimate southern productivity and labor and help prove to the satisfaction of McWhiney and McDonald that southerners did not work very hard. Planters' and farmers' diaries reveal numerous activities, such as the production of fodder, that are essential to the health of a farmstead but are not measured by the census. The disease environment for plants and animals was not the same in the North and South. Finally, farmers' proximity to transportation and markets affected the size of crops measured by the census. See the *AHR* forum "Antebellum North and South in Comparative Perspective: A Discussion," *ibid.*, 1150–66; Julius Rubin, "The Limits of Agricultural Progress in the Nineteenth- Century South," *Agricultural History*, 49 (April 1975), 362–73; Frederick F. Siegel, *The Roots of Southern Distinctiveness: Tobacco and Society in Danville, Virginia, 1780–1865* (Chapel Hill, 1987), 68–72; and *Southern Planter*, 12 (March 1852), 71. There is also a heavy reliance on travelers' narratives in McWhiney's thesis about lazy Celts. For an insightful critique of the reliability of travel literature, see Joyce E. Chaplin's chapter entitled "Being Exotic" in *An Anxious Pursuit: Agricultural Innovation and Modernity in the Lower South, 1730–1815* (Chapel Hill, 1993), chap. 3.
12. Frank L. Owsley, *Plain Folk of the Old South* (Baton Rouge, 1949); Blanche Henry Clark, *The Tennessee Yeomen, 1840–1860* (Nashville, 1942); Herbert Weaver, *Mississippi Farmers, 1850–1860* (Nashville, 1945).
13. Stephanie McCurry, *Masters of Small Worlds: Yeoman Households, Gender Relations, and the Political Culture of the Antebellum South Carolina Low Country* (New York, 1995), viii. See also Lacy K. Ford Jr., *Origins of Southern Radicalism: The South Carolina Upcountry, 1800–1860* (New York, 1988), 50–54, 56; J. William Harris, *Plain Folk and Gentry in a Slave Society: White Liberty and Black*

Slavery in Augusta's Hinterlands (Middletown, Conn., 1985) 6, 18–26, 36–39, chap. 4; Bradley G. Bond, *Political Culture in the Nineteenth-Century South: Mississippi, 1830–1900* (Baton Rouge, 1995), chaps. 1–2; Robert Tracy McKenzie, *One South or Many? Plantation Belt and Upcountry in Civil War-Era Tennessee* (Cambridge, Eng., 1994), 36–37, 44–45, 66–84; Bill Cecil-Fronsman, *Common Whites: Class and Culture in Antebellum North Carolina* (Lexington, Ky., 1992), 7–8, 31, chaps. 4–5; Donald L. Winters, *Tennessee Farming, Tennessee Farmers: Antebellum Agriculture in the Upper South* (Knoxville, 1994), chap. 7; and Richard G. Lowe and Randolph B. Campbell, *Planters and Plain Folk: Agriculture in Antebellum Texas* (Dallas, 1987), chap. 7.

14. Ann Patton Malone, "Piney Woods Farmers of South Georgia, 1850–1900: Jeffersonian Yeomen in an Age of Expanding Commercialism," *Agricultural History*, 60 (Fall 1986), 51–84.
15. Cecil-Fronsman, *Common Whites*, 106–9.
16. Frederick Law Olmsted, *A Journey in the Seaboard Stave States, with Remarks on Their Economy* (New York, 1856), 538, 540; Kay L. Cothran, "Olmsted's Contributions to Folklife Research," in Dana F. White and Victor A. Kramer, eds., *Olmsted South: Old South Critic/New South Planner* (Westport, Conn., 1979), 64; Chaplin, *Anxious Pursuit*, chap. 3.
17. I use "self-working farmers," as does Stephanie McCurry, to emphasize that these farmers worked with their own hands for a substantial part of their lives, as opposed to farmers who worked with their "invisible hands," their slaves. A slaveholding farmer might say, for example, "I plowed cotton today," meaning that one or more of his black workers had performed this task. He, however, had not touched the plow handle. See McCurry, *Masters of Small Worlds*, 47–48; and Laurence Shore, *Southern Capitalists: The Ideological Leadership of an Elite, 1832–1885* (Chapel Hill, 1986), 40.
18. John Hebron Moore, *The Emergence of the Cotton Kingdom in the Old Southwest: Mississippi, 1770–1860* (Baton Rouge, 1988), 116; Jennifer K. Boone, " 'Mingling Freely': Tennessee Society on the Eve of the Civil War," *Tennessee Historical Quarterty*, 51 (Fall 1992), 144.
19. This rich source of plain-folk recollections that sustains the interpretation of a hardworking South is *The Tennessee Civil War Veterans Questionnaires*, compiled by Gustavus W. Dyer and John Trotwood Moore (5 vols.; Easley, S.C, 1985); hereinafter cited as *TCWVQ*. Veterans responded to specific questions regarding the amount and kinds of work they and their parents performed. There were questions about the valuation of work (Was honest labor viewed as respectable?) and questions addressing opportunities for poor men. Not all veterans agreed with the interpretation of a hardworking South; some believed there was considerable idleness, although it was located mostly among slaveholders. For examples see *TCWVQ*, James M. Hill, vol. III, 1101; J. M. Johnson, vol. III, 1233. Fred Arthur Bailey provides the calculation that slightly over 80 percent of Tennessee veterans worked hard physically. See Bailey, *Class and Tennessee's Confederate Generation* (Chapel Hill, 1987), 158; and Bailey, "Tennessee's Antebellum Common Folk," *Tennessee Historical Quarterly*, 55 (Spring 1996), 45. David B. Danbom has argued the commonsense point of view that work dominated the lives of most rural people; see his *Born in the Country: A History of Rural America* (Baltimore, 1995), 95.
20. Bailey, "Tennessee's Antebellum Common Folk," 45; Cecil-Fronsman, *Common Whites*, 103. On the operation of the household economy see Sharon Ann Holt, "Making Freedom Pay: Freedpeople Working for Themselves, North Carolina, 1865–1900," *Journal of Southern History*, 60 (May 1994), 229–62.
21. Historians have engaged in a lively discussion about the production and market orientation of yeoman farmers. It might be that most farmers had experience with a

variety of market networks—with neighbors (often based upon barter or exchange of labor), with local town markets, and with the international market for cotton or tobacco. See Bradley G. Bond, "Herders, Farmers, and Markets on the Inner Frontier: The Mississippi Piney Woods, 1850–1860," in Samuel C. Hyde Jr., ed., *Plain Folk of the South Revisited* (Baton Rouge, 1997), 74–80; Bond, *Political Culture in the Nineteenth-Century South*, 53–55, 60, 66–67, 73–74; Michael Shirley, "The Market and Community Culture in Antebellum Salem, North Carolina," *Journal of the Early Republic*, 11 (Summer 1991), 220–21; McKenzie, *One South or Many?* 33–34, 54; and McCurry, *Masters of Small Worlds*, 70. For emphasis on safety-first agriculture, see Cecil-Fronsman, *Common Whites*. 98–103; and Barbara Jeanne Fields, "The Nineteenth-Century American South: History and Theory," *Plantation Society in the Americas, 2* (April 1983), 9–11. Claudia L. Bushman's account of John Walker's life as a small planter in antebellum Tidewater Virginia offers a wonderful example of complex market arrangements. Walker participated in (or benefited from) seven economies: his own farm economy (feeding and clothing his people), a market economy, a paper economy (lending and borrowing), a separate women's economy, a slave economy not part of typical field work, an economy based on hiring out slaves, and a lively barter economy within his locality. See Bushman, *In Old Virginia: Slavery, Farming, and Society in the Journal of John Walker* (Baltimore, 2002), 4–5, chap. 5.

22. Joseph Benjamin Lightsey Diary, ace. no. Z 1836 (Mississippi Department of Archives and History, Jackson, Mississippi), photocopy. Almost every diary entry adds something to the account of Lightsey's work life in this and subsequent paragraphs. For representative entries see October 4, 1849; January 14, 1850; May 14, 1850; June 10–15, 1850; September 4, 1850 ("This is my nineteen birthday I pulled fodder all day"); January 1, 1851; April 30, 1851; March 22–24, 1852; October 2, 1852; and December 9, 1853, in Lightsey Diary. Lightsey spent much of August each year pulling fodder. Near the close of the diary, letters from Joseph to his relatives provide significant details about the Lightsey family and their farm activities. See especially Joseph Lightsey to Joel W. Lightsey (cousin), March 12, 1853. A good discussion of Joseph Lightsey and family appears in Bond, *Political Culture in the Nineteenth-Century South*, 44–47.
23. Lightsey Diary, especially entries for March 1, 1850; December 18 and 23, 1850; January 1 and 25, 1851; and August 1853 (pulling fodder).
24. *Ibid.*, especially entries for December 3 and 22, 1849; January 1 and 8, and November 30, 1850; and December 30 and 31, 1853.
25. *Ibid.*, entries for November 4, 1850; and October 2, 1851.
26. *Ibid.*, entries for November 13, 1850 (first quotation); July 18, 1850 (second quotation); May 2, 1851 (third quotation); August 8 and September 4, 1850 (fourth quotation); and January 5, 1850 (fifth quotation). See also entries for October 4, 1849; January 14 and 23, and November 2 and 9, 1850; August 30 and October 3, 1851; April 4 and October 2, 1852; and November 7, 1853.
27. *TCWVQ*, William Denier Harden, vol. III, 1001; William Sidney Hartsfield, vol.III, 1037; William E. Orr, vol. IV, 1665 (first and second quotations), 1666 (third quotation); James F. Sloan journal, various entries, April 14, 1861–April 13, 1862, James F. Sloan Papers #9656 (South Caroliniana Library, University of South Carolina, Columbia); John W. Rumble, "A Carolina Country Squire in the Old South and the New: The Papers of James F. Sloan," *South Atlantic Quarterly*, 81 (Summer 1982), 324–25; Ford, *Origins of Southern Radicalism*, 79–80.
28. Entry for July 18, 1855, in Paul D. Escott, ed., *North Carolina Yeoman: The Diary of Basil Armstrong Thomasson, 1853–1862* (Athens, Ga., 1996), 89.
29. *TCWVQ*, Jeptha Marion Fuston, vol. II, 871; Samuel B. Kyle, vol. III, 1314; Lewis Crawley Howse, vol. III, 1170; N. B. Johnson, vol. III, 1236; James Stiles, vol. V, 2007;

and many other relevant examples. See also Bailey, "Tennessee's Antebellum Common Folk," 47, 49. Danbom, *Born in the Country*, 90, also argues that farm children were economic resources. Additionally, see Reverend Watkins, *The Old Pine Farm: or, The Southern Side* (Nashville, 1859), 42–43; McCurry, *Masters of Small Worlds*, 59; and Cecil-Fronsman, *Common Whites*, 148.

30. *TCWVQ*, T. J. Howard, vol. III, 1159.
31. William C. Anderson to Friend Miller, [n. d.], and Anderson to S. H. Bingham, January 11, 1871, and February 2, 1871, William Anderson Papers #8411 (South Caroliniana Library); Rumble, "Carolina Country Squire," 329; William Woodall to John Woodall, May 30, 1854 (first and second quotations), August 4, 1854 (third quotation), John Woodall Papers #5884 (Rare Book, Manuscript, and Special Collections Library, Duke University, Durham, North Carolina).
32. Lightsey Diary, entry for October 2, 1852; Ford, *Origins of Southern Radicalism*, 78. There are many references in *TCWVQ*; for examples see Charles D. Fontaine, vol. II, 829; and William J. Kirkham, vol. III, 1301.
33. James Ross, *Life and Times of Elder Reuben Ross* (1882; rpt., Nashville, 1977), 188–89.
34. Self-working farmers Daniel Cobb, Joseph Lightsey, Basil Thomasson, and John Flintoff and Virginia planter John Walker ignore and thus perhaps trivialize the contributions of women's labor, although one must admit that most diarists focus on their own activities. Cobb, a pious, self-working Virginia farmer who eventually owned eleven slaves, clearly believed that field work was more valuable than household labor, and he and Flintoff criticized their wives' tendency toward idleness. For Cobb's farm labor, work ethic, and comments on his wife, see Daniel W. Crofts, ed., *Cobb's Ordeal: The Diaries of a Virginia Farmer, 1842–1872* (Athens, Ga., 1997), xvi–xvii, 22–23, 64–83, 131, 132, and diary entries in *ibid*, for June 22, 1851, pp. 26–27; May 14, 1846, p. 32; March 3, 1858, pp. 32–33; January 5, 1858, p. 70; January 7, 1856, p. 70; February 4, 1858, p. 71; January 4, 1849. p. 72; June 10, 1843, p. 82; July 22, 1846, p. 83; and January 31, 1843, p. 17.
35. Bushman, *In Old Virginia*, 112, 116; entry for February 27, 1854, in Escott, ed., *North Carolina Yeoman*, 29. James Talleyrano McColgan recalled his mother's skill with wheel and loom and then wrote: "Remember she was the only real slave on the plantation." See *TCWVQ*, vol. IV, 1425.
36. Bushman, *In Old Virginia*, 107 (quotations), 111.
37. Jean E. Friedman, *The Enclosed Garden: Women and Community in the Evangelical South, 1830–1900* (Chapel Hill, 1985), 25.
38. *TCWVQ*, William C. Dillihay, vol. II, 692.
39. *Ibid.*, Zachary Taylor Dyer, vol. II, 748; Keith L. Bryant Jr., "The Role and Status of the Female Yeomanry in the Antebellum South: The Literary View," *Southern Quarterly*, 18 (Winter 1980), 77; Friedman, *Enclosed Garden*, 23.
40. McCurry, *Masters of Small Worlds*; Friedman, *Enclosed Garden*, 78.
41. Bushman, *In Old Virginia*, 111.
42. D. Harland Hagler, "The Ideal Woman in the Antebellum South: Lady or Farmwife?" *Journal of Southern History*, 46 (August 1980), 405, 406; *TCWVQ*, Edwin Maximilian Gardner, vol. III, 880; T. L. Johnson, vol. III, 1240 ("Mother was the best gardner on the place. . . ."); J. A. Summers, vol. V, 2016.
43. Hagler, "Ideal Woman," especially pp. 410, 412, 413 (quotation), 416.
44. *TCWVQ*, S. F. Paine, vol. IV, 1682.
45. Genovese, *Political Economy of Slavery*, 49; J. William Harris, "The Organization of Work on a Yeoman Slaveholder's Farm," *Agricultural History*, 64 (Winter 1990), 42; Ralph V. Anderson and Robert E. Gallman, "Slaves as Fixed Capital: Slave Labor and Southern Economic Development," *Journal of American History*, 64 (June 1977), 24.

46. See *TCWVQ*, N. C. Godsey, vol. III, 912; R. Z. Taylor, vol. V, 2037.
47. For discussions of personal combat and violence see Elliott J. Gorn, " 'Gouge and Bite, Pull Hair and Scratch': The Social Significance of Fighting in the Southern Backcountry," *American Historical Review*, 90 (February 1985), 18–23, 25, 28, 33–37; Edward L. Ayers, *Vengeance and Justice: Crime and Punishment in the Nineteenth-Century American South* (New York, 1984), 10–11, 20–21; and Christopher J. Olsen, *Political Culture and Secession in Mississippi: Masculinity, Honor, and the Antiparty Tradition, 1830–1860* (Oxford, Eng., 2000), 3–24.
48. *TCWVQ*, John N. Meroney, vol. IV, 1519; T. R. Ford, vol. II, 834; Major C. P. Nance, vol. IV, 1623; Theodric Ervin Lipscomb, vol. IV, 1367; William Henry Cox, vol. II, 579; Benjamin Alexander Haguewood, vol. III, 982.
49. *Ibid.*, T. L. Johnson, vol. III, 1240 (first and second quotations); J. R. Cox, vol. II, 578 (third quotation); Joe C. Brooks, vol. I, 384–85 (seventh quotation); James LindsyCochran, vol. II, 525; Pressley Neville Conner, vol. II, 545 (sixth quotation); William Jefferson Corn, vol. II, 567 (fourth and fifth quotations).
50. *Ibid.*, William Anderson Wilson, vol. V, 2222–23; J. P. Stribling, vol. V, 2011; Julius C. Martin, vol. IV, 1497; C. W. Hicks, vol. III, 1090.
51. *Ibid.*, George A. Rice, vol. V, 1835–36; John H. O'Neal, vol. IV, 1655; Peter Donnell, vol. II, 711; James Koger, vol. III, 1311; Halyard Wilhite, vol. V, 2187; Thomas Jefferson Howard, vol. III, 1163; W. J. Tucker, vol. V, 2076; McKenzie, *One South or Many?* 19.
52. Escott, ed., *North Carolina Yeoman*, esp. "Introduction," pp. xxii, xxxvi, and 276n7; and entries for November 12, 1853, p. 13; December 11, 1853, p. 17; April 18, 1854, p. 35; January 21, 1855, p. 64; July 15, 1857, p. 176; December 7, 1858, p. 223 (second quotation); January 31, 1860, pp. 268–69; October 28, 1860, p. 290 (first quotation). Despite an occasional reference to an imaginary reader, there is no indication that Thomasson ever envisioned the publication of his diary.
53. Entries for March 14, 1854, p. 30 (first quotation); May 29, 1855, p. 82; December 16, 1855, p. 107; December 17, 1855, p. 107; February 19, 1858, p. 191 (second quotation), in *ibid.*
54. *Ibid.*, xxxvii; Bertram Wyatt-Brown, *Southern Honor: Ethics and Behavior in the Old South* (Oxford, 1982).
55. Escott, ed., *North Carolina Yeoman*, xix, xlvii, xlviii (quotation); and entries for November 17, 1853, p. 14; November 28, 1853, p. 15; June 28, 29, 1859, p. 245; September 2, 1859, p. 253.
56. *TCWVQ*, George Washington Alexander, vol. I, 186; W. F. Blevins, vol. I, 336; Berry Rice Bostick, vol. I, 347; William Henry Blackburn, vol. I, 327; John Wesley Dunavant, vol. II, 735; John Franklin Clinton, vol. II, 520.
57. *Ibid.*, W. A. Duncan, vol. II, 738.
58. *Ibid.*, W. J. Tucker, vol. V, 2076–77.
59. *Ibid.*, Edwin Maximilian Gardner, vol. III, 880; George W. Samuel, vol. V, 1908; Thomas M. Patterson, vol. IV, 1704; Isaac NeKson Rainey, vol. V, 1787; Wiley Benton Ellis, vol. II, 767; James M. Nowlin, vol. IV, 1645.
60. *Ibid.*, John Vincent, vol. V, 2108 (first quotation); William Gibbs Allen, vol. I, 202 (second quotation); James Glenn Sims, vol. V, 1961 (third quotation); James Jackson Carroll, vol. II, 463; Jack Harvey Coats, vol. II, 524; Edward Jerry Davis, vol. II, 646; Benjamin Franklin Derby, vol. II, 633; James A. Delozier, vol. II, 665; Edward Silas Doe, vol. II, 702; Thomas Jefferson Howard, vol. III, 1163; N. B. Johnson, vol. III, 1236; Robert L. Morris, vol. IV, 1587; William H. Patterson, vol. IV, 1706; William H. Roach, vol. V, 1852; John K. Roberts, vol. V, 1858; J. A. Summers, vol. V, 2016; B. L. Swaffor, vol. V, 2021; W. J. Tucker, vol. V, 2076; J. M. Thurman, vol. V, 2056; J. B. Williams, vol. V, 2200; W. A. Wilson, vol. V, 2223.

61. *Ibid.*, J. L. Walton, vol. V, 2133; R. T. Mockbee, vol. IV, 1554; Edward Norville Gannaway, vol. III, 877; Gentry Richard McGee, vol. IV, 1440–41; Harrison W. Farrell, vol. II, 796; James S. Pearce, vol. IV, 1716.
62. *Tennessee Farmer*, 1 (November 1836), 371.
63. *TCWVQ*, Samuel Scoggins, vol. V, 1919 (quotation); Charles Ambrose Driskell Faris, vol. II, 790; Stephen J. Brown, vol. I, 402; Daniel Jefferson Crisp, vol. II, 590; James Jackson Carroll, vol. II, 463; Edward P. Martin, vol. IV, 1490.
64. *Ibid.*, Henry Melvil Doak, vol. II, 698, 699 (quotation).
65. *Ibid.*, C. W. Park, vol. IV, 1684.
66. *Ibid.*, James Calvin Hodge, vol. III, 1115; Ezkiel Inman, vol. III, 1203; T. J. Kersey, vol. III, 1281.
67. *Tennessee Farmer*, 1 (January [1835]), 31.
68. Susan Dabney Smedes, *Memorials of a Southern Planter*, edited with an introduction and notes by Fletcher M. Green (1887; rpt. New York, 1965), 53.
69. *TCWVQ*, Joel L. Henry, vol. III, 1080; William Grant, vol. III, 941; Thomas Jefferson Howard, vol. III, 1163; Orville Vernon Burton, *In My Father's House Are Many Mansions: Family and Community in Edgefield, South Carolina* (Chapel Hill, 1985), 75, 76; Bailey, "Tennessee's Antebellum Common Folk," 48.
70. *TCWVQ*, Zachary Taylor Dyer, vol. II, 748; R. H. Mosley, vol. IV, 1602; John S. Howell, vol. III, 1165; Isaac Butler Day, vol. II, 658; T. B. Alexander, vol. I, 191.
71. *Ibid.*, William Waller Carson, vol. II, 464–65.
72. See, among others, the entries for July 3, 1819; September 24 and 25, 1819; January 6, 1820; February 4, 1820; December 24, 1820; and July 2, 1821, in John Osbourne Diary #3397-z (Southern Historical Collection, Wilson Library, University of North Carolina at Chapel Hill). Osbourne was not the only one to express guilt at the time spent away from his fields. David Golightly Harris, a hardworking, slaveholding farmer in Spartanburg, South Carolina, expressed regret when hunting, fishing, or business or pleasure trips to town lured him from his daily routine of working in field or shop and supervising his small slave force. See Philip N. Racine, ed., *Piedmont Farmer: The Journals of David Golightly Harris*, 1855–1870 (Knoxville, 1990), entries for December 25, 1857, pp. 66–67; March 17, 1859, p. 105; March 19, 20, and 21, 1860, pp. 128–29; and April 2, 1860, p. 131.
73. William E. Hatcher, *Along the Trail of the Friendly Years* (New York, 1910), 11 (first and second quotations), 12 (third quotation).
74. *TCWVQ*, Richard Enos Sherrill, vol. V, 1947.
75. Watkins, *Old Pine Farm*, 10, 11, 18 (quotation), 20–21.
76. Memoir of Zillah Haynie Brandon (1823–1871) (Alabama Department of Archives and History, Montgomery), cited in Theda Perdue and Michael D. Green, eds., *The Cherokee Removal: A Brief History with Documents* (Boston, 1995), 86.
77. *TCWVQ*, David Shires Myers Bodenhamer, vol. I, 336, 339 (quotation).
78. Foner, *Free Soil, Free Labor, Free Men*, 13.
79. Isaac, *Transformation of Virginia*, 118–21, chap. 13; Ted Ownby, *Subduing Satan: Religion, Recreation, and Manhood in the Rural South, 1865–1920* (Chapel Hill, 1990), 14, 15; Heyrman, *Southern Cross*, 3–27; Allan Kulikoff, *Tobacco and Slaves: The Development of Southern Cultures in the Chesapeake, 1680–1800* (Chapel Hill, 1986), 217, 218; George C. Rable, *Civil Wars: Women and the Crisis of Southern Nationalism* (Urbana, 1989), 269; Beth Barton Schweiger, *The Gospel Working Up: Progress and the Pulpit in Nineteenth-Century Virginia* (New York, 2000), 7; Anne C. Loveland, *Southern Evangelicals and the Social Order, 1800–1860* (Baton Rouge, 1980), 92; Donald G. Mathews, *Religion in the Old South* (Chicago, 1977), 114.
80. Randy J. Sparks, *On Jordan's Stormy Banks: Evangelicalism in Mississippi, 1773–1876* (Athens, Ga., 1994), 149; Gregory A. Wills, *Democratic Religion: Freedom, Authority, and Church Discipline in the Baptist South, 1785–1900* (New York, 1997), 13–14, 31.

81. John B. Boles, "Evangelical Protestantism in the Old South: From Religious Dissent to Cultural Dominance," in Charles Reagan Wilson, ed., *Religion in the South* (Jackson, 1985), 26–27 (quotation); Boles, *Religion in Antebellum Kentucky* (Lexington, Ky., 1976), 124, 130–31.
82. McCurry, *Masters of Small Worlds*, 136, 158–59, 166, 169.
83. Schweiger, *Gospel Working Up*, 46; Mathews, *Religion in the Old South*, 86–87; Wayne Flynt, *Alabama Baptists: Southern Baptists in the Heart of Dixie* (Tuscaloosa, 1998), 24. Of course, in large, urban churches with imposing brick edifices, theologically trained, ordained ministers frequently preached to sophisticated congregations and received handsome salaries for their efforts. Still, these prominent southern divines often had roots in rural values and the ways of poor farm folk; many had worked early in life as farm boys or rural teachers. See Kenneth Moore Startup, *The Root of All Evil: The Protestant Clergy and the Economic Mind of the Old South* (Athens, Ga., 1997), 3; and Schweiger, *Gospel Working Up*, 3, 21, 35.
84. William M. Wightman, *Life of William Capers . . . Including an Autobiography* (1858; rpt., Nashville, 1902), 168–69, 178–79, 202–3. See also Startup, *Root of All Evil*, 119, 120; and Flynt, *Alabama Baptists*, 14–15.
85. See *TCWVQ*, I. W. Johnson, vol. III, 1231.
86. Reuben Davis, *Recollections of Mississippi and Mississippians*, rev. ed., with a new introduction by William D. McCain (1889; rpt., [Hattiesburg, Miss.], 1972), 2.
87. Ross, *Life and Times of Elder Reuben Ross*, 294–95.
88. [Watkins], *Old Pine Farm*, 20, 21 (quotations). See also Startup, *Root of All Evil*, 36–37; and Moore, *Emergence of the Cotton Kingdom*, 145.
89. Wightman, *Life of William Capers*, 180–84 (quotation on pp. 182–83).
90. Walter C. Whitaker, *Richard Hooker Wilmer: Second Bishop of Alabama* (Philadelphia, 1907), 15–17, 31, 32, 50 (second quotation), 57 (first quotation), 65.
91. Diary entries for February 13 and 14, 1863, John Frederick Mallet Papers #3473 (Rare Book, Manuscript, and Special Collections Library, Duke University).
92. *A Class-Book: Containing Directions for Class-Leaders, Ruled Forms for Leaders' Weekly Accounts, and the Rules of the Methodist Societies* (London, 1833), 5; Washington (Ga.) *Christian Index*, April 27, 1837, p. 271; Boles, "Evangelical Protestantism in the Old South," 32.
93. Quoted in Loveland, *Southern Evangelicals*, 93.
94. Thomas Smyth, "The Design and Motive of Worldly Business as Exhibited in the Bible," October 1847, in J. Wm. Flinn, ed., *Complete Works of Rev. Thomas Smyth, D.D.* (10 vols.; Columbia, S.C., 1908–1912), X, 465–68 (first quotation quoted on p. 468, second and third quotations on p. 465, fourth and fifth quotations on p. 466), 481; Smyth, "The Commercial Benefit of Christianity in Producing Integrity, Diligence and Moderation," August 1847, in *ibid.*, X, 453.
95. Loveland, *Southern Evangelicals*, 94, 97; Startup, *Root of All Evil*, 16, 21, 59, 63.
96. *Tennessee Farmer*, 1 (May 1836), 286.
97. Entry for March 30, 1856, in Escott, ed., *North Carolina Yeoman*, 132.
98. Croft, ed., *Cobb Ordeal*, xvii.
99. January 5, 1837, pp. 12–13; March 2, 1837, p. 142.
100. Startup, *Root of All Evil*, 13 (quotation), 23, 126–27, and especially chap. 4, "How Dreadful to Be Rich."
101. Hatcher, *Along the Trail*, 353; Startup, *Root of All Evil*, 78, 79 (quotation).
102. *Ibid.*, 39, 51–53, 89, 90; Wightman, *Life of William Capers*, 166–67.
103. Schweiger, *Gospel Working Up*, vii; Frederick A. Bode, "The Formation of Evangelical Communities in Middle Georgia: Twiggs County, 1820–1861," *Journal of Southern History*, 60 (November 1994), 713.
104. Rumble, "Carolina Country Squire," 334–35; Mathews, *Religion in the Old South*, 96–97; Loveland, *Southern Evangelicals*, especially pp. 148–51, 162–63.

105. Washington (Ga.) *Christian Index*, April 27, 1837, pp. 262, 268–69; Whitaker, *Richard Hooker Wilmer*, 60; Loveland, *Southern Evangelicals*, 106; Startup, *Root of All Evil*, 41; John W. Quist, "Slaveholding Operatives of the Benevolent Empire: Bible, Tract, and Sunday School Societies in Antebellum Tuscaloosa County, Alabama," *Journal of Southern History*, 62 (August 1996), 516–19.
106. Mathews, *Religion in the Old South*, 35 (first quotation), 37 (second and third quotations).
107. Davis, *Recollections of Mississippi*, 22–23; Brantley York, *The Autobiography of Brantley York* (Durham, 1910), 5; Wyatt-Brown, *Southern Honor*, 43, 273–81, 294–96, 348–61; Bode, "Formation of Evangelical Communities," 744–45; Rable, *Civil Wars*, chap. 9. Ted Ownby, in *Subduing Satan*, provides an extended analysis of the enduring battle between male and evangelical cultures in the post-Civil War South.
108. Davis, *Recollections of Mississippi*, 18.
109. Ira Berlin and Herbert G. Gutman, "Natives and Immigrants, Free Men and Slaves: Urban Workingmen in the Antebellum American South," *American Historical Review*, 88 (December 1983), especially pp. 1178–81; Michele Gillespie, *Free Labor in an Unfree World: White Artisans in Slaveholding Georgia, 1790–1860* (Athens, Ga., 2000), 42–45, 60–61, 94–95, 104–7, 146–50.
110. *TCWVQ*, Theodric Ervin Lipscomb, vol. IV, 1367.
111. *Ibid.*, John Russell Dance, vol. II, 630.
112. *Ibid.*, T. W. Walthall, vol. V, 2131–32.

Chapter 5

" 'It Was Like All of Us Had Been Raped': Sexual Violence, Community Mobilization, and the African American Freedom Struggle"

Danielle L. McGuire

From *The Journal of American History*

On Saturday, May 2, 1959, four white men in Tallahassee, Florida, made a pact, one of their friends testified in court later, to "go out and get a nigger girl" and have an "all night party." That evening, they armed themselves with shotguns and switchblades and crept up behind a car parked alongside a quiet road near Jake Gaither Park. At about 1:00 a.m. on May 3, Patrick Scarborough pressed a sixteen-gauge shotgun against the driver's nose and ordered Richard Brown and his companions out of the car. Dressed in formal gowns and tuxedoes, the four African Americans—all students at Florida A&M University who had spent the evening dancing at the Green and Orange Ball—reluctantly stepped out of the car. Scarborough forced the two black men to kneel, while his friend David Beagles held the two black women at knifepoint. When Betty Jean Owens began to cry, Beagles slapped her and told her to "shut up" or she "would never get back home." Waving his gun, Scarborough ordered Richard Brown and his friend Thomas Butterfield back in the car and told them to leave. As Brown and Butterfield began to move toward the car and then slowly drove away, Edna Richardson broke free and ran to the nearby park, leaving Betty Jean Owens alone with their attackers. Beagles pressed the switchblade to Owens's throat and growled, "We'll let you go if you do what we want," then forced her to her knees, slapped her as she sobbed, and pushed her into the backseat of their blue Chevrolet; the four men drove her to the edge of town, where they raped her seven times.[1]

Analyses of rape play little or no role in most histories of the civil rights movement, even as stories of violence against black and white men—from

Emmett Till to Andrew Goodman, Michael Schwerner, and James Chaney—provide gripping examples of racist brutality.[2] Despite a growing body of literature that focuses on the roles of black and white women and the operation of gender in the movement, sexualized violence—both as a tool of oppression and as a political spur for the movement—has yet to find its place in the story of the African American freedom struggle.[3] Rape, like lynching and murder, served as a tool of psychological and physical intimidation that expressed white male domination and buttressed white supremacy. During the Jim Crow era, women's bodies served as signposts of the social order, and white men used rape and rumors of rape not only to justify violence against black men but to remind black women that their bodies were not their own.

African American women frequently retaliated by testifying about their brutal experiences. I argue that, from Harriet Jacobs to Ida B. Wells to the women of the present, the refusal of black women to remain silent about sexualized violence was part of a long-standing tradition. Black women described and denounced their sexual misuse, deploying their voices as weapons in the wars against white supremacy. Indeed, their public protests often galvanized local, national, and even international outrage and sparked campaigns for racial justice and human dignity. When Betty Jean Owens spoke out against her assailants, and when the local black community mobilized in defense of her womanhood in 1959, they joined in this tradition of testimony and protest.

The arrest, trial, and conviction of Owens's white rapists by an all-white jury marked a dramatic change in the relations between this tradition of testimony and a tradition of silence that Darlene Clark Hine has termed the "culture of dissemblance."[4] The verdict not only broke with southern tradition but fractured the philosophical and political foundations of white supremacy by challenging the relationship between sexual domination and racial inequality. For perhaps the first time since Reconstruction, southern black communities could imagine state power being deployed in defense of their respectability as men and women. As a result, the 1959 Tallahassee rape case was a watershed event that remains as revealing now as it was important then.

The sexual exploitation of black women had its roots in slavery. Slave owners, overseers, and drivers took advantage of their positions of power and authority to rape slave women, sometimes in the presence of their husbands or families. White slave owners' stolen access to black women's bodies strengthened their political, social, and economic power, partly because colonial laws made the offspring of slave women the property of their masters.[5] After the fall of slavery, when African Americans asserted their freedom during the interracial experiment in democracy that briefly characterized Reconstruction, former slaveholders and their sympathizers used violence and terror to reassert control over the social, political, and economic agency of freedpeople. At the heart of this violence, according to Gerda Lerner, rape became a "weapon of terror" to dominate the bodies and minds of African American men and women.[6]

"Freedom," as Tera Hunter notes, "was meaningless without ownership and control over one's own body." During Reconstruction and Jim Crow, sexualized violence served as a "ritualistic reenactment of the daily pattern of social dominance," and interracial rape became the battleground upon which black men and women fought for ownership of their own bodies. Many African American women who were raped or assaulted by white men fought back by speaking out. Frances Thompson told a congressional committee investigating the 1866 Memphis race riot that seven armed white men broke into her house on a Tuesday afternoon, "drew their pistols and said they would shoot us and fire the house if we did not let them have their way with us." Four of the men raped Frances, while the other three choked and raped sixteen-year-old Lucy Smith and left her close to death. In 1871, Harriet Simril testified in front of a congressional committee investigating Ku Klux Klan terror during Reconstruction that she was beaten and "ravished" by eight men in South Carolina who broke into her house to force her husband to "join the democratic ticket." Essic Harris, appearing before the same committee, reported that "the rape of black women was so frequent" in the postbellum South that it had become "an old saying by now." Ferdie Walker, who grew up during the height of segregation in the 1930s and 1940s in Fort Worth, Texas, remembered being "scared to death" by a white police officer who often exposed himself to her while she waited at the bus stop when she was only eleven years old. The sexual abuse of black women, she recalled, was an everyday occurrence. "That was really bad and it was bad for *all black girls*," she recalled.[7]

John H. McCray, editor of the South Carolina *Lighthouse and Informer*, reported that it was "a commonplace experience for many of our women in southern towns . . . to be propositioned openly by white men." He said, "You can pick up accounts of these at a dime a dozen in almost any community." African American women that I interviewed in Birmingham, Alabama, in March 2003 echoed Ferdie Walker's and McCray's comments. Nearly all of them testified about being sexually abused or intimidated by white men—particularly bus drivers, police officers, and employers.[8]

The acclaimed freedom fighter Fannie Lou Hamer knew that rape and sexual violence was a common occurrence in the segregated South. *For Freedom's Sake*, Chana Kai Lee's biography of Hamer, is one of the few histories of the modern-day civil rights movement that openly deals with and documents the legacy of sexual assault. Hamer's grandmother, Liza Bramlett, spoke often of the "horrors of slavery," including stories about "how the white folks would do her." Bramlett's daughter remembered that "this man would keep her as long as he want to and then he would trade her off for a little heifer calf. Then the other man would get her and keep her as long as he want—she was steady having babies—and trade her off for a little sow pig." Twenty of the twenty-three children Bramlett gave birth to were products of rape.[9]

Hamer grew up with the clear understanding that a "black woman's body was never hers alone." If she was at all unclear about this lesson, the forced hysterectomy she received in 1961 and the brutal beating she received in the Winona, Mississippi, jail in 1963 left little room for confusion. After being arrested with other Student Nonviolent Coordinating Committee (SNCC) activists for desegregating a restaurant, Hamer received a savage and sexually abusive beating by the Winona police. "You bitch," one officer yelled, "we going to make you wish you was dead." He ordered two black inmates to beat Hamer with "a long wide blackjack," while other patrolmen battered "her head and other parts of her body." As they assaulted her, Hamer felt them repeatedly "pull my dress over my head and try to feel under my clothes." She attempted to pull her dress down during the brutal attack in order to "preserve some respectability through the horror and disgrace." Hamer told this story on national television at the Democratic National Convention in 1964 and continued to tell it "until the day she died," offering her testimony of the sexual and racial injustice of segregation.[10]

By speaking out, whether it was in the church, the courtroom, or a congressional hearing, black women used their own public voices to reject the stereotypes used by white supremacists to justify economic and sexual exploitation, and they reaffirmed their own humanity. Additionally, African American women's refusal to remain silent offered African American men an opportunity to assert themselves as *men* by rallying around the protection of black womanhood. Many other men, however, remained silent since speaking out was often dangerous, if not deadly. Most important, women's testimonies were a political act that exposed the bitter ironies of segregation and white supremacy, helped to reverse the shame and humiliation rape inflicts, and served as catalysts in mobilizing mass movements.[11]

Only after local and national groups were organized, black women's testimony began to spark public campaigns for equal justice and protection of black womanhood. In this respect, World War II served as a watershed for African Americans—especially in the South. Black women's testimony and the willingness of black leaders to protect black womanhood must be viewed as part of these resistance movements. For example, in Montgomery, Alabama, the organizational infrastructure that made the Montgomery bus boycott possible in 1955 stemmed in part from decades of black women's activism and a history of gendered political appeals to protect black women from sexual assault. The majority of leaders active in the Montgomery Improvement Association in 1955 cut their political teeth demanding justice for black women who were raped in the 1940s and early 1950s.[12]

In 1944, the kidnapping and gang rape of Mrs. Recy Taylor by six white men in Abbeville, Alabama, sparked what the *Chicago Defender* called "the strongest campaign for equal justice to Negroes to be seen in a decade." Taylor, a twenty-four-year-old African American woman, was walking home from the Rock Hill Holiness Church near Abbeville on September 3 when a carload of six white men pulled alongside her, pointed a gun at her head, and ordered her to get into the car. They drove her to a vacant patch of land where Herbert Lovett pointed his rifle at Taylor and demanded she get out of the car and "get them rags off or I will kill you and leave you down here in the woods." Lovett held her at gunpoint while each of the white men took turns "ravishing" her. After the men raped her, Lovett blindfolded her, pushed her into the car, and dropped her off in the middle of town. That night, Recy Taylor told her father, her husband, and Deputy Sheriff Lewey Corbitt the details of her harrowing assault.[13]

Within a few weeks, the Committee for Equal Justice for Mrs. Recy Taylor formed and was led on a local level by Rosa Parks, E. D. Nixon, Rufus A. Lewis, and E. G. Jackson (editor of the *Alabama Tribune*), all of whom later became pivotal figures in the Montgomery bus boycott. By utilizing the political infrastructure designed to defend the Scottsboro boys a decade earlier and employing the rhetoric of democracy sparked by World War II, Parks, Nixon, and their allies secured the support of national labor unions, African American organizations, women's groups, and thousands of individuals who demanded that Gov. Chauncey Sparks order an immediate investigation and trial. "The raping of Mrs. Recy Taylor was a fascist-like, brutal violation of her personal rights as a woman and as a citizen of democracy," Eugene Gordon, a reporter for the *New York Daily Worker*, wrote in a pamphlet about the case; "Mrs. Taylor was not the first Negro woman to be outraged," he argued, "but it is our intention to make her the last. White-supremacy imitators of Hitler's storm troopers [will] shrink under the glare of the nation's spotlight." Gordon closed by universalizing the rape: "The attack on Mrs. Taylor was an attack on all women. Mrs. Taylor is a Negro . . . but no woman is safe or free until all women are free."[14] Few African Americans were surprised when the Henry County Grand Jury twice failed to indict the white men—despite the governor's belief that they were, in fact, guilty. Still, Recy Taylor's testimony launched a national and international campaign for equal justice that must not be ignored.[15]

Five years later, African Americans in Montgomery, Alabama, rallied to the defense of a twenty-five-year-old black woman named Gertrude Perkins. On March 27, 1949, Perkins was walking home when she was arrested for public drunkenness and attacked by two white police officers in uniform. After forcing her into their squad car, they drove her to the edge of town and raped her repeatedly at gunpoint. Afterwards, they threw her out of their car and sped away. Somehow, she found the strength to stagger into town, where she went directly to Rev. Solomon Seay Sr.'s house. Awaking him, she told him the details of her brutal assault through sobs and tears. "We didn't go to bed that morning," remembered Seay; "I kept her at my house, carefully wrote down what she said, and later had it notarized." Seay sent Perkins's horror story to the syndicated columnist Drew Pearson, who let the whole country know what happened in his daily radio address before Montgomery's white leaders knew what hit them.[16]

The leaders of the local Interdenominational Ministerial Alliance, the Negro Improvement League, and the National Association for the Advancement of Colored People (NAACP), led by E. D. Nixon and the Reverend Mr. Seay, joined together to form the Citizens Committee for

Gertrude Perkins. Mary Fair Burks and her newly formed Women's Political Council may have been involved since one of their early goals was to "aid victims of rape." Although the community mobilized on behalf of Perkins, a grand jury failed to indict the assailants a few weeks later, despite running the full process of "the Anglo-Saxon system of justice." Still, Joe Azbell, editor of the *Montgomery Advertiser*, thought Gertrude Perkins, who bravely spoke out against the men who raped her, "had as much to do with the bus boycott and its creation as anyone on earth." The Perkins protest did not occur in isolation. In February 1951, Rufus A. Lewis, whose influence was crucial to the 1955 campaign, led a boycott of a grocery store owned by Sam E. Green, a white man, who was accused of raping his black teenage babysitter while driving her home. Lewis, a World War II veteran and football coach at Alabama State University, organized other veterans and members of the Citizens' Coordinating Committee in the successful campaign to close the store and bring Green to trial.[17]

The 1955 Montgomery bus boycott itself can be viewed as the most obvious example of the African American community coming to the rescue of a black woman, Rosa Parks, though not because of rape. When Parks sat down in a bus's "no-man's land" and was arrested for refusing to give up her seat to a white man, Montgomery blacks found the *perfect* woman to rally around. "Humble enough to be claimed by the common folk," Taylor Branch notes, Rosa Parks was "dignified enough in manner, speech, and dress to command the respect of the leading classes." Rosa Parks fit the middle-class ideals of "chastity, Godliness, family responsibility, and proper womanly conduct and demeanor" and was the kind of woman around which all the African Americans in Montgomery could rally. It is clear that her symbolic role as icon of virtuous black womanhood was decisive in Montgomery. Rev. Martin Luther King Jr.'s first speech at Holt Street Baptist Church stressed this point. "And since it had to happen," the young preacher told the crowd, "I'm happy it happened to a person like Mrs. Parks. Nobody can doubt the height of her character; nobody can doubt the depth of her Christian commitment."[18]

By selecting Rosa Parks as the symbol of segregation instead of other, less exemplary black women who had been arrested on buses earlier in 1955, black leaders in Montgomery embraced the "politics of respectability" and adhered to what Darlene Clark Hine calls the "culture of dissemblance" as a matter of political necessity amidst the burning white backlash that the 1954 Supreme Court decision in *Brown v. Board of Education* sparked.[19] The White Citizens' Councils, a kind of uptown Ku Klux Klan, led the movement for massive resistance to school integration by relying heavily on sexual scare tactics and white fears of racial amalgamation. As a result, any gender or racial impropriety on the part of African Americans could be viewed as threatening the social order. For the supporters of segregation, "integration always meant miscegenation." Headlines in the *Citizens' Council* warned that "mixed marriage," "sex orgies," and accounts of black men raping white girls were "typical of stories filtering back from areas where racial integration is proceeding 'with all deliberate speed.' "[20]

In this environment, respectability and dissemblance required that silence surround black sexuality, a "cult of secrecy" that helped counter negative stereotypes and kept the inner lives of African Americans hidden from white people. This self-imposed reticence, Hine argues, "implied that those [African American women] who spoke out provided grist for detractors' mills and, even more ominously, tore the protective cloaks from their inner selves."[21] Silence as strategy did not emerge in the mid-twentieth century; it had been a staple of black clubwomen's politics since Reconstruction, when whites continued to use racist violence and sexual abuse to shore up white supremacy.

The culture of dissemblance does not mean there was an unbroken wall of silence. There are moments in history when the pain of violation or the opportunity for justice forced women to come forward to speak out against their abusers. Yet this code of secrecy, a political imperative during the Montgomery bus boycott, helped create a void in the historical record. As a result, violence toward black women has not been as "vividly and importantly retained in our collective memory," Elsa Barkley Brown claims, as the lynching of and violence against black men.[22]

In many ways, this culture of dissemblance silenced more than the survivors of rape; it also trained historians of the black freedom struggle to ignore the subject of black women's dissemblance. Over the past two decades, historians have sharpened their focus on the gendered meanings of respectability, but they have lost sight of the role rape and the threat of sexual violence played in the daily lives of African American women as well as within the larger black freedom struggle.[23] Yet throughout the Jim Crow South African American women such as Recy Taylor in 1944, Gertrude Perkins in 1949, and Betty Jean Owens in 1959 refused to shield their pain in secrecy, thereby challenging the pervasiveness of the politics of respectability. Following in the footsteps of their Reconstruction-era counterparts, they testified about their assaults, leaving behind critical evidence that historians must find the courage to analyze.

To be sure, black women's refusal to remain silent about sexual violence during and after slavery suggests that the culture of dissemblance functioned in tension and in tandem with a tradition of testimony. Even after respectability became the key to black women's symbolic place in the civil rights movement in the early 1950s, however, a number of African American women continued to speak out publicly about being raped, and African American community members rallied to their defense. Unfortunately, too many of these stories remain buried in the archives, yellowing newspapers, or the memories of the survivors, contributing to the historical amnesia about black women's experiences. And Montgomery, Alabama, was not the only place in which attacks on black womanhood fueled protests against white supremacy. Betty Jean Owens's experience in Florida is evidence that a significant story has been missed across the South.

When the four armed white men in Tallahassee forced Thomas Butterfield and Richard Brown to get into their car and drive away, leaving Betty Jean Owens and Edna Richardson at the mercy of their assailants, the two black men did not abandon them but drove around the corner and waited. As the blue Chevrolet disappeared down the street, Brown and Butterfield hurried back to the scene. Edna Richardson, the black woman who was able to get away, saw her friends from her hiding spot, called out to them, and then ran to the car. Hoping to save Owens, the Florida A&M students rushed to the local police station to report the crime.[24]

Similar situations in other southern towns had typically left African Americans without police aid. The officer on duty that night in Tallahassee was Joe Cooke Jr., a nineteen-year-old intern from the all-white Florida State University. Much to the surprise of the three black students, he agreed to look for Owens and her assailants. After a lengthy search, one of the students finally spotted the blue Chevrolet and shouted, "That's it!" It was just after 4:00 a.m. Deputy Cooke turned on his flashers and drove alongside the car. Attempting to escape, the kidnappers led Cooke "twisting and turning through the dark streets of Tallahassee at speeds up to 100 miles per hour." One of the white men suggested "dumping the nigger," but William Collinsworth replied, "we can't now, he's on our tail." Finally, Collinsworth pulled the car to the curb, grabbed his shotgun, and got out of the car. Deputy Cooke drew his pistol and ordered all four to line up against the car or, he threatened, "I will shoot to kill."[25]

As they waited for assistance from Cooke's supervisor, they heard muffled screams coming from the car. Richard Brown and Deputy Cooke peered through the rear window and saw Betty Jean Owens, bound and gagged, lying on the backseat floorboards. Brown tried to help her out of the car, but, as her feet touched the ground, she collapsed. Cooke drove Betty Jean Owens and her friends to the local colored hospital at Florida A&M while Deputy Sheriff W. W. Slappey arrested the four white men and drove them to the jailhouse.[26]

Laughing and joking on the way to the police station, the four white men apparently did not take their arrest seriously, nor did they think they had done anything wrong. Collinsworth, for example, worried less about the charges against him than about the safety of his car. Deputy Sheriff Slappey revealed his disgust when he handed the men over to Sheriff Raymond Hamlin Jr. "They all admitted it," Slappey said; "they didn't say why they did it and that's all I'm going to say about this dirty business." William Collinsworth, David Beagles, Ollie Stoutamire, and Patrick Scarborough confessed in writing to abducting Betty Jean Owens at gunpoint and having "sexual relations" with her. When Sheriff Hamlin asked the men to look over their statements and make any necessary corrections, David Beagles, smiling, bent over the table and made one minor adjustment before he and his friends were hustled off to jail.[27]

If the four white men did not take their arrests seriously, students at Florida A&M University flew into a rage. Many of them were veterans of the Tallahassee bus boycott in 1957, a Montgomery-inspired campaign that highlighted the trend in students' preference for direct action rather than the more respectable and slower litigation favored by the NAACP throughout the 1940s and 1950s. When the students heard news of the attack on Owens and the subsequent arrest of four white men, a small group planned an armed march to city hall to let city officials know that they were willing to protect black womanhood the same way whites "protected" white womanhood—with violence or at least a show of force. Mainstream student leaders persuaded them that an armed march was "the wrong thing to do" and patched together a "Unity" demonstration on Sunday, May 3, only twelve hours after Betty Jean Owens was admitted to the hospital and the four white men were taken to jail.[28]

Fifteen hundred students filled Lee Auditorium, where Clifford Taylor, president of the Student Government Association, said he "would not sit idly by and see our sisters, wives, and mothers desecrated." Using language white men in power could understand, student leaders professed their "belief in the dignity, respect, and protection of womanhood" and announced that they would petition the governor and other authorities for a "speedy and impartial trial."[29]

Early the next day, a thousand students gathered in the university's grassy quadrangle with signs, hymns, and prayers aimed at the national news media, which sent out stories of the attack across the country. The students planned to show Tallahassee and the rest of the nation that white men could no longer attack black women without consequence. Student protesters held signs calling for "Justice"; other posters declared, "It could have been YOUR sister, wife, or mother." Some students linked the attack in Tallahassee to larger issues related to the black freedom struggle: two students held up a poster depicting scenes from Little Rock, Arkansas, which read, "My God How Much More of This Can We Take."[30]

It was the deeply personal violation that rape inflicts, however, that gave the students their focus. Patricia Stephens Due remembered feeling helpless and unsafe. She recalled, "we all felt violated, male and female. It was like all of us had been raped." The student leader Buford Gibson, speaking to a crowd, universalized the attack when he said, "You must remember it wasn't just one Negro girl that was raped—it was all of Negro womanhood in the South."[31] By using Betty Jean Owens as a black Everywoman, Gibson challenged male students to rise up in protest and then placed the protection of black womanhood in their hands. Gibson's exhortation inspired students at Florida A&M to maintain their nonviolent demonstration, unlike white men who historically used the protection of white womanhood to inspire mob violence against black men.

At about the same time, white men in Poplarville, Mississippi, used the protection of womanhood as justification for the lynching of Mack Charles Parker, a black man who was charged with the kidnapping and rape of a twenty-four-year-old white woman who could barely identify him in a police lineup. On April 25, 1959, two days before his trial, a group of eight to ten white men obtained keys to Parker's unguarded jail cell, savagely beat him, and then dragged him down three flights of stairs and out of the building while he screamed "I'm innocent." Federal Bureau of Investigation

(FBI) agents located Parker's bloated body floating in the Pearl River on May 4, 1959, just two days after four white men gang-raped Betty Jean Owens.[32] The Parker lynching cast a shadow over Tallahassee, brutally reminding the black community that white women's bodies were off limits, while the bodies of black women were fair game.

Accelerating media coverage, student-led protests, and a threat to boycott classes at Florida A&M forced Judge W. May Walker to call members of the grand jury into special session in Tallahassee on May 6, 1959. Over two hundred black spectators, mostly students, squeezed into the segregated balcony at the Leon County Courthouse to catch a glimpse of Betty Jean Owens and her attackers before they retreated into the secret hearing. Still undergoing hospital treatment for injuries inflicted during the attack and for "severe depression," Owens was accompanied to the courthouse by a nurse, the hospital administrator, and her mother.[33]

Gasps and moans emanated from the balcony when, after two hours behind closed doors, William Collinsworth, David Beagles, Patrick Scarborough, and Ollie Stoutamire emerged, calmly faced the judge, and pleaded innocent to the charge of rape, making a jury trial mandatory. African Americans in the balcony roared with disapproval. Dr. M. C. Williams, a local black leader, shouted, "four colored men would be dead if the situation had been reversed. It looks like an open and shut case." Defense attorneys for Collinsworth and Scarborough argued for a delay, insisting that public excitement threatened a fair trial, but Judge Walker ignored their objections. For the first time in Florida history, a judge sent the white defendants charged with raping an African American woman back to jail to await their trial. Echoing the sentiments of the people around him, a young boy traced "we want justice" in the dust on the railing of the segregated balcony.[34]

Justice was the last thing the black community expected. In the thirty-four years since Florida began sending convicted rapists to the electric chair instead of the gallows, the state had electrocuted thirty-seven African Americans charged, with raping white women. Before this, Florida led the country in per capita lynchings, even surpassing such notoriously violent states as Mississippi, Georgia, and Louisiana. From 1900 to 1930, white Floridians lynched 281 people, 256 of whom were African American. Throughout its history, Florida never executed or lynched a white man for raping a black woman. In this respect, Florida followed the entire region. Florida's violent history included the "little Scottsboro" case involving Samuel Shepard, Walter Irvin, and Charles Greenlee, black men accused of raping a white woman in Groveland, Florida, in 1949. After the U.S. Supreme Court overturned their guilty verdicts in 1951, Sheriff Willis McCall picked up Shepard and Irvin from Raiford State Prison to transfer them back to the county. On the way there, McCall pulled to the side of the road and asked the two handcuffed men to change the tire and then shot them both in the chest. He radioed his boss and muttered, "I got rid of them; killed the sons of bitches." Walter Irvin survived the shooting, but Samuel Shepard died that day.[35]

In Tallahassee, memories of the "little Scottsboro" case hung over many members of the African American community in 1954 when the state electrocuted Abraham Beard, a seventeen-year-old black youth accused of raping a white woman. Apart from the races of the accuser and the accused, the Beard case featured a cast of characters almost identical to that of the Tallahassee case five years later: an all-white jury had tried and convicted Beard in the same courtroom where Betty Jean Owens faced her attackers. Judge W. May Walker presided, and William D. Hopkins served as the state prosecutor. Harry Michaels, Patrick Scarborough's attorney in 1959, served as Beard's court-appointed attorney in 1954. Both the "little Scottsboro" and the Beard cases revealed the extent to which the protection of white women served as the ultimate symbol of white male power and the foundation of white supremacy. When African Americans in Tallahassee demanded equal justice for Betty Jean Owens, that foundation began to crumble.[36]

News that four white men would actually face prosecution for raping a black woman plunged both whites and blacks into largely unfamiliar territory. It not only highlighted the bitter ironies of segregation and "social equality" but allowed African Americans to publicize them. According to the *Pittsburgh Courier*, the arraignment made the "arguments for white supremacy, racial discrimination, and segregation fall by the wayside" and the arguments against school desegregation seem "childishly futile." "Time and again," another newspaper editor argued, "Southern spokesmen have protested that they oppose integration in the schools only because it foreshadows a total 'mingling of the races.' The implication is that Negroes are hell-bent for intimacy, while whites shrink back in horror." "Perhaps," the writer argued, "as Lillian Smith and other maverick Southerners have suggested, it is not quite that simple."[37]

While prominent members of the white community expressed their shock and horror at the rape, they continued to stumble into old narratives about race and sex. The indictment helped incite age-old fears of miscegenation and stereotypes of the so-called black beast rapist. William H. Chafe argues that "merely evoking the image of 'miscegenation' could often suffice to ring the alarm bells that would mobilize a solid phalanx of white resistance to change." For example, white women around Tallahassee began to speak openly about their "fear of retaliation," while young white couples avoided parking "in the country moonlight lest some Negroes should be out hunting in a retaliatory mood." Reflecting this fear as well as the larger concern with social equality, Florida legislators, like other lawmakers throughout the South, passed a series of racist bills designed to segregate children in schools by sex in order to circumvent the *Brown v. Board of Education* decision and "reduce the chances of interracial marriage."[38] The extent to which the myth of the black beast rapist was a projection of white fears was never clearer than when the gang rape of a black woman conjured up terror of *black-on-white* rape. The fact that the black community rallied around Betty Jean Owens and her womanhood threatened white male power—making the myth of the black savage a timely political tool.

Black leaders from all over the country eagerly used the rape case for their own political purposes as well. Most focused on the lynching of black men in similar cases, placing the crime against Betty Jean Owens into a larger dialogue about the power struggle between black and white men. As A. D. Williams, a black businessman in Tallahassee, put it, "the white men are on the spot." Rev. Dennis H. Jamison felt that the indictment of four white men indicated a "better chance at Justice than any involving the races in the South," but, he added, "still no white men have ever been executed." Elijah Muhammad, leader of the Nation of Islam, expressed this viewpoint forcefully. Using almost the exact same language as white supremacists, he accused the "four devil rapists" of destroying the "virginity of our daughters." "Appeals for justice," he fumed, "will avail us nothing. We know there is no justice under the American flag."[39] Nearly all the editorials in major black newspapers echoed his sentiments.

Ella Baker, director of the Southern Christian Leadership Conference (SCLC), felt that the evidence in the Tallahassee case was so strong that "not even an all white Florida jury could fail to convict." Reminding whites of their tendency to mete out unequal justice toward black men, she warned, "with memories of Negroes who have been lynched and executed on far less evidence, Negro leaders from all over the South will certainly examine every development in this case. . . . What will Florida's answer be?" The *New York Amsterdam News* called for equal justice, noting that the "law which calls for the death sentence does not say that Negro rapists should be punished by death and white rapists should be allowed to live." The *Pittsburgh Courier* bet on acquittal, despite the fact that the case "is as open and shut as a case can be."[40]

Martin Luther King Jr., at the annual SCLC meeting in Tallahassee a few days after the indictment, praised the student protesters for giving "hope to all of us who struggle for human dignity and equal justice." But he tempered his optimism with political savvy, calling on the federal government to force the country to practice what it preached in its Cold War rivalry with the Soviet Union. "Violence in the South can not be deplored or ignored," King declared, directing his criticism at President Dwight D. Eisenhower; "without effective action, the situation will worsen."[41] King exploited a political context in which America's racial problems were increasingly an international issue. The British Broadcasting Corporation (BBC) broadcast segments of the Florida A&M University student speeches condemning the rape and racial injustice, while newspapers throughout Europe closely watched the case unfold. "It is ironical that these un-American outrages occur as our representatives confer in Geneva to expand democratic principles . . . it might well be necessary and expedient," King threatened, "to appeal to the conscience of the world through the Commission on Human Rights of the United Nations." This international angle was a strategy shared by mainstream integrationists, leftist radicals, and black nationalists alike. Audley "Queen Mother" Moore, leader of the Universal Association of Ethiopian Women, Inc., petitioned the United Nations Human Rights

Commission in person to end the "planned lynch terror and willful destruction of our people." She tied issues of race, gender, sex, and citizenship together by demanding Justice Department assistance for Betty Jean Owens's rape case, an FBI investigation of the Mack Charles Parker lynching, and basic voting rights.[42]

Robert F. Williams, militant leader of the Monroe, North Carolina, chapter of the NAACP, suggested African Americans stand their ground and defend themselves. The Parker lynching, the Tallahassee rape case, and two Monroe, North Carolina, cases in which white men stood accused of attacking black women forced Williams to defend racial pride and black womanhood. On May 6, 1959, B. F. Shaw, a white railroad engineer, had been exonerated on charges of beating and kicking a black maid at the Hotel Monroe, even though he did not show up for court. That same day, white jurors giggled while Mrs. Mary Ruth Reed, a pregnant black woman, testified that Lewis Medlin, a white mechanic, beat and sexually assaulted her in front of her five children. Medlin's attorney argued that he was just having a little fun, that he was married to a "lovely white woman . . . the pure flower of life," whom he would not dare leave for "that." The jury deliberated for less than ten minutes before returning the not guilty verdict. It was the defilement of black womanhood and the humiliation of black manhood that inspired Williams to hurl his infamous vow to "meet violence with violence." His exhortation set off a national controversy, culminating at the 1959 NAACP convention where Executive Secretary Roy Wilkins suspended Williams for his remarks. Williams defended his position by citing the tragedy in Tallahassee. Had the "young black men who escorted the coed who was raped in Tallahassee" been able to defend her, Williams argued, they would have been justified "even though it meant that they themselves or the white rapists were killed."[43]

Roy Wilkins shared Williams's gender and race politics but not his methods for achieving them. In a letter to Florida governor LeRoy Collins, Wilkins invoked the lynchings of Mack Charles Parker and Emmett Till, noting that the victims' skin color alone kept them from receiving a fair trial and that their deaths threatened political embarrassment at home and abroad. "Full punishment has been certain and swift in cases involving a white victim and a Negro accused," he said, "but the penalty has neither been certain nor heavy in cases involving a Negro victim and a white accused . . . for these reasons," Wilkins warned, "all eyes will be upon the state of Florida."[44]

On June 11, 1959, at least four hundred people witnessed Betty Jean Owens face her attackers and testify on her own behalf. Owens approached the witness box with her head bowed. She wore a white embroidered blouse and a black-and-salmon checked skirt with gold earrings. The African American press had cast her in the role of respectable womanhood by characterizing her as a God-fearing, middle-class college co-ed "raised in a hard-working Christian household" with parents devoted to the "simple verities of life that make up the backbone of our democracy." Unlike white women, who were often able to play the role of "fair maiden" before a lynch mob worked its will on their alleged attackers, Betty Jean Owens had to tell her story knowing that the four white men who raped her might go unpunished. Worse, Owens had to describe the attack in front of hundreds of white people in a segregated institution that inherently denied her humanity.[45] Though it may seem unnecessary, even lurid, to bear witness to the details of her testimony today, it is crucial that we hear the same testimony that the jurors heard. Owens's willingness to identify those who attacked her and to testify against them in public broke the institutional silence surrounding the centuries-long history of white men's sexual violation of black women, made a white southern judge and jury recognize her womanhood and dignity, and countered efforts to shame or stereotype her as sexually unchaste. As a result, her testimony alone is a momentous event.

Owens remained strong as state prosecutor William Hopkins asked her to detail the attack from the moment she and her friends left the Florida A&M dance. This she did powerfully and emotionally. "We were only parked near Jake Gaither Park for fifteen minutes," she said, when "four white men pulled up in a 1959 blue Chevrolet." She identified Patrick Scarborough as the man who pressed the shotgun into her date's nose and yelled, "Get out and get out now." When Owens began to cry, David Beagles pressed a "wicked looking foot long knife" to her throat and forced her down to the ground. He then pulled her up, slapped her, and said, "You haven't anything to worry about." Owens testified that Beagles pushed her into the car and then "pushed my head down in his lap and yelled at me to be quiet or I would never get home." "I knew I couldn't get away," she stated; "I thought they would kill me if I didn't do what they wanted me to do."[46]

She continued with the horrid details. As the car pulled off the highway and into the woods, "the one with the knife pulled me out of the car and laid me on the ground." Owens was still wearing the gold and white evening gown as they tugged at the dress and "pulled my panties off." She pleaded with them to let her go and not hurt her when Beagles slapped her again. She then told how each one raped her while she was "begging them to let me go . . . I was so scared, but there was nothing I could do with four men, a knife, and a gun . . . I couldn't do anything but what they said." Owens testified that the men eagerly watched one another have intercourse with her the first time around but lost interest during the second round. "Two of them were working on taking the car's license plate off," she said, "while the oldest one" offered her some whiskey. "I never had a chance to get away," she said quietly; "I was on the ground for two or three hours before the one with the knife pushed me back into the car." After the men had collectively raped her seven times, Ollie Stoutamire and Beagles blindfolded her with a baby diaper and pushed her onto the floorboards of the car, and they all drove away. When she heard the police sirens and felt the car stop, she pulled the blindfold down and began yelling for help. After police ordered the men out of the car, Owens recalled, "I was so scared and weak and nervous that I just fell on the ground and that is the last thing I remember."[47]

Betty Jean Owens then described the physical injuries she sustained from the attack. "One arm and one leg," she said, "were practically useless" to her for several days while she was at the hospital. A nurse had to accompany her to the grand jury hearing a few days after the attack, and she needed medication for severe depression. She also had a large bruise on her breast where the bodice stay from her dress dug into her skin as the four men pressed their bodies into hers. Asking her to identify some of the exhibits, Hopkins flipped open the switchblade used the night of the attack, startling some of the jurors. Immediately the four defense attorneys jumped up and vehemently called for a mistrial, arguing that "by flashing the knife Mr. Hopkins tried to inflame the jury and this prejudiced their clients' constitutional rights to a fair trial." Judge Walker denied their motion, signaling Hopkins to continue. When asked whether she consented, Owens clearly told Hopkins and the jury, "No sir, I did not."[48]

Defense attorneys grilled Owens for more than an hour, trying to prove that she consented because she never struggled to get away and that she actually enjoyed the sexual encounter. "Didn't you derive any pleasure from that? Didn't you?" the attorney Howard Williams yelled repeatedly. He kept pressing her, "Why didn't you yell or scream out?" "I was afraid they would kill me," Owens said quietly. She showed signs of anger when Williams repeatedly asked if she was a virgin in an attempt to characterize her as a stereotypical black jezebel. Owens retained her composure, refused to answer questions about her chastity, and resisted efforts to shame her. The defense made a last-ditch effort to discredit Owens by arguing that, if the young men had actually raped her and threatened her life, she would have sustained more severe injuries.[49]

Proceeding with the state's case, William Hopkins called the doctors, both black and white, who examined Owens after the attack. They told the jury that they found her in a terrible condition and that she "definitely had sexual relations" that caused the injuries that required a five-day hospital stay. Richard Brown, Thomas Butterfield, and Edna Richardson took the stand next. They all corroborated Owens's testimony, adding that after the attack Owens was "crying, hysterical, and jerking all over." Brown testified that Scarborough pointed the shotgun into his car window and ordered him and Butterfield to kneel in front of its headlights. Defense attorney John Rudd asked Brown on cross-examination, was it a "single or double barrel shotgun they pointed into your car?" Brown replied, "I only saw one barrel, sir." Laughter rolled down from the balcony, upsetting Rudd. "I can not work with this duress and disorder at my back, a boy's life is at stake here!" Judge Walker called for order and reprimanded the spectators.[50] When the prosecution finally rested its case at 8:30 p.m. on June 11, defense attorneys moved for a directed verdict of acquittal, claiming the state failed to prove anything except sexual intercourse. Judge Walker vigorously denied the motion and insisted the defense return the next day to present their defense.

Amid a sea of people in the tiny courtroom, David Beagles, an eighteen-year-old high school student, sat rigidly on the stand, pushing a ring back and forth on his finger as he answered questions from his attorney. His mother buried her head in her arms as she listened to her son tell the jury his side of the story. Beagles testified that he had a knife and William Collinsworth had a shotgun. The four of them were out "looking around for Negroes who had been parking near Collinsworth's neighborhood and bothering them." When they came upon the Florida A&M students, Beagles admitted holding the switchblade but then said he put it away when he saw they were dressed in formal wear. He admitted that they ordered Brown and Butterfield to drive away but insisted that he "*asked* the girls to get into the car." He denied the rape, arguing that Owens consented and even asked them to take her "back to school to change her dress." Under cross-examination, Beagles admitted that he "pushed her, just once . . . not hard," into the car, that he said, "If you do what we want you to, we'll let you go," and that he blindfolded her with a diaper after the attack. Defense attorney Howard Williams then asked Judge Walker to remove the jury as Beagles detailed the confession he made the night of the crime. Williams argued that when police officers arrested the young men, they "were still groggy from a night of drinking," making their confessions inadmissible. Under Hopkins's cross-examination, however, Beagles admitted that he was not pressured to say anything, that his confession was voluntary, and that he actually looked over the written statement and made an adjustment.[51]

Patrick Scarborough, who admitted that he was married to a woman in Texas, testified that he had intercourse with Owens twice but emphatically denied using force. When Hopkins questioned him, Scarborough admitted that Owens pleaded, "please don't hurt me," but he insisted that she offered "no resistance." He denied kissing her at first and then said he kissed her on the neck while he had sex with her.[52]

Defense attorneys focused on discrediting Owens instead of defending their clients because the prosecution repeatedly drew self-incriminating information from them. State prosecutor Hopkins argued that "they simply have no defense." Defense attorneys tried to use each man's ignorance to prove his innocence, highlighting their low IQ's and poor educations. When that failed, they detailed the dysfunctional histories of each defendant, as though to diminish the viciousness of the crime by offering a rationale for the men's depravity. Character witnesses for William Collinsworth, for example, described his sordid home life and drinking problem. Nearly every member of Collinsworth's family took the stand, spilling sorrowful stories about their poverty and dysfunction. His sister, Maudine Reeves, broke down on the stand and had to be rushed to the hospital. His wife, Pearlie, told the jury through sobs and tears that he was "not himself when he was drunk," but when he was sober "you couldn't ask for a better husband." On the stand, she failed to mention what her letter to the judge had made explicit: that her husband regularly beat her. When that did not seem to work, defense attorneys switched gears and attempted to portray their clients as reputable young men who were incapable of rape. Friends and family members all testified that these young men "were good boys," and that in particular Ollie Stoutamire, a cousin of Tallahassee police chief Frank Stoutamire, had "nothing but pure and moral intentions."[53]

Finally, the defense appealed to the jury's prejudices. Collinsworth blamed his actions on the "Indian blood" pulsing through his veins; the Pensacola psychiatrist Dr. W. M. C. Wilhoit backed him up when he argued, "It is a known fact that individuals of the Indian race react violently and primitively when psychotic or intoxicated." When Collinsworth added alcohol to his "Indian blood," Wilhoit argued, "he was unable to discern the nature and quality of the crime in question." The attorney for Ollie Stoutamire, city judge John Rudd, blamed "outside agitators." The defendants are "being publicized and ridiculed to satisfy sadists and people in other places," Rudd yelled during closing arguments. "Look at that little skinny, long legged sixteen-year-old boy. Does he look like a mad rapist who should die . . . should we kill or incarcerate that little boy because he happened to be in the wrong place at the wrong time?"[54]

In their summations to the jury, defense attorneys S. Gunter Toney and Harry Michaels followed Rudd's lead. Michaels insisted that "the crime here is insignificant . . . the pressure, clamor, and furor are completely out of proportion." Pointing to Scarborough, Michaels told the jury, "his motives, intentions, and designs that night were wholesome, innocent and decent." The fact that Owens could "have easily walked ten feet into the woods where nobody could find her," Michaels said, proved she consented. Waving her gold and white gown in front of the jury, he pointed out that it was "not soiled or torn," which he said proved no brutality was involved. Finally, he called for an acquittal, arguing that the jury could not possibly convict on the basis of "only one witness—the victim, and confessions that admitted only one fact—sexual intercourse." Sitting in the segregated balcony, Charles U. Smith, a sociologist at Florida A&M University, said he gasped when he heard Howard Williams yell, "Are you going to believe this nigger wench over these four boys?"[55]

In his summation, prosecuting attorney William Hopkins jumped up, grabbed the shotgun and Betty Jean Owens's prom dress, and appealed to the jury for a conviction.

> Suppose two colored boys and their moron friends attacked Mrs. Beagles' daughter . . . had taken her at gunpoint from a car and forced her into a secluded place and regardless of whether they secured her consent or not, had intercourse with her seven times, leaving her in such a condition that she collapsed and had to be hospitalized?

Betty Jean Owens, he said, "didn't have a chance in the world with four big boys, a loaded gun and a knife. She was within an inch of losing her life . . . she was gang-raped SEVEN times." "When you get to the question of mercy," he told the jury, "consider that they wouldn't even let that little girl whimper."[56]

Restless spectators, squeezed into every corner of the segregated courthouse, piled back into their seats when jurors emerged after three hours of deliberation with a decision. An additional three hundred African Americans held a silent vigil outside. A. H. King, the jury foreman and a local plantation owner, slowly read aloud the jury's decision for all four defendants: "guilty with a recommendation for mercy." The recommendation for mercy saved the four men from the electric chair and, according to the *Baltimore Afro-American*, "made it inescapably clear that the death penalty for rape is only for colored men accused by white women." A. H. King defended the mercy ruling by arguing that "there was no brutality involved" and insisted, implausibly enough, that the decision would have been the same "if the defendants had been four Negroes."[57] Judge Walker deferred sentencing for fifteen days, cleared the courtroom, and sent the four white men to Raiford prison.

African Americans who attended the trial quietly made their way home after the bittersweet verdict. Betty Jean Owens's mother told reporters that she was "just happy that the jury upheld my daughter's womanhood." Rev. A. J. Reddick, former head of the Florida NAACP, snapped, "If it had been Negroes, they would have gotten the death penalty." "Florida," he said, "has maintained an excellent record of not veering from its pattern of never executing a white man for the rape of a Negro," but he acknowledged that the conviction was "a step forward." Betty Jean Owens showed a similar ambivalence in an interview by the *New York Amsterdam News*. "It is something," she said; "I'm grateful that twelve white men believed the truth, but I still wonder what they would have done if one of our boys raped a white girl."[58]

Florida A&M students, who had criticized Butterfield and Brown for failing to protect black womanhood a week earlier, were visibly upset after the trial. In fact, letters to the editors of many African American newspapers condemned the two men and all black men for failing to protect "their" women. Mrs. C. A. C. in New York City felt that all Negro men were "mice" and not worthy of respect because "they stand by and let the white men do anything they want to our women." She then warned all black men that they "would never have freedom until [they] learn to stand up and fight." In a letter to the *Baltimore Afro-American*, a black man accepted her challenge: "unless we decide to protect our own women," he argued, "none of them will be safe." Some African American women felt they should protect themselves. A white woman sent her black maid home one day after she came to work with a knife, "in case any white man came after her," reported the *Tallahassee Democrat*. Still, many felt that "someone should have burned."[59]

Despite their anger at the unequal justice meted out, some African Americans in the community considered the guilty verdict a victory. The Reverend C. K. Steele Jr., head of the Tallahassee chapter of the SCLC, said it showed progress, reminding others that four white men "wouldn't have even been arrested twenty years ago." The Reverend Leon A. Lowery, state president of the Florida NAACP, saw a strategy in the mercy recommendation. He thought that it could help "Negroes more in the long run" by setting a precedent for equal justice in future rape cases.[60] After Judge Walker handed down life sentences to the four white men, some African Americans in Tallahassee applauded what they felt was a significant step in the right direction; many others, however, exhibited outrage. Roy Wilkins openly praised the verdict as a move toward equal justice but acknowledged in a private letter the "glaring contrast that was furnished by the Tallahassee verdict." In light of the recent lynching of Mack Charles Parker, no one really had to wonder what would have happened had the attackers been black. Editors of the *Louisiana Weekly* called the trial a "figment and a farce" and insisted that anyone who praised the verdict "confesses that he sees nothing wrong with exacting one punishment for white offenders and another, more severe for others."[61]

Any conviction was too much for some whites who felt that sending four white men to jail for raping a black woman upset the entire foundation of white supremacy. Many believed the guilty verdict was the result of a Communist-inspired NAACP conspiracy, which would ultimately lead to miscegenation. Letters to Judge Walker featured a host of common fears and racist stereotypes of black men and women. Fred G. Millette reminded the judge that a conviction "would play into the hands of the Warren Court, the NAACP, and all other radical enemies of the South . . . even though the nigger wench probably had been with a dozen men before." Mrs. Laura Cox wrote to Judge Walker that she feared this case would strengthen desegregation efforts, posing a direct threat to white children who might attend integrated schools. "If the South is integrated," she argued, "white children will be in danger because the Negroes carry knives, razors, ice picks, and guns practically all the time." Petitioning Judge Walker for leniency, Mrs. Bill Aren reminded him to remember that "Negro women like to be raped by the white men" and that "something like this will help the Supreme Court force this low bred race ahead, making whites live and eat with him and allow his children to associate with the little apes, grow up and marry them."[62]

It is ironic that a rape case involving a black woman and four white men would conjure up images of the black brute chasing white women with the intent to mongrelize the white race. The Tallahassee case attests to the persistence of such images decades after Reconstruction, when the mythological "incubus" took flight, justifying mob violence and a reign of terror throughout the South. Anxieties about the black beast rapist and fears of miscegenation conveniently surfaced when white men feared losing their monopoly on power. As Frederick Douglass noted nearly a century earlier, the myth of the black man as a rapist was an "invention with a well defined motive."[63] The rape of Betty Jean Owens reminds us that the maintenance of white supremacy relied on *both* the racial and sexual domination of black men *and* women.

While the verdict was likely the confluence of localized issues—a politically mobilized middle-class African American community, the lower-class status of the defendants (who were politically expendable), Florida's status as a "moderate" southern state dependent on northern tourism, and media pressure—it had far-reaching consequences.[64] The Tallahassee case focused national attention on the sexual exploitation of black women at the hands of white men, leading to convictions elsewhere that summer. In Montgomery, Alabama, Grady F. Smith, a retired air force colonel, was sentenced to fourteen months of hard labor for raping a seventeen-year-old African American girl. In Raleigh, North Carolina, Ralph Lee Betts, a thirty-six-year-old white man, was sentenced to life imprisonment for kidnapping and molesting an eleven-year-old African American girl. And in Burton, South Carolina, an all-white jury sent a white marine named Fred Davis to the electric chair—a first in the history of the South—for raping a forty-seven-year-old African American woman. In each case, white supremacy faltered in the face of the courageous black women who testified on their own behalf.[65]

Betty Jean Owens's grandmother recognized the historic and political significance of the verdicts. "I've lived to see the day," she said, "where white men would really be brought to trial for what they did." John McCray, editor of the South Carolina *Lighthouse and Informer*, wondered if the convictions in Tallahassee and elsewhere pointed to "defensive steps" taken by the South to "belatedly try to disprove that it discriminates against colored people." Still, he realized the importance of guilty verdicts. "This forced intimacy," he argued "goes back to the days of slavery when our women were the chattel property of white men." For McCray, the life sentences indicated a new day: "Are we now witnessing the arrival of our women? Are they at long last gaining the emancipation they've needed?"[66]

John McCray's connection between the conviction of white men for raping black women and black women's emancipation raises important questions that historians are just beginning to ponder. How did the daily struggle to gain self-respect and dignity, rooted in ideas of what it meant to be men and women, play out in the black freedom struggle? It is not just a coincidence that black college students, struggling for their own identity and independence, sparked the sit-in movement soon after Betty Jean Owens was brutally raped. In Tallahassee, Patricia Stephens Due, who felt that the rape symbolized an attack on the dignity and humanity of all African Americans, organized the city's first Congress of Racial Equality (CORE) chapter just six weeks after Owens's trial. Florida A&M CORE members launched an uneventful sit-in campaign that fall, but, like other black students throughout the South, successfully desegregated local lunch counters, theaters, and department stores in the spring of 1960. The students later led the "jail, no bail" tactic popularized by SCLC and SNCC.[67] While the rape alone may not have been the galvanizing force that turned students into soldiers for freedom, the sexual and racial dynamics inherent in this case speak to larger themes in the African American freedom struggle.

The politics of respectability—Betty Jean Owens's middle-class background, her college education, and her chastity—may have enabled

African Americans on the local and national level to break through the "culture of dissemblance" and speak out against her rape. But it was the convergence of the politics of respectability, Owens's testimony, and African Americans' growing political influence on the national and international stage in the late 1950s that made the legal victory possible. Still, the long tradition of black women's testimony, stretching back to slavery and Reconstruction, makes it clear that some elements of the Tallahassee case were not aberrations. The testimonies and trials of Betty Jean Owens, Gertrude Perkins, and Recy Taylor, to name just a few, bear witness to these issues, forcing historians to reconsider the individual threads that make up the fabric of African American politics. Black women not only dissembled where it was necessary but testified where it was possible. Not only silence but often protest surrounded the sexualized violence against African American women. If we are fully to understand the role of gender and sexuality in larger struggles for freedom and equality, we must explore these battles over manhood and womanhood, frequently set in the context of sexualized violence, that remain at the volatile core of the modern civil rights movement.

Notes

Danielle L. McGuire is a Ph.D. candidate in history at Rutgers University. This essay received the 2004 Louis Pelzer Memorial Award.

This article would not have been possible without the gracious historians, teachers, family, and friends who always seemed willing to go out of their way to provide encouragement, support, and intellectual engagement. For this I am eternally grateful. Thank you especially to Steven Lawson, Nancy Hewitt, Tim Tyson, and Steve Kantrowitz and the Harmony Bar Writers Collective, all of whom spilled gallons of ink on this essay. They are members of a beloved community that is made up of some of the best folks around. A hearty thanks goes out to Davarian Baldwin, Martha Bouyer, Herman Bennett, David S. Cecelski, Bill Chafe, Paul Clemens, Dorothy Sue Cobble, John Dittmer, Lisa Elliott, Ann Fabian, Glenda Gilmore, Christina Greene, Darlene Clark Hine, Charles Hughes, William Jones, Temma Kaplan, Le Club, Jan Lewis, Tim and Dee McGuire, Richard and Grace McGuire, Katherine Mellen, Jennifer Morgan, Perri Morgan, Adam Rosh, Karl and Marcia Rosh, Regan Shelton, Phyllis St. Michael, Stephen Tuck, William L. Van Deburg, Craig Werner, and Deborah Gray White. I am also grateful to Joanne Meyerowitz, Kathleen Brown, Victoria Walcott, and the anonymous referees of this essay for their insightful comments and criticisms.

Readers may contact McGuire at <dmcguire@eden.rutgers.edu>.

1. *New York Amsterdam News*, June 20, 1959, p. 37. Jimmy Carl Cooper, a white youth, testified that David Beagles told him he planned to go out and get "some nigger 'stuff' " and noted that "stuff was not the word used": Trezzvant W. Anderson, "Rapists Missed Out on First Selection," *Pittsburgh Courier*, June 20, 1959, p. 3. A cleaned-up version reported that Beagles had plans to get a "Negro girl": "Four Convicted in Rape Case," *Tallahassee Democrat*, June 14, 1959, p. 7. "I Was Scared," *Pittsburgh Courier*, June 20, 1959, p. 1. "Four Begin Defense in Trial on Rape," *New York Times*, June 13, 1959, p. A13. See also criminal case file #3445, *State of Florida v. Patrick Gene Scarborough, David Ervin Beagles, Ollie Odell Stoutamire, and William Ted Collinsworth*, 1959 (Leon County Courthouse, Tallahassee, Fla.) (copy in Danielle L. McGuire's possession). Thanks to the Leon County Courthouse for

sending me the file. Because the original trial transcript is no longer available, I have had to rely on newspaper reports, particularly those in African American newspapers: the *Baltimore Afro-American*, the *Louisiana Weekly*, the *New York Amsterdam News*, the *Pittsburgh Courier*, and the *South Carolina Lighthouse and Informer*. The fact that the transcript is missing is verified in the case file notes of *Patrick G. Scarborough v. State of Florida*, 390 So. 2d 830 (Fla. Dist. Ct. App., 1980). See also Robert W. Saunders, "Report on Tallahassee Incident," May 9, 1959, box A91, series III, National Association for the Advancement of Colored People Papers (Manuscript Division, Library of Congress, Washington, D.C.). Thanks to Timothy B. Tyson for finding this information for me.

2. The murders of Emmett Till in 1955 and Andrew Goodman, Michael Schwerner, and James Chaney in 1963 are considered pivotal moments in the civil rights movement. Their stories are given prominent attention in the PBS Eyes on the Prize series and Hollywood films such as the 1988 thriller *Mississippi Burning*. For monographs on these murders, see, for example, Nicolaus Mills, *Like a Holy Crusade: Mississippi 1964—The Turning Point of the Civil Rights Movement in America* (Chicago, 1992); and Stephen J. Whitfield, *A Death in the Delta: The Story of Emmett Till* (Baltimore, 1991).
3. Historians have only recently begun to explore how gender and sexuality affected the civil rights movement. Early efforts to include gender often took the form of "a women's history tacked onto men's history of civil rights": Steven F. Lawson, "Civil Rights and Black Liberation," in *A Companion to American Women's History*, ed. Nancy A. Hewitt (Oxford, Eng., 2002), 411. On the ways women changed the civil rights movement and how it changed their lives as well, see, for example, Vicki L. Crawford, Jacqueline Anne Rouse, and Barbara Woods, eds., *Women in the Civil Rights Movement: Trailblazers and Torchbearers, 1941–1965* (New York, 1990); and Belinda Robnett, *How Long? How Long? African-American Women in the Struggle for Civil Rights* (New York, 1997). Recent works place black and white women and their long-standing traditions of community organizing and resistance in the forefront of the movement; see, for example, Charles M. Payne, *I've Got the Light of Freedom: The Organizing Tradition and the Mississippi Freedom Struggle* (Berkeley, 1995); and Barbara Ransby, *Ella Baker and the Black Freedom Movement: A Radical Democratic Vision* (Chapel Hill, 2003).
4. On the "culture of dissemblance," see Darlene Clark Hine, "Rape and the Inner Lives of Black Women in the Middle West: Preliminary Thoughts on a Culture of Dissemblance," *Signs*, 14 (Summer 1989), 912–20.
5. On the way gender and sexuality structured racial slavery, see, for example, Kathleen Brown, *Good Wives, Nasty Wenches, and Anxious Patriarchs* (Chapel Hill, 1996), 128–36; Kirsten Fischer, *Suspect Relations: Sex, Race, and Resistance in Colonial North Carolina* (Ithaca, 2002); and Deborah Gray White, *Arn't I a Woman? Female Slaves in the Plantation South* (New York, 1985).
6. Gerda Lerner, ed., *Black Women in White America: A Documentary History* (New York, 1972), 172. See also, for example, Jacquelyn Dowd Hall, " 'The Mind That Burns in Each Body': Women, Rape, and Racial Violence," in *Powers of Desire: The Politics of Sexuality*, ed. Ann Snitow, Christine Stansell, and Sharon Thompson (New York, 1983), 328–49; and Leslie A. Schwalm, *A Hard Fight for We: Women's Transition from Slavery to Freedom in South Carolina* (Urbana, 1997), 37, 44–45, 119–21.
7. Tera W. Hunter, *To 'Joy My Freedom: Southern Black Women's Lives and Labors after the Civil War* (Cambridge, Mass., 1997), 34. Winthrop Jordan, *White over Black: American Attitudes toward the Negro, 1550–1812* (Chapel Hill, 1968), 141. Frances Thompson quoted in Lerner, ed., *Black Women in White America*, 174–75; Harriet Simril quoted ibid., 183–85; see also Hannah Rosen, " 'Not That Sort of

Woman': Race, Gender, and Sexual Violence during the Memphis Riot of 1866," in *Sex, Love, Race: Crossing Boundaries in North American History*, ed. Martha Hodes (New York, 1999), 267–93. Essic Harris quoted in Elsa Barkley Brown, "Negotiating and Transforming the Public Sphere: African American Political Life in the Transition from Slavery to Freedom," *Public Culture*, 7 (1994), 112n8; Ferdie Walker quoted in William Chafe, Raymond Gavins, and Robert Korstad, eds., *Remembering Jim Crow: African Americans Tell about Life in the Segregated South* (New York, 2001), 9–10.

8. John H. McCray, "South's Courts Show New Day of Justice," *Baltimore Afro-American*, July 11, 1959. Theralene Beachem interview by McGuire, March 19, 2003, audiotape (in McGuire's possession); Gloria Dennard interview by McGuire, March 19, 2003, audiotape, ibid.; Linda S. Hunt interview by McGuire, March 19, 2003, audiotape, ibid.; Mrs. Lucille M. Johnson interview by McGuire, March 16, 2003, audiotape, ibid.
9. Chana Kai Lee, *For Freedom's Sake: The Life of Fannie Lou Hamer* (Urbana, 1999), 9. On the "perilous intersection of race, gender, and sexualized brutality," see Timothy B. Tyson, *Radio Free Dixie: Robert F. Williams and the Roots of Black Power* (Chapel Hill, 1999), 2, 94. Though over a half century old, two of the best articulations of the sexual subtext of segregation that exist are John Dollard, *Caste and Class in a Southern Town* (Madison, 1937); and Lillian Smith, *Killers of the Dream* (New York, 1949).
10. Lee, *For Freedom's Sake*, 9–10, 78–81. Although Lee argues that Hamer was "inclined to dissemble when it came to sex, race, and violence" (ibid., 78–81), Lee's own evidence suggests that Hamer testified publicly to the sexualized aspects of her beating in Winona, Mississippi, and her forced sterilization as often as she kept them hidden; see ibid., 54, 59, 79, 80–81, 89, 198n42, 196n2. See also Kay Mills, *This Little Light of Mine: The Life of Fannie Lou Hamer* (New York, 1993).
11. See Deborah Gray White, *Too Heavy a Load: Black Women in Defense of Themselves, 1894–1994* (New York, 1999), 60–66. John Lewis Adams, " 'Arkansas Needs Leadership': Daisy Bates, Black Arkansas, and the National Association for the Advancement of Colored People" (M.A. thesis, University of Wisconsin, Madison, 2003). Thanks to John Adams for sharing his research with me. On "reversing the shame," see Temma Kaplan, "Reversing the Shame and Gendering the Memory," *Signs*, 28 (Autumn 2002), 179–99. Jo Ann Robinson, *The Montgomery Bus Boycott and the Women Who Started It: The Memoir of Jo Ann Gibson Robinson*, ed. David J. Garrow (Knoxville, 1987), 37.
12. On the impact of World War II, see, for example, Timothy B. Tyson, "Wars for Democracy: African American Militancy and Interracial Violence in North Carolina during World War II," in *Democracy Betrayed: The Wilmington Race Riot of 1898 and Its Legacy*, ed. David Cecelski and Timothy B. Tyson (Chapel Hill, 1998), 254–75; and Harvard Sitkoff, "Racial Militancy and Interracial Violence in the Second World War," *Journal of American History*, 58 (Dec. 1971), 661–81. My preliminary dissertation research indicates that African Americans throughout the South used World War II as a wedge to publicize southern injustice, especially sexual violence by white men. Between 1942 and 1950, African American women accused white men of rape, testified about their assaults, and sparked community mobilization efforts in a number of southern towns, often securing convictions, mostly on minor charges with small fines assessed.
13. Fred Atwater, "$600 to Rape Wife? Alabama Whites Make Offer to Recy Taylor Mate," *Chicago Defender*, n.d., clipping, Recy Taylor case, folder 2, Administrative Files, Gov. Chauncey Sparks Papers, 1943–1947 (Alabama Department of Archives and History, Montgomery); N. W. Kimbrough and J. V. Kitchens, "Report to

Governor Chauncey Sparks," Dec. 14, 1944, ibid.; John O. Harris, N. W. Kimbrough, and J. V. Kitchens to Gov. Chauncey Sparks, "Supplemental Report, December 27, 1944," ibid. See also "Grand Jury Refuses to Indict Attackers," *Pittsburgh Courier*, Feb. 24, 1945, folder 3, ibid.; "This Evening," *Birmingham News*, Feb. 21, 1945, ibid.; and "Second Grand Jury Finds No Bill in Negro's Charges," *Dothan Eagle*, Feb. 15, 1945, ibid.

14. On Scottsboro's political infrastructure, see Dan T. Carter, *Scottsboro: A Tragedy of the American South* (New York, 1971); and James Goodman, *Stories of Scottsboro* (New York, 1994). Over thirty national labor unions and many more locals supported Recy Taylor. See "Press release," Feb. 3, 1945, folder 4, box 430, Earl Conrad Collection (Cayuga Community College Library, Auburn, N.Y.). Other organizations that played an active role in Recy Taylor's defense include the Southern Conference for Human Welfare, the National Council of Negro Women, the Southern Negro Youth Congress, the National Negro Congress, the International Labor Defense, and the Birmingham and Montgomery branches of the NAACP: "Partial Sponsor List," Dec. 28, 1944, ibid.; Earl Conrad, Eugene Gordon, and Henrietta Buckmaster, "Equal Justice under Law," pamphlet draft, ibid.
15. See Kimbrough and Kitchens, "Report to Governor Chauncey Sparks"; Harris, Kimbrough, and Kitchens to Sparks, "Supplemental Report." See also "Grand Jury Refuses to Indict Attackers," *Pittsburgh Courier*, Feb. 24, 1945; "Dixie Sex Crimes against Negro Women Widespread," *Chicago Defender*, n.d., Scrapbook Collection, Conrad Collection; "Alabama Rapists Came from Church to Join White Gang in Sex Crime," *Chicago Defender*, March 24, 1945, ibid.; and "Alabama Has No Race Problem, Claims Official," *Chicago Defender*, n.d., ibid.
16. See *Montgomery Advertiser*, April 5, 1949, p. 8A; ibid., April 6, 1949, p. 1B; ibid., April 7, 1949, p. 2A; S. S. Seay, *I Was There by the Grace of God* (Montgomery, 1990), 130–31. "Drew Pearson Changes Mind; Criticizes City," *Montgomery Advertiser*, May 3, 1949, p. 1A; ibid., May 21, 1949, p. 1A; "Anglo-Saxon System of Justice," ibid., May 22, 1949, p. 2B.
17. "Rape Cry against Dixie Cops Fall on Deaf Ears," *Baltimore Afro-American*, April 9, 1949, p. 1; Stewart Burns, ed., *Daybreak of Freedom: The Montgomery Bus Boycott* (Chapel Hill, 1997), 7; Joe Azbell quoted in "Cradle of the Confederacy," transcript, *Will the Circle Be Unbroken*, Southern Regional Council Web site (March 1997; not currently available; printout in McGuire's possession). Rufus A. Lewis story in Townsend Davis, *Weary Feet, Rested Souls: A Guided History of the Civil Rights Movement* (New York, 1998), 34.
18. Taylor Branch, *Parting the Waters: America in the King Years, 1954–1963* (New York, 1988), 130. Marissa Chappell, Jenny Hutchinson, and Brian Ward, " 'Dress modestly, neatly . . . as if you were going to church': Respectability, Class, and Gender in the Montgomery Bus Boycott and the Early Civil Rights Movement," in *Gender in the Civil Rights Movement*, ed. Peter J. Ling and Sharon Monteith (New York, 1999), 87. Branch, *Parting the Waters*, 130.
19. Black leaders in Montgomery decided against using the arrests of Claudette Colvin, an unwed pregnant teenager, and Mary Louise Smith, the daughter of a local drunk, as test cases for desegregating the buses; see Branch, *Parting the Waters*, 123–28; Lynn Olson, *Freedom's Daughters: The Unsung Heroes of the Civil Rights Movement from 1830–1970* (New York, 2001), 94–95; and Chappell, Hutchinson, and Ward, " 'Dress modestly, neatly . . . as if you were going to church,' " 84.
20. Neil R. McMillen, *The Citizens' Council: Organized Resistance to the Second Reconstruction, 1954–1964* (Urbana, 1994), 184, 186; see also Numan V. Bartley, *The Rise of Massive Resistance: Race and Politics in the South during the 1950s* (Baton Rouge, 1969), 83–84; and Tom P. Brady, *Black Monday: Segregation or*

Amalgamation, America Has Its Choice (Winona, Miss., 1955). The White Citizens' Councils counted approximately 250,000 members throughout the South.

21. Hine, "Rape and the Inner Lives of Black Women in the Middle West," 915.
22. Brown, "Negotiating and Transforming the Public Sphere," 146.
23. Historians of the modern day civil rights movement are beginning to build upon work that chronicled the ways respectability, dignity, and manhood and womanhood shaped the strategies and goals of the middle- and working-class black activists during Reconstruction and the Progressive Era; see, for example, Glenda Gilmore, *Gender and Jim Crow: Women and the Politics of White Supremacy in North Carolina, 1896–1920* (Chapel Hill, 1999); and Evelyn Brooks Higginbotham, *Righteous Discontent: The Women's Movement in the Black Baptist Church, 1880–1920* (Cambridge, Mass., 1993).
24. "Deputy Tells of Confessions," *Tallahassee Democrat*, June 12, 1959.
25. Saunders, "Report on Tallahassee Incident."
26. "Deputy Tells of Confessions," *Tallahassee Democrat*, June 12, 1959. Original reports stated that Owens was "bound and gagged," but she later testified that she was only blindfolded; after she pulled the blindfold down, she appeared to have been gagged.
27. "Four Whites Seized in Rape of Negro," *New York Times*, May 3, 1959, p. A45.
28. On the Tallahassee bus boycott, see Glenda Alice Rabby, *The Pain and the Promise: The Struggle for Civil Rights in Tallahassee, Florida* (Athens, Ga., 1999), 9–46. Robert M. White, "The Tallahassee Sit-ins and CORE: A Nonviolent Revolutionary Sub-movement" (Ph.D. diss., Florida State University, 1964), 65.
29. White, "Tallahassee Sit-ins and CORE," 65.
30. "Rapists Face Trial," *Famuan*, 27 (May 1959), 1, 3; "Negroes Ask Justice for Co-ed Rapists," *Atlanta Constitution*, May 4, 1959, p. 2; "Four Whites Seized in Rape of Negro," *New York Times*, May 3, 1959, p. A45; ibid., May 5, 1959, p. A23; "Mass Rape of Co-ed Outrages Students," *Louisiana Weekly*, May 9, 1959, p. 1; *L'Osservatore Romano*, June 12, 1959; *Heraldt Tribune-London*, June 13, 1959; "Jury to Take Up Rape of Negro Co-ed," *Atlanta Constitution*, May 5, 1959, p. 5.
31. Patricia Stephens Due telephone interview by McGuire, March 4, 1999 (notes in McGuire's possession). See also Tananarive Due and Patricia Stephens Due, *Freedom in the Family: A Mother-Daughter Memoir of the Fight for Civil Rights* (New York, 2003), 40–41. White, "Tallahassee Sit-ins and CORE," 65.
32. See Howard Smead, *Blood Justice: The Lynching of Mack Charles Parker* (New York, 1988); Tyson, *Radio Free Dixie*, 143; "Lynch Victim Mack Parker's Body Is Found," *Tallahassee Democrat*, May 5, 1959.
33. "4 Indicted in Rape of Negro Co-ed," *New York Herald Tribune*, May 7, 1959, p. 5; Moses Newson, "Leaves Hospital to Give Testimony," *Pittsburgh Courier*, May 16, 1959, pp. 1–2.
34. M. C. Williams quoted in "Packed Court Hears Not Guilty," *Pittsburgh Courier*, May 16, 1959, pp. 1–2; "Judge Instructs Jury Here," *Tallahassee Democrat*, May 6, 1959, p. 1; "Sobbing Co-ed Bares Ordeal," *Baltimore Afro-American*, May 16, 1959, p. 1; "Indictment for Rape," criminal case file #3445, *Florida v. Scarborough, Beagles, Stoutamire, and Collinsworth*; "Four Plead Not Guilty to Rape," *Tallahassee Democrat*, n.d., clipping, folder 4, box 912, W. May Walker Papers (Special Collections, Robert Manning Strozier Library, Florida State University, Tallahassee).
35. Claude Sitton, "Negroes See Gain in Conviction of Four for Rape of Co-ed," *New York Times*, June 15, 1959, p. A1. Statistics are from David R. Colburn and Richard K. Scher, *Florida's Gubernatorial Politics in the Twentieth Century* (Gainesville, 1995), 13. Willis McCall quoted in Steven F. Lawson, David R. Colburn, and Darryl Paulson,

"Groveland: Florida's Little Scottsboro," in *The African American Heritage of Florida*, ed. David R. Colburn and Jane L. Landers (Gainesville, 1995), 298–325, esp. 312.

36. See Moses J. Newson, "The Wind Blew, the Sky Was Overcast," *Baltimore Afro-American*, June 20, 1959; Moses J. Newson, "Abraham's Shadow Hangs Low over Tallahassee," ibid.; and Moses J. Newson, "His Mother Can Never Forget Him," ibid.
37. "Another Dixiecrat Headache," *Pittsburgh Courier*, June 20, 1959; "The Other Story," n.d., clipping, folder 1, box 912, Walker Papers.
38. William H. Chafe, "Epilogue from Greensboro, North Carolina," in *Democracy Betrayed*, ed. Cecelski and Tyson, 281–82. "Senate to Get Racial Measures," *Tallahassee Democrat*, June 14, 1959, p. 1; "Pent Up Critique on the Rape Case," ibid., May 14, 1959.
39. *Pittsburgh Courier*, May 30, 1959, p. 3; "Mr. Muhammad Speaks," *Pittsburgh Courier*, May 16, 1959.
40. Ella Baker quoted in *Pittsburgh Courier*, May 30, 1959, p. 3; see also Ransby, *Ella Baker and the Black Freedom Movement*, 210. "Enforce the Law," *New York Amsterdam News*, May 9, 1959; "What Will Florida Do?," *Pittsburgh Courier*, May 16, 1959.
41. "King Asks Ike to Go to Mississippi," *Baltimore Afro-American*, May 23, 1959; see also Martin Luther King Jr. to Clifford C. Taylor, May 5, 1959, in *The Papers of Martin Luther King*, ed. Clayborne Carson et al. (vol. 6, Berkeley, forthcoming). Thanks to Kieran Taylor for sending me this information.
42. "Report from Europe," *Baltimore Afro-American*, May 23, 1959; "King Asks Ike to Go to Mississippi," ibid. For the impact of the Cold War on civil rights, see, for example, Mary L. Dudziak, *Cold War Civil Rights: Race and the Image of American Democracy* (Princeton, 2000); and Thomas Borstelmann, *The Cold War and the Color Line: American Race Relations in the Global Arena* (Cambridge, Mass., 2001). "Appeal to U.N. to Stop Race Violence," *Louisiana Weekly*, May 9, 1959, p. 1.
43. Tyson, *Radio Free Dixie*, 145-51, esp. 148, 149; ibid., 163–65.
44. Roy Wilkins to LeRoy Collins, May 6, 1959, box A91, series III, NAACP Papers.
45. *Tallahassee Democrat*, May 4, 1959. On the "fair maiden," see Hall, " 'The Mind That Burns in Each Body,' " 335.
46. "I Was Scared," *Pittsburgh Courier*, June 20, 1959; see also "Did Not Consent," *Tallahassee Democrat*, June 11, 1959; "Rape Co-eds Own Story," *New York Amsterdam News*, June 20, 1959, p. 1; *Atlanta Constitution*, June 12, 1959; "Negro Girl Tells Jury of Rape by Four," *New York Times*, June 12, 1959, p. A16. Coverage of Owens's testimony was nearly identical in newspapers cited.
47. "Did Not Consent," *Tallahassee Democrat*, June 11, 1959; ibid.; ibid.; "I Was Scared," *Pittsburgh Courier*, June 20, 1959, p. 1; "Did Not Consent," *Tallahassee Democrat*, June 11, 1959; ibid.; see also *Charlotte Observer*, June 12, 1959, p. 1A.
48. "Did Not Consent," *Tallahassee Democrat*, June 11, 1959; "I Was Scared," *Pittsburgh Courier*, June 20, 1959; "State's exhibits" (knife) in criminal case file #3445, *Florida v. Scarborough, Beagles, Stoutamire, and Collinsworth*, 1959.
49. "Rape Co-eds Own Story," *New York Amsterdam News*, June 20, 1959, p. 1; "I Was Scared," *Pittsburgh Courier*, June 20, 1959, p. 1; see also "Four Begin Defense in Trial on Rape," *New York Times*, June 13, 1959, p. A13.
50. Doctors quoted in "Rape Co-eds Own Story," *New York Amsterdam News*, June 20, 1959, p. 1; also in "Four Begin Defense in Trial on Rape," *New York Times*, June 13, 1959, p. A13; friends quoted in "Did Not Consent," *Tallahassee Democrat*, June 11, 1959; John Rudd and Richard Brown quoted in "Deputy Tells of Confessions," ibid., June 12, 1959.
51. Anderson, "Rapists Missed Out on First Selection," *Pittsburgh Courier*, June 20, 1959, p. 3; "Four Begin Defense in Trial on Rape," *New York Times*, June 13, 1959,

p. A13; Howard Williams quoted in "Rape Defendants Claim Consent," *Tallahassee Democrat*, June 13, 1959.

52. "Negro Co-ed Gave Consent, Rape Defendants Tell Jury," *Atlanta Constitution*, June 13, 1959.
53. William Hopkins quoted in "Four Convicted in Rape Case; Escape Chair; 2 hr 45 min Verdict Calmly Received in Court," *Tallahassee Democrat*, June 14, 1959, p. 1; Pearlie Collinsworth and friends quoted in "Rape Defendants Claim Consent," ibid., June 13, 1959; Maudine Reeve's history of Ted Collinsworth, "State's exhibit #15," criminal case file #3445, *Florida v. Scarborough, Beagles, Stoutamire, and Collinsworth*, 1959; letter from Mrs. W. T. Collinsworth, "State's exhibit #16," ibid.
54. W. M. C. Wilhoit's testimony in "Motion for Leave to File Notice of Defense of Insanity," May 28, 1959, criminal case file #3445, *Florida v. Scarborough, Beagles, Stoutamire, and Collinsworth*, 1959. "Four Begin Defense in Trial on Rape," *New York Times*, June 13, 1959, p. A13; John Rudd quoted in "Four Guilty of Raping Negro; Florida Jury Votes Mercy," ibid., June 14, 1959, p. 1; Arthur Everett, "Four Convicted in Florida Rape Case," *Washington Post*, June 14, 1959; "Insanity Plea Prepared as Rape Case Defense," *Tallahassee Democrat*, May 28, 1959; "Mental Exam Set for Collinsworth," ibid., May 29, 1959; "Four Begin Defense in Trial on Rape," *New York Times*, June 13, 1959, p. A13.
55. "Four Guilty of Raping Negro; Florida Jury Votes Mercy," *New York Times*, June 14, 1959, p. A1. Charles U. Smith interview by Jackson Lee Ice, 1978, in Jackson Lee Ice Interviews, Florida Governors Manuscript Collection (Special Collections, Strozier Library); verified in Charles U. Smith telephone interview by McGuire, March 9, 1999 (notes in McGuire's possession).
56. "Precedent Seen in Rape Trial," *Tampa Tribune*, June 15, 1959; *Tallahassee Democrat*, June 14, 1959, p. 1.
57. "Verdict," June 14, 1959, criminal case file #3445, *Florida v. Scarborough, Beagles, Stoutamire, and Collinsworth*, 1959. "Guilty as Charged," *Baltimore Afro-American*, June 20, 1959; A. H. King quoted in "No Brutality Proof, Says Florida Jury," *Atlanta Constitution*, June 15, 1959, p. 1.
58. Sitton, "Negroes See Gain in Conviction of Four for Rape of Co-ed," *New York Times*, June 15, 1959, p. A1; "I'm Leaving Dixie," *New York Amsterdam News*, June 20, 1959.
59. Apparently students at Florida A&M ostracized Thomas Butterfield and Richard Brown for failing to protect Betty Jean Owens and Edna Richardson; students thought they ought to have shown some "physical resistance" rather than run away from the "point of a knife and gun": "I'm Leaving Dixie," *New York Amsterdam News*, June 20, 1959. "Hits Negro Men," ibid., June 6, 1959, p. 8. "Williams Was Right," *Baltimore Afro-American*, June 27, 1959; "Four Convicted in Rape Case," *Tallahassee Democrat*, June 14, 1959, p. 7; "I'm Leaving Dixie," *New York Amsterdam News*, June 20, 1959.
60. Sitton, "Negroes See Gain in Conviction of Four for Rape of Co-ed," *New York Times*, June 15, 1959, p. A1. "Negroes Say They Will Use Tallahassee Case as Precedent in Rape Trials," *Tampa Tribune*, June 15, 1959. Later that summer, Leon A. Lowery and others helped launch a successful campaign to highlight the unequal justice meted out for black men accused of raping white women. See also Trezzvant W. Anderson, "Four Florida Rapists Near Chair," *Pittsburgh Courier*, July 4, 1959.
61. Roy Wilkins to Fredrick Cunningham, June 23, 1959, box A91, series III, NAACP Papers; "This Is Not Equal Justice," *Louisiana Weekly*, July 4, 1959.
62. Fred G. Millette to Judge W. May Walker, June 15, 1959, box 912, folder 1, Walker Papers; Mrs. Laura Cox to Judge Walker, June 15, 1959, ibid.; Mrs. Bill Aren to Judge Walker, June 15, 1959, ibid.

63. On the "incubus," see Glenda Gilmore, "Murder, Memory, and the Flight of the Incubus," in *Democracy Betrayed*, ed. Cecelski and Tyson, 73–93. Frederick Douglass quoted in Martha Hodes, *White Women, Black Men: Illicit Sex in the Nineteenth-Century South* (New Haven, 1997), 206.
64. For information on Florida's "moderate" racial politics, see Tom Wagy, *Governor LeRoy Collins of Florida: Spokesman of the New South* (University, Ala., 1985); and Steven F. Lawson, "From Sit-in to Race Riot: Businessmen, Blacks, and the Pursuit of Moderation in Tampa, 1960–1967," in *Southern Businessmen and Desegregation*, ed. Elizabeth Jacoway and David R. Colburn (Baton Rouge, 1982), 257–81.
65. Cases cited in Kimberly R. Woodard, "The Summer of African-American Discontent," unpublished paper, Duke University, 1992 (in McGuire's possession). See also "Death to Be Demanded in Rape Case," *Baltimore Afro-American*, July 4, 1959; John H. McCray, "Marine Doomed to Electric Chair in S.C. Rape Case," ibid., July 11, 1959, p. 1; Clarence Mitchell, "Separate but Equal Justice," ibid.; "Girlfriend Turns in Rape Suspect," ibid., Aug. 1, 1959; Trezzvant Anderson, "Negroes Weep as Georgia White Is Acquitted," *Pittsburgh Courier*, Sept. 2, 1959.
66. "The Tallahassee Case: A Turning Point in South," *New York Amsterdam News*, July 18, 1959; John H. McCray, "South's Courts Show New Day of Justice," *Baltimore Afro-American*, June 11, 1959.
67. Richard Haley, "Report on Events in Tallahassee, October 1959–June 1960," folder 7, box 10, series 5, Congress of Racial Equality Papers (Wisconsin Historical Society, Madison).

Chapter 6

Popular Culture in the Age of White Flight: Film Noir, Disneyland, and the Cold War (Sub)Urban Imaginary

Eric Avila

From *The Journal of Urban History*

Urban life in the United States underwent a dramatic transformation toward the middle of the twentieth century. To the extent that one can think of the history of the American city as a series of successive but overlapping paradigms, the 1930s marked the beginnings of a transition from the modern, industrial, centralized city, which emerged around the turn of the century, to the postwar, decentralized urban region. The shifting concentration of public resources and private capital, coupled with federal incentives toward suburban home ownership among broader segments of the population, accelerated the pattern of decentralized urbanization in postwar America and decimated the economic and social life of the inner city. The regional biases of such development were manifest in the postwar ascendance of the Sun Belt, which cradled a compelling vision of the suburban good life, whereas an "urban crisis" took shape within the Rust Belt cities of the industrial Northeast.[1]

This transition accompanied a profound reconfiguration of social relations. In the second half of the twentieth century, after a wave of labor strikes during the mid-1940s, class gradually subsided as the discursive basis of social conflict, whereas racial and gendered divisions assumed greater prominence.[2] What role the spatial transformation of American society at midcentury played in this development, however, requires additional exploration. The postwar suburban boom created a space, literally and figuratively, for reinstating racial and sexual barriers that weakened within an ascendant urban liberalism that reached its zenith during the 1930s and 1940s. As the racially exclusive patterns of postwar suburbanization facilitated the "blackening" of American inner cities, white flight reflected and reinforced the racial resegregation of the United States. And whereas the modern city incorporated women into public life—as workers and consumers—postwar suburbanization placed greater demands on women to return to the private sphere to resume their traditional responsibilities as mothers and wives. Creating a space for a return to normalcy, the postwar suburban boom offered a setting in which to restore traditional divisions between the races and the sexes.[3]

Urban historians, geographers, and sociologists have measured and mapped the political, economic, and social transition from the modern industrial city to the decentralized urban region, but the cultural corollary to this process has been overlooked. White flight during the postwar period necessitated the formation of a new cultural order, one that marked an exchange of the heterogeneous, anonymous, promiscuous spaces of the centralized city for the contained, segregated, homogeneous experiences of the decentralized urban region.[4] This article explores that transformation through the lens of popular culture, considering the mid-1940s debut of film noir as a popular genre of film and the successive opening of Disneyland in 1955. Both cultural productions posited a critique of the modern city and its typical pattern of social relations, and both arrived alongside the heightened thrust of postwar suburbanization. If film noir situated its indictment of the racial and sexual promiscuity within the spatial context of the modern city, Disneyland offered a suburban antithesis, modeling a new sociospatial order that took shape along the fringes of the urban core. The juxtaposition of film noir and Disneyland within their historical context illustrates a key cultural tension between a reinvigorated suspicion of urban modernity, on one hand, and a suburban retreat from the black city and its disordered culture, on the other. This tension underscored the post–World War II construction of a white suburban ethos and encompassed the political unconscious of a "silent majority" still in its formative years.[5]

The Modern City, its New Mass Culture, and their Midcentury Decline

Not too long ago, a generation of historians discovered the culture of the modern city as a rich field of historical inquiry and illustrated how diverse groups of Americans collectively experienced the transition to urban modernity through a burgeoning set of cultural institutions. In world's fairs, expositions, movie palaces, amusement parks, spectator sports, and night clubs, urban Americans reveled in the "new mass culture" that electrified the landscape of the American city at the turn of the century. As the preeminent metropolis of the nineteenth century, New York City dominated this discussion as the city's cultural institutions facilitated the transition from a Victorian social order, with its strict separation of classes, races, and sexes, to a new cultural order, one that promoted a promiscuous set of interactions among a motley crowd of urban strangers. In New York City, as well as in its urban counterparts at the turn of the century, the crowded venues of the new mass culture reflected the ways in which urban Americans negotiated the perils and pleasures of the modern city.[6]

The vitality of the new mass culture, however, rested in no small part on the economic fortunes of the great industrial centers of the Northeast and Midwest, but such fortunes began to contract toward the middle of the twentieth century. The Great Depression crippled the urban economies of New York City, Philadelphia, Detroit, and Chicago, but perhaps more than any other singular event, World War II undermined the hegemony of urban industrial society and culture by initiating the deconcentration of public resources and private capital. Beginning in the early 1940s, the federal government actively promoted industrial decentralization as a strategy to protect a burgeoning military-industrial infrastructure from the event of an air attack. When the Chrysler Warren Tank Plant took advantage of federal incentives to open on an undeveloped tract of land some fifteen miles north of downtown Detroit in 1941, for example, it augmented the suburban model of postwar industrial development that weakened the economic vitality of traditional urban centers.[7]

The urban crisis initiated during the war years was as much social as it was economic. World War II unleashed a wave of racial violence in the nation's cities, demonstrating the level of discomfort that accompanied the sudden diversification of urban society. The great migration of African Americans from the rural South to wartime centers of employment in the Northeast, Midwest, and Far West "blackened" the face of American cities considerably and aroused hostility from local whites, whose sense of entitlement to defense jobs rested on an entrenched conviction of white supremacy. On June 6, 1944, for example, ten thousand white workers at Cincinnati's Wright aircraft engine plant staged a wildcat strike to protest the integration of the machine shop. Race riots exploded in cities elsewhere. The year 1943 delivered a moment of intense racial violence for the nation's cities, as race riots erupted in New York City, Detroit, and Los Angeles, where the infamous Zoot Suit Riots between white sailors and Chicano youth demonstrated the extent to which other racial groups besides African Americans were implicated within wartime racial tensions.[8]

As American cities festered with racial violence during the war years, an emergent pattern of suburbanization materialized during and after World War II and offered a setting removed from such tensions. Again, the federal government played no small part in this development. Housing policy under the New Deal administration set the stage for the postwar suburban boom and offered incentives to industrialists and aspiring home owners to abandon the nation's urban centers. In particular, the creation of the Homeowners Loan Corporation, the Federal Housing Administration, and, later, the Veterans Administration stimulated the national market for housing construction by shifting the focus of urban development away from the inner city and toward the suburbs. But, as historians have demonstrated, the discriminatory measures built into federal housing policy created the basis for the racial resegregation of postwar America. The urbanization of African Americans throughout and beyond the war years coincided with the largest phase of mass suburbanization in American history, in which millions of Americans who qualified themselves or were qualified as white realized their dream of suburban home ownership. Generally, excluded from the greatest mass-based opportunity for wealth accumulation in American history, African Americans and other minority groups largely remained concentrated within decaying cores of urban poverty. The racial dimensions of the postwar urban crisis thus gave rise to "chocolate cities and vanilla suburbs," which became the dominant paradigm of race and space after World War II.[9]

As a generation of white Americans pursued their dreams of home ownership in the suburbs and as the face of the American city blackened considerably in the aftermath of that exodus, it is not difficult to understand how the culture of industrial urbanism entered a period of decline. Reports of the demise of the new mass culture circulated throughout the networks of public discourse in postwar America, and not surprisingly race emerged as a primary explanation for this development. For example, though Coney Island at the turn of the century reigned as the capital of modern urban culture, the *New York Times* reported in 1962 "Coney Island Slump Grows Worse," drawing attention to the postwar plight of the amusement park. Amidst the many reasons cited for Coney Island's decline, "concessionaire after concessionaire" agreed "the growing influx of Negro visitors [to the park] discouraged some white persons to the area." Three years later, Steeplechase Park, the first of Coney Island's great amusement parks, became the last, closing its doors forever.[10]

Chicago's Riverview Park experienced a similar fate. Once billed as the world's largest amusement park, Riverview stood on 140 acres of land on the city's northwest region. Whereas Riverview enticed an ethnically diverse array of pleasure seekers throughout its sixty-four-year popularity, the amusement park could not withstand the changing demographics that ensued in the era of racial desegregation. By the 1960s, Riverview entered a period of rapid decline, and on October 3, 1967, Riverview closed its doors forever. The *Chicago Tribune* explained that the park's "natural defenses began to crumble. Racial tension ran rampant inside the park."[11]

Amusement parks were not the only genre of popular amusement that fell by the wayside. Urban baseball parks that grew alongside amusement parks encountered similar difficulties during the postwar period. Philadelphia's Shibe Park, for example, once hailed as the crown jewel of ballparks, lost much of its appeal among baseball fans during the 1950s. In 1970, Bob Carpenter, owner of the Philadelphia Phillies, removed his team from its inner-city locale, convinced that baseball was "no longer a paying proposition" at Shibe Park and that its location in "an undesirable neighborhood" meant that white baseball fans "would not come to a black neighborhood" to see a ball game.[12] Similarly, in the aftermath Walter

O'Malley's infamous decision to move the Dodgers from Brooklyn to Los Angeles, one disappointed fan pointed to Brooklyn's changing racial profile to explain O'Malley's decision: "I guess O'Malley was like everybody else, as long as you're not my neighbor, it was okay. But once [blacks] started to live in the neighborhood, it was time to move out."[13]

Clearly, a complex interplay of factors contributed to the decline of these cultural landmarks, but in the era of desegregation, a perception emerged that black urbanization facilitated a retreat from the modern city and its culture among a white public. Such a perception informed the tenor of American popular culture as far back as the early postwar period. Take, for example, that body of American film that critics and historians have identified as film noir. Coined by French film critics in the late 1940s, film noir describes a cycle of American film making roughly spanning the ten years following the end of World War II. Defined as a genre, a mood, a sensibility, and a movement, film noir eludes precise definition but includes a diverse array of crime dramas ranging from individual case studies of murder and criminal deviance to more general treatments of gangsters and organized crime.[14]

Historical assessments of film noir tend to emphasize the experience of the war and its effects on the nation's psyche, but when viewed through the lens of urban history, the genre reveals some striking perceptions about the American city and its culture at midcentury. One of film noir's defining characteristics, after all, is its use of the modern city as setting and subject. Unlike the gleaming spires of the *Wizard of Oz*, however, the noir city exposed the seedy side of urban life. Noir's dark urban vision resonated throughout its titles: *Dark City, City of Fear, The Naked City*, and *Cry of the City*. The noir vision of urban life drew on a representational tradition in Western culture. In contrast to the Enlightenment view of the Western city as the summit of social progress, film noir emphasized the social and psychological consequences of urban modernity. Based initially on the writings of Dashiell Hammett, Raymond Chandler, and James Cain, and with striking parallels to the paintings of Reginald Marsh, George Bellows, and Edward Hopper, noir's erotic portrait of an urban wasteland intonated a deep ambivalence toward the midcentury American metropolis. By the 1940s, as the postwar urban crisis took shape, film noir translated the literary and artistic visions of urban malaise into a more popular cinematic discourse that paralleled the midcentury fate of the American city.[15]

Film noir targeted those urban spaces that best conveyed its vision of urban malaise. The tenement, for example, is a recurrent noir setting, identified as an appropriate milieu for noir's gallery of urban deviants. Its peeling walls, dingy lighting, and rickety stairs frame the encounters between prostitutes and their johns in *Act of Violence* and hide the monstrous fetishes of child molesters in *M*. Film noir featured other spaces of the modern city in its blighted urban landscape. Desolate train stations and abandoned warehouses, vacant streetcars and late-night diners, deserted alleys and empty sewers, seedy nightclubs and tawdry amusement parks: these were the landmarks of film noir and they symbolized the brand of industrial urbanism that entered a period of decline at the outset of the postwar period.

Noir's portrait of urban life focused on the social disorder that ensued within the spatial context of the modern city. In particular, as film historians have demonstrated, noir emphasized the degraded state of sexual relations at the outset of the postwar period. Similar to African Americans, women entered urban public life in unprecedented numbers in the early 1940s, as the female workforce in the United States rose from eleven million to nearly twenty million during the war years.[16] But the very public profile of "Rosie the Riveter," particularly within the nation's cities, aroused animosity toward women who abandoned traditional social roles. As men returned from the war front to resume the routines of work and family, film noir channeled such animosities into its alluring yet disturbing portrait of a new breed of public woman—sassy, conniving, and out to undermine masculine authority through her many misdeeds. The femme fatale resurfaced with a vengeance in American culture vis-à-vis film noir, but the urban context in which she debuted underscored the dangers of a promiscuous urban world where the gendered divisions between public and private life dissolved. Film noir saw the ascendance of such actors as Joan Crawford, Barbara Stanwick, and Veronica Lake, who perfected the image of the public woman and modeled a clear contempt for the traditional role of women as guardians of the private sphere.[17]

Noir's urban vision of sexual disorder had a racial corollary as well. By the mid-1940s, amidst the blackening of American cities, film noir—translated from French as "black film"—offered a recurring portrait of the promiscuous mixing of the races. Film noir dramatized a larger discourse of race that likened the denigrated condition of blackness to white criminality. In this capacity, film noir echoed a larger discursive affinity between white deviance and black identity. For example, the National Association of Real Estate Board issued *Fundamentals of Real Estate Practice* in 1943, which advised real estate agents to be wary of those living on the margins of respectability:

> The prospective buyer might be a bootlegger who could cause considerable annoyance to his neighbors, a madam who had a number of call girls on her string, a gangster who wants a screen for his activities by living in a better neighborhood, a colored man of means who was giving his children a college education and thought they were entitled to live among whites . . . . No matter what the motive or character of the would-be purchaser, if the deal would instigate a form of blight, then certainly the well-meaning broker must work against its consummation.[18]

Within the discourse of real estate industry at midcentury, race and deviance went hand in hand. In their marketing of a suburban alternative to urban blight, real estate agents likened blacks to the city's deviants: bootleggers, madams, call girls, and gangsters. But within their definition of "blight," the racial distinctions between black people and white deviants disappear. To real estate agents and presumably their white clientele, blacks are akin to the white criminals who reside within the noir city: all are equally undesirable as neighbors.

Film noir deploys a similar discourse. In the noir city, white criminality and black identity are mutually constitutive. The morally corrupt white folks who inhabit the noir city, for example, often are viewed alongside black service workers—servants, custodians, garage attendants, shoe shine boys, Pullman porters, and jazz musicians—suggesting their ease within the city's black underworld. In *Double Indemnity*, for example, arguably the quintessential film noir, Walter Neff depends on a colored woman to look after him. After he executes his plans for murder, he relies on the black janitor of his apartment building for an airtight alibi. Throughout his many crimes, Neff's whiteness is compromised by his conspicuous position alongside African Americans. Moreover, noir's innovative and masterful use of light and shadow reinforced the symbolic blackening of white deviants. Darkness pervades the noir screen, always encroaching on the sources of light within the frame. Noir's deviants often are mired in blackened cinematic compositions as if to illuminate their corrupt souls. Throughout *He Walked by Night*, for example, the face of a violent psychopath, never seen in its totality, is marred by dark shadows, reinforcing the black connotations of white criminality.[19]

As film noir coincided with a general retreat from the blackening spaces of industrial urbanism, the genre honed in on those spaces that sanctioned racial and ethnic transgression. The nightclub and its exotic music offer a quintessential noir setting where the boundaries between whiteness and blackness blur. In *Criss Cross*, Steve Thompson wanders through downtown Los Angeles, stumbling into "the old club," where he is hypnotized by the haunting music of Esy Morales and his Rumba Band. There, Thompson reignites a relationship with an old flame that leads him to his demise. In *D.O.A.*, as Frank Bigelow sacrifices his engagement by swinging with "jive crazy" women in a San Francisco nightclub, the camera focuses tightly on the black face of a trumpeter, reinforcing the racialized milieu of urban nightlife. And in *T-Men*, as two undercover agents from the treasury department venture into a Chinatown nightclub to pursue a mob moll who fancies silk kimonos and fastens tiger lilies to her hair, a vaguely Asian music enhances the mood of mystery and danger. The nightclub, a prominent cultural institution of the Swing Era that sanctioned racial intermingling, figured prominently with noir's portrait of urban malaise.[20]

Ultimately, film noir identified a crisis of white masculinity at the outset of the postwar period, but the spatial context of that crisis demands an awareness of how filmmakers and their audiences at midcentury shared a perception of the modern city as a detriment to traditional models of social order. Noir's parade of "weak men," rendered so memorably by the acting of Fred MacMurray, Robert Mitchum, and Burt Lancaster, underscored the destabilization of the white male identity within the topsy-turvy world of the modern city. Duped by conniving women at every turn and mired within the shadows of the black city, noir's white male antiheroes met their demise within the culture of urban modernity. As many Americans craved some semblance of normalcy after the social turmoil of depression and war, and as they satisfied that yearning by removing themselves, physically, from the racialized spaces of the new mass culture, film noir prefigured the need for a "new" new mass culture, one that offered an alternative to the modern city and its degraded culture.

Disneyland and the "New" New Mass Culture of Postwar America

Recent scholarship emphasizes the degree to which black urbanization and white suburbanization belonged to a larger set of social, economic, and political processes that enabled the transition from the centralized metropolis to the decentralized urban region. For this reason, popular culture in the age of white flight included a suburban antithesis to its noir vision of urban life. If film noir dramatized the degraded condition of the black city, Disneyland premiered the cultural mythography of suburban whiteness. Arguably the preeminent cultural impresario of postwar America, Walt Disney took deliberate steps to model his theme park as the very antithesis of its New York predecessor, Coney Island. In its proximity to freeways, its highly disciplined ordering of space, its validation of patriarchy and the nuclear family, and its thematic emphasis on racial distinctions, Disneyland provided a spatial articulation of a new suburban ethos that millions of Americans adopted in their claim to home ownership after World War II.

Disney's decision to locate his new theme park in Orange County, California, underscores the significance of that region to the shifting basis of cultural capital in postwar America. Whereas Detroit suffered the most severe effects of the postwar urban crisis, Orange County profited handsomely from the westward migration of federal defense expenditures during the cold war. In the decades following World War II, the region sheltered the development of a vast military industrial complex that for decades provided Orange County's main source of income. The growth of a regional defense industry, in turn, spurred suburban development, as ranchers turned property developers and real estate speculators marketed affordable, suburban tract housing units for an expanding middle-class population. Orange County's expansion during the postwar period was nothing short of spectacular. While in 1940, 130,760 people made their homes in Orange County, that total reached nearly 1.5 million by 1970.[21]

The very newness of Orange County's suburban communities created a cultural space for the resurrection of traditional social values that seemed to dissipate within the promiscuous spaces of the noir city. Removed from Southern California's dominant urban center and far distant from the cosmopolitan culture of eastern cities, Orange County fostered a distinctive political identity that increasingly appealed to groups of Americans disaffected from decades of New Deal liberalism. In a region sustained by a militarized economy, a staunch nationalism and a rigid defense of the American way took shape against the presence of un-American outsiders, whereas the privatized nature of suburban growth in the region nurtured a homegrown appreciation for the values of privacy, individualism, and property rights. The region's remarkable social homogeneity, moreover, coddled an antipathy toward the expansion of a collectivist welfare state and a repudiation of federal interventions on behalf of civil rights activists and other special interest groups. By the 1960s, Orange County sheltered a conservative populism that catapulted New Right ideologues such as Ronald Reagan into California's and ultimately, the nation's, highest public office. With 72 percent of its electorate voting for Reagan in California's 1966 gubernatorial election, Orange County first emerged as "Reagan Country" toward the end of the postwar period.[22]

Orange County sustained a political culture amenable for not only Reagan's postwar metamorphosis from a crusader for the New Deal to an ideologue of the New Right but also Walt Disney's foray into other cultural enterprises besides filmmaking. In fact, as if to underscore the ideological affinities between the two men, Reagan "starred" at the opening ceremonies of Disneyland held on June 17, 1955. Both Reagan and Disney emerged as men of their time, embracing a set of values that resonated with an expanding middle class who sought refuge from the disordered culture of the modern city within the well-ordered landscapes of suburbia. Not unlike Reagan, Disney underwent a political transformation during the cold war, in which his hostility grew toward those groups whose gains during an era of New Deal reform threatened to undermine the postwar prospects for resurrecting the American way: intellectuals, racial and ethnic groups, labor unions, and, most of all, Communists. After an embittering experience with labor unions during the war years and at the height of cold war anxiety, Disney retreated into a vision of a homogeneous WASP folk who for him embodied the traditional values of hard work, rugged individualism, tightly knit families, and traditional gender roles. Such values inspired the basis for not only a spate of Disney films including *Davy Crockett, Swiss Family Robinson*, and *Pollyanna* but also the creation of Disneyland.[23]

As postwar Americans withdrew from the racialized spaces of the modern city, Disney labored to create a cultural alternative to its noir culture. The war years left Walt Disney Productions in financial disarray, prompting company executives to seek alternate venues in which to market Disney products. Following his foray into television, Disney began to think seriously about the creation of an amusement park, and he expressed the "need for something new" but admitted that he "didn't know what it was." He was clear, however, about his aversion toward that paragon of urban industrial culture: Coney Island. The showman once remarked that Coney Island and its generation of amusement parks were "dirty, phoney places run by tough looking people." After visiting a dilapidated Coney Island in the course of planning Disneyland in the mid-1950s, Disney recoiled from "its tawdry rides and hostile employees." Subsequent admirers of Disneyland affirmed Disney's indictment of Coney Island. *New York Times* reporter Gladwin Hill asserted that Disneyland marked a departure from "the traditionally raucous and oft times shoddy amusement park," delighting in the fact that Disneyland eliminated the "ballyhoo men to assault [the visitor's] ears with exhortations to test his strength, skill, courage, digestion or gawk at freaks or cootch dancers."[24]

Disney repudiated the slick cynicism of the noir city and sought to restore the innocence and wonder that seemed lost on generations of urban Americans. Raised by a strict father who cautioned against the "corruptive influences of a big city," Disney remained suspicious of modern urban culture throughout his life. His disdain for New York City, for example, became public after the success of Disneyland. When asked by a reporter to consider New York as the site for a second theme park, he dismissed that suggestion in large part because he doubted the capacity of New Yorkers to embrace the Disney worldview.[25] "He said that audience is not responsive," recalled Disneyland's chief architect and Disney's close associate, John Hench, "that city is different." Hench also elaborated on Disney's conviction that urban modernity preyed on the moral conscience of Americans:

> In modern cities you have to defend yourself constantly and you go counter to everything that we've learned from the past. You tend to isolate yourself from other people . . . you tend to be less aware. You tend to be more withdrawn. This is counter life . . . you really die a little . . . . I think we need something to counteract what modern society—cities—have done to us.[26]

Having to "defend yourself constantly" became a hallmark experience of the noir city, especially at places like Coney Island, where women, particularly unescorted women, were forced into a defensive posture against the unwanted advances of lustful men. As Kathy Peiss discovered in her study of working women and popular amusements in New York at the turn of the century, the typical shopgirl at Coney Island was "keen and knowing, ever on the defensive . . . she distrusts cavaliers not of her own station."[27]

Disney deplored modernity's sacrifice of innocent virtue. The average citizen, he once remarked, "is a victim of civilization whose ideal is the unbotherable, poker-faced man and the attractive, unruffled woman." Disney's revulsion toward the poker-faced man and the unruffled woman echoed earlier cultural anxieties about "confidence men" and "painted women" in antebellum America. Much like the trickster figure of various folk cultures, the confidence man was the seducer who preyed on the naïveté of the strangers, particularly women, for self-aggrandizement. The confidence man, however, unlike the trickster, owed his existence to the modern city in the first half of the nineteenth century, where individuals could lay claim to new and higher social status through deceit and manipulation. In her study of middle-class culture in nineteenth-century America, Karen Haltunnen located cultural anxieties about confidence men and painted women within the rapid expansion of the city and its ambiguous social milieu. "Hypocrisy," the art of deceit and manipulation mastered by the confidence man, "paid off in an urban environment." Though removed from the historical context in which middle-class moralists denounced the rise of confidence men and painted women, Disney, in his critique of phony amusement parks, poker-faced men, and unruffled women, shared a similar antipathy toward the hypocrisy and deception that defined social relations in the urban world of strangers.[28]

To combat the dissonance and heterosociality of the noir city, Disneyland presented a counterculture of visual order, spatial regimentation, and social homogeneity. Reacting against what Disney criticized as the "diffuse, unintegrated layout" of Coney Island, the park's designers sought to maximize control over the movement of the crowd through the meticulous organization of space. Whereas Coney Island had multiple entrances and exits, Disneyland offered only one path by which visitors could come and go. Upon entering the park, visitors began their day in Main Street, USA, a central corridor built as a replication of a small-town commercial thoroughfare that channeled pedestrians toward the central hub of the park, "from which the other lands radiate out like spokes in a wheel"—Tomorrowland, Fantasyland, Frontierland, and Adventureland. The spatial organization of Disneyland reflected the designers' intentions to direct the continual movement of people with as little indecision as possible. "Each land is easy to enter and easy to exit," asserted one Disney official in a speech to the Urban Land Institute, a national organization of urban developers, "because everything leads back to the central hub again. The result is a revelation to anyone who has ever experienced the disorientation and confusion built into world's fairs and other expositions."[29]

Disneyland's location alongside the Interstate 5 freeway, moreover, underscored the degree to which park designers situated Disneyland within the burgeoning spatial order of the postwar urban region. As Southern California garnered state and federal monies toward highway construction during the 1950s, freeways increasingly dictated regional patterns of development. Following the advice of the Stanford Research Institute—a think tank promoting industrial development in California—Disney strategically situated his theme park alongside the proposed route of Santa Ana freeway and built what was the largest parking lot in the nation at the time. So vital was the freeway to the success of Disneyland that it earned a permanent place inside the park. Among the thirteen original attractions included in the park's opening in 1955, the Autopia Ride in Tomorrowland was a "real model freeway," not unlike the "motorways of the world of tomorrow" that highlighted the "Futurama" exhibit of the 1939 New York World's Fair. Situated between a rocket-ship ride and the "Voyage to the Moon" attraction, the Autopia Ride demonstrated Disney's optimistic vision of the future and how freeways constituted an integral part of that vision. Like almost every other attraction within the park, and very much unlike the titillating sensations of Coney Island rides, the Autopia Ride had a didactic function, "constructed to acquaint youngsters with traffic conditions on the highways of tomorrow."[30]

The location and layout of Disneyland reflected a larger spatial culture that took shape within the myriad suburban communities that sprouted across the terrain of the decentralized urban region. Lakewood, (figure 6.1) for example, emerged alongside Disneyland in the early 1950s, and it reflected the intense preoccupation with order that followed the heyday of the noir city. Like the designers of Disneyland, the builders of Lakewood positioned their development in between the proposed routes for two major freeways and incorporated the principles of efficiency, uniformity, and predictability into its design. Typical of postwar suburban development, Lakewood was built on the grid system, a fraction of a larger grid on which Southern California's decentralized urban region took shape. At the center of Lakewood's grid stood Lakewood Center, an outdoor pedestrian mall featuring one hundred retail shops and a major department store. Similar to the way in which the designers of Disneyland organized space to exert maximum control over the vision and movement of the crowd, the architects of Lakewood Center implemented a rigid spatial order to create a self-contained environment dedicated wholly to consumption.[31]

Figure 6.1 Visiting Model Homes in Lakewood, ca. 1951. Potential buyers of Lakewood's tract houses walked through a street of model homes, furnished by local retailers, on their way to the Lakewood Park sales office. Tens of thousands of aspirant, working-class husbands and wives passed through the model houses on weekends in 1950 and 1951.

Source: City of Lakewood Historical Collection.

Lakewood also implemented a set of innovations in municipal government that effected a more homogeneous social environment. In 1954, the developers of Lakewood struck a deal with the county of Los Angeles. For minimal costs, Los Angeles County would provide vital services (fire, police, library) to Lakewood, which incorporated as an independent municipality. Contracting services from county government without submitting to its authority, the citizens of Lakewood escaped the burden of supporting county government and enjoyed a greater degree of control over the social composition of their community. "Local control" became a mantra among suburban Southern Californians, whose widespread use of the Lakewood Plan minimized the kind of racial heterogeneity that characterized the modern city and its culture. Given the degree to which the Lakewood Plan effected racial segregation within the context of Southern California's increasingly diverse urban region, one policy expert concluded, "The Lakewood Plan cities were essentially white political movements."[32]

If the Lakewood Plan enforced a literal distance between white and nonwhite people within the postwar urban region, Disneyland underscored that development by asserting a figurative distinction between suburban whiteness and racial otherness. Race and racial difference figured prominently among Disneyland's many themes. Frontierland, for example, described by publicity materials as "a land of hostile Indians and straight shooting pioneers," featured Indians among its main attractions. There one also could find Aunt Jemima's Pancake House, a recreation of a southern plantation where an African American woman, dressed as "Aunt Jemima did . . . on the plantation . . . was on hand everyday to welcome visitors warmly." Aside from featuring a southern mammie, Disneyland included other stereotypes of African Americans. Adventureland, for example, beckoned visitors to "the sound of native chants and tom-tom drums," where the Jungle Cruise attraction featured "wild animals and native savages [that] attack your craft as it cruises through their jungle privacy."[33]

The racial dimensions of the Disneyland experience surfaced not only in those places of the park where images of blacks and Indians prevailed but also where such images did not appear. Main Street, USA, promoted as "everybody's hometown," and "the heartline of America," reiterated Disney's populist idealization of a WASP folk. Richard Hofstader noted in the *Age of Reform* the latent xenophobia within the populist sensibility, which, although seeking to maintain "the primary contacts of country and village life" also cherished a vision of "an ethnically more homogeneous nation." That vision guided the design of Main Street, USA, where the absence of mammies, Indians, and savages reified Disney's racialized and deeply nostalgic vision of the American "folk." The exclusion of African Americans and their history from the representational landscape of Main Street was most glaring in the "Great Moments with Mr. Lincoln" exhibit, which debuted in Disneyland in 1966. The "Audio Animatronic" Lincoln recited a speech designed to elicit patriotic sentimentality, although making no mention of such divisive conflicts as slavery or the Civil War.[34]

The point here is not to elicit scorn or indignation but rather to understand such racialized representations within their spatial and historical context. White Americans have long maintained a fascination with race and its representation in popular culture, but the contours of race relations had changed significantly in postwar America. After World War II, which brought unprecedented levels of racial cohabitation in American cities, a new generation of white Americans, or at least those who qualified themselves as such, looked to the decentralized urban region as a place that could maintain separate and not necessarily equal communities. In the aftermath of the Supreme Court's 1948 ruling against racially restrictive covenants in *Shelley vs. Kraemer*, and amidst an explosion of civil rights activism, cultural stereotypes of nonwhite racial groups affirmed the racial distinctions that seemed to dissipate within the politically charged climate of a nascent civil rights era. Disneyland, removed from the "darker" shades of the inner city in Orange County yet permeated with representations of racial difference, provided a space where white Southern Californians could reaffirm their whiteness against the fictions of the racial other.[35] Given the battles that Southern California's white home owners subsequently waged against such public initiatives as fair housing, busing, and affirmative action, it is not difficult to comprehend how Disneyland's racial representations prefigured the racial underpinnings of a white suburban identity.

If the presence of Aunt Jemima at Disneyland signaled the subordinate position of blacks within Disney's vision of social order, it also symbolized the subservient position of women in that order as well. Disneyland's delineation of a social order appropriate to the tastes and values of an expanding suburban middle class included an emphasis on patriarchal social relations and the centrality of the nuclear family.[36] Suburbanization provided a setting in which postwar Americans could confront their anxieties about the changing position of women in American society, seeking comfort in cultural representations of domesticated housewives and stable nuclear families. Disney's effort to position the "typical family of four" at the center of the Disneyland experience signaled yet another departure from amusement parks of Coney Island's generation. The *New York Times*, for example, described Disneyland "not as a place where anyone would casually go to take a roller coaster ride or buy a hot dog, but as the goal of a family adventure."[37]

Paradoxically, it was in that section of the theme park touted as a "show world of the future" where park designers chose to insert a traditional vision of gender roles. Tomorrowland featured as its centerpiece the "Monsanto House of the Future," which invited park visitors to preview "how the typical American family of four will live in ten years from now." When the house opened to the public on June 12, 1957, models Helen Bernhart and John Marion acted the part of the model couple at home. Photographs depicted the husband relaxing in the "psychiatric chair," which afforded "therapeutic relief after a hard day at the office," with his aproned wife standing in the "Atoms for Living Kitchen." Adhering to the reigning vision family life in postwar America, the interior space of the House of the Future was divided according to the individual needs of family members. The home's cruciform plan ensured "added privacy for various family activities," separating the children's room from the master bedroom. A step-saver kitchen opened onto the family-dining room, an arrangement "convenient and perfect for party entertainment." As postwar Americans looked to suburban home ownership as means of restoring some sense of normalcy, Disneyland's House of the Future depicted a futuristic setting where women could return to traditional gender roles.[38]

Moreover, the emphasis on domesticity and private life at Disneyland signaled a shifting cultural focus away from the urban spaces of working-class culture and toward the suburban spaces of middle-class home ownership. In the modern city of the nineteenth and early twentieth centuries, private life belonged to those privileged enough to enjoy the comforts of a townhouse, a carriage, or a private club, whereas the city's working class crowded within the congested spaces of tenements houses, streetcars, and entertainment venues. In the postwar urban region, as greater numbers of Americans attained suburban home ownership through a generous set of public policies, the focus of American popular culture, as Disneyland demonstrated, gradually shifted away from the public venues of the noir city to the private spaces of the home. Thus the park's emphasis on familial domesticity reflected not only a desire to return to traditional gender roles but also a more general valorization of private life that appealed to growing numbers of Americans who entered, or at least aspired to, the ranks of the middle class after World War II.

Disneyland is a complex cultural phenomenon, and there are other aspects of the theme park that underscore its significance to the transformation of urban culture and society at midcentury. Nonetheless, when viewed comparatively alongside simultaneous cultural developments, the theme park illustrates a broader cultural transformation that accompanied the changing configuration of the postwar American city. In its spatial organization, as well as in its thematic emphases, Disneyland asserted a repudiation of the noir sensibility that captivated the American public at the outset of the postwar period. By the mid-1950s, as the heyday of film noir began to wane, a new set of film genres won favor with the public—science fiction, musicals, westerns—that not only upheld traditional models of social order but also delivered the kind of happy endings that were absent from film noir. Disneyland appeared at this cultural moment, delivering its own happy ending to the midcentury transformation of urban life, at least for those who acquired the privileges and comforts of suburban home ownership. As film noir rendered its obituary for the modern city and its new mass culture, Disneyland heralded a new spatial culture that stressed order without complexity, pleasure without danger, and sociability without diversity.

The new suburban cultural order exhibited in film noir and at Disneyland also included other cultural institutions. Television's ascendance as a dominant cultural medium during the 1950s lowered the curtain on the grand movie palaces of the nation's inner cities and rendered the experience of going out on the town an inconvenient waste of time. Suburban shopping malls similarly offered a car-friendly alternative to the downtown department store, where the dire shortage of parking repelled a generation of Americans increasingly wedded to their automobiles. Freeways emerged on top of defunct streetcar lines, introducing a more privatized means of moving rapidly through urban space. The interior settings of the "new" new mass culture provided that very refuge that film noir dramatized a necessity for. Its disciplined, contained, and detached spaces removed consumers from the public realm of decaying cities and modeled idealizations of a new cultural order that captivated a new generation of home owners eager to create their own suburban retreat from the noir city.[39]

These idealizations, moreover, delivered more than mere entertainment. They also provided a blueprint for a nascent political subjectivity that surfaced in places like Southern California during the 1960s, where a new conservative idealism took shape that aimed to restore traditional patterns of racial and gendered relations. No one better personified that new subjectivity than Ronald Reagan, who championed such principles as property rights, private enterprise, law and order, family values, and small government in his political metamorphosis from New Deal Democrat to New Right Republican. Well attuned to the dawning sensibilities of an expanding suburban public, and affiliating himself with the spectacles of the "new" new mass culture Reagan fashioned a new political agenda by channeling the values hovering within the larger culture. Film noir, fixated on the disordered culture of the black city, corroborated Reagan's claim in the aftermath of Los Angeles's Watts riots that the urban "jungle is waiting to take over" white suburban communities, whereas Disneyland modeled the very order that his core constituency aspired to.[40] Both cultural productions articulated a deep-seated hostility to urban modernity, both stressed a return to traditional patterns of social order, and both pandered to the political aspirations of an emerging silent majority that retreated from the public culture of the noir city into the private realm of suburban home ownership. Popular culture in the age of white flight thus exposes the linkages between structure and culture during the post–World War II period. Disneyland, like film noir, owed its existence to the very real transformations that wrought new patterns of urban life in postwar America. Disneyland's calculated proximity to new freeways and its suburban location underscored the park's anticipation of accelerated patterns of decentralized development, whereas film noir refined its techniques of on-location shooting to capture an authentic portrait of urban malaise. In their vital relationship to the postwar transformation of the American city—and it is well to remember that that process happened not simply through the collusion of unseen, abstract social forces but rather through the very conscious efforts of developers, planners, policy makers, and home owners—film noir and Disneyland codified the anxieties and ambitions, as well as the perceptions and assumptions, widely shared by a public who abandoned their cities for suburban jobs and housing. Their relationship to the postwar emergence of "chocolate cities and vanilla suburbs" was neither incidental nor merely reflective. In modeling popular aspirations toward a new sociospatial order, popular culture in the age of white flight thus enabled the very realization of that order.

The cultural history of the American city illuminates how previous generations of Americans have imagined city form, social order, and the proper relations between the two. Urban imaginings are indeed slippery subjects for the historian to grasp, but popular idealizations of urban life often shape the very real process of making cities. Daniel Burnham's *White City*, for example, which debuted so triumphantly at Chicago's Columbian Exposition in 1893, inspired a generation of urban planners who brought the classical imagery of the Beaux Arts style to bear on the landscape of the American city at the turn of the century. And for better or for worse, few can doubt the impact Disneyland has had on the contours of contemporary urbanism in the United States. Urban cultural history provides a window onto the urban mythography of the past and present—that catalog of simulations and hallucinations that contain our deep-seated fantasies and anxieties about the metropolis and its place in American society.[41]

Notes

Eric Avila is a cultural historian, studying the historical relationship between urban space, social identity, and cultural representation. His book *Popular Culture in the Age of the White Flight: Suburbanism and Postwar Los Angeles* (University of California Press, 2004) traces the post–World War II formation of a white suburban identity within the landscapes of popular culture in postwar Los Angeles. Currently he is an assistant professor of Chicano studies and history at the University of California, Los Angeles. Recent publications include *The Chicano Studies Reader: Anthology of* Azlatán, *1970–2000* (coedited with Chon Noriega, Chela Sandoval, Rafael Pérez Torres, and Karen Mary Dávalos); "Dark City: White Flight and Urban Space Fiction Film in Postwar America," in *Classic Whiteness: Race and Holluwood Studio System*, ed. Daniel Benardi (University of Minnesota Press, 2002); and "The Folklore of Freeway: Space, Identity and Culture in Postwar Los Angeles," *Azlatán: A Journal of Chicano Studies*, 23 no. 1 (1998).

1. Sam Bass Warner, *Streetcar Suburbs: The Process of Growth in Boston, 1870–1900* (Cambridge, MA: Harvard University Press, 1962); Kenneth Jackson, *Crabgrass Frontier: The Suburbanization of the United States* (New York: Oxford University Press, 1985); Mark I. Gelfand, *A Nation of Cities: The Federal Government and Urban America, 1933–1965* (New York: Oxford University Press, 1975); Carl Abbot, *The Metropolitan Frontier: Cities in the Modern American West* (Tucson: University of Arizona Press, 1993); and Thomas Sugrue, *The Origins of the Urban Crisis: Race and Inequality in Postwar Detroit* (Princeton, NJ: Princeton University Press, 1996).
2. The heightened racial consciousness of postwar America, though typically associated with African Americans and the civil rights struggles of racialized minority groups, also encompassed a new generation of white suburban home owners who defended their interests in racial terms. Becky Nicolaides, for example, argues that suburban

home owners, "grasping willfully for middle class lives in a town with working-class roots," evoked "the language of white rights" to offset racial encroachment by the early 1960s. Similarly, Lisa McGirr locates the origins of a conservative populism in Orange County, which asserted a white backlash to the civil rights gains won by African Americans and other racialized minorities. See Becky Nicolaides, *My Blue Heaven: Life and Politics in the Working Class Suburbs of Los Angeles, 1920–1965* (Chicago: University of Chicago Press, 2002); and Lisa McGirr, *Suburban Warriors: The Origins of the New American Right* (Princeton, NJ: Princeton University Press, 2001). Other social historians recognize the national bases by which racial and gender division attained greater recognition. See Thomas J. Sugrue, "Crabgrass–Roots Politics: Race, Rights, and the Reaction against Liberalism in the Urban North, 1940–1964," *Journal of American History* (September 1995): 551–78; Nelson Lichtenstein, "From Corporatism to Collective Bargaining: Organized Labor and the Eclipse of Social Democracy in the Postwar Era" in *The Rise and Fall of the New Deal Order, 1930–1980*, ed. Steve Fraser and Gary Gerstle (Princeton, NJ: Princeton University Press, 1989); Jonathan Reider, "The Rise of the 'Silent Majority,' " in *The Rise and Fall of the New Deal Order, 1930–1980*; and Elaine Tyler May, *Homeward Bound: American Families in the Cold War Era* (New York: Basic Books, 1988).

3. On postwar urbanization and racial segregation, see Michael N. Danielson, *The Politics of Exclusion* (New York: Columbia University Press, 1976); Douglas Massey and Nancy Denton, *American Apartheid: Segregation and the Making of an Underclass* (Cambridge, MA: Harvard University Press, 1993); Arnold Hirsch, *Making the Second Ghetto: Race and Housing in Chicago, 1940–1980* (Chicago: University of Chicago Press, 1998); and Thomas J. Sugrue, *The Origins of the Urban Crisis: Race and Inequality in Postwar Detroit* (Princeton, NJ: Princeton University Press, 1996). For a contrast between the role of women within a changing urban context, see Kathy Peiss, *Cheap Amusements: Working Women and Leisure in Turn of the Century New York* (Philadelphia: Temple University Press, 1986); and May, *Homeward Bound*.
4. To a certain extent, this new cultural order provides the focus of John Findlay's rigorous study *Magic Lands*. Although Findlay identifies the distinct spatial character of postwar culture and its relationship to new modes of urbanization in the Far West, his analysis does not emphasize the dynamics of race, class, and gender embedded within these cultural forms and their significance to the shifting (geographic and ideological) bases of national political power. See John M. Findlay, *Magic Lands: Western Cityscapes and American Culture after 1940* (Berkeley: University of California Press, 1992).
5. Frederic Jameson deployed the term "political unconscious" to describe the political meanings embedding within literary forms. Subsequently, the term has been applied to other cultural forms. See Frederic Jameson, *The Political Unconscious: Narrative as a Socially Symbolic Act* (Ithaca, NY: Cornell University Press, 1981). For the relationship between postwar popular culture and the formation of a new white suburban identity, see Eric Avila, *Popular Culture in the Age of White Flight: Suburbanism in Postwar Los Angeles* (University of California Press, 2004).
6. John Kasson identifies Coney Island as exemplifying the new mass culture that emerged within the context of industrial urbanization and Kathy Peiss describes the "heterosocial" nature of urban popular culture at the turn of the century, emphasizing the role of women within that culture. See John Kasson, *Amusing the Million: Coney Island at the Turn of the Century* (New York: Hill and Wang, 1978); and Peiss, *Cheap Amusements*. Other scholars who have surveyed the history of the new mass culture include David Nasaw, *Going Out: The Rise and Fall of Public Amusements* (New York: Basic Books, 1993); Gunther Barth, *City People: The Rise of Modern City*

Culture in Nineteenth Century America (New York: Oxford University Press, 1982); Neil Harris, *Cultural Excursions: Marketing Appetites and Cultural Tastes in Modern America* (Chicago: University of Chicago Press, 1990); Lawrence Levine, *Highbrow/Lowbrow: The Emergence of Cultural Hierarchy in America* (Cambridge, MA: Harvard University Press, 1988); Timothy J. Gilfolye, *City of Eros: New York City, Prostitution and the Commercialization of Sex, 1790–1920* (New York: Norton, 1992); George Chauncey, *Gay New York: Gender, Urban Culture, and the Making of the Gay Male World, 1890–1940* (New York: Basic Books, 1994); and Karen Haltunnen, *Confidence Men and Painted Ladies: A Study of Middle Class Culture in America, 1830–1870* (New Haven, CT: Yale University Press, 1982).

7. Sugrue, *The Origins of the Postwar Urban Crisis*, 127–30.
8. Howard Chudacoff and Judith Smith, *The Evolution of American Urban Society*, 5th ed. (Upper Saddle River, NJ: Prentice Hall, 2000), 263–67; John Teaford, *The Twentieth Century American City*, 2nd ed. (Baltimore: Johns Hopkins, 1993), 94–95.
9. The terms "chocolate city" and "vanilla suburbs" are taken from George Clinton, leader of the outrageous funk ensemble, Parliament, which issued its hit "Chocolate City" on Casablanca Records in 1975. The song celebrates black political power in American cities, describing black urbanization as a takeover of the nation's cities. In contrast to the disparaging and often dehumanizing portraits of the racialized inner city issued by the nation's leading social scientists, "Chocolate City" asserts the strength of the black ghetto as a bulwark against the hostility of a racist society. Subsequently, the geographer Reynolds Farley used the term "chocolate city" to frame his account of racial segregation within urban America. See Reynolds Farley, Howard Schuman, Suzanne Bianchi, Diane Colasanto, and Shirley Hatchett, " 'Chocolate City, Vanilla Suburbs': Will the Trend toward Racially Separate Communities Continue?" *Social Science Research* 7 (1978): 319–44; and William H. Frey, "Central City White Flight: Racial and Nonracial Causes," *American Sociological Review* 44 (1979): 425–48. On the racial barriers built into postwar suburbanization, see Kenneth T. Jackson, "Race, Ethnicity, and Real Estate Appraisal: The Home Owners Loan Corporation and the Federal Housing Administration," *Journal of Urban History* 6 (1980): 419–52. See also Melvin L. Oliver and Thomas M. Shapiro, *Black Wealth/White Wealth: A New Perspective on Racial Inequality* (New York: Routledge, 1995), 15–18; George Lipsitz, *The Possessive Investment in Whiteness: How White People Profit from Identity Politics* (Philadelphia: Temple University Press, 1998), 5–7.
10. "Coney Island Slump Grows Worse," *The New York Times*, July 2, 1964, 1.
11. *Chicago Tribune Magazine*, May 16, 1976.
12. Quoted in David Nasaw, *Going Out: The Rise and Fall of Public Amusements* (New York: Basic Books, 1993), 252. For a more in-depth analysis of the fate of Shibe Park, see Bruce Kuklick, *To Everything a Season: Shibe Park and Urban Philadelphia, 1909–1976* (Princeton, NJ: Princeton University Press, 1991).
13. Peter Golenbock, *An Oral History of the Brooklyn Dodgers* (New York: Putnam, 1984), 38.
14. The literature on film noir is extensive and growing. Foster Hirsch, *Film Noir: The Dark Side of the Screen* (New York: Da Capo, 1981); Paul Schrader, "Notes on Film Noir," in *Film Noir: A Reader*, ed. Alain Silver and James Ursini (New York: Limelight Editions, 1997), 53–64; A. M. Karimi, *Toward a Definition of the American Film Noir (1941–1949)* (New York: Arno, 1976); Alain Silver and Elizabeth Ward, eds., *Film Noir: An Encyclopedic Reference to the American Style* (New York: Overlook Press, 1979); Spencer Selby, *Dark City: The Film Noir* (Jefferson, NC: McFarland, 1984); James Naremore, *More Than Night: Film Noir in*

Its Contexts (Berkeley: University of California, 1998); and Frank Krutnik, *In a Lonely Street: Film Noir, Genre, Masculinity* (London: Routledge, 1991).

15. Foster Hirsch, *Film Noir: The Dark Side of the Screen*, 82.
16. American Social History Project, *Who Built America? Working People and the Nation's Economy, Politics, Culture and Society, Volume Two: From the Gilded Age to the Present* (New York: Pantheon Books, 1992), 457.
17. Hirsch, *The Dark Side of the Screen*, 152–57; and May, *Homeward Bound*, 62–63.
18. Quoted in Arnold R. Hirsch, "With or without Jim Crow: Black Residential Segregation in the United States," in *Urban Policy in Twentieth Century America*, ed. Arnold R. Hirsch and Raymond A. Mohl (New Brunswick, NJ: Rutgers University Press, 1993), 75.
19. Eric Lott, "The Whiteness of Film Noir," in *Whiteness: A Critical Reader*, ed. Mike Hill (New York: New York University Press, 1997), 93–94. Lott draws on the work of film historian and critic Richard Dyer, who argues that film noir is part of a broader "culture of light" in the West, in which light and dark are invested with social meanings. In a racialized democracy that values "white over black," to borrow Winthrop Jordan's famous characterization of Anglo-American social values, the delineation of light in the representation of the social world is structured by racial hierarchies that place amoral premium on whiteness and light. The cinematic combination of white skin and light evoke ethical connotations that associate whiteness with moral purity and spiritual hygiene and, conversely, the absence of light, or the abundance of shadows, conveys a denigrated state of moral ambiguity. Within the history of portraiture, photography, film, and other aspects of Western visual culture, the uses of light speak not only to Western notions of the racial other but also to the West's conception of itself. See Richard Dyer, *White* (London: Routledge, 1997).
20. On the jazz and the urban nightclub, see Louis Erenberg, *Swingin' the Dream: Big Band Jazz and the Rebirth of American Culture* (Chicago: University of Chicago Press, 1998).
21. Security First National Bank, *The Growth and Economic Stature of Orange County*, May 1967, 12–15.
22. McGirr, *Suburban Warriors*, 209.
23. Richard Schickel, *The Disney Version: The Life, Times, Art and Commerce of Walt Disney* (Chicago: Ivan R. Dee, 1997); and Stephen Watts, "Walt Disney: Art and Politics in the American Century," *Journal of American History* 100, no. 2 (1995): 84–110.
24. Schickel, *The Disney Version*, 310; *The New York Times*, February 2, 1958; "The Never-Never Land Khrushchev Never Saw," *The New York Times*, October 4, 1959, 22.
25. Schickel, *The Disney Version*, 47.
26. John Hench, interview by Jay Horan, December 3, 1982, transcript, Walt Disney Archives, Burbank, CA.
27. Quoted in Peiss, *Cheap Amusements*, 127.
28. "The Wisdom of Walt Disney," *Wisdom* 32 (December 1959): 77; and Haltunnen, *Confidence Men and Painted Women*, 192–93.
29. "Disney's 'Magical Little Park' after Two Decades," *Los Angeles Times*, July 6, 1975, pt. 10, p. 1; Carl Walker, speech to Urban Land Institute, October 5, 1975, quoted in Findlay, *Magic Lands*, 84.
30. *Disneyland News*, n.d., Regional History Archives, Anaheim Public Library.
31. Richard Longstreth, *From City Center to Regional Mall: Architecture, the Automobile and Retailing in Los Angeles, 1920–1950* (Cambridge, MA: MIT Press, 1997), 336–40.

32. Gary Miller, *Cities by Contract: The Politics of Municipal Incorporation* (Cambridge, MA: MIT Press, 1981), 135; and Mike Davis, *City of Quartz: Excavating the Future in Los Angeles* (New York: Vintage, 1992), 165–69.
33. *News from Disneyland*, Walt Disney Productions 1965, Anaheim History Room—Anaheim Public Library; *Disneyland News*, August 7, 1956; *News from Disneyland*, n.d., Public Relations Division, Disneyland, Inc., Anaheim History Room—Anaheim Public Library.
34. Hofstadter, quoted in Stephen Watts, "Walt Disney: Art and Politics in the American Century," 97; and "Moving Right Along: Disneyland Grows Ever More Sophisticated," *Los Angeles Times Magazine*, July 13, 1986, 8. Text of speech from "Great Moments with Mr. Lincoln," Anaheim History Room—Anaheim Public Library.
35. Disneyland's symbolic delineation of racial hierarchy suited cold war conceptions of racial difference. By contrast, when the City of Los Angeles commissioned local artist Bernard Rosenthal to create a sculpture for the new downtown police department building, the resulting piece incited a local uproar among conservative groups. Rosenthal's piece—titled *The Family*—depicted human figures without a specific racial character. The racial vagueness of Rosenthal's figures led one public official to denounce *The Family* as a "shameless, soulless, faceless, raceless, gutless monstrosity that will live in infamy." In Los Angeles, abstract art aroused intense opposition among cold warriors for its subversive potential, but humanistic representations of racial ambiguity also aroused considerable protest. See Sarah Schrank, "Art and the City: The Transformation of Civic Culture in Los Angeles, 1900–1965," (Ph.D. diss., Department of History, University of California, San Diego, 2002).
36. May, *Homeward Bound*, 3–15.
37. *The New York Times*, February 2, 1958, sec. 2, pt. 2, p. 1.
38. "Monsanto Chemical Co.," *Disneylander*, March 1958, 2. Disneyland Collection, Anaheim History Room, Anaheim Public Library. See also "Disneyland's First Ten Million," *The New York Times*, February 2, 1958. For an illuminating analysis of the gendered assumptions built into residential architecture after World War II, see Dolores Hayden, "Model Houses for the Millions: Architect's Dreams, Builder's Boasts, Residents' Dilemmas," in *Blueprints for Modern Living: History and Legacy of the Case Study House* (Cambridge, MA: MIT Press, 1989), 197–212.
39. Avila, *Popular Culture in the Age of White Flight.*
40. Reagan, quoted in Lisa McGirr, *Suburban Warriors*, 204.
41. Mike Davis, *Ecology of Fear: Los Angeles and the Imagination of Disaster* (New York: Metropolitan Books, 1998), 392. On the relationship between cultural history and urban history, see Timothy J. Gilfoyle, "White Cities, Linguistic Turns, and Disneylands: The New Paradigms of Urban History," *Reviews in American History* 26 (1998): 175–204.

7

Sing Sheng vs. Southwood: Residential Integration in Cold War California

Charlotte Brooks

From *The Pacific Historical Review*

On a Saturday afternoon in early 1952, residents of South San Francisco's all-white Southwood housing tract voted on whether to accept or reject a Chinese American family that wanted to move to the neighborhood. After reading each homemade ballot aloud, volunteer counters working at a table in a neighbor's garage announced their final tally: The Shengs had lost by 174 votes to 28. "I congratulate those who voted against me, and I hope you will enjoy living here," said Sing Sheng bitterly, as Grace, his crying wife, stood by his side. "May your property values go up every three days." Sheng had proposed the poll himself, after putting a deposit on a West Orange Avenue home and receiving threats from white neighbors. But speaking to local reporters after the vote, he was more disappointed than angry. Those white residents who claimed that a Chinese American family would lower property values, he declared, should "find out a little of what we're fighting for in Korea." Sing Sheng, who had come to the United States just a few years earlier, soon discovered that much of America agreed with him. After the story of an immigrant family that had lost its bet on democracy became nationwide news, white Americans from around the country condemned the Southwood residents for the message their votes might send to Asia. Yet such outrage also revealed that, while the Cold War and domestic racial tensions were improving Asian American housing opportunities, they were not lessening white support for residential discrimination in general.[1]

By the early 1950s U.S. policymakers and citizens had become increasingly preoccupied with Asia. The U.S. government was trying to contain communism in the region through a combination of foreign aid, diplomatic pressure, and, in the case of Korea, military force. Public interest in Asia reflected this foreign policy, as well as the growing presence of Asia in American cultural, social, and political life. U.S. soldiers brought back thousands of "war brides" from Japan, China, the Philippines, and Korea. Publisher Henry Luce used his tremendously popular magazines *Time* and *Life* to create sympathy for Taiwan's dictator, Chiang Kai-shek. American movies focused both on the recent war against Japan and contemporary struggles in Asia. And conservative Republicans attacked the Truman administration for being "soft" on communism in the region.[2]

Americans' increasing interest in Asia during the 1950s had significant consequences for Asian Americans, who knew that many of their fellow citizens considered them foreigners—or at least not really American.[3] Only a few years earlier, at the beginning of World War II, the U.S. government had imprisoned the Japanese American population of the West Coast. When the People's Republic of China (PRC) entered the Korean War, Chinese Americans worried that officials would put them in concentration camps too. Although government officials publicly voiced confidence in Chinese American loyalty, the Federal Bureau of Investigation and the Immigration and Naturalization Service harassed Chinese American leftists and monitored Chinatowns.[4] Still, nationwide reaction to the Southwood incident demonstrated that "foreign" ties did not always have negative consequences for Asian Americans in the Cold War United States. Relationships between the United States and various Asian governments had long influenced white Americans' treatment of Asian Americans. Before World War II, such relationships were usually unequal or inharmonious.[5] By the late 1940s, however, American officials attempting to counter Soviet influence in Asia were wooing governments in the region. And as the United States started to treat Asian nations with growing respect, white Americans began viewing Asian Americans more favorably as well.[6]

Even so, Asian Americans had little reason to expect that white Californians' attitudes would change in the same way. For decades before World War II, white Californians had singled out Asian Americans as the primary threats to white privilege in the state.[7] Many prominent officials, including several governors, belonged to anti-Asian organizations that accused the Chinese of being immoral, dirty, and unassimilable. Such groups also considered the Japanese to be racial inferiors and called on other whites to "hold California for the white race." Unsurprisingly, a large majority of white Californians approved of the incarceration of Japanese Americans in 1942.[8]

Yet support for the Sheng family was at least as strong in California as elsewhere in the nation, suggesting a remarkable shift in white opinion there. While many historians have noted that Asian Americans enjoyed a dramatic expansion of rights and opportunities in the West after World War II, few have offered more than the most general reasons for this change. This essay argues that scholars of Asian American history must examine the effects of black migration on white opinion in postwar California. At the same time, they need to explore the connections between U.S. foreign policy and domestic civil rights debates, something historians of the Cold War and African American activism have recently begun to do. In order to understand the impact of such varied factors, this article uses organizational and government records, private and official correspondence, contemporary studies, and English and Chinese language newspapers, which together bring a diversity of perspectives to a largely unstudied aspect of Asian American history.[9]

* * *

Although most Chinese Americans in the 1950s were American-born, Sing Sheng had been born in China and had grown up in Shanghai. During China's war against Japan, he served as a captain in the intelligence branch of the Chinese Nationalist forces. Sheng's wife Grace, a Missouri-born Chinese American, had also grown up in Shanghai, but she returned to the United States after the war to attend Indiana's Earlham College. Sing Sheng joined her there, studying international relations and dreaming of a career in China's diplomatic corps. But when the Chinese Communists took over the Mainland, the newlywed Shengs decided to remain in America. To support his family, Sing Sheng accepted a job as an accountant with Greyhound Bus Lines and studied engine repair in his spare time.[10]

Their backgrounds aside, Sing and Grace Sheng had much in common with many young white married couples in 1950s California. Like numerous men his age, Sing Sheng was a war veteran and a union member, having gotten a job as an aircraft mechanic after completing his engine repair training. The Shengs had also started a family, and while Sing Sheng worked fulltime at Pan American Airways, Grace stayed home with the couple's young son, Richard, in their small apartment in San Francisco's Twin Peaks district. Once the Shengs learned that Grace was pregnant again, they decided to buy a home in the suburbs to accommodate their growing family. Southwood, a moderate blue- and white-collar neighborhood just ten minutes from the airport, seemed ideal. In fact, some of Sing Sheng's Pan Am coworkers already lived there.[11]

Had Sing and Grace Sheng grown up in California, however, they would have known that what they did not share with young white couples was a wide choice of housing. In prewar California, residential discrimination against people of Asian ancestry was the rule rather than exception. In Los Angeles and the East Bay, Chinese Americans lived among other nonwhite residents and poorer whites in the most rundown districts. White San Franciscans limited the housing options of Chinese Americans even more drastically. Almost none of the 20,000 Chinese American residents of San Francisco in 1940 lived outside the Chinatown area.[12] Across the country, and particularly in the urban Northeast and Midwest, other nonwhite Americans of the time faced persistent housing discrimination as well. Outside the Pacific Coast states, African Americans encountered the most tenacious white resistance to integration. In cities such as St. Louis,

Cleveland, and Boston, blacks of all backgrounds and social classes crowded out of necessity into the same rundown ghetto areas. Whites used not just violence but the law to keep them there; until the U.S. Supreme Court's 1948 *Shelley v. Kraemer* decision, courts upheld devices such as racial restrictive covenants, which were contracts that white neighbors signed promising not to sell to nonwhites. While white homeowners unable to find white buyers sometimes broke the covenants, homeowners' associations, realtors, builders, and lenders worked together to keep numerous inner-city neighborhoods all-white for many years.[13]

After 1948, with judges no longer enforcing restrictive covenants, whites and African Americans increasingly clashed over residential and racial boundaries. Clerics in cities such as Philadelphia and Cicero, Illinois, reported that many of their white parishioners strongly opposed housing integration. In Dallas, white elites pushed for the creation of black subdivisions to avoid it altogether, but whites living near the planned sites fought these developments. Many white residents became active in homeowners' associations, such as Detroit's Northwest Civic Association, which struggled to keep blacks out. Some whites turned to vandalism and violence, as in Baltimore, where vigilantes broke the windows of a black family's home and painted "KKK" on it. Most, however, simply abandoned their old neighborhoods in places like Miami, Los Angeles, Brooklyn, and Chicago, and fled to suburbs that excluded nonwhites.[14]

As recent arrivals in America, Sing and Grace Sheng were not prepared for this. Even their lives in California—from their apartment in Twin Peaks to Sing Sheng's job—reflected the gains nonwhites had made in the state during the war.[15] As a result, the couple was surprised when white neighbors confronted them and warned them not to move to the neighborhood. Belligerent residents also phoned the Shengs, threatening to dump garbage on their lawn and harm their children. After some thought, Sing Sheng suggested that the neighborhood vote on his family, and he tied the poll directly to what he considered an important contemporary test of American principles—the ongoing Korean War. Speaking with reporters, he asserted that, "if the votes are not in my favor, it is a good indication that this war is being fought in vain." In a letter to the Southwood homeowners, Sheng used even stronger language. "The present world conflict is not between individual nations, but between communism and Democracy," he argued. "We think so highly of democracy because it offers freedom and equality . . . Do not make us the victims of false democracy."[16]

While Sheng's actions betrayed some naiveté, he did not suggest a referendum merely because of his anti-communist beliefs or faith in American democracy. According to a Chinese-language paper, the Southwooders' comments about the Chinese had particularly irked him. "Truly it would be infuriating for any living member of the Chinese race!" declared Sheng. "It makes my head spin, to use us to oppose Chinese people with such a tone." Sheng wanted to teach his opponents not just about democracy but about the desirability of the Chinese. "I was sure everybody really believed in democracy, so I thought up this vote as a test," he said to a reporter for an English-language paper. "Whichever way it turns out, I will have done my little share for this democracy." But a Chinese-language paper noted that Sheng told his sister he also hoped to show Southwood that anti-Chinese discrimination "had to be given up."[17]

Southwood refused to give it up. When Sing Sheng told the neighbors gathering to vote that "democracy is in a fight with communism and I believe that if I am defeated here it will be a defeat for democracy the world over," the angry Southwooders shouted him down.[18] They had little patience for appeals to their patriotism. For them, the vote was purely local. It allowed them to show Sheng that he was not wanted. Perhaps the poll would encourage him to spread the word to other nonwhite home buyers he might know. Beyond that, they maintained, it had no significance.

* * *

Thirty years earlier, they would have been right. As the major focus of white supremacist activity in California for almost a century, Asian Americans faced greater discrimination in most areas of prewar California than did other nonwhites, including African Americans. In the early twentieth century, the California legislature passed numerous laws to prevent Asian immigrants from owning land and entering certain professions. White homeowners in California's cities used these statutes and the well-developed anti-Asian nativist networks to keep Asian Americans segregated. In prewar San Francisco, African Americans enjoyed significant residential mobility even as Chinese Americans remained segregated in Chinatown.[19]

But by the late 1930s events overseas had begun to alter white perceptions of Chinese Americans, even in nativist California. In agricultural regions of the state, where growers competed with Japanese farmers and fought Japanese and Filipino strikers, many whites mourned the disappearance of the supposedly docile Chinese.[20] This local nostalgia turned statewide after 1937, when Japan launched its brutal invasion of China proper. The Japanese government spent millions of dollars to tell its side of the story in the United States, while China's impoverished government remained largely silent. But as State Department official William Daughtery noted, foreign reporters, missionaries, businesspeople, and other observers "gave to the outside world the shocking account that they had been forced to witness [in China]." In the process, they helped create a great deal of American sympathy for the occupied nation.[21]

Chinese Americans used concern for China and public disgust with Japan to achieve both charitable and political goals in California. With the support of prominent citizens and thousands of white residents, San Francisco's Chinese Americans held "Rice Bowl" rallies to raise money for Chinese refugees. Canny community activists also used growing American sympathy for China to advance a domestic agenda. After the passage of the 1937 U.S. Housing Act, the San Francisco Housing Authority ignored Chinese

American requests for a Chinatown housing project until white civic organizations pressed the Authority to reconsider the idea. And to counter Japanese American dominance of bazaars on Grant Avenue, the main tourist thoroughfare of San Francisco's Chinatown, Chinese American merchants handed out literature and posted signs overtly comparing their rivals to the invading armies of Imperial Japan.[22]

America's entry into World War II transformed China from an admirable underdog into an actual ally, reinforcing the connection many Americans made between Chinese Americans and China. Ironically, prominent California nativists helped strengthen this link by defending on racial grounds the U.S. government's decision to intern the Japanese American population. Attorney General Earl Warren, who later became California's governor, summed up the prevailing sentiment. "When we are dealing with the Caucasian race we have methods that will test [their] loyalty," he claimed. "When we deal with the Japanese we are in an entirely different field and we cannot form any opinion that we believe to be sound." Chinese Americans at the time benefited from such racist, if ultimately double-edged, "logic" about Japanese Americans. Many even wore buttons identifying themselves as Chinese to ensure their own safety. Publications such as *Time* also printed pseudo-scientific articles intended to help other Americans tell the difference between Chinese and Japanese. For example, *Time* maintained that "the Chinese expression tends to be more placid, kindly, open; the Japanese, more positive, dogmatic, arrogant."[23]

During the war, Chinese Americans continued to use public assumptions about their foreign connections for decidedly domestic purposes. When Madame Chiang Kai-shek visited the United States in early 1943, Chinese Americans urged her to call for a repeal of the old law that barred virtually all Chinese immigration. Congress eventually passed a bill allowing token Chinese immigration and letting Chinese aliens become naturalized citizens; they could also bring their Chinese spouses and children into the country. President Franklin D. Roosevelt signed it out of consideration for America's ally China, but Chinese Americans were the bill's main beneficiaries. Similarly, the federal government did not attempt to segregate Chinese Americans who enlisted in the armed forces; unlike African Americans and Japanese Americans, they served in white units.[24]

White citizens also singled out Chinese Americans for fairer treatment. During World War II, government officials and many civic leaders in California called for greater racial tolerance and formed local organizations to promote interracial harmony. The federal Fair Employment Practices Committee (FEPC) also pressed companies to hire nonwhites and responded to workers' discrimination complaints. But even without such encouragement, employers who had long shunned Chinese Americans turned to them first when the draft and the new war industries created a serious labor shortage in California. Chinese American communities responded enthusiastically; in 1943 San Francisco's Chinese American leaders estimated that a third of Chinatown's 20,000 residents worked in defense industries. And

Chinese Americans often found the kinds of skilled jobs that employers did not offer other nonwhite workers, especially the thousands of African Americans migrating to California's cities. Despite severe wartime housing shortages and increased black segregation in California, Chinese Americans even began to find homes in all-white middle-class neighborhoods.[25]

By war's end, Chinese Americans were enjoying more rights than ever before, but these rights often depended on perceptions of Chinese Americans as foreign. In numerous cases, they received better treatment because white Americans identified them as allies rather than as fellow citizens. At the Mare Island shipyards, supervisors chose one of the Chinese American workers to christen a ship. "China has done such a good job of keeping the Japanese on the move," explained the employee who suggested the idea. "It would be a good way for *our people* to show their appreciation and reaffirm their faith in China." Discussing the planned "Ping Yuen" housing project in Chinatown, San Francisco Housing Authority representatives promised that architects would "orientalize and embellish the exterior of the apartments [because] 'Ping Yuen' must be truly representative of our Chinese war ally." When describing a Chinese American veteran who faced housing discrimination in southern Los Angeles, the black-owned *Los Angeles Sentinel* argued that "the Chinese were our noble allies during the war [but] the so-called white Americans who live [on West 56th Street] . . . don't share these feelings." The "noble ally" at the center of the controversy had been born and raised in the United States.[26]

Like these predecessors, numerous observers commented on Southwood as if it were as much a foreign policy issue as a matter of civil rights. A *Life* magazine editorial argued that, after Southwood, "in Asia they will . . . be asking whether American democracy is still worth betting on." Former First Lady Eleanor Roosevelt noted that "all those things do us harm. The Soviets circulate them widely [in Asia]." Across the nation, lesser-known Americans reacted similarly.[27]

* * *

In a sign of just how much public opinion had changed in a few years, white Californians were louder than anyone in their criticism of the Southwood residents and the message they had supposedly sent to Asia. The morning after the vote, the *San Francisco Chronicle* editorialized that "Southwood has undone the long and tedious work of the Voice of America, of Radio Free Asia, and even of American men who have been fighting in Korea." The *Chronicle* had long supported Asian American rights, but even the once virulently anti-Asian *Sacramento Bee* asserted that the Southwood vote "will be received gleefully in Moscow and exploited for all it's worth wherever the army of Red agents are seeking to arouse distrust, engender suspicion, and create hate for the United States." Similarly, columnist Raymond Lawrence of the *Oakland Tribune* contended that "no incident I can think of provides the reds in Asia more powerful ammunition than the Sing Sheng case."[28]

California officials across the political spectrum agreed. Twain Michelsen, a San Francisco superior court judge, complained that the Southwooders' vote "will, of course, be taken up and played upon by the evil forces that reside behind the Iron Curtain." Senator William Knowland believed that Southwood "will undoubtedly be put to the worst possible use by communist propaganda in Asia." Governor Earl Warren personally apologized to the Shengs for the Southwood residents' vote. "I agree with you that it is just such things that the Communists make much of in their efforts to discredit our system," he noted.[29]

If large numbers of white Californians sympathized with the Shengs, however, they were reacting not just to foreign policy concerns but also to broader racial shifts in the state. Until the 1940s Asian Americans had outnumbered blacks in most of California's urban areas. During the war, however, hundreds of thousands of African Americans came to California to work in its booming industries, and most stayed on after the conflict. Indeed, the mass migration of blacks into the state's urban areas continued into the 1950s.[30] With white Californians now considering African Americans the principal threat to their homes and neighborhoods, black-white tensions over housing soon became as common in Los Angeles and the San Francisco Bay Area as they were in cities east of the Mississippi River. At the same time, white homeowners in California proved increasingly open to arguments about Asian American desirability.

The November 1946 election, in which voters considered two explicitly racial initiatives, suggested the shift taking place. One initiative, Proposition 15, sought to make anti-Japanese American Alien Land Acts part of the California constitution. Prop. 15's advocates used explicitly nativist arguments in an attempt to whip up the old anti-Japanese American hatred in California. The other race-based measure on the ballot was Proposition 11. Widely associated with the National Association for the Advancement of Colored People (NAACP), the initiative sought to create a permanent FEPC in California. Voters overwhelmingly rejected Proposition 11, but they also failed to endorse the anti-Japanese American Proposition 15. The vote showed that the heroism of the all-Japanese American 442nd battalion, the most decorated unit of its size during World War II, had created enough fair play sentiment in California to defeat the state's traditional nativism. But it also suggested that, while Californians refused to sanction blatantly discriminatory laws aimed at a particular group, they also refused to support positive legislation that limited white "choice."[31]

By 1951 a group calling itself "America Plus" formed to take advantage of white Californians' concerns about black ambitions in the state. America Plus's primary organizer, a virulent anti-Semite named Aldrich Blake, claimed that African Americans could not reach "the high peak of equality with the whites." But the group's platform glossed over Blake's racial views. Instead, America Plus literature referred to "democratic liberties and property rights," which the group equated with restrictive covenants and the repeal of civil rights legislation. And in December 1951 America Plus announced plans to gather signatures to place a "Freedom of Choice" initiative on the November 1952 California ballot. The initiative would have invalidated the state's existing civil rights laws and guaranteed every citizen the right to discriminate against anyone else in employment, housing, and other areas.[32]

Civil rights groups worried that America Plus could win in California by fusing the ongoing red scare with issues such as "choice" and property values. Conservative politicians had already red-baited many of the racially progressive organizations active in wartime and postwar California. In addition, America Plus had secured the backing of State Senator Jack Tenney, a headline-craving white supremacist who was also the former leader of the State Committee on Un-American Activities.[33] Franklin H. Williams of the West Coast NAACP asserted that "Freedom of Choice" could "undo every civil rights advantage that has been gained over the last 50 years . . . and just about completely destroy any hope of further civil rights advances for many years to come." Other organizations, including the Japanese American Citizens' League (JACL), the American Jewish Council, and the California Federation for Civic Unity, scrambled to raise money for an anti-America Plus campaign.[34]

In this context, the Southwood vote, which three decades earlier would have attracted little attention, became a de facto test of the popularity of "Freedom of Choice" in communist-fearing 1950s California. Indeed, what had begun as a rather common incident of housing segregation had quickly grown into something much larger. Within days of the referendum, the key issue was no longer whether Sing Sheng and his wife would move to the suburbs, but the meaning of democracy itself.

Echoing America Plus's rhetoric about freedom of association and choice, Southwood's defenders claimed that democracy equaled the right to select one's own friends and neighbors. Jack Stockton, who lived on the street where the Shengs hoped to move, argued that "I, as an American, like to live with my own race of people." According to William Grapengeter, Jr., another resident, "now that the world is criticizing Southwood for this election, I have come to feel that the world is trying to take away my vote and my right to say what I think." Tenney, who praised Sing Sheng for submitting the issue to a vote, felt similarly: "If people don't have the right to vote on their neighbors, they don't have the right to vote on their president," he claimed.[35]

In a nation where residential segregation was pervasive—indeed, where it was often official policy—the 178 families who had voted against Sing Sheng were surprised to find that they had few defenders. "Aren't there other neighborhoods where Chinese, Negroes, and minorities are excluded?" a Southwood neighbor asked during a meeting convened several days after the vote. "Of course there are," replied another. "Only nobody ever hears about it . . . it all happens very quietly." *San Francisco Chronicle* reporter Bernard Taper observed that if the Southwooders could ask the nation one question, it would be: "How would you have voted if you had been in our position?" As Southwood resident Felix Surmont contended, "the true hypocrites and bigots [are] these smug people who have persecuted us from behind the flag or the church with bold and gratuitous statements while living in their own restricted homes." Other residents agreed, and those attending the post-referendum meeting reaffirmed their original anti-Sheng stand.[36]

To bolster their arguments, Southwood residents used the kind of property values language they felt many other white Americans would understand. After all, white housing professionals had long insisted that nonwhites hurt prices, and realtors, bankers, and insurance agents continued to claim this after the *Shelley* decision. So Southwood resident and spokesman Clinton Kenney asserted that "when one oriental or any one of a minority group comes into an area others follow. The property value then drops correspondingly." The Southwooders even blamed their property value concerns and their votes not on personal prejudice, but on the sentiments of other white people. According to Kenney, the Shengs' arrival would have left Southwood families with homes "materially depreciated through no fault of [our] own but through the racial prejudices of others." Only after the furor over Southwood died down did neighbors confess their real feelings about the Shengs. A group of sociology students taking a survey in the area heard a common refrain:

> Sheng would be paving the way for his own countrymen and for Negroes. Our children don't know the difference and might marry one of them someday . . . Chinamen can live on ten cents a day . . . . [T]hey would move three families into one house in order to finance it . . . . [T]hey don't live as we do. No Chinamen have money, except the gamblers.

Apparently, many white Southwood neighbors shared the very prejudices they disavowed.[37]

If the Southwooders' property "values" involved much more than money, the tract's residents were hardly alone. Like the Southwood neighbors, white segregationists across America considered home ownership symbolic not just of their financial stability, but of their morality, character, and social status. In his study of postwar Detroit, historian Thomas Sugrue describes this world view:

> To white Detroiters, the wretched conditions in Paradise Valley and other poor African American neighborhoods were the fault of irresponsible blacks, not greedy landlords or neglectful city officials . . . . Many Detroit whites interpreted [these] poor housing conditions as a sign of personal failure and family breakdown.

In other words, the "values"—or lack of them—that many white Detroit residents ascribed to blacks contrasted markedly with the values they saw themselves embodying. Similarly, as Becky Nicolaides has shown, postwar white working-class homeowners in Los Angeles County simultaneously "embraced self-reliance, independence, Americanism, familism, and racial separation." The first four ideals depended to a significant extent on the fifth. White homeowners like the Southwooders feared that racial mixing—with interracial marriage the inevitable endpoint—threatened the rest. It certainly threatened their ability to claim these values as racially unique.[38]

By using arguments about property "values" against a Chinese American family, however, the Southwooders stumbled into a Cold War trap. President Harry S. Truman had sent American troops to Korea, and many Republican politicians were now demanding that the United States protect Taiwan as well. In 1952 much of the black population of the South could not vote; in the North, many local officials and community leaders fought residential integration. Yet at the same time, American policymakers were sacrificing white American lives for Asian freedom and democracy. This was a strong statement. If Asians did not share the very American "values"—independence, individualism, and self-reliance—that white Americans so often refused to see in blacks, then this sacrifice was pointless. Even American foreign policy priorities emphasized this distinction: The U.S. government actively intervened in Asia but largely ignored Africa.[39]

Furthermore, many Americans identified the suburban good life as part of what soldiers were fighting and dying to defend in Asia. The Cold War was not just a competition between the U.S. and Soviet governments but between two kinds of economies—command and capitalist. As historian Stephen Whitfield has shown, "domestic patterns of consumption [became] a manifestation of American supremacy" in the minds of many citizens. No one expressed this view better than Vice President Richard Nixon. During Nixon's 1959 "kitchen debate" with Soviet leader Nikita Khrushchev, the vice president "insisted that American superiority in the cold war rested not on weapons, but on the secure, abundant family life of modern suburban homes." By barring the Shengs from sharing this kind of life, the Southwooders were mocking the sacrifices American troops were making in Korea.[40]

The Sheng supporters' constant references to the family's origins reinforced this idea of shared values. Southwood critics frequently linked the family directly to the Chinese Nationalist struggle against communism. "The Chinese people have many many friends in America who value their qualities and appreciate their aid during World War Two and who want to see them again freed from domination," wrote Harold Mansfield of Seattle's China Club in an open telegram to the Shengs. Columnist Karl Bennet Justus argued that the Shengs "believe in our democratic way of life . . . . [Sing Sheng] is still an ally of ours in the struggle against communism." The communist newspaper *People's Daily World* cracked that "one might think the Sheng case is a semi-military exercise in the cold war rather than a problem of discrimination in California."[41]

Indeed, citizens, journalists, and officials branded the unrepentant Southwood residents inadvertent communist collaborators. A local journalist reported that "so acute had the situation become in the schools that South

San Francisco's school superintendent [told students to] 'lay off the Southwood kids.' " When national magazines and the press misidentified South San Francisco as "south San Francisco" or simply "San Francisco", the San Francisco Board of Supervisors considered a citizen's request to demand that South San Francisco change its name. Meanwhile, mayoral secretary Max G. Funke assured angry but misinformed correspondents that "the incident to which you refer occurred in South San Francisco [which] is not even in our county."[42]

Now shouted down themselves, the Southwooders protested that they were not traitors. Perhaps, some ventured, Sing Sheng was a communist sent to provoke an incident. Mrs. William Beam, a tract resident, warned that "these people who are calling us names [should] look a little deeper and find the true culprits who are behind all this." Other neighbors recognized Sheng's impeccable anti-communist credentials and his popularity with the public; they suggested that communist agents had manipulated both the Southwood voters and the Shengs to stir up trouble. "It seems to us," commented one, "that Mr. Sing [*sic*] as well as we ourselves have been used as unwitting tools by subversive elements who want to create dissension in America." But Southwood had already lost the battle for public opinion.[43]

* * *

Ironically, only those who had experienced residential discrimination first-hand supported the Southwooders' contention that the vote was simply about racial prejudice in the United States. Few African American activists in California regarded Southwood with any interest. The obstacles blacks encountered in gaining access to decent housing throughout the state dwarfed what the Shengs had experienced in South San Francisco. Most California public housing projects segregated African Americans, and, in the years after World War II, blacks seeking homes in the state faced not just Southwood-style threats but actual violence and arson. The Rev. Frederick D. Haynes, a San Francisco civil rights leader, called for an official investigation of what he termed "the campaign to intimidate citizens of South San Francisco" into rejecting the Shengs. But Haynes was an exception among African American activists. Even the local NAACP paid little attention to the Southwood incident and offered no official comment.[44]

The black press reacted similarly. While the *New York Times* followed Southwood for a week, the *Los Angeles Sentinel*, one of California's leading black newspapers, ignored the incident altogether. The black-owned *California Eagle* used what little space it devoted to Southwood to argue that the tract's residents merely represented the white mainstream. In an editorial, the *Eagle* noted that:

> We suspect that most of the people who voted for a lily white neighborhood are just average, everyday Americans who could be counted on to come to the aid of a distressed friend and who are good friends and good citizens. We don't think they are Fascists or Klansmen. They are just badly informed.

The *Eagle*, which carried stories of violence against the state's black homeowners almost weekly, reserved its criticism for Sing Sheng. Since he had the right to live in Southwood, concluded the *Eagle*, he should have exercised it.[45]

Many African American organizations and activists ignored Southwood for the same reasons that Tenney and his allies cheered the vote results. America Plus saw Southwood's informal referendum as a harbinger of November. If the group managed to get "Freedom of Choice" on the ballot, members believed that whites throughout California would act as the Southwooders had. For their part, black activists pointedly avoided using California's referendum system for the same reason. William Byron Rumford, a prominent African American activist who served in the state legislature and later in Congress, recalled that many black politicians had actually opposed putting the FEPC on the ballot in 1946. "Any time you put any rights issue on the ballot, it's going to be defeated," he argued.[46] For many black Californians, Southwood seemed to foreshadow what would occur if "Freedom of Choice" became a ballot initiative. Sing Sheng, however well-intentioned, had actually imperiled all nonwhite residents; rights existed for the protection of minorities and not at the pleasure of majorities, but his vote proposal suggested otherwise.

If blacks remained largely silent about Southwood, Asian Americans worried for weeks about an incident many felt affected all of them, regardless of ethnicity. Chinese Americans were particularly concerned. Since the late 1940s, Chinese American leaders had been working to change public perceptions of their community's relationship with China. The *Chinese Press* counseled Chinese Americans to turn away from Chinatowns altogether. "Work and live among other Americans," urged its editors. "They too will know you as Americans." Chinese American Citizens Alliance president Y. C. Hong asserted that "many of us are third or fourth generation Americans [and] owe allegiance only to the Government of the United States." The *Chinese News* featured a photo of a veterans' color guard marching in a Chinese New Year parade, commenting that it was a "symbol of the new Chinatown which is all-American in heart and deeds." By the mid-1950s even the conservative Chinese Consolidated Benevolent Association was developing what members called "a continuing program of public relations for the . . . Chinese community in the United States" to highlight that community's loyalty and Americanness.[47]

Japanese Americans also paid close attention to the reactions the Southwood vote generated. Seven years after World War II, much of the white public had resumed referring to people of Asian ancestry as "Orientals," regardless of ethnicity. Southwood residents knew that Sing Sheng was Chinese American; after all, he used his own life story to argue for tolerance in the tract. But such familiarity was not necessarily common in postwar California. White residents and scholars usually spoke of integration involving "Orientals," not "Chinese" or "Japanese." Pondering Southwood, the *New York Times* wondered whether it was "indicative of a marked resurgence of anti-Oriental feeling on the West Coast"—not anti-Chinese sentiment during the Korean War. Scholar Yen Le Espiritu has argued that Asian American community activists did not embrace "panethnicity" until the mid-1960s. But Asian American leaders of the early 1950s certainly understood how the public perceived them. In 1953 *Chinese News* editor Charles Leong wrote to Japanese American journalist Harry Honda about "the Nisei group whose problems are more parallel to ours than any other racial group." When the Japanese American magazine *Scene* discussed racial segregation, its articles often described the prejudices that Americans of "Oriental" or "Asiatic" descent faced. The Japanese American Citizens League newspaper *Pacific Citizen* occasionally referred to Chinese Americans as "Chinese Nisei." By 1954 the *Chinese News* was praising the success of Korean American diving champion Sammy Lee as beneficial to "all Oriental minorities" in America. And some of the most detailed accounts and lengthy editorials about Southwood appeared in the Japanese American press, whose reporters understood the importance of the Sheng story to their readers.[48]

Japanese American and Chinese American journalists almost unanimously described the Southwood vote as a terrible idea. The *Pacific Citizen* warned about "the danger in establishing a precedent in a neighborhood vote to accept or reject a minority group." The liberal Chinese-language *Chinese-Pacific Weekly* agreed. "[Our] fundamental rights very much rely on freedom of residence," noted editor Gilbert Woo. "The Constitution bestows this right. It should not be given to other people to vote on and decide." The conservative Nationalist Party organ *Young China* praised the Shengs but editorialized that, "if we take a firm stand on morality and the law, we need not adopt a negative attitude of 'meek acceptance,' nor the negative attitude, 'despite our numbers, we will let such things pass.' " Like their African American counterparts, these Asian American observers sensed that Southwood's real danger lay as much in the lesson it sent about rights to white America as in the one it sent about democracy to the world.[49]

Individual Asian Americans residents of the Bay Area also avoided making Southwood into an international incident. Churchill T. Chiu of San Francisco thanked the Shengs for making "a very good case for all of us who are of Chinese ancestry" but added that "for the next step, I would suggest you select a nice home at about the same price in another district of South San Francisco, and demonstrate to them that we can get along with our neighbors." Alfred B. Chan of San Francisco confessed that "I don't think I will ever be able to understand [freedom and democracy] if this is part of the American way of life." Lim P. Lee, a prominent Democrat who would later become San Francisco's first Chinese American postmaster, briefly acknowledged that Southwood could embarrass the United States in front of the world. But he noted that federal agencies bore the blame for sanctioning all-white communities in the first place. Lim Lee contended:

> A benevolent government that makes it easy for the veterans and citizens to own their own homes through liberal provisions of underwriting by the VA

> [Veterans' Administration], FHA [Federal Housing Administration] or California Vet. program, makes possible . . . 'restricted residential districts.' Our government should not be used to perpetuate a legal wrong.[50]

* * *

If Asian American journalists and citizens worried about the precedent Southwood might set, so did many white Californians, albeit for different reasons. No town wanted to be the next Southwood. In March 1952 a Chinese American named Freddie Wing who had bought a home in an all-white neighborhood of Sonoma sent out 200 invitations to his housewarming party. According to the *New York Times*—which rarely covered Sonoma housewarmings—everyone Wing invited came, including the town's mayor, the heads of both its banks, and the widow of famed wartime general Henry "Hap" Arnold. In October of that year, twenty-four residents of a San Jose neighborhood signed a petition objecting to a Japanese American family, the Yoshiharas, who had just bought a home there. Sam Yoshihara, a disabled World War II veteran, confessed to the *San Jose Mercury* that he worried about moving to such a hostile place. But when Yoshihara supporters announced that, "in these days when Democracy is under attack all over the world, such action as was taken against Sam Yoshihara is to be deplored," the residents relented. They claimed that the first petition had been a "misunderstanding" and quickly signed a second one welcoming the Yoshiharas to the neighborhood.[51]

Long after Southwood, the Cold War continued to inform the way the press and much of the public viewed publicized incidents of housing discrimination against Asian Americans. During the Southwood furor, the *Chinese-Pacific Weekly* predicted that "after the uproar is over, this new and unusual flavor will be gone. This rice can't be stir-fried again." But apparently it could. In 1953 a Chinese American couple building a home in a Watsonville subdivision received a threatening letter and forwarded it to the local paper. "Watsonville citizens will perhaps come to the same conclusion that citizens of South San Francisco did," argued the *Watsonville Register-Pajaronian*. "It takes only a few crackpots to give a community a black eye [and] to do immeasurable damage to the cause of the United States." When Palo Alto realtors backed out of a 1954 home deal with Dr. William Lee, a Stanford University research chemist, scores of people called the Lees to apologize and to offer them homes for sale. The following year Earl LaCount received a death threat when he sold his San Leandro home to Japanese American dentist Satoru Larry Aikawa. A veteran who canvassed the neighborhood to gather support for the Aikawas complained that such incidents squandered the "millions of dollars [America spends] all over the world to combat Communist propaganda." Meanwhile, the Southern Alameda County Real Estate Board publicly denied encouraging such discrimination, while the Aikawas received dozens of home offers.[52]

The case of Sammy Lee overshadowed all these incidents, however. A two-time Olympic gold medalist, Lee was also an Army major and doctor who had traveled across Asia promoting democracy for the State Department. In 1955 Lee made plans to leave the Army and set up a private practice in Orange County, California. But agents at two tracts in the county's Garden Grove suburb refused to sell a home to his family. Friends of the Lees eventually leaked the story to the *San Francisco Chronicle*, which helped make it front-page news across the state. In its editorials, the *Chronicle* used language that could have come directly from its Southwood articles. "Here was an American of Oriental descent demonstrating to Asians that despite Communist propaganda the United States is a land of tolerance and opportunity," scolded the *Chronicle*. "The story of Major Lee's reception in Garden Grove will embarrass our country in the eyes of the world." Both tracts' developers quickly announced their willingness to sell a home to the Lees, and the couple received scores of other home offers as well. Equally significant, the FHA's local office stepped in to investigate the matter. Governor Goodwin Knight urged Garden Grove to "uphold the finest traditions of Americanism and freedom." Even Vice President Nixon, a California native, became involved, telling reporters he was "shocked" at the treatment the Lees had received. "I reflect the majority of my state when I say that I would be proud to have Sammy Lee as my neighbor," said Nixon. The Lees eventually bought a home in an all-white neighborhood of nearby Anaheim.[53]

Numerous white Californians still saw Asian Americans as foreigners, but with Japan, South Korea, the Philippines, and Taiwan now allies, and the rest of Asia seemingly up for grabs, the significance of being "foreign" had changed since the early twentieth century. "Foreignness" set Asian Americans apart from African Americans, Mexican Americans, and other nonwhite Californians.[54] This supposed foreignness, together with American foreign policy, changed the meaning and acceptability of discrimination against Asian Americans. In 1942 thousands of white Americans believed that all Japanese Americans were Japanese spies or saboteurs because of their ancestry and wholeheartedly supported their internment. By the 1950s thousands of white Americans believed—indeed, given the casualties of the Korean War, they had to believe—that Sing Sheng, the Yoshiharas, the Aikawas, Sammy Lee, and many other Asian Americans deserved a place among white Americans because of their shared values and because of what they symbolized abroad.

When reporters and officials criticized anti-Asian American discrimination as unpatriotic, however, they implied that accepting residential integration was a "sacrifice" whites sometimes had to make for the nation—not a right all citizens should enjoy, regardless of color. By the early 1950s mainstream black groups, fearful of red-baiting, had largely stopped criticizing American foreign policy, but they still tried to use concern about America's image abroad to push for greater civil rights at home.[55] White Californians remained largely impervious to such African American arguments.

Discrimination against Asian Americans, many reasoned, might have real and direct consequences and thus require "sacrifices," but America was barely involved in colonial Africa. Conveniently, this "logic" also happened to conform to prevailing white racial fears and racial assumptions in postwar California.

Many of the white Californians who eventually accepted Asian American neighbors thus continued to reject African American ones, often quite violently. Less than a month after the Sheng referendum, white vigilantes firebombed the home of a black teacher who had moved into a formerly all-white neighborhood of Los Angeles. When three state assemblymen submitted a resolution arguing that "such incidents are not in keeping with the American tradition and way of life and furnish material to be used as propaganda by the Communists," the measure died in committee. Its demise attracted little attention, nor did scores of editors, citizens, and elected officials across the nation rush to condemn the vigilantes of Los Angeles.[56]

Indeed, publicized incidents of anti-Asian American housing discrimination drew widespread condemnation throughout the 1950s while African Americans and many Mexican Americans who faced harsher prejudice received comparatively little sympathy. A little more than a year after Southwood, the Taylors, a black family, bought a home in another South San Francisco tract. The *Watsonville Register-Pajaronian* may have believed that South San Francisco had learned its lesson, but close to 300 white neighbors quickly met to plan their response to the unwanted newcomers. While residents acknowledged the Taylors' legal right to move in, they promised that "we'll let them know we won't serve them ice cream every night." Despite such threats, the incident received little attention. The *Palo Alto Times* also erred when it claimed that the public outcry over the William Lee affair was "heartening evidence that this type of prejudice is on its way out." A year later, realtors blockbusted the Belle Haven tract on the border of Menlo Park and Palo Alto; the neighborhood became virtually all-black within two years. Perhaps the *Palo Alto Times* should have specified that anti-Asian American prejudice was on its way out. After all, white residents of the new Monterey Park subdivision of Los Angeles paid little attention to the Mexican Americans and Asian Americans moving to the tract. They began to protest only when blacks tried to buy homes there as well.[57]

The aftermath of the Sammy Lee case once again highlighted the divergent treatment of Asian Americans and African Americans. Two years after Sammy Lee moved to Anaheim, African American Army lieutenant Harold Bauduit purchased a home in Lee's neighborhood. Many of the same residents who had welcomed Lee and his Chinese American wife now formed a committee to force out Bauduit, apparently little concerned about the message they were sending to the world. Nor did star power mean a great deal in such situations. When Willie Mays moved to San Francisco with the former New York Giants, white neighbors in the posh St. Francis Wood district objected to the black baseball star's attempts to buy a home there. The NAACP and Mayor George Christopher intervened, but Mays received little of the sympathy and none of the home offers that Lee had. No one suggested that Jim Crowing Willie Mays made America look bad overseas. Neither Vice President Nixon nor the FHA investigated the Mays case; the governor said nothing, and even Mayor Christopher admitted that he was powerless to do anything but try to negotiate. While Mays finally got his home, many of his neighbors never accepted his presence among them; vigilantes were still throwing bottles through his windows a year later.[58]

The Southwood affair ended better, creating publicity that destroyed America Plus. Until the tract vote became national news, the group's organizers believed they could collect the necessary money and signatures to get their proposition on the California ballot in November 1952. But Southwood showed how "Freedom of Choice" might look in practice. Once Americans began attacking the Southwooders for creating communist propaganda, America Plus's fortunes quickly faded. Widespread support for a Chinese American family thus crippled an organization formed largely to check African American civil rights gains. America Plus soon relocated to Tulsa, Oklahoma.[59]

The Sheng family also had a happy ending to their story. After baby Fred arrived, Sing and Grace Sheng started their home search anew and eventually purchased a house in an all-white section of the growing San Francisco Peninsula town of Menlo Park. The relative ease with which they bought their home highlighted once again the changing attitudes of white homeowners in 1950s California. Before the end of World War II, restrictive covenants had prevented all nonwhites except servants from living almost anywhere on the Peninsula. Yet by the early 1950s, Asian Americans were moving into several Peninsula towns without incident, and no one protested the Shengs' arrival in Menlo Park. Having outgrown their home, the Shengs moved on in 1955. So did many of their white neighbors, albeit for a different reason: Their tract was very near Belle Haven, which white realtors were aggressively blockbusting. The Shengs had inadvertently joined the tide of white flight. And in the late 1950s residents and realtors in Menlo Park and neighboring communities were still fighting the black "influx" that they so feared.[60]

* * *

Foreign policy concerns were obviously not the only factors influencing white homeowners' perceptions of other racial groups and their comparative desirability in 1950s California. Wartime migration had changed the demographics of the urban state: African Americans had become the largest minority group in many California cities, especially in the Bay Area.[61] And white homeowners, whether migrants or oldtimers, frequently came to believe the same ideas about racial values and comparative desirability so common elsewhere in the nation. Authorities often encouraged such feelings. Federal housing officials and their local agents segregated black migrants and oldtimers in public and subsidized private housing during and after the war. The FHA endorsed redlining, restrictive covenants, and similar housing practices in California's booming suburbs as well.[62]

Still, American foreign policy played a significant role in helping Asian Americans escape the segregation that trapped so many blacks in postwar California's inner cities. During World War II, federal officials reinforced white perceptions of Asian Americans as foreign through their treatment of both Japanese American "enemies" and Chinese American "allies." After the war, as racial conflict over housing became widespread, the U.S. government endorsed positive ideas about the values and desirability of Asians by helping them fight communism. American policymakers wanted to contain communism more than promote democracy; their support for dictators such as South Korea's Syngman Rhee and Taiwan's Chiang Kai-shek demonstrated as much. But the millions of Americans whose friends and loved ones were fighting in Korea, who believed in President Dwight D. Eisenhower's domino theory and who worried about domestic communist influence, likely took America's professed ideals very seriously.

As a result, the Cold War affected African American and Asian American opportunities quite differently. Conservative legislators, particularly Southerners, routinely red-baited black civil rights activists. During a debate about a permanent FEPC bill, Georgia Senator Richard B. Russell even claimed that "we are told that we must pass the FEPC bill because the communists are in favor of it."[63] Asian Americans did not face the same organized legislative resistance as they sought increased rights.[64] Western legislators had abandoned anti-Asian politics; California's Senator Knowland did not stop supporting the Nationalist government in Taipei just because political opponents dubbed him the "senator from Formosa." Asian Americans also faced less hostility than blacks did from the executive branch. Historian Penny Von Eschen has argued that after World War II the Truman administration sought "the systematic repression of . . . anticolonial activists" and tried to make "the oppression of Africans and people of African descent a secondary issue." Presidents Truman and Eisenhower both had significantly different agendas for Asia.[65]

Asian Americans continued to view the connection between their rights and foreign policy with discomfort, however. White neighbors sometimes treated them with more consideration than African Americans or Mexican Americans. They found that their status as "different" nonwhites could help them get jobs in industries hostile to other minorities. They bought homes in some districts where white vigilantes firebombed black neighbors. Yet Asian Americans, whether of Chinese, Korean, Japanese, Filipino, or Indian descent, still rejected the perception that they were foreigners, even when that perception created unique opportunities for them. They knew all too well the dangers of shifting public opinion and political rhetoric. More importantly, they were U.S. citizens, and many were tired of waiting—as some had for several generations—for their fellow Americans to recognize that fact.

Notes

The author is a member of the history department at the University of Albany, State University of New York.

I am very grateful to Richard Sheng for making his family's Southwood materials available to me. In addition, I would like to thank David K. Johnson, Wallace Best, Karen Leroux, Brett Gadsden, Michael S. Sherry, Josef Barton, the four anonymous *Pacific Historical Review* readers, and Nancy K. MacLean for their suggestions and comments on earlier drafts of this article.

1. "Homeowners Ballot, Keep Chinese Out," *San Francisco Examiner*, Feb. 17, 1952, p. 1; "Sing [*sic*] Family Gets Host of Offers," *San Mateo Times*, Feb. 18, 1952, p. 1; " 'Democracy Vote' Rejects Chinese," *New York Times*, Feb. 17, 1952, p. 18; "Chinese Couple Accepts Vote Barring New Home," *San Francisco News*, Feb. 18, 1952, Richard Sheng collection (in possession of author), hereafter referred to as Sheng Collection. As the Southwooders discovered later, their neighborhood was not as racially pure as they believed; a mixed-race Hawaiian couple owned a house in the tract. In 1952 they were renting the house to a white family, but they had lived in it themselves in the late 1940s. Bernard Taper, "Southwood Finds Out It Isn't an 'All White' Community, After All," *San Francisco Chronicle*, Feb. 22, 1952, p. 1.
2. Robert M. Blum, *Drawing the Line: The Origins of American Containment Policy in East Asia* (New York, 1982), 5; Andrew J. Rotter, *The Path to Vietnam: Origins of the American Commitment to Southeast Asia* (Ithaca, N.Y., 1987), 1–2, 75–79, 123, 171, 180; Michael H. Hunt and Steven I. Levine, "The Revolutionary Challenge to Early U.S. Cold War Policy in Asia," in Warren I. Cohen and Akira Iriye, eds., *The Great Powers in East Asia, 1953–1960* (New York, 1990), 15, 19–21; Gary Hess, "The American Search for Stability in Southeast Asia: The SEATO Structure for Containment," in Cohen and Iriye, eds., *The Great Powers*, 288; Evelyn Nakano Glenn, *Issei, Nisei, Warbride: Three Generations of Japanese American Women in Domestic Service* (Philadelphia, 1986), 8; Yen Le Espiritu, *Filipino American Lives* (Philadelphia, 1995), 18; Xiaojian Zhao, *Remaking Chinese America: Immigration, Family, and Community, 1940–1965* (New Brunswick, N.J., 2002), 1; Ji-Yeon Yuh, *Beyond the Shadow of Camptown: Korean Military Brides in America* (New York, 2002), 1; Stephen J. Whitfield, *The Culture of the Cold War* (Baltimore, 1991), 160. Movies dealing with World War II in the Pacific and postwar American involvement in Asia include *From Here to Eternity* (Columbia Pictures Corporation, 1953); *China Venture* (ibid., 1953); *The Bamboo Prison* (ibid., 1954); *Okinawa* (ibid., 1952); *Halls of Montezuma* (Twentieth Century Fox, 1951); *Hell and High Water* (ibid., 1954); *Blood Alley* (Warner Brothers, 1955); and scores of others.
3. Mae M. Ngai, "The Architecture of Race in American Immigration Law: A Reexamination of the Immigration Act of 1924," *Journal of American History*, 86 (1999), 67–92, discusses the origins of the perception of all Asian Americans as perpetual foreigners. Arguably, attitudes about Asian American "foreignness" have not changed greatly since the 1950s. See, for example, Frank H. Wu, *Yellow: Race in America Beyond Black and White* (New York, 2002), 79–129; Neil T. Gotanda, "Citizenship Nullification: The Impossibility of Asian American Politics," in Gordon H. Chang, ed., *Asian Americans and Politics: Perspectives, Experiences, Prospects* (Stanford, Calif., 2001), 91; Helen Zia, *Asian American Dreams: The Emergence of an American People* (New York, 2000), 44.
4. Renqiu Yu, *To Save China, To Save Ourselves: The Chinese Hand Laundry Alliance of New York* (Philadelphia, 1992), 183–194. Other studies of government harassment of Chinese Americans during the Cold War include Peter Kwong, *Chinatown, U.S.A.: Labor and Politics, 1930–1950* (New York, 2001); Mae M. Ngai, "Legacies of

Exclusion: Chinese Illegal Immigration during the Cold War Years," *Journal of American Ethnic History*, 18 (1998); and Him Mark Lai, "To Bring Forth a New China, to Build a Better America: The Chinese Marxist Left in America to the 1960s," *Chinese America: History and Perspectives*, 6 (1992). For examples of official praise of Chinese Americans during the Korean War, see "California's Gov. Warren Assures Chinese-Americans," *Chinese Press*, Dec. 8, 1950, p. 1; "Mayor Talks on Chinese Contribution," ibid., Feb. 9, 1951, p. 1.

5. Two of the best examples of the impact of America's relationships with various Asian nations are the World War II internment of Japanese Americans and the tacit official tolerance of anti-Chinese violence in the West between the 1850s and the turn of the twentieth century (due to the weakness of the faltering Chinese empire). See also Robert S. Chang, *Disoriented: Asian Americans, Law, and the Nation-State* (New York, 1999), 16–38.
6. Hess, "The American Search for Stability," 273.
7. Studies of the development of white Californians' racial attitudes in the nineteenth and early twentieth centuries include Tomás Almaguer, *Racial Fault Lines: The Historical Origins of White Supremacy in California* (Berkeley, 1994); Roger Daniels, *The Anti-Japanese Movement in California and the Struggle for Japanese Exclusion* (Berkeley, 1962); and Alexander Saxton, *The Indispensable Enemy: Labor and the Anti-Chinese Movement in California* (Berkeley, 1971).
8. K. Scott Wong, "Cultural Defenders and Brokers: Chinese Responses to the Anti-Chinese Movement," in K. Scott Wong and Sucheng Chan, eds., *Claiming America: Constructing Chinese American Identities During the Exclusion Era* (Philadelphia, 1998), 5; John S. Chambers, "The Japanese Invasion," *Annals of the American Academy of Political and Social Science*, 93 (1921), 28; back cover, *Grizzly Bear*, Aug. 1924. John Modell, *The Economics and Politics of Racial Accommodation: The Japanese of Los Angeles, 1900–1942* (Urbana, Ill., 1977), 181–188, discusses the evolution of public opinion against the Japanese Americans in California between 1941 and 1942.
9. Scholars who argue that Asian American life improved and offer only general reasons for this change include Ronald Takaki, *Strangers from a Different Shore: A History of Asian Americans* (New York, 1990), 416–418; Sucheng Chan, *Asian Americans: An Interpretive History* (New York, 1991), 140–142; Gloria Heyung Chun, *Of Orphans and Warriors: Inventing Chinese American Culture and Identity* (New Brunswick, N.J., 2000), 70–96; and Zia, *Asian American Dreams*, 44–46.
10. Recent works connecting international relations to domestic racial issues include Mary L. Dudziak, *Cold War Civil Rights: Race and the Image of American Democracy* (Princeton, N.J., 2002); Thomas Borstelmann, *The Cold War and the Color Line: American Race Relations in the Global Arena* (Cambridge, Mass., 2001); Penny M. Von Eschen, *Race Against Empire: Black Americans and Anticolonialism, 1927–1957* (Ithaca, N.Y., 1997); Brenda Gayle Plummer, *Rising Wind: Black Americans and U.S. Foreign Affairs, 1935–1960* (Chapel Hill, N.C., 1996); and Renee Romano, "No Diplomatic Immunity: African American Diplomats, the State Department, and Civil Rights, 1961–1964," *Journal of American History*, 87 (2000). Each of these works considers civil rights in the United States as an African American issue and does not examine the impact of foreign policy on Asian Americans. One recent work that goes beyond a black-white view of this issue is Justin Hart, "Making Democracy Safe for the World: Race, Propaganda, and the Transformation of U.S. Foreign Policy during World War II," *Pacific Historical Review*, 73 (2004), 49–84.
11. Elaine Tyler May, *Homeward Bound: American Families in the Cold War Era* (New York, 1988), 3–5; "Democracy in Southwood," *Time*, Feb. 25, 1952, p. 27.

12. Charlotte Brooks, "Ascending California's Racial Hierarchy: Asian Americans, Housing, and Government, 1920–1955" (Ph.D. dissertation, Northwestern University, 2002), 19–66. U.S. Census numbers in 1940 broke down California's counties by race, counting people of Chinese, Japanese, and Native American ancestry separately. However, census tracts were reported as "white" and "nonwhite." Works Progress Administration, *1939 Real Property Survey, San Francisco, California* (San Francisco, 1940), includes the five census tracts with the most substandard housing—one of which was Chinatown—and reports 71 Chinese American-occupied units outside of Chinatown and 4,787 within it.
13. Kenneth T. Jackson, *Crabgrass Frontier: The Suburbanization of the United States* (New York, 1985), 241–242; Arnold R. Hirsch, "With or Without Jim Crow: Black Residential Segregation in the United States," in Arnold R. Hirsch and Raymond A. Mohl, eds., *Urban Policy in Twentieth-Century America* (New Brunswick, N.J., 1993), 73–75.
14. John T. McGreevy, *Parish Boundaries: The Catholic Encounter with Race in the Twentieth-Century Urban North* (Chicago, 1996), 88–98; William H. Wilson, *Hamilton Park: A Planned Black Community in Dallas* (Baltimore, 1998), 12–15; Douglas S. Massey and Nancy A. Denton, *American Apartheid: Segregation and the Making of the Underclass* (Cambridge, Mass., 1993), 56; Thomas J. Sugrue, *The Origins of the Urban Crisis: Race and Inequality in Postwar Detroit* (Princeton, N.J., 1996), 214; W. Edward Orser, *Blockbusting in Baltimore: The Edmondson Village Story* (Lexington, Ky., 1994), 68; Jackson, *Crabgrass Frontier*, 227; Arnold Hirsch, *Making the Second Ghetto: Race and Housing in Chicago, 1940 –1960* (Chicago, 1998), 15; Marvin Dunn, *Black Miami in the Twentieth Century* (Gainesville, Fla., 1997), 208–209. Frequently the developers of subdivisions excluded nonwhites by instructing their salesperson to refuse to sell homes to nonwhite buyers. Regardless of such discrimination, the Federal Housing Administration (FHA) was often the institution insuring the mortgages on such tracts.
15. Gerald D. Nash, *The American West Transformed: The Impact of the Second World War* (Lincoln, Nebr., 1985), 214 –215; Chris Friday, " 'In Due Time': Narratives of Race and Place in the Western United States," in Paul Wong, ed., *Race, Ethnicity, and Nationality in the United States: Toward the Twenty-First Century* (Boulder, Colo., 1999), 132–135.
16. Sing Sheng to the author, p. 1; "Democracy in Southwood," 27; "Sing [*sic*] Family Gets Host of Offers," 1–2; Sing and Grace Sheng to Southwood residents, Feb. 5, 1952, Sheng Collection.
17. "Zhongzu qishi zai jiujinshan!" ["Racial discrimination in San Francisco!"], circa March 1952, unidentified Chinese-language newspaper, Sheng Collection. I have translated into English all quotations from Chinese language sources. "A District Votes on 'Restriction,' " *San Francisco Chronicle*, Feb. 16, 1952, Sheng Collection.
18. "Community Opposes Letting Chinese Move In," *South Pasadena Record*, Sheng collection; " 'Democracy Vote' Rejects Chinese," 18.
19. Douglas Henry Daniels, *Pioneer Urbanites: A Social and Cultural History of Black San Francisco* (Philadelphia, 1980), 102; Albert S. Broussard, *Black San Francisco: The Struggle for Racial Equality in the West, 1900 –1954* (Lawrence, Kans., 1993), 44; Rick Moss, "Not Quite Paradise: The Development of the African American Community in Los Angeles through 1950," *California History*, 75 (1996), 229; Lawrence Brooks de Graaf, "Negro Migration to Los Angeles, 1930 to 1950" (Ph.D. dissertation, University of California, Los Angeles, 1962), 88; Marilynn S. Johnson, *The Second Gold Rush: Oakland and the East Bay in World War II* (Berkeley, 1993), 55; Brooks, "Ascending California's Racial Hierarchy," 39–51. Daniel Widener,

" 'Perhaps the Japanese Are to Be Thanked?' Asia, Asian Americans, and the Construction of Black California," *Positions: East Asia Cultures Critique*, 11 (2003), 145, also discusses "the Afro-Asian city" of Los Angeles.

20. Yuji Ichioka, *Issei: The World of the First Generation Japanese Immigrants, 1885–1924* (New York, 1988), 91–145, details the history of Japanese laborers' involvement in various unions throughout the West. Cletus E. Daniels, *Bitter Harvest: A History of California Farmworkers, 1871–1941* (Ithaca, N.Y., 1981), 72–74, analyzes the reasons many growers considered the Chinese "docile" workers; most had to do with the workers' relative powerlessness.
21. William Daugherty, "China's Official Publicity in the United States," *Public Opinion Quarterly*, 6 (1942), 72–73; Quincy Wright and Carl J. Nelson, "American Attitudes Toward Japan and China, 1937–1938," in ibid., 3 (1939), 48–50; Hadley Cantril, Donald Rugg, and Frederick Williams, "America Faces the War: Shifts in Opinion," in ibid., 4 (1940), 655.
22. "Rice Bowl: Money by Sheaf and Handful Pours into Chronicle Office," *San Francisco Chronicle*, Feb. 9, 1940, p. 7; Yu, *To Save China*, 82– 83; Arthur Caylor, "Behind the News," *San Francisco News*, July 8, 1939, p. 13; Tad Uyeno, "Lancer's Column," *Rafu Shimpo*, Nov. 24, 1940, p. 4.
23. Michi Nishiura Weglyn, *Years of Infamy: The Untold Story of America's Concentration Camps* (Seattle, 1996), 38; Yong Chen, *Chinese San Francisco, 1850–1943: A Transpacific Community* (Stanford, Calif., 2000), 246; "How to Tell Your Friends from the Japs," *Time*, Dec. 22, 1941, p. 33.
24. Chen, *Chinese San Francisco*, 246; Judy Yung, *Unbound Feet: A Social History of Chinese Women in San Francisco* (Berkeley, 1995), 251, 253. Chinese aliens were prohibited from becoming citizens before 1943, and American citizens could not bring Chinese alien wives into the country.
25. Dolly Rhee, "Chinese Home Front," *San Francisco Chronicle*, Dec. 24, 1942, p. 6; Takaki, *Strangers from a Different Shore*, 373 –374; Johnson, *The Second Gold Rush*, 63; Davis McEntire, *Residence and Race: Final and Comprehensive Report to the Commission on Race and Housing* (Berkeley, 1960), 46.
26. Marie Carey, "Chinese Girl to Christen Next Ship," *San Francisco Chronicle*, Dec. 3, 1942, p. 10 (emphasis added); "Authority Starts Postwar Slum-Clearance Program," *San Francisco Housing Authority News*, 2 (Aug.–Sept. 1945), 3; Grace Simons, "56th Street Whites Fight Chinese, Too," *Los Angeles Sentinel*, May 30, 1946, p. 2.
27. "The Shengs and Democracy," *Life*, March 3, 1952, p. 19; "Mrs. FDR Here, Says Truman News Isn't Surprising," *San Francisco Chronicle*, March 30, 1952, p. 7. See also Ellen Watamull to editor, in ibid., Feb. 19, 1952, p. 16; "A Dream Destroyed," *Pittsburgh Post-Gazette*, Feb. 20, 1952, Sheng Collection; "Offers of Welcome Received by Excluded Chinese Family," *Milwaukee Journal*, in ibid.; Mario J. Canabba (Grand Rapids, Mich.), to editor, *San Francisco Examiner*, Feb. 23, 1952, p. 12.; Joan W. Snell (Rochester, Minn.), to Sing and Grace Sheng, March 3, 1952, Sheng Collection.; John Kenneth Hyatt, Jr. (Annapolis, Md.), to editor, *Time*, March 10, 1952, p. 8; R. M. Barnard (Seattle), to editor, *San Francisco Chronicle*, Feb. 21, 1952, p. 13. The Sheng family received about 400 letters from supporters in California and across the United States.
28. "Southwood to the World," *San Francisco Chronicle*, Feb. 19, 1952, p. 16; "Another Disservice Is Rendered to Democracy," *Sacramento Bee*, Feb. 20, 1952, p. 42; Raymond Lawrence, "At Home and Abroad—The Vindication of Sing Sheng," *Oakland Tribune*, Feb. 20, 1952, p. 60. For examples of pro-Asian American articles in the *San Francisco Chronicle*, see "Intermarriage of Chinese Is Still Banned," *San Francisco Chronicle*, Jan. 22, 1944, p. 7; "Citizens' Return," in ibid., Dec. 14,

1944, p. 12; Tedd Thomey, "The Guerreros Only Want to Make S.F. Landlords Understand—That They, Too, Are Americans," in ibid., June 23, 1943, p. 11.

29. Twain Michelsen to Emmons McClurg, Feb. 17, 1952, Sheng Collection; "State's Leaders Deplore Ban on Chinese Family," *Oakland Tribune*, Feb. 20, 1952; Gov. Earl Warren to Sing Sheng, Feb. 18, 1952, Sheng Collection.
30. Aside from those cited above, newer studies that examine the impact of black migration on Northern California include Shirley Ann Wilson Moore, *To Place Our Deeds: The African American Community in Richmond, California, 1910–1963* (Berkeley, 2000); Gretchen Lemke-Santangelo, *Abiding Courage: African American Migrant Women and the East Bay Community* (Chapel Hill, N.C., 1996); and Robert Owen Self, *American Babylon: Race and the Struggle for Postwar Oakland* (Princeton, N.J., 2003). Fewer studies of Los Angeles and the black migration have been published in the past two decades, but Scott Kurashige, "Transforming Los Angeles: Black and Japanese American Struggles for Racial Equality in the Twentieth Century" (Ph.D. dissertation, University of California, Los Angeles, 2000) deals with this period, as do Josh Sides, *L.A. City Limits: African American Los Angeles from the Great Depression to the Present* (Berkeley, 2003), and Kevin Allen Leonard, "Years of Hope, Days of Fear: The Impact of World War II on Race Relations in Los Angeles" (Ph.D. dissertation, University of California, Davis, 1992). An older source that deals specifically with the wartime migration is Keith Edison Collins, "Black Los Angeles: The Maturing of the Ghetto, 1940–1950" (Ph.D. dissertation, University of California, San Diego, 1975).
31. State of California, Nov. 1946 ballot. For more discussion of this period, see Kevin Allen Leonard, " 'Is That What We Fought For?' Japanese Americans and Racism in California: The Impact of World War II," *Western Historical Quarterly*, 21 (1990), 463—482, and Daniel Widener, " 'Perhaps the Japanese Are to Be Thanked?' " 167.
32. Nash, *The American West Transformed*, 94 –106; Friday, " 'In Due Time,' " 132; "Fact-Sheet #1: America Plus," Jan. 21, 1952, pp. 1– 4, "Housing" file, carton 1, California Federation for Civic Unity Papers, Bancroft Library, University of California, Berkeley (hereafter Civic Unity Papers); Earl C. Behrens, " 'America Plus' Urges Haste on Petitions," *San Francisco Chronicle*, Dec. 10, 1951, p. 1.
33. Josh Sides, " 'You Understand My Condition': The Civil Rights Congress in the Los Angeles African-American Community, 1946 –1952," *Pacific Historical Review*, 67 (1998), 251–257. Edward L. Barrett, *The Tenney Committee: Legislative Investigation of Subversive Activities in California* (Ithaca, N.Y., 1951), offers a critical examination of Jack Tenney's record.
34. Franklin H. Williams to Walter White, Roy Wilkins, Thurgood Marshall, Gloster Currant, Henry Lee Moon, and Clarence Mitchell, Dec. 31, 1951, "American [*sic*] Plus, 1951–1953" file, carton 43, National Association for the Advancement of Colored People-West Coast Branch Papers, Bancroft Library (hereafter NAACP-WC Papers). "Memo to Edward Howden," March 21, 1952, ibid.; "Gongmin tuanjie hui huabu quanjuan shu" ["Civic Unity Council Chinatown letter urges donations"], *Taiping Yang Zhoubao* (*Chinese- Pacific Weekly*, San Francisco), March 1, 1952, p. 26.
35. Bernard Taper, "South S.F. City Council Deplores Exclusion Vote," *San Francisco Chronicle*, Feb. 19. 1952, p. 1, and Taper, "New Action on 'Test of Democracy,' " Feb. 22, 1952, Sheng Collection; "Council Disavows Ban on Chinese," *Oakland Tribune*, Feb. 19, 1952, p. 1.
36. "Southwood is Exclusive—But Sing Sheng Haunts It," *San Francisco Chronicle*, Feb. 25, 1952, Sheng Collection; "Southwood Residents Strike Back at Critics," *San Francisco Examiner*, Feb. 22, 1952, p. 3; "Homeowners Reaffirm Stand Against Sheng," ibid., Feb. 24, 1952, p. 3.

37. "Southwood Residents Strike Back at Critics," 3; Luigi Laurenti, *Property Values and Race: Studies in Seven Cities* (Berkeley, 1961), 18; "Community Opposes Letting Chinese Move In," Sheng Collection; Robert Lee, "Community Exclusion: A Case Study," *Phylon*, 15 (1954), 205.
38. Sugrue, *The Origins of the Urban Crisis*, 216–217; Becky M. Nicolaides, *My Blue Heaven: Life and Politics in the Working-Class Suburbs of Los Angeles, 1920–1965* (Chicago, 2002), 5.
39. Gayle B. Montgomery and James W. Johnson, *One Step from the White House: The Rise and Fall of Senator William F. Knowland* (Berkeley, 1998), 89; Raymond A. Mohl, "Shifting Patterns of American Urban Policy Since 1900," in Hirsch and Mohl, eds., *Urban Policy in Twentieth-Century America*, 15–17. As Andrew Rotter has shown, Asia eclipsed Africa in the minds of American policymakers not just because the latter was largely under European rule in the 1950s but also because the success of the communist revolution in China drew U.S. officials' attention to the other underdeveloped nations in Asia. Rotter, *The Path to Vietnam*, 31.
40. Whitfield, *The Culture of the Cold War*, 71; May, *Homeward Bound*, 17–18.
41. Harold Mansfield to Sing and Grace Sheng, Feb. 17, 1952, Sheng Collection; "Pulse of the Public: Southwood's Treatment of Sing [*sic*] Family Brings Many Bitter Protests," *San Francisco News*, Feb. 20, 1952, ibid.; "The Sheng Case," *People's Daily World*, Feb. 21, 1952, p. 3.
42. "Southwood Is Exclusive," 1; "The Shengs and Democracy," 19; "Democracy in Southwood," 27; Louise R. Hewlett to editor, *Life*, March 10, 1952, p. 12; Bob Sturia, "So. S.F. 'Apologizes' to Voted-Out Chinese," *San Francisco News*, Feb. 19, 1952, Sheng Collection; Max G. Funke to Joan W. Snell, March 7, 1952, in ibid.
43. Anonymous Southwood resident to editor, *San Francisco Examiner*, Feb. 25, 1952, ibid.; "Southwood Residents Strike Back at Critics."
44. Brooks, "Ascending California's Racial Hierarchy," 311–313, 347–348; "Warren Hits Decision," *San Francisco Examiner*, Feb. 20, 1952, p. 3.
45. "Victims of Propaganda," *California Eagle*, Feb. 28, 1952, p. 5.
46. William Byron Rumford interview by Joyce A. Henderson, Amelia Fry, and Edward France, 1970–1971, Earl Warren Oral History Program (files online, Berkeley, accessed Oct. 1, 2002), http://sunsite.berkeley.edu:2020/dynaweb/teiproj/oh/blackalum/rumford/.
47. Zia, *Asian American Dreams*, 45; Chun, *Of Orphans and Warriors*, 76 –77; "The People Say . . .," *Chinese Press*, May 4, 1951, p. 1; Y. C. Hong, "A New Year's Message to Chinese-Americans," in ibid., Jan. 5, 1951, p. 1; *Chinese News*, Feb. 27, 1954, p. 2; Howard Freeman to Joseph A. Quan, June 11, 1956, p. 1, file 30, carton 3, Charles Leong Papers, Ethnic Studies Library, University of California, Berkeley (hereafter Leong Papers).
48. See, for example, Laurenti, *Property Values and Race*, 18; Catherine Bauer Wurster, *Housing and the Future of Cities in the San Francisco Bay Area* (Berkeley, 1963), 13; Wilson Record, *Minority Groups and Intergroup Relations in the San Francisco Bay Area* (Berkeley, 1963), 13–14; "The Sheng Story: Scientific Study Shows Property Loses No Value When Races Mix," *San Francisco Chronicle*, Feb. 21, 1951, p. 4; Davis McEntire, "A Study of Racial Attitudes in Neighborhoods Infiltrated by Nonwhites: San Francisco, Oakland, and Berkeley" (1955), pp. 127–129, "*Bay Area Real Estate Reporter*" file, carton 43, NAACP-WC Papers; Lawrence E. Davies, "Case of the Sing Shengs Has Aroused West Coast," *New York Times*, Feb. 24, 1952, Sheng Collection; Yen Le Espiritu, *Asian American Panethnicity: Bridging Institutions and Identities* (Philadelphia, 1994), 20–32; Charles Leong to Harry Honda, March 3, 1953, file 31, carton 3, Leong Papers. See also "Our Achilles Heel," *Scene*, Oct. 1950, p. 26; editorial in ibid., July 1950, p. 26; "Anonymous Letter

Objects to Chinese Nisei Home Plans," *Pacific Citizen*, July 24, 1953, p. 4; "New-Style Ambassadors," *Chinese News*, April 10, 1954, p. 10; and "Chinese-Japanese Legion Auxiliary Formed in Denver," in ibid., March 25, 1949, p. 1. Star Chinese American and Japanese American basketball teams also played an annual "Oriental championship" game during the 1950s.

49. Him Mark Lai, "The Chinese Press in the United States and Canada Since World War II: A Diversity of Voices," *Chinese America: History and Perspectives*, 9 (1990), 111; "The Sing Shengs and Democracy," *Pacific Citizen*, Feb. 23, 1952, p. 4; Jing Nan, "Suibi" (Essay), *Taiping Yang Zhoubao*, Feb. 23, 1952, p. 17; "Sheng an zhuanhao: lun zhongzu pianjian" ["Special Sheng case focus: a discussion of racial prejudice"], *Shaonian Zhongguo Nongbao* [*Young China*, San Francisco], Feb. 21, 1952, p. 3.
50. Churchill T. Chiu to Editor, *San Francisco Examiner*, Feb. 25, 1952, Sheng Collection; Alfred B. Chan to editor, *San Francisco Chronicle*, Feb. 20., 1952; Lim P. Lee to editor, ibid., Feb. 20, 1952.
51. "Chinese Welcomed to California Home," *New York Times*, March 13, 1952, p. 3; "24 Against Nisei As Neighbor," *San Jose Mercury*, Oct. 9, 1952, p. 1; "Neighbors Welcome Yoshihara," ibid., Oct. 10, 1952, pp. 1– 4.
52. "Sheng An de Zhongzhong" ["Straight talk on the Sheng case"], *Taiping Yang Zhoubao*, Feb. 23, 1952, p. 3; "Anonymous Letter," *Pacific Citizen*, p. 4; "Anti-Chinese Attitude Not Popular Here," *Daily Palo Alto Times*, June 28, 1954, p. 6; "Japanese Dentist Gets Dozens of Home Offers," *San Francisco Chronicle*, March 19, 1955, pp. 1–13. The anonymous caller who threatened Earl LaCount warned him against selling to "orientals."
53. "Not a Story to Hide," *San Francisco Chronicle*, Aug. 19, 1955, p. 1; Michael Harris, "Diving Champ Gets Bias-Case Support," in ibid., Aug. 20, 1955, p. 1, and "Nixon Shocked by Bias Against Dr. Sammy Lee," in ibid., Aug. 21, 1955, pp. 1– 4; Robert Bland, "Report on Garden Grove," circa 1957, pp. 1–3, file 6, box 30, American Civil Liberties Union-Southern California papers, Special Collections, University of California, Los Angeles.
54. The situation of Mexican Americans, particularly in Southern California, was complex and involved factors such as skin color, income, and neighborhood. For this reason, I have not attempted to deal at length here with Mexican American housing issues.
55. Von Eschen, *Race Against Empire*, 107; Plummer, *Rising Wind*, 211–212.
56. California State Assembly, House Resolution 33, March 19, 1952.
57. "Neighbors Object to Negro Family," *San Francisco Chronicle*, Dec. 11, 1953, p. 6; "Anti-Chinese Attitude Not Popular Here," 6; Timothy Fong, *The First Suburban Chinatown: The Remaking of Monterey Park, California* (Philadelphia, 1994), 21–23.
58. Bland, "Report on Garden Grove," 1–3; David Perlman, "Willie Mays Is Refused S.F. House—Negro," *San Francisco Chronicle*, Nov. 14, 1957, pp. 1, 22; Steve W. LaBounty, "Willie Mays on Miraloma Drive," in *Streetwise* [online journal] (San Francisco, 2000, accessed May 2, 2003); available from http://www.outsidelands.org/sw5.html.
59. Notes, circa Feb. 1952, "Housing" file, carton 1, Civic Unity Papers.
60. "Editorials," folder 567, "Discrimination—Racial—General—Housing 1940–1950 clippings," American Civil Liberties Union-Northern California papers, North Baker Library, California Historical Society, San Francisco; "Sad Story Has Happy Ending," *San Francisco News*, Jan. 11, 1954, Sheng Collection; Elaine D. Johnson, "Survey of Peninsula Realtors," Nov. 6, 1957, p. 1, "Survey of Peninsula Realtors" file, carton 45, NAACP-WC Papers. In two September 1999 e-mails to the author, Richard Sheng noted that his family moved in 1955 and that he recalled no other

nonwhite family living in his neighborhood up to that point. The *1960 U.S. Census* (Washington, D.C., 1960), 56 –57, suggests that Asian Americans but not blacks were able to find homes on the Peninsula by 1960. "Other" races were evident in significant numbers in Menlo Park neighborhoods in which no African Americans lived, or in which only one or two lived. The same was the case for San Mateo, Redwood City, and similar towns. The 1950 census did not include breakdowns for the San Francisco Peninsula. However, the *Chinese Press* of June 30, 1950, featured articles on Chinese American life in Peninsula towns with few if any blacks.

61. Mexican Americans were the largest minority group in the Los Angeles area at this time and had been the largest minority group in Los Angeles County (but not the city) before the war. However, census officials classified Mexican Americans as "white" between 1930 and 1960, making their movements more difficult to track from census tract to census tract.
62. Brooks, "Ascending California's Racial Hierarchy," 207.
63. Quoted in Dudziak, *Cold War Civil Rights*, 89.
64. One notable exception was Southern white opposition to Hawaiian statehood. This opposition was based almost entirely on the racial diversity of the territory's population, almost half of which was of Asian origin.
65. Von Eschen, *Race Against Empire*, 3.

Chapter 8

Murder and Biblical Memory: The Legend of Vernon Johns

Ralph E. Luker

From *The Virginia Magazine of History and Biography*

In the dark hours after the assassination of Martin Luther King, Jr., in Memphis, Tennessee, a television reporter sought to interview his best friend, Ralph D. Abernathy. As riots tore through Baltimore, Chicago, New York, Washington, and dozens of other cities and left thirty-nine people dead, Abernathy was unresponsive to the reporter's questions. He was lost in reverie. The reporter asked about the assassination, plans for the future, and memories of historic events between 1955 and 1968. In shock, King's best friend retreated to another place, telling stories about an earlier best friend in the ministry, Vernon Johns (figure 8.1), who was unknown to the reporter. More than a decade later, King biographer Taylor Branch reviewed footage of that interview. It inspired the brilliantly written first chapter of his Pulitzer Prize-winning book, *Parting the Waters: America in the King Years, 1954–1963*. Grandly conceived, it may be the most beautifully written book on the modern civil rights movement. Its stunning opening chapter on Johns, King's less-well-known predecessor at Montgomery, Alabama's Dexter Avenue Baptist Church, makes the Vernon Johns story a dramatic prelude to the mid-century crisis in race relations.[1]

Branch rightly began his story with Vernon Johns. In the eighteen months between becoming the pastor of Dexter Avenue and the beginning of the bus boycott that put his name in headlines across the land, King knew that Johns was a more prominent figure in the Afro-Baptist world than he was. Inviting princes of its pulpit to Montgomery as guest speakers, he identified himself as Johns's successor because his predecessor's name was much more recognizable than his own. "My immediate predecessor was your friend, Dr. Vernon

Figure 8.1 Vernon Johns, ca. 1959.
Source: Oberlin College Archives.

Johns," King told Howard Thurman, dean of Boston University's Marsh Chapel. "You will probably remember me from my recent studies [there]."[2]

More importantly, having helped to launch a movement with which he could only hope to stay abreast, Martin Luther King drew the associates of his predecessor at Dexter Avenue around him. His closest friend in the movement, Abernathy, had spent two years as Vernon Johns's understudy before King came to Montgomery.[3] When his Southern Christian Leadership Conference (SCLC) seemed to flounder between 1957 and 1960, King sought as its chief operating officer other men who had apprenticed with Johns, John Lee Tilley and Wyatt Tee Walker.[4] Before their appointments, both men had won laurels for leadership in the movement. Tilley had led a successful voter registration drive in Baltimore, but when his leadership failed to breathe life into SCLC, King recruited the younger and more aggressive Walker. As pastor of Petersburg, Virginia's historic Gillfield Baptist Church, Wyatt Walker was an active state and local leader in the Congress of Racial Equality, the National Association for the Advancement of Colored People, and SCLC. He had become the embodiment of the movement in Virginia. Unlike Tilley, Walker was willing to leave his pastorate, move to Atlanta, and put all of his abundant energy and talent at the disposal of King and SCLC.

Johns, King, Abernathy, Tilley, and Walker were all Afro-Baptist preachers whose paths frequently intersected. When Johns left Montgomery in 1953, he shuttled between his Virginia farm; Baltimore, where he succeeded Tilley as director of the Maryland Baptist Center; and Petersburg, where his wife taught music at Virginia State College and directed the children's choir at Walker's church.[5] By 1960, the legend of Vernon Johns was fixing itself in the firmament of the Afro-Baptist preachers who made up the core of King's SCLC. In a circle where such relationships were important, he was, after all, King's predecessor, the mentor of Ralph Abernathy and Wyatt Walker, and the successor of John Tilley. The legend was nurtured by Vernon Johns's commanding presence, but nothing entertained his fellow Baptist preachers more than Wyatt Walker's perfect mime of Johns's rural Virginia accent or Ralph Abernathy's latest Vernon Johns story. Walker said that Johns was simply "the greatest preacher I've known, living, dead or unborn." When they spoke of his role in history, the biblical analogy seemed obvious. Johns had long been "preparing the way," said Abernathy. He was a John the Baptist, they believed, "a forerunner of the whole civil rights movement."[6] As forerunner, Vernon Johns figured in both the NAACP's litigation leading to *Brown v. Board of Education* in 1954 and the Montgomery Improvement Association's nonviolent direct action in the bus boycott of 1955 and 1956.

If successions, associations, and forerunning are important, there was also the direct plea for help. In October 1963, as Wyatt Walker prepared to leave the SCLC staff, Martin Luther King and the nation had endured a remarkable emotional roller coaster. The previous six months had been the most exhilarating and exhausting in SCLC's brief history. During massive spring demonstrations in Birmingham, King and Walker had collaborated to produce the "Letter from the Birmingham Jail." Concurrent protests in Cambridge, Maryland; Jackson, Mississippi; Savannah, Georgia; and Greensboro, North Carolina, tested the distinction between peaceful demonstration and riot. This hazy line was then eradicated in the riots that broke out after the announcement of a "settlement" in Birmingham. The violence continued to swirl around the movement, as Medgar Evers was assassinated in Jackson and Fannie Lou Hamer beaten in Winona, Mississippi, by the time King recycled an old speech, "I Have a Dream," for the March on Washington at the end of August.[7] Two weeks later, Vernon Johns closed a revival at the Atlanta church of King's best friend in college and seminary, Walter McCall, with the announced subject, "Here Comes the Dreamer."[8]

That Sunday morning, Birmingham's Sixteenth Street Baptist Church was bombed, and four church school students were killed. King preached a eulogy for them. In the previous six months, he had produced both texts by which he is now best remembered. Yet, just then, Branch tells us, King felt "demoralized and stale," exhausted, emotionally drained, and uncertain about the future of the movement. He was in need of fresh words of judgment and hope. When SCLC failed to locate Vernon Johns to preach for its late September convention in Richmond, King sent his personal attorney, Chauncey Eskridge, on a mission to Petersburg. The urbane Chicago lawyer had heard colorful stories about Virginia's vagabond preacher and relished the task of tracking him down.[9]

Eskridge was unprepared, however, to find the Reverend Johns tending a "squatter's vegetable stand" in the muddy vacant lot of an abandoned gas station in Petersburg. From the stubble of a white beard to the rumpled shirt and pants and the rough brogans unrefined by socks or strings, the old man might have been mistaken for a wino on the street corner. Yet, Eskridge had come, not to offer help, but to seek it. "He wants you to give me all your notebooks for your Sunday sermons," said the attorney. "Dr. King sent you to me for that?" Johns asked. The preacher recited titles, reliable texts from Scripture and snatches of sermons. They lived with the cloud in his head, he told Eskridge. Finally, moved by Eskridge's serious purpose, Johns parted the clouds and launched into an oft-repeated stemwinder. The attorney listened patiently and asked the preacher to send along whatever notes he had. Nothing came of the request, says Branch, and Eskridge concluded that the notebooks "did not exist—always his sermons returned to the air from which they had come." King, however, insisted that there must be notebooks. When Johns died twenty months later, he asked again and Eskridge repeated that nothing had come in the mail.[10]

Clearly, if we hope to understand the roots and spirit of the movement that Martin Luther King led and if his judgment is any measure of it, we need to understand who this enigmatic preacher from the backwater of Virginia was, what moved him, and what he had to say. Taylor Branch made a major contribution to that end by drawing him to our attention, but his careless methods undermined the achievement.[11] In order to understand Vernon Johns, it is necessary to recapitulate the legend he created and deconstruct Branch's version of it.

Nowhere is Branch more eloquent than in his narrative of murders committed by Vernon Johns's two grandfathers, one white and one black, with its suggestion that both were done for a moral purpose.

> Vernon Johns was merely another invisible man to nearly all whites, but to the invisible people themselves he was the stuff of legend. The deepest mysteries of existence and race rubbed vigorously together within him, heating a brain that raced constantly until the day he died. His ancestry was a jumble of submerged edges and storybook extremes. During slavery, his father's father was hanged for cutting his master in two with a scythe, and even eighty years later it was whispered in the Johns family that the hunting dogs would not approach the haunted spot where the murder had occurred.
>
> Johns's maternal grandfather was a white man named Price, of Scottish descent, who maintained two entirely separate families—one white, one Negro. This type of bi-patriarchy, though fairly widespread, was never publicly acknowledged in either culture. The Negro children handed down stories about how Price became one of the first inmates at the new Virginia State Penitentiary for killing another white man he caught trying to rape his slave mistress. He protected the mistress "just like she was a white woman." For this he was admired by some Negroes, but he was by nature a mean, violent, complicated man. When his Negro wife died in the 1870s, he took all his Negro children into the other household to be raised by his childless white

> wife, "Miss Kitty." Vernon Johns's mother, Sallie Price, made this transfer as a little girl, and years later she told her family how the taboos had been respected against all opposing reality, even in the intimacy of the home. She never called her father "father," for decency required the Negro children to be orphans and the white couple to be missionary dispensers of foster care. When Price died about 1900, Sallie Price Johns went to the funeral with her young son Vernon and her husband Willie, son of the hanged slave, and sat through the burial services in a separate-but-equal family section, just across the gravesite from Miss Kitty and the white relatives.
>
> Willie Johns died not long afterward, and in due course Sallie Johns married her dead husband's younger brother. So Vernon Johns finished his youth as the stepson of his uncle, and grandson of a slave who killed his master and of a master who killed for his slave. Only in the Bible did he find open discussion of such a tangle of sex, family, slavery, and violence.[12]

Here, a master storyteller gives us a narrative with the ring of poetic truth that serves well as a prologue to the great human rights struggle of mid-twentieth century America. Yet, most of this narrative is no nearer the truth than Warner Brothers' version of *The Color Purple* to Alice Walker's novel or Hollywood's "Mississippi Burning" is to Mississippi reality. Vernon Johns did have a white and a black grandfather, his white grandfather did kill at least one person, and Johns did believe that the trauma of his own story was prefigured in biblical history.

Branch's interviews with Vernon Johns's children and members of SCLC's inner circle told a version of Vernon Johns's family myth. A primal murder, an act of alcoholic rage, was a source of public embarrassment to the family's first generation. It became two very different things to the next generation. On the one hand it was a private scandal that some, like Vernon Johns's genteel wife Altona Trent Johns, chose not to discuss. Thus, her narrative of the family history makes no reference to sex or murder. On the other hand, though he never mentioned his white grandfather in public, for Vernon Johns the past served as a stimulus for reflections on biblical teachings about human communities and what might justify an act of murderous violence. In doing so, he created a family myth that transfigured a tragic legacy into a redemptive heritage. Nurtured between those two different instincts and piecing together bits of what they had been told, Vernon and Altona Johns's children and Vernon Johns's associates at SCLC told Branch the stories of two murders, committed by two different grandfathers, both committed with moral purpose and projected back many years earlier than the primal events, into a past well beyond their memories.

A memoir by Altona Trent Johns about her husband's family is among the sources that Branch cites for this remarkable tale. It refers to the paternal grandfather of color by name, Monroe Johns, and tells us—not that he was hanged as a slave for killing his slave master—but that he lived a quiet life beyond emancipation as a shoemaker and cook to nurture a large family into the twentieth century.[13] Pull that thread and others offer themselves for the pulling. The resulting fabric is closer to the truth, even more instructive, and still fascinating. It also suggests important lessons about how and why a family might mislead a historian, how Branch came to believe his fabrication, and the proper relationship of oral history sources to documentary evidence.

The original source of the story of a slave who killed his master was certainly Vernon Johns. In his maturity, Johns often told the story of a slave who cut his master in two "with a scythe or wheat cradle." Sometimes, he said that the slave was his grandfather; sometimes, he said that the slave was hanged for murder; and, sometimes, he said that it happened near the location of Prince Edward County's Robert Russa Moton High School. In none of his versions of this story, however, did Johns refer to the slave by name. Branch heard the story repeated by Vernon Johns's children and associates. It was a cornerstone of the legend that Johns nurtured and that took root among his children and in SCLC's highest circles.[14] The apparent contradiction between Vernon and Altona Trent Johns's stories about his grandfather of color, to whom they both refer, is illuminated by the story of his white grandfather, of whom neither of them was ever known to speak in public.

Thomas W. Price, Vernon Johns's white grandfather, died at Virginia's state prison farm at Goochland—not as Branch has it "about 1900"—but in 1923. More threads. Little Vernon, his father and mother, Willie and Sallie Branch Price Johns, could not have attended his graveside burial and sat across from "Miss Kitty" and the white Price family because Vernon Johns was thirty-one years old and both "Miss Kitty" Price and Willie Johns were dead by the time Tom Price died. He was buried on the day of his death, probably in a pauper's grave, in Richmond.[15] If Branch's account of Vernon Johns's family background is so flawed, we need to understand the actual story because it registered deeply in the mind of Tom Price's grandson and fed his thinking about race, religion, and violence in America.

In the summer months of 1865, after Robert E. Lee surrendered his remaining troops at nearby Appomattox Courthouse, the newly elected Prince Edward County Court replaced its old slave patrols with new patrols to police the countryside. In Darlington Heights, a remote Prince Edward community, the court named a white farmer, Tom Price, to serve on the patrol.[16] Before the Civil War, Price had married a white woman by the name of Catherine, who became known as "Miss Kitty" Price to all who knew her. More than ten years older than her husband, Miss Kitty would have no children, but she and Tom owned seven male and five female slaves. In May 1861, he enrolled as a private in Company I of the 23d Virginia Regiment of the Army of Northern Virginia and was detailed as a wagoner. Suffering from chronic diarrhea and epilepsy, Tom Price spent much of his time as a Confederate soldier in hospitals at Charlottesville and Lynchburg. In August 1862, he received a disability discharge from Confederate service and returned to the farm in Prince Edward County.[17]

By then, the oldest of Tom Price's female slaves, Dolly, had given birth to a child. After emancipation, she took the name of an African American consort and became known as Dolly Gaines. By 1870, she was the mother of four daughters, who ranged in age from newborn Frances to nine-year-old Ada.[18] In 1875, Dolly Gaines gave birth to a son, Peter; and, in February 1879, to a second son, Henry. Seven months later, Miss Kitty Price reported that Dolly Gaines had died of consumption and the infant of pneumonia.[19] Other women in the neighborhood, however, believed that Tom Price had become enraged by rumors that the child was not his son. Their grapevine said that, as a slave, Dolly Gaines had children both by Tom Price and her African American consort, Richard Gains, and that Tom Price had sold the children he did not father and separated their parents. Enraged that they had reunited to conceive another child, Price "violated" Dolly Gaines with a stick and she bled to death.[20] Clearly, Tom Price did not kill "another white man he caught trying to rape his slave mistress." Nor did he protect his "mistress 'just like she was a white woman.' " Apart from Miss Kitty's report that Dolly Gaines died of consumption, which may have been a cover story for her husband's violent murder of his former slave mistress, the documentary evidence substantiates the neighborhood grapevine's version of their relationship. Tom Price's subsequent history of violence and his wife's willingness to tell a cover story for him also lends credibility to it.[21]

The Price and Gaines households changed dramatically after the death of Dolly Gaines. Tom Price's seventy-four-year-old mother, Sallie B. Price, moved in with him and Miss Kitty. Dolly Gaines's two older daughters either died or left home by 1880, when the Gaines family included Lizzie, 13; Frances, 11; Sallie, 9; Pattie, 7; and their young brother, Peter, 5. Unlike his predecessor, the census taker in 1880 carefully noted that these children were "mulattoes."[22] By then, the Prices had accepted responsibility for Tom's children with Dolly Gaines. After all, Sallie was named for her white grandmother and Pattie for her white aunt, the wife of Tom's brother, A. J. And all the children assumed their white father's last name by 1882. In time, the memory of their mother, Dolly Gaines; her African American lover, Richard Gains; and that they had ever been known by any other last name were almost forgotten within the family. By then, the younger Sallie had married and would be known by all who knew her as Sallie Branch Price Johns.[23]

The Johns family was the third household in the human drama in Darlington Heights. There were white Johns families throughout central Virginia, and there had been free Johns people of color in the counties south and west of Richmond for more than 150 years. Some men of color by that name had served in the Revolutionary War.[24] There were no free families named Johns in Prince Edward County in 1860, however. Both Monroe and Harriet Womack Johns were of bi-racial background and, in 1860, were among the fourteen slaves owned by John Dillon, whose farm lay adjacent to the Price's. Harriet was born about 1840, probably on the other side of the Price's place from the Dillon farm on David Womack's plantation where sixty-five slaves lived by 860.[25] Monroe Johns was born about 1835, possibly on the Buckingham County farm of Melville Monroe Johns, and like his wife, had been sold by 1860 to John Dillon.[26] Harriet gave birth to their first child, Carter, by 1861 and their second, William Thomas, in 1864. At emancipation, Monroe and Harriet asserted their freedom by shunning Dillon's name. After emancipation, Monroe worked as a farm laborer and a shoemaker, keeping house and cooking for his wife and their five sons and four daughters. Harriet Womack Johns continued to work for wages on the Dillon family farm in Arlington Heights after emancipation.[27]

In the 1880s, the Johns men knit the fabric of family with the Price women. On 2 November 1882, Harriet and Monroe Johns's oldest son, Carter, married Tom Price's most eligible daughter, seventeen-year-old Lizzie. When the marriage was officially recorded in Prince Edward County's records, her parents were listed as "T & D Price." Carter and Lizzie Price Johns would name one of their daughters Dolly. On 18 December 1889, Lizzie's younger sister, Sallie Branch Price, married Carter Johns's younger brother, William Thomas Johns, who was known to all as Willie. Their children's double first cousin would be the family's last surviving link to the slave woman, Dolly, who bore Tom Price's children and may have died from wounds he inflicted.[28]

After their marriage, Willie and Sallie Branch Price Johns farmed and became the parents of five sons and two daughters. Their oldest son, Vernon Napoleon Johns, was born on 22 April 1892. The middle name became a thorn in his side. After 1925, he never used it, and it was known only to the immediate family.[29] Even in 1892, the legacy of slavery still cast a long shadow over Prince Edward County. The old court ledger in which the birth of "Bernard Johns" was recorded still offered the option of listing a child of color as having been born a slave. If no children were so listed, the New South's pale substitutes for slavery were all too evident. In 1894, an African American convict brought into the county on a chain gang to do road construction escaped and shed his telltale prison stripes, only to be caught in naked flight through Darlington Heights. Two years later, Elisha Johnson, a black man, was arrested, charged with assault and robbery of two white men, and jailed at the county seat in Farmville. A mob of white men intent on lynching him gathered there four days later. Unable to break into the jail to seize him, the mob began shooting at Johnson who lay on the cot in his cell. Gunfire blew a hole in the jail's stovepipe and shattered Johnson's bedposts, but he escaped with minor wounds by rolling under the bed.[30]

In 1898, young Vernon Johns enrolled in a rough, one-room elementary school for African American students near Darlington Heights. Prince Edward County had a prominent visitor that year, the brilliant young black sociologist, W. E. B. Du Bois, who came to Farmville to study its African American community. His study did not extend to the rural community of Darlington Heights. But that summer, when Vernon Johns's white grandfather, Tom Price, was nearing seventy, he drew unsettling attention to it. On Thursday, 28 July, Price and twenty-one-year-old Hall Carter, a white farm laborer, hitched Price's horse to Carter's buggy and rode into Farmville together. In that regional center of the tobacco trade, they each withdrew

$25 of their money from the tobacco commissioner. Apparently on good terms, they bought some whiskey and left town together, reaching home in the early evening. By then, Price admitted, he was so drunk that he fell into bed still wearing his clothes and boots, while Carter drove the horse and buggy off to a prayer meeting at the Spring Creek Baptist Church. Hall Carter returned to Price's house for work very early the next day—sometime before sunrise, Miss Kitty testified. Expecting to be fed, he called into the bedchamber to ask if Price was going to fix breakfast. Still feeling the effects of the previous day's whiskey, the old man said he did not feel like it and asked where his horse was. Everyone agreed that Tom Price was mean tempered when he was drunk and that a struggle ensued. A strong man for his age, of middling height with a full flowing beard, Price was yet no match for the much younger man in a fistfight. Miss Kitty Price claimed to be the sole witness to the struggle. She told investigators that Hall Carter had come into the bedchamber, cursed her husband, and said he would fix his own breakfast. When Price threatened to shoot the young man if he did not leave the house, Carter threw the old man to the floor, choked him, and threatened to kill him with a butcher knife. Again, she said, Price ordered the farm worker out of the house. When he refused, the two men struggled over a gun, and it fired, mortally wounding Carter. Despite her assertion, it seems that Miss Kitty was not the only eyewitness. A black farmhand, Spencer Hill, claimed to have seen the fight. Hill said that, when he entered the cookroom, Hall Carter was fixing breakfast and arguing with Tom Price, who was still in bed in Miss Kitty's chambers. Price came down to the cookroom, called Carter a "dam son of a bitch," Hill said, and threatened to "cut his dam guts out" with a knife. After disarming the old man, Carter began eating breakfast, and Price returned to the bedchamber. Hill reported that he and Carter heard Miss Kitty ask Price what he was doing with his gun and that when Carter rose from the table Price fired at him.[31]

News of the death of Hall Carter spread rapidly through Darlington Heights on 29 July. Only Price's arrest by lawmen saved him from the threat of lynching for killing the popular young farm worker. In subsequent weeks, the case dominated local newspaper headlines. Charged with first-degree murder, Price was tried in Farmville between 17 and 19 August 1898. Crowds of people "from every quarter of the county . . . thronged the town and court-room." Public interest in the case was so widespread, said the newspaper, that "the trial and the court-room is crowded from morning till adjournment, while a number of attorneys from a distance are in attendance." For the defense, Tom and Miss Kitty both repeated her original claim that he had only acted in self defense. As its primary witness, the prosecution brought Spencer Hill, whose testimony expanded on the statement he had given on the day of the murder.[32]

In Prince Edward County, race was not far removed from anything, even when one white man was accused of murdering another white man. Would the jury accept the word of a black field hand against the sworn testimony of a white property owner and his wife? Among other witnesses for the prosecution, both black and white, Tom Price's own relatives of color offered convincing testimony. The local newspaper did not use her full name, but since he made no secret of her paternity, neighbors in the courtroom may have whispered knowingly as his daughter, Frances Price Womack, took the witness stand against her father. Vernon Johns's aunt testified that Miss Kitty Price's testimony contradicted other statements she made in the days after the shooting. Frances Price Womack's husband, General Womack, testified that two weeks before the murder Tom Price had threatened to kill Hall Carter for abusing Price's horse. Willie Johns's older brother, Carter Johns, was summoned to testify for the prosecution, but his testimony was apparently not thought necessary because other witnesses tended to sustain Spencer Hill's account of events. The jury found Tom Price guilty of premeditated murder, and the judge ordered him to die by hanging.[33]

When Price's attorney appealed the decision, a circuit court ordered the case remanded to the Prince Edward County court for retrial. The court convened in Farmville on 16 April 1899 to hear the case again. Unable to seat a jury from Prince Edward County because of the case's local notoriety, the court imported and empaneled jurors from Lynchburg to hear it. The second trial differed little from the first, except that Miss Kitty did not testify on her husband's behalf. On the evening of 20 April, the jury found Price guilty. His attorney's motion for a new trial was denied and, on 26 April, Price was again sentenced to die by hanging. In subsequent weeks, Tom Price's attorney and his brother, A. J. Price, gathered signatures on a petition asking Virginia's governor, J. Hoge Tyler, for clemency in Price's case. "Out of a total of white votes in the county of 956," said the local newspaper, "eight hundred and eighty-eight signed the petition." The petition for clemency also bore the signatures of seven of the twelve jurors in the first trial and all twelve jurors in the second trial. Some of Price's nearest neighbors, however, asked the governor not to intervene. At the last minute, they alleged that Miss Kitty Price admitted her husband had killed another man, John Baker, "seven or eight years ago by striking him over the head with a stick of wood." Reports in the neighborhood said that Price may have disposed of the body by dumping it in a well. When reporters inquired about the charge, Miss Kitty denied it. The petitioners against her husband had promised to take care of her every need, said Miss Kitty, if she would stand by the accusation. In August 1899, in light of Price's advanced age, Governor Tyler commuted his sentence to life in prison.[34]

Vernon Johns's maternal white grandfather did not, as Branch says, go to prison for "killing another white man he caught trying to rape his slave mistress." She had been dead, possibly by his own hands, for twenty years when Tom Price was twice convicted of the murder of a white man. Far from protecting a slave mistress "just like she was a white woman," Price's murder of a white field hand was an act of alcoholic rage that may have had its root in the treatment of a horse. An invalid for many years, Miss Kitty Price was more than eighty years old when the murder occurred and may have died soon thereafter, for she disappeared from the census records in

1900. As they followed his trial for the murder of Hall Carter, however, Tom Price's daughters may have recalled the reports that he had murdered their African American mother, Dolly Gaines. Like other residents of the remote agricultural community, however, Willie and Sallie Branch Price Johns returned to their seasonal routines. For years thereafter, the older folk would talk in hushed tones about the violence that briefly drew attention to the informal biracial family arrangements in Darlington Heights. Willie and Sallie Johns's son, Vernon, would ponder it over the years. He remembered that his white grandfather—a strong man for his age, of middling height with a full flowing beard—was sentenced to die by hanging for his senseless brutality. Johns was never known to refer to the old man in public, but he processed the memory in other ways.

If Taylor Branch's rendering of Vernon Johns's family legend is deeply flawed, other historians have raised questions about discrete inaccuracies and broader flaws in his brilliant narrative.[35] The pattern in his work is that a good story gets told even if there is reason to doubt it. Journalist Harry Ashmore was finishing a biography of his longtime mentor, Robert Maynard Hutchins, when he read *Parting the Waters*. He was startled by Branch's account of the relationship between Hutchins and Johns when the two were students at Oberlin College. It claimed that Johns had "displaced" Hutchins in the competition for college honors, that Hutchins said that "no country Negro could make the grades Johns was making without cheating," and that, when Johns heard of it, he sought out the future president of the University of Chicago, called him a "son of a bitch," and "punched him in the mouth." When Ashmore heard Branch repeat the story in an interview, he told him that its premise was obviously incorrect. Johns and Hutchins were contemporaries at Oberlin, but they did not compete for honors with each other because Hutchins was an undergraduate when Johns was taking classes in the college's theological seminary. Moreover, the story was out of character both with Ashmore's thirty-year recollection of Hutchins and the memories of Oberlin staff members who knew both Johns and Hutchins. "This bit of apocrypha," Ashmore guessed, "is the product of embroidery of family history on the part of some of the Johns' family."[36]

Replying to Ashmore, Branch thanked him for correcting the claim that, as students, the two men had been academic competitors. Yet, he rejected both Ashmore's dismissal of the story as a "bit of apocrypha" and his criticism of *Parting the Waters*' heavy reliance "on interviews rather than standard historical reference materials."

> [T]his means that the entire field of cross-racial history is necessarily risky. Vernon Johns does not exist in the standard references. These materials are generally limited, indeed almost defined, by the range of cultural comfort within the predominant society. Historical texts have excluded persons such as Vernon Johns and therefore much of the texture of black society . . . . To fill this historical gap, writers must rely on the memory of witnesses.[37]

And yet, as standard a historical reference as *Who's Who in America* included biographical information on Vernon Johns for twenty years. It may be just as well that Branch ignored *Who's Who*, because for twenty years Johns submitted misleading information to it that obscured the glitches in his career. Citing Altona Trent Johns's memoir, Branch ignored questions it should have raised about his oral history reports about the life and death of her husband's grandfather of color. Had Branch read the best history of Prince Edward County, he would have found a more reliable account of the murder by Vernon Johns's white grandfather, his trial, and his death many years later, than his interviews yielded. In short, the documentary record by and about African Americans and their kin is deeper and richer than Branch's apologia suggests, but all sources, written and oral, primary and secondary, must be used critically.

Branch's account of Vernon Johns's relationship to Martin Luther King's trial sermon at Dexter Avenue is another case of his telling a good story from oral sources, even when he had in hand evidence calling it into question. Based exclusively on an interview with Ralph Abernathy, Branch tells us that on Saturday, 16 January 1954, as King was preparing to leave Atlanta for Montgomery to give his trial sermon the next day, he received a telephone call: "Young King, this is Vernon Johns. I hear you're going to preach at my former church in Montgomery tomorrow. I'm supposed to preach myself at [Abernathy's] First Baptist, but I'm sort of stranded here in Atlanta. You think I could hitch a ride over to Montgomery with you?" There follows four pages of entertaining reconstructed dialogue and a detailed menu of the meal Mrs. Abernathy served to the three Baptist preachers at Abernathy's parsonage when King and Johns arrived. In fairness, Abernathy was undoubtedly there and he certainly told Branch much or all of this because he repeated a similar account of King's arrival in Montgomery in his own autobiography. Branch's endnote admits that King's autobiography, *Stride Toward Freedom*, says that King drove to Montgomery alone, but he privileges Abernathy's recollection thirty years later over King's recollection within five years of the event for four pages of detailed dialogue over "steak and onions, turnip greens and cornbread, and a dozen kindred delights."[39]

King's account was, of course, more accurate. On Saturday, 16 January 1954, he was actually preparing to give a trial sermon the next day at First Baptist Church in Chattanooga, Tennessee. His trial sermon at Dexter Avenue came a week later. But Vernon Johns did play a role in Martin Luther King's trial run in the Dexter Avenue pulpit. Martin Luther King, Sr., wished to be fully informed about any church that might hire his older son as its pastor. He knew that Dexter's deacons had unceremoniously relieved Vernon Johns of his responsibilities there only eight months earlier. On Sunday, 24 January 1954, while Martin Luther King, Jr., preached on "The Three Dimensions of the Complete Life" in Montgomery, Vernon Johns preached on "Segregation After Death" at Atlanta's Ebenezer Baptist Church. Probably, Johns enjoyed a fine meal with the older Kings after the service and, as likely, there was frank conversation about certain deacons in Montgomery. Abernathy's memory was remarkably flawed, especially in his last years when Branch interviewed him and his autobiography was published. In it, he referred to Vernon Johns's wife as "Alternate Johns."[40]

In ways Abernathy did not intend, much about Altona Trent Johns was alternate to her husband's background and temperament. In 1927, four years after Tom Price's death, Vernon Johns married Altona Malinda Trent. He had courted several other women, including Alroy Spencer, the daughter of Lynchburg poet Anne Spencer, and Sue Bailey, who would marry his friend, Howard Thurman, but Johns married Altona Trent. They came from very different backgrounds. He came from a farm family in the backwater of Prince Edward County. She was part of a family of urban black middle-class professionals.

In 1925, Altona Trent's father, William Johnson Trent, left a career as a secretary of African American branches of the YMCA to become the fourth president of his alma mater, Livingstone College in Salisbury, North Carolina. He would be its president for the next thirty-two years. In 1944, his son, William Johnson Trent, Jr., became the founding executive director of the United Negro College Fund. Nineteen years later, he became the assistant personnel director at Time, Inc., its senior African American executive. By contrast, Vernon Johns never held a job for more than seven years, and most of his pastorates were much shorter than that. Symptomatic of the temperamental differences between the Trents and the Johnses is that in 1951, William Johnson Trent, Sr., became the first African American appointed to the public school board in Salisbury. That same year, Vernon Johns's niece, Barbara Johns, led African American students in a boycott of the Robert Russa Moton High School in Farmville, which led to the NAACP's challenge to racial segregation in Prince Edward County's public schools.[41] The Trents were cautious, consummate insiders, respectable conservatives. The Johnses were erratic, roughhewn outsiders. The Trents undoubtedly thought that Altona was marrying beneath herself. Vernon Johns undoubtedly thought that the Trents were "spitzterinktum Negroes," members of a black elite who were blindly preoccupied with their social status.[42]

Like the marriage of Coretta Scott to Martin Luther King, Jr., twenty-six years later, the marriage of an attractive AME Zion woman to a handsome Baptist preacher was a rite of passage performed on her family's turf. Like Coretta Scott, however, Vernon Johns was from the country and was marrying into a family more sophisticated than his own. Both he and she had to audition for their prospective in-laws. There is no indication that either Altona Trent or Martin Luther King, Jr., even bothered to meet their future in-laws before the marriage took place. Both weddings were models of bourgeois respectability. Society page accounts of the marriage of Vernon Johns and Altona Trent do not even say whether anyone else from his family was present.[43]

For Altona Trent Johns, nurtured in conservative, respectable, and stable middle-class values, the marriage was a loving, but often turbulent, ride. A woman of accomplishment in her own right, she graduated from Atlanta

University in 1925 and taught music and foreign languages at Bennett College in Greensboro, North Carolina, before her marriage. Between 1928 and 1938, she gave birth to three sons and then to three daughters. As the youngest of them entered school during World War II, Altona Johns returned to her career in music and teaching. She earned a graduate degree in music education at Columbia University's Teacher's College, published several books and articles, and taught in Prince Edward County's public schools and at Virginia State College, Alabama State College, and Southern University in Baton Rouge.[44] An accomplished pianist, she toured the black church, college, and university circuits, as her husband toured the lecture and preaching circuits. Occasionally, they appeared jointly for her concerts and his poetry readings.[45]

We do not fully know what Altona Trent Johns knew of her husband's family background, but her discussion of it confirms all that we know about her own background and temperament. The less said about Tom Price and his "tangle of sex, family, slavery, and violence" with Dolly Gaines, her bourgeois morality told her, the better. So, she made no reference to them. It was as if her mother-in-law, Sallie Branch Price Johns, had appeared by some immaculate conception or virgin birth. Rather, Altona emphasized the continuity and stability of Monroe Johns nurturing a large family of property-owning children into the twentieth century. It was as if she wished to re-create the Johns family background in the Trent family image.[46] Even her sanitized version of the Johns family background, however, should have alerted Branch that his uncritical acceptance of Vernon Johns's family myth was mistaken.

For Altona Johns's husband, Vernon, his white grandfather's murder of a twenty-one-year-old white farmhand in Prince Edward County was a traumatic childhood memory. It was made no easier by the fact that his aunt, Frances Price Womack, Tom Price's daughter of color, and her husband, General Womack, were key witnesses for the prosecution in the case that twice convicted Price of first-degree murder. Beyond that, we cannot fully know what Vernon Johns knew about his family background. He did know both his grandfather of color, Monroe Johns, and his white grandfather, Tom Price, in his early childhood. He did know that Monroe Johns was not hanged for cutting his master in two with a scythe. He did know that Price did not go to prison for defending his paramour of color.[47]

Branch correctly identifies one key to Vernon and Altona Johns's shared silence about his white grandfather and the disparity between their accounts of Monroe Johns's life: "Only in the Bible did [Vernon Johns] find open discussion of such a tangle of sex, family, slavery, and violence." For the mature Baptist preacher, if sense could be made of this legacy, it was to be found in scripture. Late in life, Vernon Johns told an interviewer as much. He recalled as a boy being sent to do chores in the tobacco barn, losing himself in reading a book and pondering large questions. "[I] was watching fires in the tobacco barn and reading the New Testament," Johns said. "That was when I discovered Christianity. I discovered that Christianity was entirely different than I had supposed. I had been led to think that you couldn't do some things to folk because they were white. I found that Christianity didn't observe that distinction." Many other southerners, white and black, read the same New Testament without feeling obliged to ignore racial privilege, but Johns read it against the background of a family history in which the distinctions had long been blurred and the experience of a mother who bristled at any hint of racial discrimination or privilege.[48]

In his college and seminary years, Vernon Johns espoused a muscular Christianity that delighted in athletic competition and supported American entry into World War I, but he vigorously attacked race prejudice both in athletics and the military.[49] Barred from military service by poor eyesight, Johns began teaching and preaching in Lynchburg. His first great success was the publication of a sermon, "Transfigured Moments," which appeared with those of Harry Emerson Fosdick, Reinhold Niebuhr, and other princes of the American pulpit in Joseph Fort Newton's Best Sermons series. It celebrates the moment in which human hearts are kindled by a vision of human brotherhood.[50] The sermon included an odd reference to Sinclair Lewis's novel, *Babbitt*. It occurred in the context of a distinction that Johns drew between Peter, the rock, a "foundation man," who had the courage to speak the best that he knows in difficult moments, and ordinary disciples

> who guard their words very zealously in tense situations, and for fear they may say something indiscreet . . . . They talk most when there is but little need to say anything, and the topic of their conversation is not likely to be material which will spread fire in the earth or set a father against his son, or make a man's enemies those of his own household. There are some things "that Babbitt will not talk about."[51]

The reference to George F. Babbitt is odd because the quotation is not from the novel, and nowhere in it does Babbitt refuse to talk about anything. *Babbitt's* plot hinges on a central scene, in which Babbitt visits the jail cell of his best friend, Paul Reisling, who refuses to talk to Babbitt about having shot his nagging wife, Zilla. Subsequently, Reisling is sentenced to prison for attacking his wife and this "death" of his best friend sends Babbitt into a mid-life crisis.[52] Johns's homiletic misattribution of silence to Babbitt in the face of spousal abuse, imprisonment, identity crises, and impending death may be either rhetorical carelessness or necessity. It serves no homiletic purpose to explain to a congregation who Paul Reisling is. Yet, it may have also anticipated ways in which Johns would negotiate similar issues in his own family history. Crucial silences and transfers of identity would enable him to be a foundation man, fully prepared "to spread fire in the earth."

In other sermons of the period, Johns praised men of heroic action and condemned the "insane hatred between the races" as "the nastiest and deadliest problem before the world today." Noting that lynching occurred most commonly in regions where conventional Christianity prevailed, Johns argued that the Ku Klux Klan was more effective than the church in mobilizing human communities. "True religion," by contrast, he insisted, "provides humanity with both the revolutionary ideals and the revolutionary power which become the bone and sinews of progress."[53] Yet, in these years just after the death of Tom Price, Johns sounded like the apostle of nonviolence. He dismissed disarmament agreements as "halfway measures" and renounced armed self-defense. "I have an acquaintance, a practical man, who is alarmed that I travel much without a pistol," he noted.

> I need one he thinks to fight off robbers. Thus far, I have not encountered any robbers; when I do, and the robbers go off with my money, I want them to leave me intact. Staging a pistol duel with a gunman, with my pocket change as the stake, strikes me as nonsense. My honor? I can find better ways to be honorable. My courage? Courage is not properly measured by the notches on the butts of our guns. Not the injuries we inflict on others in alleged defenses of ourselves, but what we suffer ourselves to make a fairer world with a finer humanity; that is the courage from which redemption comes. Jesus enjoins the principal of sacrifice in substitution of the old principle of defense.[54]

As the immediate memory of his white grandfather receded and racial violence continued, however, Vernon Johns became the apostle of armed racial self-defense and made the transition via a critique of relations within the African American community. He cited an incident in the Deep South in which the husband of a black woman who was cooking for a white man was seized, beaten, and forced to flee from the community, leaving his wife in the hands of her employer. It is "hard" and "depressing" to know that such a tragedy could befall a black brother "in this white land," he admitted, but that was only a "partial" and "sentimental" view. A "less partial, "more factual" and "somewhat fairer" view would ask: what else could he expect? "The colored lady involved was a black man's *wife* but she was a white man's *cook*," he noted, "and we black men can not forever expect our wives and sweethearts to go on *taking their living from white men and their loving from black men*. It is natural and somewhat fair for a lady to look to the same source for her living and her loving."[55]We do not know whether Vernon Johns knew what the neighborhood grapevine said about Tom Price and Richard and Dolly Gaines, but if he did, he was holding Richard Gains partially responsible for failing to relieve his consort from her dependence on Tom Price for sustenance.

Subsequently, Johns made clear that his criticism of the failure of African American men to free their women from economic dependency was no apologia for the behavior of white men. Rather, black men should be prepared to "Select Carefully Your Time and Place To Die." "[W]e fume and blaze (at a safe distance) about the brutality of white mobs that butcher and burn Negroes at will, whether they be guilty or innocent, whether the alleged crime be great or small," he wrote. "A mob gathered at my home in Virginia to lynch Sam Ford because he had seen a white couple in a compromising position. The lynching did not materialize!" Wanting not to be directly quoted as advocating armed self-defense, Johns nonetheless made his position quite clear. "I must not put naughty ideas into those little roundish objects that stand atop our colored necks," he wrote, "but it would be easy and comparatively safe to do something to a mob that would keep a considerable portion of the bold peasantry out of the next one that formed. That something could be done from behind a tree, log, barn or out of a gully, and could be done by one colored gentleman without taking a single brother into his confidence. It was one lone Negro who turned the trick that stopped the lynching of Sam Ford. And by the way I was not that lone Negro. Don't forget that!"[56]

Two weeks later, Johns first referred to his story of biblical memory. Arguing that African Americans should stake their claim in vast parts of the country where white folk were thinly settled, he cited the example of Moses and the children of Israel. "Moses, a well favored young Hebrew, killed one of the Egyptian masters while the latter was in the act of beating a slave, and took to the woods without leaving his address," Johns wrote. "After forty years of wilderness experience he ripened a plan for drawing the slave population away from Egypt, and settling it outside of civilized strongholds, where there would be opportunity for freedom and independent development."[57]

In a smart review of historians' recent interest in "memory," Jacquelyn Hall says that "every narrative depends on the suppression and repression of contrary, disruptive memories—other people's memories of the same events, as well as the unacceptable ghosts of our own pasts."[58]Biblical memory is a peculiar subset of memory in that respect. It filters and refracts the pain and anguish of human experience through a lens of biblical narrative to give meaning to experience that may be otherwise disabling. One of the most prominent themes in African American preaching is the biblical memory of the Moses narratives. The Moses narratives are so rich and diverse, however, that they offer many lenses. A biblical scholar recently observed that white folk commonly think of Moses as the lawgiver and black folk commonly think of Moses as the liberator. But Moses is available to us in many forms: Moses the foundling and Moses the prince in Egypt, Moses who wanders in the desert and Moses who does not reach the Promised Land. King, for instance, recurred to the last of these when, on the eve of his assassination, he told a mass meeting in Memphis: "I may not get there with you . . . ."[59]

Historians are rightly skeptical of arguments from silence. Vernon Johns is not ever known to have referred to his white grandfather in public, much less to reports that he murdered Johns's grandmother of color, that he was twice condemned to die by hanging twenty years later for the murder in an alcoholic rage of a white man, or that his grandfather's own relatives of color provided key testimony to convict him. Yet, Vernon Johns knew Tom Price in a childhood spent in a small rural community in which Price played a large role. For a year of Johns's formative childhood, these events were headlined in the local press and disrupted the community's normal patterns of seasonal work. In light of the variety of forms in which Moses is available and the context in which those events took place, it is no mere coincidence that Vernon Johns's story of biblical memory recalled Moses the Righteous Murderer.[60]

The elements of Vernon Johns's transfiguration from an apostle of nonviolence to an apostle of armed racial self-defense were already there in a 1934 article he wrote in the *Philadelphia Tribune*. His people needed deliverance from oppression, and his own story resonated powerfully with biblical memory. His grandfather, like Moses, had killed a man. In some circumstances, such as protecting the honor of a woman or striking a blow against oppression, the willingness to kill and be killed was not just acceptable; it was obligatory. In Moses, God had made use of such a man. Like Moses, his own mother had been "adopted into the house of Pharaoh." If God had spoken to Moses from a burning bush, He had spoken to Vernon Johns from smoldering embers in a tobacco barn. It would be another fifteen years before Johns publicly acknowledged that he had a grandfather who killed a man. He would do so in his own version of the story.

In the intervening years, while Sallie Branch Price Johns and Altona Trent Johns raised his children, Vernon Johns farmed, cut and sold pulpwood, and owned and operated a grocery store in Darlington Heights. More commonly, he traveled the lecture and preaching circuits and won and lost several prized pulpits. Wherever he went, Johns condemned the soul-crippling acquiescence in racial discrimination that the white South demanded of black southerners in return for allowing their bodies to survive. He celebrated those moments when "the little rebel" challenged "Mr. Charlie Big Brute," but his critique of violence in the African American community was also unsparing. "If the bodies of Negroes lynched by white mobs were piled together and, beside these, the bodies of Negroes murdered by other Negroes," he told readers in Charleston, West Virginia, "the former would make a hill and the latter a mountain."[61] When he was a pastor in Lynchburg, a shooting at an African American recreational facility in the city, Happyland Resort, resulted in the death of one man, the arrest of two for his murder and the conviction of one of them for involuntary manslaughter. For the foolish violence, Vernon Johns's sermon heaped coals of biblical fire on the heads of "Dogpatch Negroes at 2 A.M."[62]

After he became the pastor of Dexter Avenue in 1948, Vernon Johns would say publicly that he had a grandfather who killed a man. Seventy years had passed since the death of Dolly Gaines, fifty years since Tom Price had murdered a white field hand in Prince Edward County, and twenty-five years since the old man had died at the Virginia State Prison Farm. By then, Vernon Johns was fifty-six years old, his mother and stepfather, Sallie Branch Price and Robert Johns, were nearing their own deaths, and his children spanned the adolescent range from ten to twenty. By then, he kept—not a pistol—but a loaded double-barreled shotgun in the white Mercury he drove across the South.[63]

There is, however, another key to understanding how Vernon Johns could transfigure a haunting past: his belief in the power of dreams to construe reality as it ought to be. Addressing a Lynchburg mass meeting on

14 May 1961, Johns defined that as the essence of faith. "Faith means that anything which ought to be, can be. That is exactly what faith means. Anything that ought to be, can be." Recalling his days as a student at an impoverished college in Lynchburg, he argued that a dream can transform present reality. "You know, ah, anything can happen in a dream," he said.

> In our waking hours, we have to keep to the facts, but when we go to sleep, we don't bother about facts . . . when I was at Virginia Seminary, on Sunday nights, we used to have a slice of lightbread for supper, that was all, with a spot of black molasses in the center that varied in size from a nickel to a half a dollar, [laughter] according to whether or not the cook cared for you. [laughter] If the cook cared, it might be the size of a half a dollar. [Lord, have mercy] I came in a minute late from my Sunday night, ah, speech and Dean Woody had eaten it up. Well, I couldn't do a thing. I didn't have a penny to buy any with and I was too weak to fight. [laughter] So, I, I climbed the stairs and went to bed and as soon as my eyes were closed, the darkness got hold of me. Ah, man, I was half [inaudible words] this world. I dreamed, I dreamed that I was a chef on a gravy train [laughter] and that I was the only passenger on that train. [laughter] And I, I woke up and in my dreams a gust of chickens flew off trees. And that I was out under a chicken tree and gravy was dripping all over. [laughter] Anything can happen in a dream. [laughter]

Dreams, Johns continued, were transfiguring future reality. He was addressing a mass meeting in Lynchburg in the midst of sit-in demonstrations. Freedom riders had recently passed through the city and, even as he spoke, one of their buses was burning outside Anniston, Alabama. "Ah, who would have believed, who would have believed twenty years ago?" he asked.

> Young men walking around, black men in the University of Virginia, in the medical department, with, ah, stethoscopes [inaudible words]. The first time my wife went to the University of Virginia, to the hospital. I walked in and said, "Ah, may I see Mrs. Johns?" "Who?" [laughter] "May I see Mrs. Johns? How is Mrs. Johns?" "Altona is doing fine." The last time I went up there, Negroes walking around with stethoscopes, examining white patients. Who could have believed? Who could have believed? Who could have believed that, ah, all over the South kids would walk into white places that they were not allowed and sit down without saying grace? Why, twenty years ago, they would have knocked their brains out as fast as. . . . . [Oh yeah!][64]

If dreams could remake the present and reshape the future, dreams could also redeem the past. In a dream, a man could have truly grand-fathers, heroic men of faithful action. Biblical memory could transfigure a tragic heritage into a redemptive legacy.[65]

In a 1949 baccalaureate address at Tuskegee Institute, Johns spoke of Moses as "The Man Who Started Freedom." There, he distinguished between the common virtue of reliable workmen on whom our regular lives depend—ordinary disciples: a Moses tending the flocks of his father-in-law, Jethro, or a Monroe Johns plying his skill at the hearth and in the field to nurture a family into the twentieth century—and the transforming action of a Moses who turns aside from normal routines to hear the voice from the burning bush and obeys its command to strike out for freedom. "Moses was a man capable of violence and religion," Johns told the Tuskegee graduates. "He picked a time for the homicide when there would be no eye witness except the mistreated slave, God and Satan, and none of them objected. The Bible raises no question of the morality of this homicide!" True nonviolence "belongs with the highest expression of idealism," he granted, but it has "nothing to do with the man who cringes before brute power for fear of his life." Only the man, only a people who absorb the fact that death is universal and are willing to make it serve some redemptive purpose are capable of making history. "When Moses picked up a corner of one of the bricks which his people had made without straw and threw it with all the force that he could command at the head of an autocratic brute, the higher powers directed the missile and the brickbat lodged in history." "Religion and violence are not the same thing," Johns acknowledged;

> but they have their roots in the same soil. Both are usually in dead earnest. Both feel passionately. Both embrace death in their scheme. The man who has gotten past fear is closer to God than the coward. There is something essentially spiritual about any person who has achieved a working adjustment to the worst that the world has to offer. This much is certain: there never could have come the measure of liberty which the world knows but for bondsmen who kill to be free and free men who would kill to remain and to further freedom.[66]

Early in March 1951, Johns was the speaker for Religious Emphasis Week at Morehouse College in Atlanta. There, Abernathy first heard him preach. The subject was: "Constructive Homicide."[67] Only the title of the sermon survives, but it is enough to tell us that the text for the sermon very likely was Exodus 2:11–12: "One day, when Moses had grown up, he went out to his people and looked on their burdens; and he saw an Egyptian beating a Hebrew, one of his people. He looked this way and that, and seeing no one he killed the Egyptian and hid him in the sand." Two paragraphs from another sermon, published five months later, however, give us the essence of Johns's commentary on the righteous murder.

> "Moses went out when he became a man to see how it was with his brethren." He didn't go far before he saw. "He noted the loads they had to bear." "He saw an Egyptian beating a Hebrew"; not a man to man fight by any means; for the master was laying it on as masters had always done, and the cringing slave was taking it, lying down, as slaves were supposed to do. Moses was hot, but not incautious. "He looked this way and that, and when he saw that no one was looking," he took one of the brick bats which his people had made without either straw or pay and facing the arrogant, unjust master he said, "I'll give one brute what he deserves"; and with a majestic sweep of the arm, he committed an holy, constructive homicide.
>
> It was a revelation to the slaves that death could be the ally of the oppressed as well as the oppressors. They got important ideas. Later in

> life, God rebuked Moses for striking a rock, but there was never any divine disapproval of striking the Egyptian. Instead, God got Moses' address and kept it on file in heaven, until the other Israelites were ready for freedom.[68]

In the months between Johns's sermon on "Constructive Homicide" and publication of his commentary on Moses's righteous murder of the Egyptian, his niece, Barbara Johns, led students in a boycott of Prince Edward County's overcrowded Robert Russa Moton High School, and the NAACP intervened to file a case that became known as *Davis v. County School Board of Prince Edward County, Virginia*. It eventually forced the desegregation of public schools in the only county in the United States to resist the order by closing them for years.[69] Vernon Johns might have said that his niece, the great-granddaughter of Monroe and Harriet Womack Johns and of Tom Price and Dolly Gaines, had "lodged a brickbat in history."

In 1953, a year after Johns's mother died and after the rest of his family returned to Virginia, the deacons at Dexter Avenue accepted one of Johns's resignations. He tarried around Montgomery long enough to appear at the inauguration of his fellow Virginian, Luther Foster, Jr., as president of Tuskegee Institute. There, said one observer, the sixty-one-year-old preacher began his sermon with: "When my grandfather was hanged for cutting his master in two with a scythe, they asked him on the gallows if he had anything to say. He said 'Yes, I'm just sorry I didn't do it thirty years before.' And they dropped the trapdoor."[70] In a dream, a man could have truly grand-fathers, heroic men of faithful action, and biblical memory could transfigure a tragic heritage into a redemptive legacy. Vernon Johns would have had a child's memory of his two grandfathers, Monroe Johns and Tom Price. The slave turning aside from his work in the fields, hearing the voice of God, and striking a blow against oppression became a type of Gabriel Prosser or Nat Turner. The oppressor is more difficult to redeem, and Vernon Johns made no public reference to him, but he knew from his reading of history that some white men were capable of seizing their own death to strike a blow for the freedom of oppressed people. His favorite example was John Brown. Like Johns's white grandfather, he was a strong man for his age, of middling height with a full flowing beard.[71]

For his family, his friends at SCLC, and his audience, Vernon Johns transfigured both of his grandfathers. Monroe Johns, the steady workman at home and in the field, became a sort of Nat Turner, who heard the voice of God and died for slaying a brutal slavemaster; and Tom Price was disowned. In his place on the gallows stood John Brown, who heard the voice of God and died for the freedom of the slaves. In the dark hours after the assassination of Martin Luther King in Memphis, Ralph Abernathy returned to the place of mind where Vernon Johns had told him that violent death might have redemptive purpose.

Notes

Ralph E. Luker is an Atlanta historian, the editor of the Vernon Johns Papers, and founder of CLIOPATRIA: A History Group blog (http://hnn.us/blogs/2.html).

1. Taylor Branch Interview conducted by Kenneth Fink, Summer, 1989, copy of transcript in possession of the author; Taylor Branch, *Parting the Waters: America in the King Years, 1954–1963* (New York, 1988), pp. 1–26.
2. Martin Luther King, Jr. (hereafter cited as MLK) to Howard Thurman, 31 Oct. 1955, in Clayborne Carson, Ralph E. Luker et al., eds., *The Papers of Martin Luther King, Jr.* (5 vols.; Berkeley, 1991-), 2:583. See also MLK to Mordecai Johnson, 14 July 1955 and W. T. Handy, Jr., to MLK, 24 Oct. 1955, in Dexter Avenue-King Memorial Baptist Church Papers, Montgomery, Alabama; and MLK, *Stride Toward Freedom: The Montgomery Story* (New York, 1958), pp. 36–39, 41, and 152.
3. Ralph David Abernathy, *And the Walls Came Tumbling Down: An Autobiography* (New York, 1989), pp. 116–28. As noted elsewhere, however, Abernathy's memoirs must be used cautiously.
4. On the awkward floundering of SCLC's early years, see David Garrow, *Bearing the Cross: Martin Luther King, Jr., and the Southern Christian Leadership Conference* (New York, 1986), pp. 97–125; Adam Fairclough, *To Redeem the Soul of America: The Southern Christian Leadership Conference and Martin Luther King, Jr.* (Athens, Ga., 1987), pp. 37–55; and Papers of MLK, 4:1–38.
5. Between June 1953 and 1956, Johns moved between his farm in rural Prince Edward County, where he raised cattle under the auspices of Virginia Farm and City Enterprises, Inc.—of which he was part-owner—and Petersburg, where his wife, Altona Trent Johns, taught music at Virginia State College. From 1956 to 1959, he moved between his wife's home in Petersburg and Baltimore, where he was the director of the Maryland State Baptist Center and School of Religion and where he opened a restaurant under the auspices of Maryland Farm and City Enterprises, Inc. Tilley was Johns's predecessor at the Maryland State Baptist Center and an officer of Maryland Farm and City Enterprises. Walker was an officer in Johns's Virginia Farm and City Enterprises. See Johns to MLK, 27 Sept. 1956, Martin Luther King, Jr., Collection, Howard Gotlieb Archival Research Center, Boston University; Vernon Johns, Form Letter, 28 Jan. 1958, John Lee Tilley Papers, Amistad Research Center at Tulane University, New Orleans, Louisiana; *Norfolk Journal and Guide*, 21 June 1958; *Papers of MLK*, 4:441n; and Wyatt Walker Interview conducted by Kenneth Fink, Summer 1989, copy of transcript in possession of the author. Vernon Johns's circle of influence in the civil rights movement was primarily ministerial. Beyond SCLC's inner circle, it included Harold Carter, Herman Dreer, R. James Glasco, Leslie Francis Griffin, J. Raymond Henderson, Lester Kendal Jackson, Mordecai Johnson, Thomas Kilgore, Martin Luther King, Sr., Benjamin Mays, John Porter, Adam Clayton Powell, Sr. and Jr., Samuel Proctor, Solomon Snowden Seay, Charles Sherrod, Nelson H. Smith, C. Kenzie Steele, Leon Sullivan, Gardner Taylor, and Virgil Woods. Among the laity, Mary Fair Burks, Rufus Lewis, E. D. Nixon, James Pierce, Richmond Smiley, and Jo Ann Robinson all acknowledged Johns's pioneering role in Montgomery's civil rights movement.
6. Wyatt Walker Interview (Fink); Ralph Abernathy Interview conducted by Kenneth Fink, Summer 1989; Gardner Taylor Interview conducted by Kenneth Fink, Summer 1989 (copies of transcripts in possession of the author). See also James Pierce Interview conducted by Norman Lumpkin, 23 Apr. 1973, in the Alabama Oral History Project, Alabama State University Archives, Montgomery; Vernon Dobson Interview conducted by Kenneth Fink, Summer 1989; John Porter Interview conducted by Kenneth Fink, Summer 1989; and Richmond Smiley Interview conducted by Kenneth Fink, Summer 1989 (copies of transcripts in possession of the author). See also Ralph E. Luker, "Johns the Baptist: A Profile of Vernon N. Johns," *AME Church Review* 118 (2002): 26–31.

7. The best studies of the "Letter from Birmingham Jail" and the "I Have a Dream" speech are S. Jonathan Bass, *Blessed Are the Peacemakers: Martin Luther King, Jr., Eight White Religious Leaders, and the "Letter from Birmingham Jail"* (Baton Rouge, 2001); Keith D. Miller, *Voice of Deliverance: The Language of Martin Luther King, Jr., and Its Sources* (New York, 1992); and Richard Lischer, *The Preacher King: Martin Luther King, Jr., and the Word That Moved America* (New York, 1995).
8. *Atlanta Daily World*, 8, 20 Sept. 1963. Beyond the similarity of title, there is no textual relationship between King's "I Have a Dream" and Johns's "Here Comes the Dreamer." Both addresses were standard fare in their respective repertoires.
9. Branch, *Parting the Waters*, pp. 901–2; Andrew Young Interview conducted by Kenneth Fink, Summer 1989, copy of transcript in possession of the author. See also Garrow, *Bearing the Cross*, pp. 294–302.
10. Branch, *Parting the Waters*, p. 902. I am skeptical of Branch's reconstructed conversations, except where I find documentary evidence in support of them. On "the cloud" in Johns's head, see Vernon Johns, "The Romance of Death," in Samuel Lucius Gandy, ed., *Human Possibilities: A Vernon Johns Reader, Including an Unfinished MS., Sermons, Essays, Addresses, and a Doggerel* (Washington, D.C., 1977), pp. 115–16. King had reason to believe that such notebooks existed, for when Johns left Montgomery, he had left behind fragmentary sermon notes that King may have seen and that are in the archives of Dexter Avenue-King Memorial Baptist Church. More substantial notebooks existed in Petersburg at the time of Chauncey Eskridge's mission, but the old preacher was unwilling to turn his livelihood over to King. See also note 47 below. In "Quoting, Merging, and Sampling the Dream: Martin Luther King and Vernon Johns," *Southern Cultures* 9 (2003): 28–48, I compared some of the rhetorical strategies of the two Afro-Baptist preachers.
11. On the failure of contemporary popular historical narratives to ask critical questions of their sources, see Sean Wilentz, "America Made Easy: McCullough, Adams, and the Decline of Popular History," *New Republic*, 2 July 2001, pp. 35–40.
12. Branch, *Parting the Waters,* pp. 7–8.
13. Altona Trent Johns, "As I Remember," in Gandy, ed., *Human Possibilities*, p. vii. Branch cites the Gandy anthology as a source of information on the Johns family background (*Parting the Waters*, p. 927n). A death date for Monroe Johns cannot be firmly fixed, but he appears as a head of household in Prince Edward County in the censuses of 1870 and 1880 and reappears in the census of 1900, living in the household of his son, John (United States Census, 1870, 1880 and 1900, Buffalo Township, Prince Edward County, Virginia). A search of the primary sources and secondary literature on slave resistance and rebellion in the late antebellum period produced no case even similar to the one attributed to Vernon Johns's grandfather, Monroe Johns. One cannot prove a negative, but the fact that Monroe Johns lived quietly beyond emancipation to nurture a family into the twentieth century makes Branch's account very unlikely. It is even unlikely that any of Vernon Johns's great grandfathers had killed a master with a scythe. At least one of them was and as many as three of them may have been white. Even so, the story may have been passed down from an earlier generation of the family, perhaps related to Nat Turner's Rebellion or Gabriel's Rebellion early in the nineteenth century, when, as one historian puts it, Richmond-area slaves turned their "plowshares into swords." See Philip Schwarz, *Twice Condemned: Slaves and the Criminal Laws of Virginia, 1705–1865* (Baton Rouge, 1988); Douglas R. Egerton, *Gabriel's Rebellion: The Virginia Slave Conspiracies of 1800 and 1802* (Chapel Hill, 1993); James Sidbury, *Plowshares into Swords: Race, Rebellion, and Identity in Gabriel's Virginia, 1730–1810* (New York, 1997); and Midori Takagi, *"Rearing Wolves to Our Own Destruction" Slavery in Richmond, Virginia, 1782–1865* (Charlottesville, 1999).

14. In an interview with Lamont H. Yeakey on 19 November 1976, Lewis W. Jones told of hearing Vernon Johns attribute the murder to his slave grandfather in a sermon at Tuskegee Institute about 1 November 1953; and, without attribution to his grandfather, Johns told the story of a slave who cut his master in two "with a scythe or wheat cradle" to Robert Collins Smith in an interview on 9 January 1962 (Yeakey, "The Montgomery Bus Boycott, 1955–56" [Ph.D. diss., Columbia University, 1979], p. 110; Robert Collins Smith, *They Closed Their Schools: Prince Edward County, Virginia, 1951–1964* [Chapel Hill 1965], p. 78). Branch heard the story of the murder attributed to Johns's slave grandfather from two of Vernon Johns's daughters in interviews on 31 January and 16 February 1984 (Branch, *Parting the Waters*, p. 928n). Wyatt Walker told the same story in an interview with Kenneth Fink in 1989 (Wyatt Walker Interview [Fink]) and with me in 1998 (Wyatt Walker Interview conducted by Ralph E. Luker, 17 Sept. 1998, tape and transcript in possession of the author).
15. Herbert Clarence Bradshaw, *History of Prince Edward County, Virginia, From Its Earliest Settlement through Its Establishment in 1754 to Its Bicentennial Year* (Richmond, 1955), pp. 588–91, 818n; Certificate of Death (Thomas William Price), Virginia Death Certificate #7254, Goochland County, Virginia, Library of Virginia, Richmond (hereafter cited as LVA). On the state prison farm in Goochland County during Tom Price's imprisonment, see Paul W. Keve, *The History of Corrections in Virginia* (Charlottesville, 1986), pp. 92–95, 124–25, 130, 202–6.
16. Bradshaw, *History of Prince Edward County*, p. 415.
17. United States Census, 1860, 1870, 1880, Prospect Depot Post Office and Buffalo Township, Prince Edward County, Virginia; Compiled Service Records of the Confederate Soldiers Who Served in Organizations from the State of Virginia (M324, Roll 667), Record Group 109, National Archives and Records Administration, Washington, D.C. See also Anthony J. Gage, Jr., *Southside Virginia in the Civil War: Amelia, Brunswick, Charlotte, Halifax, Lunenburg, Mecklenburg, Nottoway, and Prince Edward Counties* (Appomattox, Va., 1999), pp. 73, 78, 94, 148. The census records of 1860, 1870, and 1880; his discharge certificate of 1862; and his death certificate report birth dates for Tom Price ranging from 1826 to 1838. The census records report birth dates for Miss Kitty Price ranging from 1819 to 1827, making her anywhere from nine to seventeen years older than her husband.
18. United States Census, Slave Schedule, 1860, Prince Edward County, Virginia; United States Census, 1860, 1870, Prince Edward County, Virginia, Prospect Depot Post Office and Buffalo Township.
19. The birth report in February 1879 specified no father of the child; but in September 1879, Miss Kitty Price reported that the father of the dead infant was "R. Gains" (Register of Births, 1879; Register of Deaths, 1879, Prince Edward County, Virginia, LVA).
20. Elizabeth Johns Roebuck Interview conducted by Ralph E. Luker, 1, 5 Oct. 2000, tapes and transcripts in possession of the author. Mrs. Roebuck says that she heard this story from her mother, Agnes Lewis Johns, the wife of Willie and Robert Johns's younger brother, Monroe. There is no head of household by the name of "Gains" or "Gaines" in the census of 1860 for Prince Edward County, but in the census of 1870 there is a forty-year-old African American by the name of "Richard Gains" listed in the Buffalo Township household of an elderly Zack Womack, his wife, and their grandchildren. Nearby, a sixteen-year-old Richard Gaines lived in the household of seventy-year-old Adonis Gaines and his wife. There was also an eighteen-year-old Nancy Gaines living as a domestic worker in a Farmville household (United States Census, 1860, 1870, Prince Edward County, Virginia). It seems likely that, as slaves, Richard and Dolly Gaines had become parents to children in the 1850s and that, as the oral tradition reports, Tom Price dispersed this slave family to make way for a family of his own by Dolly Gaines.

21. Branch, *Parting the Waters*, p. 7. The second quotation is from Branch's interview with Vernon Johns's oldest son, Vernon "Increase" Johns, on 14 February 1984. Like evidence from oral history sources, evidence from primary documents may, on occasion, be misleading. Yet, the evidence from primary documents overwhelmingly shows that Branch's version of Vernon Johns's family background, based almost exclusively on oral history sources, cannot be accurate.
22. The names of Dolly Gaines, her two oldest children, Ada and Charlotte, and her infant son, Henry, do not appear in the census record of 1880 (United States Census, 1880, Prince Edward County, Virginia, Buffalo Township).
23. Register of Marriages, Prince Edward County, Virginia, 1882, p. 58 (Johns-Price), LVA; "Johns Family History as told to Jackie Pitts by Mrs. Clytie Johns, 1 July 1986," copy of typescript document in possession of the author. For the family's recollection of this transformation, see Branch, *Parting the Waters*, p. 7. On A. J. and Pattie Price, see *Farmville Herald*, 5 Aug. 1898; and Bradshaw, *History of Prince Edward County*, p. 456.
24. Paul Heinigg, *Free African-Americans of North Carolina and Virginia* (Baltimore, 1997), pp. 421–23. See also [Carter G. Woodson], "Free Negro Owners of Slaves in the United States in 1830," *Journal of Negro History* 9 (1924): 81; Woodson, *Free Negro Heads of Families in the United States in 1830* (Washington, D.C., 1925), p. 169; Luther Porter Jackson, *Free Negro Labor and Property Holding in Virginia, 1830–60* (New York, 1942), p. 128; and Smith, *They Closed Their Schools*, p. 76.
25. United States Census, Slave Schedule, 1860, Prince Edward County, Virginia; United States Census, 1860, 1870, Prince Edward County, Virginia, Prospect Depot Post Office and Buffalo Township; Register of Births, Prince Edward County, 1862 and 1865, LVA; H. Jacob, "Jacob's Official Map of Prince Edward County, Virginia, 1878," LVA. The census taker of 1870 designated Monroe Johns as "mulatto" and his wife as "black." The census taker of 1880 reversed the designations, making Monroe "black" and Harriet "mulatto" (United States Census, 1870, 1880, Prince Edward County, Virginia, Prospect Depot Post Office and Buffalo Township).
26. John Dillon owned no male slave whose age corresponded to that of Monroe Johns in 1850, but there was a male slave and a female slave on the Dillon farm in 1860 whose ages corresponded to those of Harriet Womack and Monroe Johns. Prince Edward County birth records list a son born to them in 1861 and a daughter born in 1865, when John Dillon registered the births to "Harriet and Monroe Dillon" (Johns, "As I Remember," p. vii; United States Census, Slave Schedule, 1840, 1850, Buckingham County, Virginia; United States Census, Slave Schedule, 1850, 1860, Prince Edward County, Virginia; United States Census, 1850, 1860, 1870, Prince Edward County, Virginia, Prospect Depot Post Office and Buffalo Township; Register of Births, Prince Edward County, Virginia, 1865, LVA; Elizabeth Johns Roebuck Interview conducted by Ralph E. Luker, 9 July 2000, tape and transcript in possession of the author. I am deeply indebted primarily to the genealogical research of Brigitte Burkett of Richmond and Elizabeth Johns Roebuck of Darlington Heights, Virginia, and, secondarily, to the memories of Cula Berryman of Darlington Heights and the research of Khalid Hashim Bey of Brooklyn, New York, and Lawrence Johns of Roanoke, Virginia, for this family background.
27. United States Census, 1860, 1870, 1880, Prince Edward County, Virginia, Prospect Depot Post Office and Buffalo Township; United States Census, Slave Schedule, 1860, Prince Edward County, Virginia; Johns, "As I Remember," p. vii.
28. Register of Marriages, Prince Edward County, Virginia, 1882, p. 58 (Johns-Price), LVA; "Johns Family History"; Register of Marriages, Prince Edward County, Virginia, 1889, p. 311 (Johns-Price), LVA.
29. His middle name gave writers about Johns much difficulty. A college president and a newspaper reporter who interviewed Vernon N. Johns identified him as

Vernon L. Johns; an editor of his work referred to him as Vernon S. Johns; a close friend in the ministry believed he was Vernon T. Johns; editors of the *Norfolk Journal and Guide* and of the Martin Luther King, Jr., Papers identified him as Vernon H. Johns; and a biographer wrote that Johns "had no middle initial" (Florence Matilda Read, *The Story of Spelman College* [Atlanta, 1961], p. 381; Smith, *They Closed Their Schools*, p. 272; Herman Dreer, *American Literature by Negro Authors* [New York, 1950], p. 210; Wyatt Walker Interview conducted by Ralph E. Luker, 18 Sept. 1998, tape and transcript in possession of the author; *Norfolk Journal and Guide*, 13 Sept. 1930; Papers of MLK, vol. 3; Charles Emerson Boddie, *God's Bad Boys* [Valley Forge, Pa., 1972], p. 62).

30. Register of Births, Prince Edward County, Virginia, Circuit Court, 1892, LVA; United States Census, 1900, Prince Edward County, Virginia, Buffalo Township; Johns, "As I Remember," p. viii; Bradshaw, *History of Prince Edward County, Virginia,* pp. 588, 592–93. The circuit court register lists the birth of "Bernard Johns" on 5 April 1892, but it almost certainly is a record of the birth of Vernon Johns who invariably listed his birth date as 22 April. I am indebted to James E. Coleman of Lynchburg, who made copies of the Prince Edward County Circuit Court records available to me.
31. William Edward Burghardt Du Bois, *The Negroes of Farmville*, Virginia (Washington, D.C., 1898), pp. 3–6; "Mrs. T. K. [sic] Price's evidence taken in her room on July 29th 1898 . . . by B. F. Hurst, J.P." and "Evidence of Spencer Hill taken at the house of Thos. W. Price July 29th 1898 . . . by B. F. Hurst, J.P.," *Commonwealth v. Thomas W. Price*, Prince Edward Court Records, 1898, LVA.
32. *Farmville Herald*, 5–19 Aug. 1898; Bradshaw, *History of Prince Edward County*, pp. 588–91.
33. *Commonwealth v. Thomas W. Price*; *Farmville Herald*, 19–26 Aug., 30 Sept. 1898; Bradshaw, *History of Prince Edward County*, pp. 588–91, 818n.
34. *Commonwealth v. Thomas W. Price*, Prince Edward Court Records, 1899, LVA; *Farmville Herald*, 30 Sept. 1898, 14 Apr.–25 Aug. 1899; *Richmond Times*, 2 Aug. 1899; Bradshaw, *History of Prince Edward County*, pp. 588–91, 818n; Elizabeth Johns Roebuck Interview conducted by Ralph E. Luker, 11 Oct. 2000, tape and transcript in possession of the author; Khalid Hashim Bey, "Stories about Thomas W. Price Handed Down from my great grandmother Alice Gilliam Carrington Scott to her Son Robert James Scott to his daughter Wilsie E. Scott Midgett," copy of typewritten document in possession of the author. Without naming the victim, the "body in the well" story persists in Darlington Heights oral traditions about Tom Price. Whether it refers to Baker, who was named in the *Farmville Herald* and *Richmond Times* stories, or to yet a fourth victim of Price's violence is uncertain.
35. See, for example, Charles M. Payne, *I've Got the Light of Freedom: The Organizing Tradition and the Mississippi Freedom Struggle* [Berkeley, 1995], pp. 419–20, 424.
36. Branch, *Parting the Waters*, p. 9; Harry Ashmore to Taylor Branch, 27 Feb. 1989, copy in possession of the author.
37. Taylor Branch to Harry Ashmore, 19 Apr. 1989, copy in possession of the author. Vernon Johns is the likely original source for the story of his fight with Robert Maynard Hutchins at Oberlin because it is told both by his children and his friends. Oberlin sources make no mention of it. Yet, the contrast between Hutchins's and Johns's own experiences as college presidents at the outset of the Depression may have influenced the story's "improvement" with each telling. In 1929, when Hutchins was named president of the University of Chicago, Vernon Johns became president of his own alma mater, Virginia Theological Seminary and College in Lynchburg. Already deeply in debt when Johns assumed office, the small African American college struggled through four years of his leadership before its students

and faculty forced his ouster late in 1933. At that point, Virginia Seminary had four faculty members, fewer than fifty students, and severely decayed facilities. See William Henry Rowland Powell, "On Being a 'Part-Time President' " [Lynchburg, 1946], p. 10. As Johns pondered the disparity of resources between the two institutions and the contrast between his own debacle and the rising star of America's "Mr. Higher Education," there may have been consolation in recalling a time when he had bested Hutchins both in the classroom and at fisticuffs.

38. *Who's Who in America* (Chicago, 1934–54), vols. 18–28.
39. Branch, *Parting the Waters*, pp. 104–10, 937; Abernathy, *And the Walls Came Tumbling Down*, pp. 123–28.
40. *Atlanta Daily World*, 23 Jan. 1954; "Ebenezer Baptist Church Financial Statement, 1/24/54," Ebenezer Baptist Church Papers, Ebenezer Baptist Church, Atlanta; King, *Stride Toward Freedom*, pp. 15–18; Abernathy, *And the Walls Came Tumbling Down*, p. 119.
41. "William Johnson Trent," in Joseph J. Boris, ed., *Who's Who in Colored America* (New York, 1927), pp. 204–5; O. Rudolph Aggrey, "William Johnson Trent, Sr.," in Rayford W. Logan and Michael R. Winston, eds., *Dictionary of American Negro Biography* (New York, 1982), p. 601; Aingred G. Dunston, "William Johnson Trent, Jr.," in Charles D. Lowery and John F. Marszalek, eds., *Encyclopedia of African-American Civil Rights: From Emancipation to the Present* [Westport, Conn., 1992], p. 526; Smith, *They Closed Their Schools*.
42. For Johns's use of the term, see Vernon Johns, "It Could Be So," *Philadelphia Tribune*, 28 July 1934 and Branch, *Parting the Waters*, p. 12. In Branch, it is "spingsterinkdum Negroes."
43. *Norfolk Journal and Guide*, 31 Dec. 1927; Johns, "As I Remember," pp. ix–x.
44. Altona Trent Johns, *Play Songs of the Deep South* (Washington, D.C., [1944]); Johns and Vivian Flagg McBrier, *Finger Fun with Songs to be Sung* (New York, 1949); Altona Trent Johns, "Henry Hugh Proctor," *Black Perspectives in Music* 3 (1975): 25–32.
45. See, for instance, *Spelman Messenger* 68 (1952): 35, 69 (1953): 35; *Papers of MLK*, 4:43; Altona Trent Johns to MLK, 30 Apr. 1957, King Papers, Boston University; Ralph Simpson, "A Superb Pianist-A Master Musician," *Dexter Echo*, 1 May 1957; MLK to Altona Trent Johns, 15 May 1957; Annual Report, Dexter Avenue Baptist Church, 23 Oct. 1957, in Papers of MLK, 4:201–2, 288; and *Norfolk Journal and Guide*, 8 Mar. 1958.
46. Johns, "As I Remember," pp. vn–xii.
47. Vernon Johns's papers were twice destroyed, once in a 1943 fire that burned the family home in Darlington Heights and once after his death in 1965 by a tenant acting without the family's permission. Reconstruction of what he thought and said must necessarily be limited to scattered survivals in manuscript and print, on tape, and in human memory.
48. Vernon Johns Interview conducted by Robert Collins Smith, 9 Jan. 1962, quoted in Smith, *They Closed Their Schools*, p. 77. See also Boddie, *God's Bad Boys*, p. 64.
49. Vernon Johns, "Defends VA. Seminary," *Richmond Planet*, 2 Jan. 1915, p. 8; Vernon N. Johns, "Concerning a Sort of Patriotism," *Oberlin Review* 44 (1917): 2.
50. Johns, "Transfigured Moments," in Joseph Fort Newton, ed., *Best Sermons*, 1926 (New York, 1926), p. 348.
51. Johns's reference to George F. Babbitt in the 1926 sermon is not repeated in his surviving work until his last sermon, "The Romance of Death," preached three weeks before Johns's own death in 1965. In it, he said "Death is one of the things that Babbitt will not talk about" (Johns, "Transfigured Moments," in Newton, ed.,

Best Sermons, p. 337; Johns, "The Romance of Death," in Gandy, ed., *Human Possibilities*, p. 116).

52. See Sinclair Lewis, *Babbitt* (New York, 1922), pp. 41, 61–67, 248–49, 264–69, 280.
53. Johns, "Rock Foundations," in Gandy, ed., *Human Possibilities*, p. 63; Johns, "The Men Who Let Us Drink," in ibid., p. 96; Johns, "Religion and the Open Mind," in ibid., p. 86.
54. Johns, "Transfigured Moments," p. 344; Johns, "Rock Foundations," pp. 60–61.
55. Johns, "It Could Be So," *Philadelphia Tribune*, 13 Sept. 1934.
56. Johns, "It Could Be So," ibid., 27 Sept. 1934. "Sam Ford" may be a pseudonym, but there is no recollection of this story in the Johns family. The closest parallel to it involved Vernon Johns's uncle, General Womack. When advised that a mob was after him, Womack secured his family and put out the word that he was prepared to meet the mob, which then dispersed.
57. Johns, "It Could Be So," ibid., 11 Oct. 1934.
58. Jacquelyn Dowd Hall, " 'You Must Remember This': Autobiography as Social Critique," *Journal of American History* 85 (1998): 440.
59. Maurice Luker to Ralph E. Luker, 21 July 2001, in possession of the author; MLK, "I See the Promised Land," in James Melvin Washington, ed., *A Testament of Hope: The Essential Writings of Martin Luther King, Jr.* (San Francisco, 1986), p. 286. On African American experience and biblical memory, see Genevieve Fabre and Robert O'Meally, eds., *History & Memory in African American Culture* (New York, 1994); Albert J. Raboteau, "African Americans, Exodus, and the American Israel," in David G. Hackett, ed., *Religion and American Culture: A Reader* (New York, 1995), pp. 73–86; Vincent L. Wimbush, ed., *The Bible and the American Myth: A Symposium on the Bible and Constructions of Meaning* (Macon, Ga., 1999); and Wimbush, ed., *African Americans and the Bible* (New York, 2000).
60. The story of Vernon Johns's transition from an apostle of non-violence to an advocate of armed racial self-defense joins a growing body of work that challenges superficial interpretations of the civil rights movement's non-violence. See, for example, Gail Williams O'Brien, *The Color of the Law: Race, Violence, and Justice in the Post-World War II South* (Chapel Hill, 1999) and Timothy Tyson, *Radio Free Dixie: Robert F. Williams and the Roots of Black Power* (Chapel Hill, 1999). In Montgomery, E. D. Nixon's refusal to espouse more than a tactical non-violence, King's and Abernathy's applications for gun permits after the bus boycott began, and the armed guards around King's house after it was bombed should not be seen as anomalies, but as indicators of a broad willingness to defend the black community with guns if necessary. That makes King's emergence as a disciplined spokesman for a non-violent mass movement all the more remarkable.
61. Johns, "Please Be Seated . . .," *West Virginia Digest*, 17 Feb., 2, 23 Mar. 1940.
62. *Norfolk Journal and Guide*, 31 May 1941, 30 May, 27 June, 14 Nov. 1942; Works Projects Administration, *The Negro in Virginia* (New York, 1940), p. 344; Virginia Hughes Interview conducted by Ralph E. Luker, 22 July 1998, tape and transcript in possession of the author. Also see the account of Johns's subsequent public rebuke of a prominent member of Dexter Avenue, Dr. R. T. Adair, for the murder of his wife in Branch, *Parting the Waters*, pp. 15, 107, 116.
63. Henry Powell, "Remembering Vernon Johns," p. 18 (copy of this 1995 typescript memoir in possession of the author).
64. Vernon Johns, "Here Comes the Dreamer," 14 May 1961, audio recording, Black Church Sermon Collection, Ambrose Swasey Library, Colgate Rochester Crozer Divinity School, Rochester, N.Y. Johns's definition of faith appears as early as Johns, "Religion and the Open Mind," in *Negro Pulpit Opinion: An Interpretation of Christianity by Colored People* (n.p., [c. 1927]).

65. On dreams as religious experience, see Ann Taves, *Fits, Trances, and Visions: Experiencing Religion and Explaining Experience from Wesley to James* (Princeton, 1999) and Mechal Sobel, *Teach Me Dreams: The Search for Self in the Revolutionary Era* (Princeton, 2000). Influenced by William James, but untouched by Sigmund Freud, Johns continued an African American preaching tradition that took dreams seriously as religious experience. See Gandy, ed., *Human Possibilities*, pp. xi, 2, 7–8, 103, 119, 159–67 and Johns, "Here Comes the Dreamer." Equally afreudian, King's "The American Dream" and "I Have a Dream," nevertheless, refer to dreams only in an attenuated sense of aspiration.
66. Vernon Johns, " 'The Man Who Started Freedom,' Baccalaureate Sermon Delivered at Tuskegee Institute . . . Sunday, May 15, 1949," carbon copy of a typescript, Baccalaureate Service Records, Tuskegee University Archives, Tuskegee, Ala.
67. *Atlanta Daily World*, 3 Mar. 1951; Abernathy, *And the Walls Came Tumbling Down*, pp. 119–20; Abernathy Interview.
68. Vernon Johns, "A Jew Discovers the Ground the Negro Should: Sermon Prospectus for a Corporation Aimed at Uniting Rural Production with Urban Distribution" ([Montgomery, Ala.], c. 1951). Also see Vernon Johns, "Human Possibilities: Prophetic Interference in Old Testament Politics," in Gandy, ed., *Human Possibilities*, pp. 26–27.
69. On Barbara Johns and the Prince Edward County school desegregation case, see Robbins L. Gates, *The Making of Massive Resistance: Virginia's Politics of Public School Desegregation, 1954–1956* (Chapel Hill, 1964); Richard Kluger, *Simple Justice: The History of Brown v. Board of Education and Black America's Struggle for Equality* (New York, 1975); Benjamin Muse, *Virginia's Massive Resistance* (Bloomington, Ind., 1961); Smith, *They Closed Their Schools*; R. C. Smith, "Prince Edward County: Revisited and Revitalized," *Virginia Quarterly Review* 73 (1997): 1–27; and Raymond Wolters, *The Burden of Brown: Thirty Years of School Desegregation* (Knoxville, 1984).
70. Jones Interview, quoted in Yeakey, "Montgomery, Alabama, Bus Boycott, 1955–56," p. 110. The text of Johns's March 1951 sermon, "Constructive Homicide," may have included reference to a murder by Johns's slave grandfather. Also see note 14 above. Wyatt Walker, who also reports having heard Vernon Johns tell this story, did not know him before 1948, so there is no known evidence that Johns told it before then.
71. For Johns's admiration of John Brown, see Johns, "The Man Who Started Freedom"; "May Judges Come to Hate Slavery," *Montgomery Advertiser*, 7 Aug. 1950; untitled notes, Manuscript Sermons and Notes, Dexter Avenue-King Memorial Baptist Church Papers, Dexter Avenue-King Memorial Baptist Church, Montgomery, Ala.; Johns, "Here Comes the Dreamer"; [Johns], "He Made the War That Made Us Free," "They Redeemed Brown's Sacrifice from Destruction," both in Second Century 1 (1961): 5–6; and "A Religious History of the Civil War," ibid., 2 (1962): 4–10.

Chapter 9

Affirmative Action from Below: Civil Rights, the Building Trades, and the Politics of Racial Equality in the Urban North, 1945–1969

Thomas J. Sugrue

From *The Journal of American History*

In April 1963 it was impossible to ignore the tragic events in Birmingham, Alabama, where civil rights protesters faced fire hoses and attack dogs. The clash between unchecked police brutality and nonviolent protest marked a watershed in the battle against Jim Crow. Television news crews and print journalists from around the world descended on Birmingham. Their reports and photographs provided indelible images of the black freedom struggle. A thousand miles to the northeast, overshadowed by events in Alabama, an equally momentous wave of protests swept through Philadelphia, as activists from local chapters of the Congress of Racial Equality (CORE) and the National Association for the Advancement of Colored People (NAACP) began a two-month-long siege of city-sponsored construction projects. Beginning in early April, protesters marched in front of Mayor James Tate's modest North Philadelphia row house, staged a sit-in at city hall, shut down construction of the city's Municipal Services Building, battled with police and white unionists at the site of a partially built school, and unleashed an intense debate about racial politics, discrimination, and employment. The Philadelphia protests had national resonance. On June 22, 1963, President John F. Kennedy issued Executive Order 11114, calling for a still vaguely defined "affirmative action" in government-contracted construction employment. Later that summer, activists in Harlem and Brooklyn in New York City; Newark and Trenton, New Jersey; and Cleveland, Ohio, staged similar protests at construction sites. For the next several years, building trades unions remained a major target of northern civil rights protesters.[1]

Just a little over six years after the Philadelphia protests, on June 27, 1969, the administration of Richard M. Nixon announced the Philadelphia Plan, an administrative order designed to open jobs in the white-dominated construction industry to members of minority groups. The Philadelphia Plan, first applied to construction contractors in the City of Brotherly Love, became the blueprint for federally mandated affirmative action in employment. In a terse, jargon-laden memo, Assistant Secretary of Labor Arthur Fletcher denounced the "exclusionary practices" of several nearly all-white trades—the ironworkers, plumbers and pipe fitters, steam fitters, sheet metal workers, electrical workers, roofers, and elevator construction workers. It would take "special measures" to open jobs in those trades to nonwhite workers. Specifically, the Philadelphia Plan required all contractors bidding on government-funded construction projects to submit an "affirmative action program" that included "goals" and "targets" for "minority manpower utilization." The most controversial element of the plan, finalized in September 1969, established numerical targets, defined as a percentage range of minority workers to be employed from a particular trade on each contract. Employers were required to provide statistical evidence of their compliance. Noncompliance could lead to the loss of federal contracts or litigation and legal penalties under federal civil rights laws.[2]

Affirmative action has been the most fiercely contested legacy of the civil rights era. The policy has been the subject of polemical books and articles for over thirty years. The conventional narratives about affirmative action emphasize its role in the fragmentation of an interracial New Deal coalition, its entanglement with growing black racial consciousness, and its challenge to an allegedly long-standing policy of "color blindness." Nathan Glazer, one of the most prolific commentators on the policy, argued that with the rise of affirmative action, "we shifted from being color blind to color conscious." Affirmative action, it is argued, led to the collapse of integrationist liberalism and the rise of identity politics, culminating in an unprecedented expansion of notions of "rights" and a substitution of the principle of equality of outcome for that of equality of opportunity. It jettisoned "merit" for the preferential hiring of historically underrepresented minority groups, regardless of their qualifications. Affirmative action, Stephan Thernstrom and Abigail Thernstrom have contended, was "racial engineering of a new and radical sort" that grew out of a "racism implicit in the notion that blacks were too crippled to be judged on their individual merit." Working-class whites, others argued, had "to absorb the penalties for past discrimination by other whites, ceding opportunities for employment and promotion to competing blacks." Embittered by affirmative action, disaffected whites embraced the New Right.[3]

Such views of affirmative action are insufficiently historical. The best histories of affirmative action, part of a rich literature on bureaucracy and policy formation, have taken an inside-the-beltway perspective. In these accounts, grass-roots activism is a distant backdrop. Hugh Davis Graham saw affirmative action as part of "the quiet revolution in the American regulatory state," as government bureaucrats fashioned an "equal results approach" that rested on statistical measures of group representation. In a nod to the importance of protest, John David Skrentny interpreted affirmative action as a tool for "crisis management" in the riot-torn 1960s but, like Graham, emphasized "administrative innovation" and "pragmatism" and downplayed protest. However important the role of federal bureaucrats in shaping affirmative action, policy formation is not simply a top-down process. As Steven F. Lawson has powerfully argued, we need civil rights histories that "connect the local with the national, the social with the political."[4]

The history of affirmative action is part of the still-incomplete history of the northern freedom struggle. Affirmative action emerged amid a great and unresolved contest over race, employment, and civil rights that played out on the streets, in the union halls, and the workplaces of the urban North—a conflict that began well before the 1960s and resonated long after. Turning back to the decades that preceded the development of a national policy of affirmative action complicates our understanding of this most controversial policy. Adopting a local vantage point, this chapter will trace the struggle over employment-discrimination policy from its origins in World War II through the racial liberalism of the postwar years to the militant protests and counterprotests in the 1960s. The key actors in this story were racial liberals who shaped antidiscrimination policies in the postwar years, civil rights activists who chafed at the limitations of liberalism, and white construction unionists who fought to maintain the status quo. Their stage was Philadelphia, Pennsylvania, where protesters and counterprotesters set the terms of the ongoing debate about affirmative action.[5]

Jobs and Freedom: From Militancy to Gradualism

The protests that rocked Philadelphia in the spring of 1963 grew out of an unfinished quest for "jobs and freedom" in the North that had begun during the Great Depression and World War II. In the 1930s local activists led "Don't Buy Where You Can't Work" campaigns to break down the barriers of workplace discrimination. The coming of World War II accelerated civil rights protests. In 1941, facing the threat of a "march on Washington" led by the Brotherhood of Sleeping Car Porters president A. Philip Randolph, President Franklin D. Roosevelt signed Executive Order 8802, creating a Fair Employment Practices Committee (FEPC), the first federal agency since Reconstruction to handle matters of civil rights. Despite the FEPC's weakness, trade union and civil rights activists used it as a tool to challenge workplace discrimination. Leading the push for equal employment opportunity in Philadelphia were left-labor activists, in the local chapter of the NAACP and in key trade unions such as the National Alliance of Postal Employees, the Transport Workers Union, and the Industrial Union of Marine and Shipbuilding Workers of America, who challenged discrimination in the city's post offices, shipyards, telephone company, and, in the face of violent white resistance, the Philadelphia Transit Corporation. World War II unleashed great expectations about the possibility of racial equality in the North. Black war workers and returning veterans alike demanded that the federal government live up to the rhetoric of democracy and equality that it had deployed against fascism. Increasingly, they couched their demands in a new, powerful rhetoric of "rights," drawing in particular from the conception of positive rights eloquently articulated in Franklin Delano Roosevelt's wartime "Second Bill of Rights." Roosevelt's promise of "economic rights," such as the right to a remunerative job, security, and equality, spoke to the aspirations of blacks who demanded equal employment opportunity.[6]

Yet for blacks in Philadelphia and their counterparts throughout the urban North, war and the postwar economic boom had mixed results. At the end of the war, blacks' economic opportunities had improved, particularly in unskilled and semiskilled industrial work. But a 1945 state-sponsored study found that Pennsylvania's blacks continued to experience "employment marginality" and were "disproportionately concentrated in the most unremunerative and insecure occupations" where "upgrading [was] slow." Efforts to challenge that marginality moved to the forefront of the postwar civil rights agenda. But as the Cold War chill descended on Philadelphia, the militant wartime demand for jobs and freedom gave way to a restrained integrationism. Whereas wartime activists had targeted discriminatory employers with protests and walkouts, postwar activists adopted the quieter tactics of moral suasion. Radical activists were purged from trade unions and from Philadelphia's NAACP branch. In place of an economic analysis of racial inequality emerged an understanding of racism as at root an individual pathology, an anomalous feature of American society, which could be eradicated through education and persuasion. "The Negro problem," wrote Gunnar Myrdal, in his pathbreaking *An American Dilemma*, the single most influential guide for postwar integrationists, "is a problem in the heart of the American. It is there that the interracial tension has its focus. It is there that the decisive struggle goes on."[7]

Myrdalian rhetoric pervaded the postwar struggle for black employment opportunity in the North. From the mid-1940s through the early 1960s, Philadelphia's major civil rights groups—the NAACP, the Committee on Equal Job Opportunity (CEJO), the Armstrong Association (Philadelphia's Urban League affiliate), and the American Friends Service Committee (AFSC)—set out, through hundreds of behind-the-scenes meetings, to persuade employers to hire blacks for "breakthrough" jobs, primarily ones involving contact with whites, such as those of department store salesclerks, telephone operators, secretaries, and bank tellers. The presence of black pioneers in formerly all-white occupations would demonstrate that blacks were capable of work in any sector of the economy. If white co-workers or customers had face-to-face contact with blacks in nonstereotypical situations, they would face the irrationality of their prejudices and eventually jettison their belief in white superiority.[8]

The breakthrough job campaigns eschewed the militant tactics of depression-era and wartime civil rights activists. When thirteen civil rights organizations launched an effort in 1953 to open department store jobs to blacks, they kept a low profile, "avoiding all publicity and keeping clear of any coercive action such as picketing and boycotts." Activists returned their monthly bills emblazoned with stickers that read, "I should like to see qualified Negroes included in your sales force," while leaders met behind the scenes with employers and enlisted the aid of the prominent white judge Curtis Bok, who held a dinner party for department store officials to persuade them to hire blacks. The AFSC launched "merit employment" projects, using the increasingly influential rhetoric of meritocracy to persuade employers that discrimination was irrational and immoral. CEJO activists reached out to business groups and churches, screened *Fair Play*, a film that depicted the travails of a frustrated black job seeker, and distributed civil rights publications to employers. The results were meager. The department store campaign led to a few black hires, mainly in temporary positions. In 1954, a typical year, Armstrong Association conferences with 89 employers yielded about 150 jobs, primarily for "those with above average skills." After hundreds of meetings with employers between 1951 and 1955, the AFSC staffer Jacques Wilmore conceded that "placements are not outstanding."[9]

While breakthrough employment efforts faltered, civil rights activists pushed for the creation of a permanent FEPC after Congress disbanded the antidiscrimination agency in 1946. On the federal level, it proved impossible to pass FEPC legislation, since southern members of Congress thwarted all efforts. Increasingly, pro-FEPC forces turned to state and local governments, which they hoped would be more hospitable.[10] In 1948 Philadelphia's city council enacted a fair employment practices (FEP) ordinance in the context of an intense partisan struggle for the loyalty of black voters, still only tenuously attached to the Democratic party. The revised City Charter of 1951 created a Commission on Human Relations (CHR) and empowered it to investigate violations of Philadelphia's FEP law. The law, like its counterparts throughout the North, mandated nondiscrimination in all employment in the city. The CHR approached discrimination on a case-by-case basis, placing the burden of proof on individual complainants. A firm might completely exclude minorities, but unless a single worker came forward and documented his or her claim, that firm's discriminatory practices went unchallenged. The CHR lacked the staff and funding to investigate civil rights violations systematically. In addition, the CHR had no enforcement powers. Its charge was to "seek to adjust all complaints of unfair employment practices." Any employer who did not comply could be fined up to $100, if successfully prosecuted by the city solicitor, which seldom occurred. The primary strategy of the city FEP law was "the use of education to reduce prejudice and fears." In its first five years, the CHR processed 1,172 employment discrimination complaints, but it found that only 389 cases (about 33 percent) were grounded, and it prosecuted no employers.[11]

On the state level, civil rights advocates battled for a decade to create an FEPC. In Pennsylvania, as in most northern states, the FEP law was the product of compromise. Fearful that a law that would interfere with managerial prerogative, Republicans thwarted efforts to pass a state FEP law five times between 1945 and 1955, before a tepid version passed in October 1955. Liberals, already inclined toward gradualism, watered down FEP legislation to win over moderate Republicans. The FEP law was passed in a non-election year (as were similar laws in most northern and western states) in a session marked by unusually high absenteeism.[12] Underfunded and understaffed, the state FEP program made only a small dent in the problem of workplace discrimination. Adjudication was time-consuming and difficult. Under Pennsylvania's FEP law, the Pennsylvania Human Relations Commission (PHRC) handled 1,416 employment discrimination cases in its first seven years and ruled on behalf of the complainants in 564 cases. But the agency did not use state power to compel employers to stop discrimination. It issued no cease and desist orders, took no employers to court, and held only 19 public hearings. Instead it "adjusted" most cases through "informal conference [with employers] and persuasion." Under such constraints, it was virtually impossible to attack the systematic exclusion of blacks from certain jobs. At best, the PHRC accomplished the placement of a token number of blacks. But however ineffective state FEP laws were, they raised expectations that job discrimination would soon be a thing of the past. FEP made the state an ally—however weak—of civil rights groups in the struggle for equal employment opportunity.[13]

The New Militants

The postwar years witnessed real gains for black workers, particularly in industrial employment. But in an increasingly affluent, suburbanizing region, they remained disproportionately poor, unemployed, and confined to the least secure jobs. Relative to their share in the population, blacks were overrepresented in unskilled industrial and service jobs and underrepresented in sales, management, and the professions—those jobs targeted by the breakthrough campaigns. The number of blacks in the skilled trades rose significantly, but most of the gain came in traditionally black crafts, such as brick laying and roofing, and in non-unionized construction. As a result, skilled black construction workers earned on average only $3,792 per year, whereas whites earned $5,192. Stuck overwhelmingly in the lowest-level jobs, blacks were vulnerable to layoffs, particularly when firms moved to overwhelmingly white suburban and rural areas. The rate of black unemployment in Philadelphia mirrored a nationwide trend: it hovered at one-and-a-half to double that of whites in the boom years from 1946 to 1953 and double that of whites from the 1954 recession through the late 1960s.[14]

By the late 1950s civil rights activists in Philadelphia had grown increasingly frustrated with the limitations of gradualist liberalism and the persistence of workplace discrimination. In 1959 a newly formed group of black Philadelphia ministers, the Committee of 400, launched a four-year "selective patronage" campaign against discriminatory employers. Impatient with the glacial pace of racial change in the work-place, they revived the tactics of the "Don't Buy Where You Can't Work" protests, using their churches as the base of operations. "We just felt that government wasn't fast enough," charged one campaign supporter. Their goal, recalled Rev. Leon H. Sullivan, a founder of the committee, was nothing short of "breaking down [a] company's entire pattern of discriminatory practices." To that end, Sullivan and the rest of the 400 defended what he called "discrimination in reverse," that is, upgrading blacks ahead of whites with seniority. "Black men have been waiting for a hundred years," argued Sullivan, "white men can wait for a few months."[15]

Their first target was the Tasty Baking Company, makers of the sugary Tasty Kakes. Tasty had many black employees, but mainly in inferior jobs. Rather than demanding the hiring of a token black or two, as breakthrough advocates had, the 400 demanded that sizable numbers of blacks be hired at every level in the firm, including for work as bakers, delivery people, chemists, and clerical staff. When Tasty's management refused to cooperate, the ministers launched a boycott. One newspaper estimated that 80 percent of black Philadelphians joined the campaign. Signs reading "We don't sell it and we don't buy it" replaced displays of Tasty's desserts. After six months, the Tasty Baking Company capitulated and hired 2 black truck drivers, 2 black clerical workers, and 4 black women production workers, the first women on a racially mixed but gender-segregated shop floor. Emboldened by their victory, the ministers launched successful boycotts of twenty-nine other firms, including Pepsi-Cola, Sun Oil, Gulf Oil, A&P, the *Philadelphia Bulletin*, and Breyers Ice Cream.[16]

Selective patronage advocates repudiated gradualism. "TOKENISM IS NOT ENOUGH," read one poster at protests outside the *Bulletin*'s offices. In their campaign against Philadelphia-based Sunoco, they demanded a "crash program" for hiring black workers and, stopping just short of a call for quotas, a "minimal acceptable standard" for the number of blacks hired. One boycotter argued, "We're tired of hearing times are changing. How long is long? And how gradual is gradual?" The selective patronage boycotts were more effective than earlier breakthrough campaigns. Leon Sullivan estimated that two thousand blacks moved into new jobs as a result of the boycotts. But even more important, the Committee of 400's increasingly militant language and confrontational strategy emboldened a younger, more working-class cadre of activists to push even harder for change.[17]

Inspired by the selective patronage campaign, established civil rights groups refashioned their strategies. Philadelphia's CORE chapter, started in the 1940s, dormant through most of the postwar years, and revived in 1960, was a quiet band of interracial activists, many of them Quakers, who advocated peaceful persuasion and education rather than confrontation and protest. In the wake of the selective patronage campaign, the chapter took a more militant tack. A small organization without the connections and legitimacy of the ministers who formed the Committee of 400, CORE met with limited successes at first, but the chapter became more visible when a group of predominantly working-class blacks joined. Beginning in 1961, CORE activists picketed stores and restaurants and vocally entered the debate about workplace discrimination in the city.[18]

Philadelphia's NAACP chapter also attracted a new generation of militants. By the late 1950s Philadelphia's NAACP was a relatively conservative organization, largely committed to fund raising for national civil rights efforts. Its middle-class leadership was steeped in 1950s-era racial liberalism, preferring behind-the-scenes negotiation to confrontation. In 1959, after the election of the lawyer A. Leon Higginbotham as president, the organization began to shift to a more activist stance. Higginbotham was barely thirty and a top Yale Law School graduate. His establishment credentials were reassuring to the old guard in Philadelphia's NAACP. But because he was too young to have taken part in the factional disputes that had cleaved the NAACP in the late 1940s and early 1950s, Higginbotham was free to push Philadelphia's branch in a more militant direction, without the taint of Communism. Under Higginbotham's leadership, the Philadelphia branch began to repudiate the gradualism of its earlier antidiscrimination campaigns. In 1962 Higginbotham's handpicked executive director, Thomas H. Burress, expressed frustration with "past approaches" that had challenged employment discrimination on an "individual, case-by-case basis." Burress demanded "accountability" on the part of employers. The burden of responding to racial inequality should be borne by firms, he argued, not by aggrieved workers.[19]

Philadelphia's NAACP chapter underwent even more sweeping changes in 1962 when Higginbotham resigned to take a Kennedy administration appointment. Waiting in the wings were black insurgents who had tried to wrest control of the chapter from its middle-class leadership in the late 1950s. Impatient and suspicious of the cautious reformism of the city's black bourgeoisie, the insurgents staged a coup. In the fall of 1962, the irascible Cecil B. Moore, a North Philadelphia lawyer, was elected Higginbotham's successor. Moore pledged to turn the NAACP into an aggressive, protest-oriented organization. Moore, a loquacious orator, earned the enmity of racial liberals by his rough language (including anti-Semitic and antiwhite comments), his defiance of authority, and his imperious style. Moore reserved particular vitriol for black moderates. CHR members Sadie Mossell Alexander and Christopher Edley were "little Uncle Toms" and "occasional Negroes." But Moore's streetwise demeanor boosted his popularity in poor and working-class neighborhoods. A Moore supporter from North Philadelphia frankly acknowledged that the NAACP president was "an arrogant foul mouth radical" but praised Moore for his interest in the "rank-and-file negro," an approach "much needed . . . among a restless people." It was Moore's brashness and concern for what he fondly called his "barbecue, porkchops, and collard-green-eating people" that won the support of blacks who bore the brunt of racial discrimination and whom the cautious racial liberalism of the 1950s had only alienated.[20]

The newly militant civil rights organizations took a bold step in 1962 and 1963. They turned to protest to challenge building trades unions and their allies in both local and federal governments. Their strategy was ingenious. They targeted an industry notorious for racial homogeneity at its most vulnerable point: its dependence on government largess. By the late 1950s, national civil rights organizations had begun to complain about discrimination in construction work. A 1957 Urban League report documented barriers to black employment in the construction industry. In a 1960 report the NAACP labor director, Herbert Hill, criticized discrimination in union-run apprenticeship programs. And in 1960, when A. Philip Randolph launched the Negro American Labor Council, he lambasted the building trades and lashed out against "tokenism and gradualism." Local activists moved a step further. They decided to tackle the problem through direct action. By protesting discrimination in government contracts, they attacked the very core of postwar Keynesian economics: businesses and unions reliant on government spending. In so doing, they unleashed what would become the affirmative action debate.[21]

The Building Trades

CORE and the NAACP went after the building trades at one of the best moments in American history to be a construction worker. Historically, construction work in the United States had been insecure, sensitive to economic fluctuations, dangerous, and seasonal.[22] In the aftermath of the New Deal, building trades work grew more secure. Few sectors of the economy benefited more from state support. Federal and state prevailing-wage (or Davis-Bacon) laws guaranteed high wages and benefits in government-funded construction. Beginning in the New Deal, the federal government had supported apprenticeship training programs, with the Philadelphia school district paying instructors' salaries and providing classrooms.[23] Above all, the construction industry profited from the New Deal's pro-growth policies. Congress created the Federal Housing Administration, the Home Owners' Loan Corporation, and the Federal Public Housing Authority in large part to revitalize the flagging construction industry. Federal, state, and local tax incentives also spurred new construction. Shopping malls supported by government-built infrastructure sprawled across former farmlands alongside new suburban housing developments underwritten by government loan guarantees; both were accessible via federally funded expressways. An expansive government channeled billions of dollars into airports and military bases, federal offices, urban renewal projects, hospitals, universities, and schools. Big government was the health of the building trades.[24]

By the early 1960s, Philadelphia was in the midst of a federally subsidized construction boom. In Center City, several new office towers, projected to cost $45 million, were rising, including the new Municipal Services Building that civil rights protesters would target. Federal urban renewal funds supported the new Penn Center complex and a regional IBM headquarters. As federal education spending skyrocketed under President Kennedy, new public schools went up in neighborhoods throughout the city. And that was just the beginning. In 1963 construction began on the Eastwick Project, slated to be the largest urban renewal site in the country. The city built new public housing; announced plans for the revitalization of the declining Market East shopping district; cleared a "blighted" district in Society Hill to make way for an apartment complex designed by I. M. Pei; broke ground for a new U.S. Mint; and launched several federally subsidized hospital and university expansion projects.[25]

Particularly galling to blacks—26 percent of the city's population in 1960—was that the work crews on Philadelphia's unionized construction sites were overwhelmingly white. Compounding black discontent at "Negro removal" (as urban renewal was derisively nicknamed), projects seldom created jobs in black neighborhoods. More than 10 percent of Philadelphia's black men had experience in construction—most in non-union jobs. From the 1940s through the 1960s, with rare exceptions, Philadelphia's black construction union members were concentrated in a few racially segregated locals of the laborers' and hod carriers' unions, confined to unskilled jobs with little opportunity for advancement. A few blacks belonged to the plasterers', carpenters', roofers', and bricklayers' unions. Even where they had a beachhead of membership, black crafts workers still faced systematic discrimination and harassment. In 1954 and 1955, for example, black carpenters complained to the NAACP that they faced arbitrary layoffs and were turned away at the hiring hall despite their union credentials. Carpenters' union officials, they contended, unhesitatingly accepted contractors' requests not to "send any Niggers to this job." Even the token hiring of blacks faced fierce resistance. William Taylor, the sole black carpenter placed at a construction site after negotiations between the union and the Armstrong Association, faced the wrath of a superintendent who told him, "You forced your way in here, I'll get you out." Even in unions with sizable black memberships, blacks were trapped in the worst jobs. In 1963 nearly one-third of Roofers Local 160 members were black, but every black member was classified as a helper, earning two dollars per hour less than mechanic roofers, all of them white.[26]

Economics and culture—interest and identity—powerfully combined to keep the building trades overwhelmingly white. The key to high wages and job security in the building trades was the constriction of the labor supply through exclusionary barriers. The shape and form that exclusion took grew out of a deeply rooted culture of race, gender, ethnicity, and family. Building trades unions practiced preferential hiring. Many skilled trades unions perpetuated a father-son tradition, recruiting new workers through family connections. In 1964, for example, all thirty-two apprentices in International Brotherhood of Electrical Workers (IBEW) Local 32 were sons or nephews of union members. Forty percent of Philadelphia's plumbers had sons in the trade. The Operative Plasterers and Cement Masons Local 8 gave first preference to sons of contractors, and second to sons of its members. When the Pennsylvania labor leader James L. McDevitt was first elected an officer of Local 8, fellow unionists joked that "his family vote was enough to elect him." McDevitt's great-grandfather, father, uncle, three cousins, and brother were all plasterers.[27] Some of the larger unions recruited more widely, drawing members from ethnic associations, Catholic parishes, and neighborhood social networks. Most Tile Layers' Local 6 members were Italian; most Sheet Metal Workers Local 19 unionists were of Scottish, Irish, or German descent. Structural and Ornamental Iron Workers' Local 401 required that every apprentice applicant have two sponsors from the union before screening by an interview committee made up of three union officials and three contractors.[28] Exclusive hiring practices reinforced the ties of ethnicity and community. Unionists strengthened their sense of exclusiveness and solidarity through elaborate hazing rituals on the job site. Friendship and kin networks in the building trades were a nearly insurmountable barrier for black workers, since blacks and whites almost never intermarried and, in the heavily segregated city, seldom lived in the same neighborhoods or belonged to the same churches and clubs.[29]

Philadelphia's segregated building trades unions were invulnerable to 1950s-era racial gradualism. Craft unions and contractors simply disregarded civil rights organizations and their breakthrough campaigns. When CEJO held a conference on construction apprenticeship in 1954, only two of thirty invited unions bothered to send representatives. The same year, IBEW Local 98 officials ignored CEJO officials' calls and letters asking for a meeting. In response to mounting accusations that they practiced racial discrimination, contractors and unions denied culpability. Contractors passed the blame for hiring practices to the building trades unions, although in most trades contractors helped select apprentices and screen journeymen through joint union-contractor councils. Unions similarly disavowed discriminatory intent, arguing that their nepotistic hiring practices were race-neutral. They were not prejudiced: blacks simply did not apply.[30]

FEP laws barely affected the building trades. In 1963 a Philadelphia building trades union official proudly noted that only a tiny percentage of FEP cases involved construction work. Few blacks filed grievances against exclusive craft unions because they had no access to information about union construction jobs and apprenticeship programs, not to mention connections at union hiring halls. Success in a FEP case required evidence that a contractor or union had deliberately, consciously discriminated by race. But building trades seldom resorted to overt methods of discrimination. They recruited through word of mouth rather than formal advertisement. Since craft unions and contractors tapped informal networks, their hiring policies escaped legal remedy. But in an era of growing civil rights consciousness, the lack of black faces in the construction industry did not go unnoticed. As black activists began to fashion new strategies in the struggle for racial equality, they moved inexorably toward a collision with the building trades.[31]

Whose Rights?

In spring 1963 civil rights protests shattered the insular world of the building trades. The battle had been long in coming. In early 1962, as part of his campaign to refashion the NAACP as "an aggressively militant organization," Thomas Burress called for an "all out attack on discriminatory practices in government agencies." At the same time, Philadelphia's Negro Trade Union Leadership Council, a coalition of unionists mostly from racially mixed industrial unions, demanded the inclusion of blacks in apprenticeship programs and in skilled trades. In 1962 the mainstream CEJO called for cooperation between federal officials and contractors in antidiscrimination efforts. In February 1963 *Greater Philadelphia Magazine*, a boosterish periodical targeted toward white professionals, published a searing exposé of Jim Crow in the city's building trades. Later that month, the Human Rights Committee of the Pennsylvania American Federation of Labor–Congress of Industrial Organizations (AFL-CIO) issued a report denouncing "our failure to break the pattern of segregated locals and to change the discriminatory membership practices of certain unions." In March 1963 the CHR criticized two electrical workers' locals, a plumbers' local, and a steam fitters' local for "Negro exclusion." In April 1963 a group of prominent black Baptist ministers, many of whom had participated in the selective patronage campaign, demanded that the city prohibit discrimination on publicly funded construction sites.[32]

Philadelphia's CORE chapter became the vanguard of the struggle against construction industry discrimination. Louis Smith, a vacuum cleaner repairman who had become director of Philadelphia's CORE chapter in 1962, accused the city of unjustly channeling "taxpayers' money to builders who hire from discriminating unions" and demanded that the city stop awarding contracts to firms with few or no black workers. The official response was tepid. Mayor James J. Tate, a stalwart of Philadelphia's Democratic machine and a resident of an all-white neighborhood that many skilled craftsmen called home, was silent. Like most northern Democrats, he supported civil rights in the South, but from the mid-1950s through the mid-1960s, as a city council member and in his first year as mayor, Tate had largely ignored race issues in his backyard. CHR head George Schermer reported, "Never once in the seven years I had to deal with him did I get the slightest hint that he had any concern" about civil rights.[33]

CORE confronted the mayor in April 1963, demonstrating in the narrow street outside Tate's row house, picketing at city hall, and occupying the mayor's reception room in an hour-long sit-in. "Why do you have to do things like this?" the exasperated Tate asked Smith. However annoyed Tate was, the protests jarred him from complacency. As Schermer recalled, Tate "never did anything until the day CORE picketed his house." The sudden appearance of the civil rights movement on his doorstep forced Tate to confront an issue that he had hoped would simply go away. Tate's frustration was common to many other Democrats in the early 1960s. The demand for an end to Jim Crow on city contracts pitted two core Democratic constituencies against each other. As a Democrat in a city that was over one-quarter black, Tate could scarcely afford to ignore civil rights. Yet in a majority-white, heavily working-class city, he feared alienating his most loyal supporters. Tate faced the dilemma of resolving irreconcilable demands: African Americans sought construction jobs; white craftsmen sought to protect the security and fraternity of their trades.[34]

Tate moved hesitatingly toward a middle ground. Hoping to defuse the protests, he instructed the city's Board of Labor Standards and CHR to investigate the hiring practices of contractors and trade unions working on city contracts. Barnet Lieberman, the city's commissioner of licenses and inspections, criticized civil rights advocates, claiming that Philadelphia officials "had made assiduous effort to protect equal employment opportunities for all persons in our city." To Lieberman, accusations of Jim Crow in city employment were "partisan pleading in its most reprehensible form." The CHR held hearings on employment discrimination in early May while city construction projects continued uninterrupted. Asked about the civil rights protesters, Tate told reporters, "I am in sympathy with them, but I can't do anything." Tate's equivocation and his aides' obstinacy infuriated civil rights activists. CORE accused the mayor of "inaction," charging him with "putting politics before the welfare of the Negro citizens of the city."[35]

In early May civil rights protests accelerated. Cecil Moore and his NAACP chapter joined (and tried to co-opt) the CORE effort. At a downtown rally in support of the victims of police brutality in Birmingham, Moore railed against discrimination in city contracts. "The only difference between Birmingham and Philadelphia is geography . . . . Like in Birmingham, we are willing to go to jail for what is right." Moore also denounced the CHR for holding hearings, voicing militants' impatience at the gradualist tactics of racial liberals. The public hearings were an "unnecessary stalling tactic," shouted Moore. "We're tired of conferring. We're not going to waste time discussing labor unions or cops who beat us up, we're going to do something about it." Moore's threat was not idle.[36]

On May 14, fifteen demonstrators from CORE occupied the mayor's offices for twenty-one hours. Singing "Freedom, Freedom" and "We Shall Overcome," they demanded an immediate end to discrimination on city-funded construction. After a meeting with Tate, the protesters left city hall. For the first time, Tate criticized craft unions and asked them to "do their duty and meet their responsibilities as Americans to admit Negroes to membership." In a press conference, Tate again deployed patriotic rhetoric to challenge discrimination in city contracts, citing Philadelphia's "heritage of freedom and equal rights for all men" and calling on "all members of the community to support our efforts to underscore the thought that all men are created equal." Outside protests continued, led by Moore, who demanded an immediate halt to construction work until black craftsmen were hired. Backed into a corner, the reluctant Tate stopped construction on the Municipal Services Building "until all persons are offered employment opportunities." Tate later told reporters that the protests "made us fear another Birmingham, and that's why we shut down work on the project."[37]

That civil rights activists had stopped work on a construction site outraged unionists. Counterprotesters at city hall waved signs that read, "Tate puts men out of work for votes." James Jones, a black steelworker and civil rights activist, took a middle ground, in support of the campaign against discrimination but critical of the work stoppage. He worried that "a lot of good unions" would suffer because of the shutdowns. Emotions were raw. In a dramatic moment of ill timing, building trades workers waiting to meet with city officials faced off with Cecil Moore, fresh from a meeting with Tate, in the corridor outside the mayor's office. Fifteen tense minutes of "shouting, arm-waving, and denunciation from both sides" followed. Angry workers yelled, "Why are you shutting us down?" "Why are you stopping us from working?" Thomas Dugan, business manager of the Steamfitters Union, confronted Moore: "Who says the unions are guilty?" Moore shot back, "Until you put black faces out there, you're guilty." Dugan replied, "You're depriving men of jobs." Moore rejoined, "You're segregated as Alabama." The "noisy confrontation" continued until police intervened.[38]

The day after the sit-in at the mayor's office, Moore gathered several hundred NAACP members in front of the Municipal Services Building construction site. NAACP and CORE leaders warned government officials that unless blacks were hired in the building trades unions, they would expand their protests to other construction sites. The Committee of 400 pledged to support the protests "to the point of using their own bodies" to shut down construction sites. Ten days after the city hall sit-in, picketers organized by the NAACP surrounded a school under construction in Philadelphia's Strawberry Mansion section. They were joined by neighbors incensed at the sight of white-dominated work crews in the predominantly black community. The crowds were diverse. One rainy afternoon, housewives led "an umbrella-studded procession." A contingent of Philadelphia's most prominent black lawyers joined the protests. In a theatrical inversion of the police brutality in Birmingham, black schoolchildren marched with "fierce-looking mastiffs." The school protest turned violent. Police officers, unionists, and demonstrators clashed. White construction workers leaped over fences to avoid picketers, a teamster drew his shotgun to threaten protesters who blocked a service entrance, and, finally, 140 police officers formed a flying wedge to break the picket line. Altogether, sixteen people were injured in the clashes. Police officers slapped a black schoolgirl and "slugged" a black minister. Two members of the Revolutionary Action Movement, a fledgling black power organization, were arrested when they confronted bricklayers and police.[39]

The protesters couched their demands in an assertive language of rights and citizenship. "We pay as much taxes as everybody else," declared Delores Gordon. "We certainly deserve something for them. We'll keep marching peacefully until we get our rights." Another marcher, Aurelia O'Kedas, was hopeful. "They've got to come around pretty soon. America is waking up to the idea that there can't be any such thing as second-class citizens." Marchers chanted, "We're tired of carrying bricks; we want to lay them," and, "We want freedom now." One activist pointed out the hypocrisy of American Cold War rhetoric, a sensitive topic in the early 1960s: "Man we're just blowing Dixie to foreign countries when we tell them that this is the Land of Opportunity."[40]

Toward Affirmative Action

Civil rights groups used their newfound clout to push for preferential hiring policies. CORE demanded racial quotas for city contracts and apprenticeship programs "to make up for years and years of exclusion of Negroes from the skilled trades." The group would be satisfied with nothing less than the allocation of 15 percent of construction jobs to black workers. Moore, who had declared victory when a few black construction workers were hired, belatedly joined the call for quotas. Finally, in late June, CORE's national director, James Farmer, echoed the local demand for quotas in testimony before the House Judiciary Committee. Only the CHR refrained from calling for quotas, instead asking contractors to hire a "reasonable number" of black skilled workers.[41]

As the Philadelphia protests continued, Kennedy administration officials announced a new antidiscrimination initiative that targeted construction unions. From the first months of his presidency, JFK's liberal advisers had advocated an executive order dealing with discrimination in the construction industry, but the president, reluctant to weaken his shaky hold over southern Democrats, had held back. But the wave of unrest in spring 1963 pushed him to act. Worried that the "successes of Birmingham, Philadelphia, and elsewhere" would spur more protests, Kennedy administration officials moved decisively. On June 4 Kennedy announced his opposition to discrimination on federal construction projects, singling out "economic distress and unrest." Unnamed administration sources suggested that the president's statement was "partly in response to violence in Philadelphia."[42] In addition, Kennedy ordered Secretary of Labor Willard Wirtz to enforce nondiscrimination in federally sponsored apprenticeship programs. Wirtz immediately created a task force to survey minority employment by federal construction contractors. Wirtz presented his findings in a memorandum to the president a week later. In twenty cities examined, blacks were wholly unrepresented in nine trades. Seven in ten black construction workers were mere laborers. In mid-June, Kennedy met with union leaders to discuss Wirtz's findings and dispatched cabinet officials to several cities to discuss "greater employment opportunities for Negroes." The destinations included Philadelphia, one of five cities that his advisers singled out as "danger spots." On June 22 the president issued Executive Order 11114, prohibiting discrimination against minorities on government-contracted construction projects.[43]

Kennedy's executive order did not, however, curb protests. Construction site pickets continued in Philadelphia throughout the summer. The Philadelphia protests had a ripple effect throughout the North. On June 8 NAACP labor secretary Herbert Hill encouraged New York activists "to stage mass protest demonstrations" at construction sites, using the Philadelphia protests as a model. In June, protesters led a "mammoth demonstration" at Harlem Hospital, still under construction. NAACP activists in Trenton, New Jersey, also targeted government-funded construction projects beginning in mid-June. Inspired by its Philadelphia counterpart, the Newark, New Jersey, CORE chapter blockaded a school construction site in July. In Cleveland, Ohio, CORE and NAACP branches orchestrated a march of twenty-five thousand against building trades discrimination. In August, spurred by the small local CORE chapter, Brooklyn ministers protested at the partially completed Downstate Medical Center.[44]

In Philadelphia officials struggled mightily to defuse construction site protests. To halt the school pickets, Mayor Tate brokered an agreement with the NAACP to put five blacks on city construction sites right away. But Tate could not keep the lid on. In late June CORE coordinated a thousand-person march and sit-in at city hall, again demanding a shutdown of all city-funded construction sites. Over the summer, both state and city human relations officials entered into prolonged negotiations with building trades unions. State officials examined the statistical representation of minorities in the building trades and other industries and, armed with data, bargained with union leaders over the "voluntary acceptance" of affirmative action plans. In July Philadelphia Board of Education officials pledged to close apprenticeship programs that excluded blacks. And in August the U.S. Department of Labor threatened to withhold its certification of union-sponsored apprenticeship programs if they were segregated.[45]

Even those relatively mild versions of affirmative action outraged many building trades unionists. Thomas Dugan belligerently told his rank and file that he "was not going to be dictated to by any minority group." Although there were no blacks in Dugan's twenty-two-hundred-member local, he claimed, "We never discriminated and never intend to. We want to do everything that is right and just"—with the qualification that "we are not going to be badgered into placing just anybody in the union." Joseph Burke, president of Sheet Metal Workers Local 19, claimed, "I've never discriminated personally or officially against a man because of the color of his skin." But Burke drew a color line when it came to hiring. "They are asking me to say to a working white man, 'Get off the job because I want to put a Negro on.' I can never say that. Nor can I say to people out of work 'I can't put you to work because I have to put a Negro to work.' " Burke's and Dugan's claims were disingenuous. They drew lines all the time—making distinctions between workers, offering a preference to the son or brother of a current member, favoring one worker on a job over another. To tell a worker, "I can't put you to work because I have just given someone else a job" would describe the turn of events on any slow day in the hiring hall. But with the word "Negro" inserted, the ordinary act of turning away a prospective worker became, in Burke's view, an injustice he could not commit. The difference here was racial, pure and simple. At the very core of resentment of affirmative action among workers in the building trades was an unacknowledged white identity politics. White building trades workers had so long benefited from the exclusion of African Americans that they could not conceive of their position as one that reflected patterns of racial separation and privilege. Rather, they saw the racial segregation of craft unions as the outcome of a natural process of group identification and affiliation.[46]

Building trades unionists attacked antidiscrimination policies in the potent language of rights. "The established and well-earned rights of white people are being imperiled in the fight of Negro leadership against unions," argued Burke. Contractors joined in the criticism, denouncing desegregation measures as "discrimination against white persons." At the same time, building trades unionists came to view government as their enemy and fiercely resisted its intervention in their apprenticeship and hiring programs. Plumbers denounced federal antidiscrimination measures as "undemocratic, unreasonable, unwarranted, and unworkable" and pledged that "we will accept no dictation from any government agency." In their view antidiscrimination efforts were part of an insidious expansion of government power that threatened to overwhelm workers' cherished independence. Peter Schoemann, national president of the plumbers' union, echoed local opposition to federal demands for affirmative action. "We resent the use of the equal employment campaign as a reason for a federal takeover in an area where government does not belong." The notion of union autonomy, central to the ideology of the building trades (even if such autonomy was largely fictitious in the heavily subsidized construction sector), was put to the test by government nondiscrimination mandates. That the federal government should regulate the employment policies of the building trades was a logical outgrowth of its already-intense involvement in the construction industry. But building trades unionists built a fire wall around their apprenticeship and hiring policies. Attempts to "force" the hiring of blacks threatened the job security that they expected the government to protect.[47]

After months of civil rights protests, Philadelphia's building trades unions made concessions—on their own terms. At the national level, the AFL-CIO encouraged construction unions to adopt antidiscrimination language in their contracts. Philadelphia locals complied. By summer's end, all but the Sheet Metal Workers had signed an agreement with the CHR that they would "accept Negro journeymen and desegregate their apprenticeship programs." By the following winter, a similar agreement had been reached with the Pennsylvania Human Relations Commission. Those agreements represented a new strategy by craft unions that was imitated throughout the North from late 1963 through the adoption of the Philadelphia Plan in 1969: they pledged nondiscrimination on the basis of race, creed, or color and emphasized the right of individual, aggrieved minority applicants to appeal union hiring decisions. Belatedly, they had embraced the rhetoric of 1950s-style racial gradualism in hopes of avoiding the quotas and targets for Negro hiring that CORE and other activists demanded. Such union antidiscrimination agreements emphasized process, not outcome. They had no mechanisms for measuring progress, for ensuring that building trades jobs were indeed open to black applicants. Adoption of antidiscrimination language allowed building trades unions to emphasize their good intentions without being held accountable for results. Above all, they hoped that their voluntarism would keep the federal government at bay.[48]

In the face of growing pressure from civil rights protesters, the building trades began to support "outreach" and "pre-apprenticeship" programs that targeted minorities. Unions found allies in black social service groups that eschewed militant protest and instead advocated programs to "uplift" the black poor through job training and education. The Urban League, for example, which had sponsored "job fairs" throughout the postwar years, hosted events where black youth could learn about apprentice opportunities. Agencies such as Philadelphia's Opportunities Industrialization Center used federal job-training funds and foundation grants to prepare blacks for work in the skilled trades. By 1967 and 1968, many building trades unions began to fund those programs from their own budgets in the hope that their outreach programs (which union leaders considered voluntary affirmative action) would deflect protest and dissuade federal officials from intervening in the hiring hall.[49]

The efficacy of union antidiscrimination policies provoked great debate. In 1966, the AFL-CIO's Building and Construction Trades Department proudly pointed to the fact that only ten complaints involving the construction industry had been filed with the federal government. Again and again, union officials asserted their innocence, snidely dismissing "discrimination" (their quotation marks) as the product of poor black education and disingenuously claiming that "THERE ARE MORE NEGROES in skilled jobs in the construction industry than in most other industries." But those claims rang hollow to most civil rights advocates, who saw union efforts as tokenism. Even with outreach in place, blacks trickled into apprenticeship programs a few at a time. In 1963, there were no black journeymen or apprentices in the plumbers', steamfitters', sheet metal workers', roofers', ironworkers', and elevator constructors' unions in Philadelphia and only 2 electricians' apprentices. In 1964, 2 blacks gained apprenticeships in plumbing and 2 as electricians; the other apprenticeship programs remained all-white. In 1966 the sheet metal workers brought aboard 2 black apprentices. In April 1967, those seven unions, with a total membership of 9,162, had 20 black journeymen and 14 black apprentices. Blacks remained clustered in the trowel trades and as laborers.[50]

Protest and Policy Making

Union antidiscrimination efforts did not quell black discontent. Throughout the country, civil rights activists kept the issue of workplace discrimination in the limelight. In 1964, 1965, 1966, and 1967, construction site protests erupted in Philadelphia, Pennsylvania; Newark, New Jersey; New York, New York; New Rochelle, New York; Cleveland, Ohio; Cincinnati, Ohio; Oakland, California; and St. Louis, Missouri, where, in a dramatic act of civil disobedience, a protester chained himself to the top of the Gateway Arch. In 1967 the NAACP announced a national campaign to open up the building trades. Federal officials took note of the protests. "The absence of non-whites among construction trades workers," wrote a Labor Department official in 1967, "has been a focal point for racial unrest" and "a prime symbol of the lack of equal employment opportunity." Officials in the newly created Equal Employment Opportunity Commission gathered volumes of statistical data to document the point. In Philadelphia, Labor Department officials accused construction unions of "dragging their feet" on minority employment.[51]

Protests and policy innovations reinforced each other in a feedback loop. In 1965 President Lyndon B. Johnson issued Executive Order 11246, which enabled the newly created Office of Federal Contract Compliance of the Department of Labor to terminate government contracts with firms that did not practice "affirmative action" in employment. What "affirmative action" and "compliance" meant would be defined in 1966 and 1967 in policy experiments in four metropolitan areas that had been rocked by construction site protests. In the aftermath of the Gateway Arch demonstrations, federal officials fashioned a St. Louis Plan that demanded that contractors provide "pre-award" evidence of their efforts to hire minorities—the awarding of a federal contract was contingent on the recruitment of underrepresented minorities. When a St. Louis contractor hired three blacks to comply with the plan, white workers walked out, leading to years of litigation. In California's Bay Area, in the wake of black-led protests against the Bay Area Rapid Transit (BART) system, the 1966 San Francisco Plan obligated contractors to document their efforts to train, hire, and place minority construction workers. But Labor Department officials criticized Bay Area contractors for "paper compliance"; the plan led to nominal changes. In 1967, in another city that had been rocked by huge antidiscrimination protests, federal officials mandated a Cleveland Plan that required pre-award "manning tables" specifying how many minority workers would be hired on federally funded job sites and what positions they would hold. Finally, in March 1967, Johnson administration officials announced a Philadelphia Plan requiring "affirmative action" in hiring on all federal contracts in that city, with pre-award manning tables to be enforced by federal officials who would visit job sites and conduct head counts of minority workers.[52]

The Johnson administration had two goals: to stem growing black discontent and to fashion a proposal that would not alienate building trades unionists. Straddling the fence proved difficult. Defending the Philadelphia and Cleveland plans to skeptics at the AFL-CIO, Secretary of Labor Willard Wirtz stated that the government had singled out the two cities for their intense racial tension—and suggested that it would not impose such plans on other cities. The unionists were not convinced; they saw the city plans as the beginning of a federal assault on union hiring practices and continued to protest federally mandated affirmative action. Complicating the scenario was an internecine battle within the Johnson administration over the legality of the Philadelphia Plan. While Wirtz continued to defend the affirmative action proposal as a necessary tool to open construction employment to minorities, Comptroller General Elmer Staats expressed skepticism about the Philadelphia Plan and finally, in November 1968, ruled that it was illegal. The fate of affirmative action would be left to Johnson's successor in the White House. In the meantime, the prospect of a federal affirmative action program with teeth sparked a new wave of protests at northern construction sites. Philadelphia's activists protested at local hospitals, the University of Pennsylvania, the Philadelphia School Board, and, in a reprise of earlier demonstrations, the U.S. Mint site. They demanded immediate remedies, not gradual change. When Richard M. Nixon took office, they pushed again and used the threat of racial unrest as a bargaining chip. In April and May 1969 a delegation of Philadelphia civil rights activists lobbied Nixon officials with the grim prediction of a new outbreak of riots if the administration did not revive the plan.[53]

In June 1969 the Nixon administration resurrected the Philadelphia Plan. The key to the "revised Philadelphia Plan" was specific "goals" and "timetables," that is, percentage ranges of minority workers to be hired on construction jobs, accelerating over time. By deploying percentage ranges, the plan attempted to meet civil rights protesters' demands for quantitative evidence of minority employment while skirting the hot-button issue of quotas that raised constitutional questions and irked trade unions. But with quotas or not, the Philadelphia Plan sparked conflict. Black activists stepped up their protests against construction discrimination in cities across the country, culminating in calls for a "nationwide black walkout" in late September. Many of the protests turned violent as hardhats and picketers clashed. Building trades unionists continued to insist on their good intentions and claimed that they were the true victims of discrimination. AFL-CIO president George Meany (himself a plumber) bitterly denounced those who charged construction unions with discrimination.

> We still find the Building Trades being singled out as being "lily white" as they say, and some fellow the other day said it was "the last bastion of discrimination." Now this is an amazing statement, when you figure how small participation of Negroes and other minorities is in, for instance, the banks in this country, the press . . . . I resent the action of government officials—no matter what department they are coming from—who are trying to make a whipping boy out of the Building Trades.

The Philadelphia Building and Construction Trades Council argued that the plan was "discriminatory against members of building trades unions" and contended that "discrimination because of race, color, religion, and ethnic origin has not existed in our trades for years past." Increasingly, white unionists saw civil rights as a zero-sum game. Sensitive to charges of racism, C. J. Haggerty, the AFL-CIO's top building trades official, inarticulately avoided the word "whites" in addressing the union's annual convention just after Nixon officials had announced the Philadelphia Plan. Haggerty charged that affirmative action "would in effect exclude others or bar others" from construction jobs. Especially unsettling to white unionists was their perception that government had unfairly "sided" with blacks. Above all, they began to view affirmative action as part of a larger cultural attack on the white working-class world, launched by protesters and abetted by "liberals" in the federal government. "We are constantly harassed by bureaucrats and so-called 'liberals,' " lamented the head of the carpenters' union in a speech attacking the Philadelphia Plan. In the thirty years following the election of FDR, government had often been an ally of white workers. Affirmative action weakened that alliance.[54]

By the Nixon years, new, bleak economic realities had raised the stakes in the affirmative action debate. As the Vietnam War progressed, the economy soured. Under Nixon federal spending on construction projects plummeted. The economic pinch was particularly acute in the older industrial cities of the Northeast and Midwest—places such as Philadelphia—which benefited relatively little from defense spending while struggling with capital flight, urban disinvestment, and a diminishing tax base. As they clung to their construction jobs, buffeted by inflation, federal cutbacks, and layoffs, building trades workers blamed civil rights for their fate. Long-term economic restructuring was inscrutable to most white workers. But affirmative action was an easy target.[55]

There is no single explanation for Nixon's support for the Philadelphia Plan. The newly elected president hoped to prevent a repeat of the "long hot summers" of urban riots that had plagued Johnson. Moreover, key Nixon administration officials, particularly Secretary of Labor George Shultz and Assistant Secretary Arthur Fletcher, were long-standing supporters of civil rights. Shultz argued that blacks should benefit from $600 million in federal funds to be spent on thirty-eight projects in Philadelphia. Fletcher hoped the plan would help lift blacks from an ongoing economic "depression" and solve the problem of the "hard-core unemployment" of young blacks. Shultz, a labor economist of the Chicago school, had other motives as well: he hoped to lower construction industry wages by increasing the supply of construction laborers. The exclusion of blacks, he believed, inflated labor costs on government-funded projects. Shultz and Fletcher also shared a suspicion of unions, which they blamed for inflation. Many Nixon aides also saw electoral benefits to the plan: it would mortally wound the New Deal coalition by dividing working-class whites and blacks—a division that had been foreshadowed in the acrimonious construction site protests. When federal courts upheld the constitutionality of the Philadelphia Plan, Nixon's administration, in the words of his aide Laurence Silberman, sowed Philadelphia Plans "across the country like Johnny Appleseed." In January 1970, Order 4 extended the principles of the Philadelphia Plan to all government contracts of $50,000 or more; in December 1971 it was amended to incorporate women. Affirmative action, Philadelphia Plan–style, now covered a large swath of the American economy.[56]

Affirmative action was the distinctive product of Johnson and Nixon administration policy makers. But local civil rights activists and construction unionists had thrust the battle over employment discrimination onto the national stage, with lasting consequences. Looking backward and situating affirmative action in the postwar struggle for civil rights helps make sense out of this controversial policy. Affirmative action grew out of the unfinished struggle for racial equality in the workplace after World War II. To cast the history of affirmative action as the story of a radical shift from color blindness to color consciousness effaces the complex lived reality of race in the urban North. There was nothing de facto color-blind about the exclusion of African Americans from Philadelphia's building trades. That the construction industry remained a bastion of white privilege was the consequence of the separation of blacks and whites in nearly every arena of everyday life in the postwar city. Civil rights activists demanded policies that broke open the closed circle of nepotism, friendship, and race that kept blacks out of one key sector of the urban economy. The threat to that closed world sparked a powerful reaction from building trades unionists and their supporters, who belatedly adopted the rhetoric and strategies of postwar racial gradualism to defend their position. Although they lost their battle to thwart the Philadelphia Plan, their arguments—particularly their insistence on their racial innocence, their critique of affirmative action's "discrimination" against whites, and their resentment of government—continue to shape the affirmative action debate.[57]

This account of Philadelphia's battle over affirmative action aims to offer a model for still-to-be-written histories of policy making from the bottom up. It is impossible to explain the timing, the form, and the target of early affirmative action programs without attention to grass-roots politics. Local civil rights activists—Leon Sullivan of the Committee of 400, Cecil B. Moore of the Philadelphia branch of the NAACP, and Louis Smith of CORE—did much to unravel the gradualist racial liberalism of the 1940s and 1950s. They demanded that racial equality in the workplace be measured by results—the number of minority workers on a job site. They would not be satisfied with antidiscrimination statements or token hiring. The protesters who blockaded Philadelphia's construction sites in the 1960s and their counterparts in St. Louis, Oakland, Cleveland, and elsewhere were not, in a strict sense, the architects of affirmative action. They did not draft executive orders and federal regulations. But by taking their grievances to the streets and construction sites, they fundamentally reoriented the civil rights debate. The legacy of their protests continues to shape America's unfinished struggle over race, rights, and politics.

Notes

Thomas J. Sugrue is Bicentennial Class of 1940 Professor of History and Sociology at the University of Pennsylvania.

For comments, criticism, and support, thanks to Susan Armeny, Dana Barron, Jim Borchert, Michelle Brattain, Tony Chen, Matthew Countryman, Jefferson Cowie, Paul Frymer, Gerald Gill, Larry Hunter, Thomas Jackson, Lynn Johnson, Jacqueline Jones, Felicia Kornbluh, Robert Korstad, Peter Levy, Glenn Loury, Regina Morantz-Sanchez, Joanne Meyerowitz, Pap Ndiaye, Gunther Peck, Emily Pollack, Fran Ryan, Robert Self, Peter Siskind, John Skrentny, Amy Dru Stanley, Daniel Tichenor, Joe Trotter, and audiences at the Atlanta Seminar on the Comparative History of Labor, Industry, Technology, and Society; Boston College; Boston University; Brandeis University; the University of California, San Diego; Carnegie Mellon University; the University of Chicago; Duke University; Ecole des Hautes Etudes en Sciences Sociales; the Massachusetts Historical Society; the University of Michigan; New York University; the University of Pennsylvania; Rutgers University; the Thomas Campbell Cleveland Seminar on the City; Union College; and the College of William and Mary.

Readers may contact Sugrue at <tsugrue@sas.upenn.edu>.

1. For a detailed discussion of Philadelphia's 1963 protests, see below. George Straus and Sidney Ingerman, "Public Policy and Discrimination in Apprenticeship," in *Negroes and Jobs: A Book of Readings*, ed. Louis A. Ferman, Joyce L. Kornbluh, and J. A. Miller (Ann Arbor, 1968), 313; Exec. Order No. 11,114, 28 Fed. Reg. 6485 (June 22, 1963).
2. "Memorandum to heads of all agencies from Arthur Fletcher, Subject: Revised Philadelphia Plan for Compliance with Equal Employment Opportunity Requirements of Executive Order 11246 for Federally-Involved Construction, June 27, 1969," reprinted in U.S. Congress, Senate, Committee on the Judiciary, Subcommittee on Separation of Powers, *Hearings on the Philadelphia Plan: Congressional Oversight of Administrative Agencies (the Department of Labor)*, 91 Cong., 1 sess., Oct. 27–28, 1969, pp. 26–30, esp. 26, 27, 28; "Order to heads of all agencies from Arthur Fletcher, Subject: Establishment of Ranges for the Implementation of the Revised Philadelphia Plan, Sept. 23, 1969," ibid., 30–38, esp. 34; John David Skrentny, *The Ironies of Affirmative Action: Politics, Culture, and Justice in America* (Chicago, 1996), 136–38, 193–98; Hugh Davis Graham, *The Civil Rights Era: Origins and Development of National Policy, 1960–1972* (New York, 1990), 322–45.
3. Nathan Glazer, *Ethnic Dilemmas, 1964–1982* (Cambridge, Mass., 1983), 159; Stephan Thernstrom and Abigail Thernstrom, *America in Black and White: One Nation Indivisible* (New York, 1997), 171–80, 423–61, esp. 172, 179; Thomas Byrne Edsall and Mary D. Edsall, *Chain Reaction: The Impact of Race, Rights, and Taxes on American Politics* (New York, 1991), 124. See also Jonathan Reider, "The Rise of the Silent Majority," in *The Rise and Fall of the New Deal Order, 1930–1980*, ed. Steve Fraser and Gary Gerstle (Princeton, 1989), 243–68; Herman Belz, Equality *Transformed: A Quarter-Century of Affirmative Action* (New Brunswick, 1991); Terry Eastland, *Ending Affirmative Action: The Case for Colorblind Justice* (New York, 1996); and Jennifer Hochschild, "Affirmative Action as Culture War," in *The Cultural Territories of Race: Black and White Boundaries*, ed. Michele Lamont (Chicago, 1999), 343–68.
4. Graham, Civil Rights Era, 462, 468; Skrentny, *Ironies of Affirmative Action*, 67–144, esp. 68, 111, 125; Steven F. Lawson, "Freedom Then, Freedom Now: The Historiography of the Civil Rights Movement," *American Historical Review*, 96 (April 1991), 456–71, esp. 457. Other leading histories of affirmative action include

John David Skrentny, *The Minority Rights Revolution* (Cambridge, Mass., 2002); Hugh Davis Graham, *Collision Course: The Strange Convergence of Affirmative Action and Immigration Policy in America* (New York, 2002); Dean J. Kotlowski, "Richard Nixon and the Origins of Affirmative Action," *Historian*, 60 (Spring 1998), 523–41; Paul Burstein, *Discrimination, Jobs, and Politics: The Struggle for Equal Employment Opportunity in the United States since the New Deal* (Chicago, 1985); and Jill Quadagno, *The Color of Welfare: How Racism Undermined the War on Poverty* (New York, 1994).

5. An important starting point is Jeanne F. Theoharis and Komozi Woodard, eds., *Freedom North: Black Freedom Struggles Outside the South, 1940–1980* (New York, 2003).
6. Richard M. Dalfiume, "The 'Forgotten' Years of the Negro Revolution," *Journal of American History*, 55 (June 1968), 90–106; Harvard Sitkoff, "Racial Militancy and Interracial Violence in the Second World War," ibid., 58 (Dec. 1971), 661–81; Exec. Order No. 8,802, June 25, 1941, General Records of the United States Government, RG 11 (National Archives, Washington, D.C.); Allen Winkler, "The Philadelphia Transit Strike of 1944," *Journal of American History*, 59 (June 1972), 75–89; Neil A. Wynn, *The Afro-American and the Second World War* (New York, 1976); Merl E. Reed, "Black Workers, Defense Industries, and Federal Agencies in Pennsylvania, 1941–45," *Labor History*, 27 (June 1986), 356–84; Vincent P. Franklin, *The Education of Black Philadelphia: The Social and Educational History of a Minority Community, 1900–1950* (Philadelphia, 1979), 122–26, 161–62; Franklin D. Roosevelt, "Message to Congress on the State of the Union," 1944, in *The Public Papers and Addresses of Franklin D. Roosevelt*, ed. Samuel Rosenman, vol. XIII (New York, 1950), 41–42.
7. *The Urban Negro in Pennsylvania: A Summary of the Findings and Recommendations of the Pennsylvania State Temporary Commission on the Conditions of the Urban Colored Population* (Philadelphia, 1945), folder 210, box 12, Philadelphia Urban League Papers (Temple University Urban Archives, Philadelphia, Pa.); Gunnar Myrdal, An *American Dilemma: The Negro Problem and Modern Democracy* (2 vols., New York, 1944), I, xliii (italicized in the original); Walter A. Jackson, *Gunnar Myrdal and America's Conscience: Social Engineering and Racial Liberalism, 1938–1987* (Chapel Hill, 1990), esp. 272–311; Stephen Steinberg, *Turning Back: The Retreat from Racial Justice in American Thought and Policy* (Boston, 1995), 21–67.
8. See "Activities of CEJO, 1949–50," news release, May 16, 1949, folder 5, box 34, Fellowship Commission Papers (Temple University Urban Archives); *CEJO News Letter*, [Jan. 1955], folder 6/II/117, box 5, Philadelphia Branch National Association for the Advancement of Colored People Papers, ibid.; "CEJO Program for 1952–1953," ibid.; Jacques E. Wilmore, "A Final Report on Philadelphia Program Activities, 1951–1955," box: Employment 1955, American Friends Service Committee, American Section (American Friends Service Committee Archives, Philadelphia, Pa.); and Patricia A. Cooper, "The Limits of Persuasion: Race Reformers and the Department Store Campaign in Philadelphia, 1945–1948," *Pennsylvania Magazine of History and Biography*, 126 (Jan. 2002), 97–126.
9. Wilmore, "Final Report on Philadelphia Program Activities, 1951–1955"; "News Release—Fair Employment Practices in Department Stores Committee," folder 5, box 34, Fellowship Commission Papers; Wayne Hopkins et al. to Thomas Wriggins Jr., Oct. 20, 1953, folder 6/I/117, box 5, Philadelphia Branch NAACP Papers; Charles A. Shorter to Lewis C. Davis, Oct. 29, 1954, ibid.; "Comprehensive Report of Administrative and Program Improvements of the Armstrong Association," Feb. 1, 1955, folder 30, box 2, Philadelphia Urban League Papers; Hopkins to DeHaven Hinkson, memorandum, folder 196, box 11, ibid.; Reports of the Employment

Department, 1954–57, folder 197, ibid.; Wilmore, "Final Report on Philadelphia Program Activities, 1951–1955."

10. Anthony S. Chen, "From Fair Employment to Equal Opportunity Employment and Beyond: Affirmative Action and Civil Rights Politics in the New Deal Order, 1941–1972" (Ph.D. diss., University of California, Berkeley, 2002); Sidney Fine, *"Expanding the Frontiers of Civil Rights": Michigan, 1948–1968* (Detroit, 2000); Paul Moreno, *From Direct Action to Affirmative Action: Fair Employment Law and Policy in America, 1933–1972* (Baton Rouge, 1997).
11. "City of Philadelphia, Fair Employment Practice Ordinance," folder 6-157, box 8, Philadelphia Branch NAACP Papers; "Provisions of the Commission on Human Relations," *Philadelphia Home Rule Charter* Philadelphia, 1959), secs. 4-700–701; Commission on Human Relations, Staff Responsibilities and Procedure, folder 6/I/95, box 4, Philadelphia Branch NAACP Papers; Franklin, *Education of Black Philadelphia*, 161–62.
12. "Death of FEPC—A Drama in 3 Acts," *Philadelphia Bulletin*, June 19, 1955; "Legislature Passes FEP Bill," *Philadelphia Legal Intelligencer*, Oct. 26, 1955; Eric Ledell Smith and Kenneth C. Wolensky, "A Novel Public Policy: Pennsylvania's Fair Employment Practices Act of 1955," *Pennsylvania History*, 69 (Fall 2002), 489–523; Duane Lockard, *Toward Equal Opportunity: A Study of State and Local Antidiscrimination Laws* (London, 1968), 76–97.
13. City of Philadelphia, Commission on Human Relations, *Annual Report*, 1953, folder 6/I/98, box 4, Philadelphia Branch NAACP Papers; Pennsylvania Human Relations Commission, *Seventh Annual Report*, 1962 (Harrisburg, 1963), 11, 21, 25–26; Alfred W. Blumrosen, *Black Employment and the Law* (New Brunswick, 1971), 13; George Schermer, "Effectiveness of Equal Opportunity Legislation," in *The Negro and Employment Opportunity: Problems and Practices*, ed. Herbert R. Northrup and Richard L. Rowan (Ann Arbor, 1965), 74–75, 79–81; Herbert Hill, "Twenty Years of State Fair Employment Practice Commissions: A Critical Analysis with Recommendations," *Buffalo Law Review*, 14 (Fall 1965), 22–69.
14. City of Philadelphia, Commission on Human Relations, *Philadelphia's Non-White Population 1960, Report No. 3: Socioeconomic Data* (Philadelphia, 1962); Zachary Yale Dyckman, "An Analysis of Negro Employment in the Building Trades" (Ph.D. diss., University of Pennsylvania, 1971), 202.
15. Hannah Lees, "The Not-Buying Power of Philadelphia Negroes," *Reporter*, May 11, 1961, pp. 33–35; Leon H. Sullivan, *Build, Brother, Build* (Philadelphia, 1969), 65–84, esp. 74, 79; Matthew J. Countryman, "Civil Rights and Black Power in Philadelphia, 1940–1971" (Ph.D. diss., Duke University, 1998), 168–91.
16. Judge F. Allen to Mr. [Lewis] Carter, memo, June 23, 1960, folder 22, box 2, Philadelphia Urban League Papers; Carter to Robert L. Taylor, Aug. 10, 1960, ibid.; " 'Buy Where You're Hired' Campaign Getting Results," *Philadelphia Tribune*, June 11, 1960; "Tastykake Co. Surrenders to Phila. Pastors," ibid., Aug. 9, 1960; Sullivan, *Build, Brother, Build*, 83–84; "Nationally Known Breyer's Ice Cream Company Capitulates," [c. March 1962], Philadelphia: January–June 1962 folder, box C137, group III, National Association for the Advancement of Colored People Papers (Manuscript Division, Library of Congress, Washington, D.C.); "Spreading Negro Boycott," *Greater Philadelphia Magazine*, 57 (May 1962), 53–58; "Ministers Hail Success; End A&P Boycott," *Pennsylvania Guardian*, Feb. 8, 1963.
17. Chester Branch, NAACP, "A Statement of Policy," Philadelphia, April–August 1961 folder, box C136, group III, NAACP Papers; Sullivan, *Build, Brother, Build*, 74, 76–77.
18. Cooper, "Limits of Persuasion," 97–100, 112, 121–22; August Meier and Elliott Rudwick, *CORE: A Study in the Civil Rights Movement, 1942–1968* (New York, 1973), 121, 187–88, 199.

19. Thomas H. Burress III to Gloster B. Current, Aug. 17, 1962, Philadelphia Branch, July–Dec. 1962 folder, box C137, group III, NAACP Papers; Countryman, "Civil Rights and Black Power in Philadelphia," 158–67.
20. "Support These Candidates Because They Believe as You Believe," Philadelphia 1959 folder, box C136, group II, NAACP Papers; "Moore Tells Cheering Throng about Family Threats," *Philadelphia Tribune*, June 1, 1963; "Congressman Nix, Mrs. Alexander Blasted by CBM," ibid., June 11, 1963; "Cecil Moore Takes a Look at 'His City,' " *Pennsylvania Guardian*, June 7, 1963; James R. Moses to Roy Wilkins, [received] Sept. 16, 1964, Philadelphia, July–Sept. 1964 folder, box C137, group III, NAACP Papers; Gaeton Fonzi, "Cecil Storms In," *Greater Philadelphia Magazine*, 58 (July 1963), 20–23, 45–57. For the best discussion of Moore's leadership, see Countryman, "Civil Rights and Black Power," 215–37, 278–87. See also Paul Lermack, "Cecil B. Moore and the Philadelphia Branch of the National Association for the Advancement of Colored People: The Politics of Negro Pressure Group Organization," in *Black Politics in Philadelphia*, ed. Miriam Ershkowitz and Joseph Zikmund II (New York, 1973), 145–60; and Arthur C. Willis, *Cecil's City: A History of Blacks in Philadelphia, 1638–1979* (New York, 1990).
21. National Urban League, *Negroes and the Building Trades* Unions (New York, 1957); "NAACP Study Concerning Trade Union Apprenticeship," 1960, Labor—Apprenticeship Training folder, box A180, group III, NAACP Papers; *Proceedings of the Fourth Constitutional Convention of the AFL–CIO*, Miami Beach, December 7–13, 1961, in *Black Workers: A Documentary History from the Colonial Times to the Present*, ed. Philip S. Foner and Ronald L. Lewis (Philadelphia, 1989), 556.
22. Michael Kazin, *Barons of Labor: The San Francisco Building Trades and Union Power in the Progressive Era* (Urbana, 1987); Richard Schneirov, *Pride and Solidarity: A History of the Plumbers and Pipefitters of Columbus, Ohio, 1889–1989* (Ithaca, 1993); Mark Erlich, *With Our Hands: The Story of Carpenters in Massachusetts* (Philadelphia, 1986).
23. Mark Erlich, *Labor at the Ballot Box: The Massachusetts Prevailing Wage Campaign of 1988* (Philadelphia, 1990), 105–10; Addendum to Standard Contract Requirements, City of Philadelphia, folder 6/I/228, box 12, Philadelphia Branch NAACP Papers; Philadelphia Advisory Committee for Vocational Education, Minutes, Jan. 20, 1948, folder 64, box 4, Philadelphia Urban League Papers; "International Brotherhood of Electrical Workers Union, Electrical Contractors Association of Philadelphia," memo, April 30, 1954, folder 16, box 32, Fellowship Commission Papers; Graham, Civil Rights Era, 64, 114; Quadagno, *Color of Welfare*, 74.
24. William E. Leuchtenburg, *Franklin D. Roosevelt and the New Deal, 1932–1940* (New York, 1963), 134–35; Gail Radford, *Housing Modern America: Radical Proposals and New Deal Policy* (Chicago, 1996); Kenneth T. Jackson, *Crabgrass Frontier: The Suburbanization of the United States* (New York, 1985); Mark H. Rose, *Interstate: Express Highway Policy, 1941–1956* (Lawrence, 1979); Thomas W. Hanchett, "U.S. Tax Policy and the Shopping Center Boom of the 1950s and 1960s," *American Historical Review*, 101 (Oct. 1996), 1082–1110.
25. Joseph S. Clark Jr. and Dennis J. Clark, "Rally and Relapse, 1946–1968," in *Philadelphia: A Three-Hundred-Year History*, ed. Russell Weigley et al. (New York, 1983), 670, 683, 685–86, 695–703; John F. Bauman, *Public Housing, Race, and Renewal: Urban Planning in Philadelphia, 1920–1974* (Philadelphia, 1987), 158; Guian McKee, "Liberal Ends through Illiberal Means: Race, Urban Renewal, and Community in the Eastwick Section of Philadelphia, 1949–1990," *Journal of Urban History*, 27 (July 2001), 547–83; "Jim Crow's Sweetheart Contract," *Greater Philadelphia Magazine*, 58 (Feb. 1963), 29; Conrad Weiler, *Philadelphia: Neighborhood, Authority, and the Urban Crisis* (New York, 1974), 112–16, 128–55.

26. List of unions, policies, and membership [first page missing], c. 1940, folder 76, box 4, Philadelphia Urban League Papers; "Selected Highlights of Findings of Inquiry Concerning Negro Workers Employed in the Apprenticeable Occupations," 1950, folder 210, box 12, ibid.; Minutes of the Committee Meeting, Vocational Services Department, May 16, 1957, folder 146, box 9, ibid.; "Report on Instances of Discriminatory Practices Directed at Negro Carpenters," folder 228, box 12, Philadelphia Branch NAACP Papers; *CHR Inside Facts* (Jan. 1956), newsletter, folder 6/I/98, box 4, ibid.; "Jim Crow's Sweetheart Contract," 29; Dyckman, "Analysis of Negro Employment in the Building Trades," 110, 115; "Craft Union Bias Blamed on Wish to Stymie Rivals," *Philadelphia Tribune*, May 14, 1963; "NAACP Study Concerning Trade Union Apprenticeship," 48–49; Department of Industrial Relations, National Urban League, "Summary Report: Apprenticeship and Training Opportunities for Negro Youths in Selected Urban League Cities," Feb. 15, 1961, folder A10–17, box 46, Detroit Urban League Papers (Michigan Historical Collections, Bentley Library, University of Michigan, Ann Arbor).
27. "NAACP Study Concerning Trade Union Apprenticeship," 34–38; Dyckman, "Analysis of Negro Employment in the Building Trades," 208; "Agreement between Local 8 and Contracting Plasterers and Lathers," 1958, box 7, Operative Plasterers and Cement Masons International Union Local 8 Papers (Temple University Urban Archives); International Brotherhood of Electrical Workers Union/Electrical Contractors Association of Philadelphia, Committee on Apprenticeship Training, Minutes, April 30, 1954, folder 16, box 32, Fellowship Commission Papers; Pennsylvania Federation of Labor, *Fraternally Yours, James L. McDevitt* (Harrisburg, 1956), 31; F. Ray Marshall and Vernon M. Briggs Jr., *The Negro and Apprenticeship* (Baltimore, 1967), 36; Straus and Ingerman, "Public Policy and Discrimination in Apprenticeship," 310–11.
28. Walter C. Wynn to Jack [Jacques] Wilmore et al., memo, re: Interview with Leonard P. Mahoney, June 1, 1954, folder 6/I/117, box 5, Philadelphia Branch NAACP Papers; "The Apprentice Story," *Philadelphia Bulletin*, June 10, 1963; membership lists in Tile Layers' Union, Pennsylvania Bricklayers and Allied Trades, Local 6 Papers (Temple University Urban Archives). Walter Reeder to Floyd L. Logan, May 13, 1963, Philadelphia Plan folder, box 3, Floyd Logan Papers, ibid.; Walter Licht, *Getting Work: Philadelphia, 1840–1950* (Cambridge, Mass., 1993), 98–121.
29. Joshua B. Freeman, "Hardhats: Construction Workers, Manliness, and the 1970 Pro-War Demonstrations," *Journal of Social History*, 26 (Summer 1993), 725–44; Schneirov, *Pride and Solidarity*, 3–12; Suzanne Model, "The Ethnic Niche and the Structure of Opportunity: Immigrants and Minorities in New York City," in *The "Under-class" Debate: Views from History*, ed. Michael B. Katz (Princeton, 1993), 161–93; Karl E. Taeuber and Alma F. Taeuber, *Negroes in Cities: Residential Segregation and Neighborhood Change* (Chicago, 1965), 39.
30. Walter Wynn, testimony before the Commission on Human Relations, May 3, 1963, folder 23, box 30, Fellowship Commission Papers. The two unions were the Painters' Union and the Reinforced Concrete Steel Workers Union. See "Minutes, Conference on Apprenticeship Opportunities in the Building Trades of Philadelphia," March 13, 1954, Executive Secretary File (Unions 1954), box 21, Philadelphia Branch NAACP Papers; and "Court Orders Go Out to Unions," *Philadelphia Tribune*, May 11, 1963.
31. Milo Manly to Charles A. Shorter, May 10, 1954, folder 6/I/94, box 4, Philadelphia Branch NAACP Papers; Daniel Neifeld, "Civil Rights: Philadelphia," *Labor Today*, 2 (Aug.–Sept. 1963), 18.
32. Burress to Current, Aug. 17, 1962, Philadelphia Branch, July–Dec. 1962 folder, box C137, group III, NAACP Papers; Negro Trade Union Leadership Council (NTULC)

1963 Membership Campaign Brochure, NTULC folder, box 10, Harold Ash Papers (Temple University Urban Archives); James Jones to Fellow Trade Unionist, May 8, 1963, ibid.; Wynn to John Yoshino, memo, March 1, 1962, ibid.; "Jim Crow's Sweetheart Contract," 28–31, 96–99; AFL–CIO Human Rights Committee to Executive Board, Philadelphia AFL–CIO Council, Feb. 27, 1963, folder 23, box 30, Fellowship Commission Papers; "Negro Enrollment Is Asked in Apprentice Classes," *Philadelphia Bulletin*, March 5, 1963; "4 Building Trades Accused by City of Barring Negroes," ibid., March 13, 1963; Wynn to George Schermer, March 28, 1963, folder 23, box 30, Fellowship Commission Papers; CEJO press release calling for public hearings, n.d., folder 5, box 34, ibid.; John E. Means, "Fair Employment Practices Legislation and Enforcement in the United States," in *Negroes and Jobs*, ed. Ferman, Kornbluh, and Miller, 476–78.

33. "Local CORE Officers Named," *Independent*, Nov. 11, 1961; "CORE Demands Action on Bias Charge," *Philadelphia Bulletin*, March 31, 1963; "Rights Committee Nears End Waiting to Hear from Mayor," *Pennsylvania Guardian*, Nov. 15, 1963. On James Tate's mayoralty, see Weiler, Philadelphia, 166; and Clark and Clark, "Rally and Relapse," 661–66.
34. "CORE Pickets Tate's Home and City Hall," *Philadelphia Bulletin*, April 14, 1963; "CORE Says It Will Prod Tate until City Job Bias Ends," ibid., April 17, 1963; "CORE Stages Hour Sitdown in Mayor's Room at City Hall," ibid., April 19, 1963; "CORE Protests City Job Bias," ibid., April 20, 1963; "Rights Committee Nears End Waiting to Hear from Mayor, Pennsylvania Guardian, Nov. 15, 1963; Burton Chardak, "Sleeping Giant: The Negro Electorate," *Greater Philadelphia Magazine*, 57 (Jan. 1962), 49, 101–7; Oscar Glantz, "Recent Negro Ballots in Philadelphia," in *Black Politics in Philadelphia*, ed. Ershkowitz and Zikmund, 60–72; William J. McKenna, "The Negro Vote in Philadelphia Elections," ibid., 73–83.
35. "CORE Demands Action on Bias Charge," *Philadelphia Bulletin*, March 31, 1963; "CORE Pickets Tate's Home and City Hall," ibid., April 14, 1963; "CORE Stages Hour Sitdown," ibid., April 19, 1963; "CORE Protests City Job Bias," ibid., April 20, 1963; "Labor Board Tells Mayor It Can't Ban Bias," ibid., April 23, 1963; "Mayor's Office Sit-In Forces Building Trades Study," *Philadelphia Tribune*, April 27, 1963; "CORE Urges City Take Over Project Hiring," *Philadelphia Bulletin*, May 6, 1963; D. Herbert Lipson, "Off the Cuff," *Greater Philadelphia Magazine*, 58 (May 1963), 1.
36. "500 Picket City Hall Here in Protest over Birmingham," *Philadelphia Bulletin*, May 12, 1963; Countryman, "Civil Rights and Black Power in Philadelphia," 246.
37. "20 from CORE Stage Sit-In in Tate's Office," *Philadelphia Bulletin*, May 14, 1963; "Sit In at Tate's Office," ibid., May 15, 1963; "Mayor Asks Support for Effort to End Bias," ibid., May 15, 1963; "He Tells CORE Unions Must Admit Negroes," ibid.; "Pact Reached in Work Bias," ibid., May 23, 1963.
38. "City Won't Pay 5 Unions Idled in Shutdown," *Philadelphia Bulletin*, May 17, 1963; "McShain's Crew Is Pulled off Job," ibid., May 16, 1963.
39. "CORE Tells City It Plans to Picket All Projects," *Philadelphia Bulletin*, May 19, 1963; "Youth 22, Beaten at NAACP Picket," *Philadelphia Tribune*, May 28, 1963; "Average Joes Star in Demonstrations," ibid.; "Commissioner Apologizes to Irate Crowd," ibid.; "NAACP Leaders Plead for No Violence," ibid., June 1, 1963; "Rain Fails to Dampen Ardor of Pickets," ibid.; "School Kids Show Up Bringing Dogs," ibid.
40. "NAACP Ranks Swelled by Dedicated Supporters," *Philadelphia Tribune*, June 1, 1963.
41. "CORE Tells City It Plans to Picket All Projects," Philadelphia Bulletin, May 19, 1963; "Negro Labor Quota on Jobs Set by CORE," ibid., May 22, 1963; "Pact Reached in Work Bias," ibid., May 23, 1963; "All Night Talks Reach Pact," ibid.,

May 31, 1963; "Talks End Bias Violence, Four Negroes Are Hired," *Philadelphia Inquirer*, June 1, 1963; "Put Negroes in 15% of Jobs, Bias Panel Told," *Philadelphia Bulletin*, June 20, 1963; Graham, Civil Rights Era, 128–29.

42. *Public Papers of the Presidents of the United States: John F. Kennedy, 1963* (Washington, 1963), 439 (June 4, 1963); "Kennedy Acts to Curb Bias in U.S. Work," *Philadelphia Bulletin*, June 4, 1963; "Kennedy Prohibits Job Discrimination," *New York Times*, June 5, 1963; Lee C. White, "Memorandum for the President," June 4, 1963, Civil Rights: General folder, 1/1/63–6/4/63, box 97, President's Office Files (John F. Kennedy Library, Boston, Mass.).
43. Thompson Powers, "Memorandum for Lee White," June 7, 1963, Civil Rights, 6/1–6/15/63 folder, box 9, Robert F. Kennedy Papers (Kennedy Library). The five "danger spots" were Atlanta, Chicago, Detroit, Los Angeles, and Philadelphia. Willard Wirtz, "Memorandum to the Attorney General," June 5, 1963, Civil Rights: Governmental Agencies folder, box 11, ibid.; Wirtz to Robert F. Kennedy, June 12, 1963, ibid.; Willard Wirtz, "Memorandum for the President," June 13, 1963, Civil Rights Meeting with Union Leaders folder, box 97, President's Office Files; White House Press Release, "Executive Order 11114," June 22, 1963, folder 55, box 8, Tile Layers, Union Local 6 Papers; Joseph D. Dolan to Frank Stinson, Aug. 12, 1963, ibid.; Graham, *Civil Rights Era*, 66–67, 85, 279.
44. "Negroes Advised on Job Protests," *New York Times*, June 9, 1963; "Discrimination Protests Rising in Newark," ibid., June 16, 1963; "Birmingham Heightens Struggle in North," *New America*, June 18, 1963, pp. 6–7; Velma Hill, "Harlem Pickets Force City to Halt Project," ibid., June 10, 1963, p. 6; Gertrude Samuels, "Even More Crucial Than in the South," *New York Times Magazine*, June 30, 1963, pp. 13, 24; John T. Cumbler, *A Social History of Economic Decline: Business, Politics, and Work in Trenton* (New Brunswick, 1989), 173–74; Meier and Rudwick, CORE, 227–28, 231, 236–37, 371; Clarence Taylor, *The Black Churches of Brooklyn* (New York, 1994), 139–63.
45. "Sit-Ins Besiege City Overnight," *Philadelphia Bulletin*, June 25, 1963; "Sit-Ins End after City Acts to Halt Jobs," ibid., June 27, 1963; Pennsylvania Human Relations Commission, *Eighth Annual Report* (Harrisburg, 1964), 7–8. "Schools Push Integration of Union Classes," *Philadelphia Bulletin*, July 30, 1963; "U.S. Orders Unions Here to Integrate Apprentices," ibid., Aug. 6, 1963; "OK Accord with City, Deny Bias," ibid., Aug. 20, 1963; "Plumbers Reject Compulsory Rule against Bias," ibid.; "CHR, 5 of 6 Unions OK Bias Agreement," *Philadelphia Tribune*, Aug. 20, 1963; "Apprentice Guidelines Set to End Bias," *Philadelphia Bulletin*, Oct. 20, 1963.
46. "Steamfitters Back Refusal to Join Truce," *Philadelphia Bulletin*, June 5, 1963; Roger Waldinger and Thomas Bailey, "The Continuing Significance of Race: Racial Conflict and Racial Discrimination in Construction," *Politics and Society*, 19 (Sept. 1991), 291–323.
47. "Trades Unions Oppose Recall of Schermer," *Philadelphia Bulletin*, June 6, 1963; "Lawyer Contends Apprentice Rule Is Discrimination against Whites," ibid., Aug. 7, 1963; "CHR, 5 of 6 Unions OK Bias Agreement," *Philadelphia Tribune*, Aug. 20, 1963; "OK Accord with City, Deny Bias," *Philadelphia Bulletin*, Aug. 20, 1963; "Plumbers Reject Compulsory Rule against Bias," ibid.
48. "Construction Industry Joint Conference," Aug. 9, 1963, folder 55, box 8, Tile Layers' Union Local 6 Papers; "Agreement between Pennsylvania Human Relations Commission and Building and Construction Trades Council," Dec. 12, 1963, folder 56, ibid.
49. "600 Negroes Enroll in New Program Teaching 'Pride' and 'Self-Respect,' " Philadelphia Bulletin, Sept. 10, 1964; "Minorities Wooed to Trades," *Philadelphia Inquirer*, June 17, 1966; "Apprenticeship Program Seeks Minority Youth," *Labor*

Education Newsletter, Nov. 1968, box 5, Operative Plasterers and Cement Masons International Union Local 8 Papers; "Provisions of Voluntary Program for Affirmative Action," *Building and Construction Trades Bulletin*, 21 (Feb. 1968), 2–3; "Building Trades Say 'Enter Negroes,' " *New York Times*, Feb. 18, 1968; "Building Trades Vote to Take More Negroes," *Philadelphia Bulletin*, May 2, 1968; Marshall and Briggs, *Negro and Apprenticeship*, 227; Dyckman, "Analysis of Negro Employment in the Building Trades," 42–43, 209.

50. "E Pluribus Unum," *Building and Construction Trades Bulletin*, 19 (July 1966), 1; "Key Factor of 'Discrimination,' " ibid., 20 (May 1967), 1; "There Are More Negroes," ibid., 21 (Jan. 1968), 1; "Few Negroes in City Enrolled as Apprentices," *Philadelphia Bulletin*, May 21, 1964; "Only 2 Negroes Become Metal Worker Apprentices," *Philadelphia Inquirer*, June 12, 1966; "Minorities Wooed to Trades," ibid., June 17, 1966; "2 Negro Electricians Contest Firing from Mint Job," *Philadelphia Bulletin*, June 7, 1968; Logan to Richardson Dilworth, June 15, 1968, Philadelphia Plan folder, box 3, Logan Papers; "Apprenticeship Training Programs—School District of Philadelphia," June 1968, ibid.; Dyckman, "Analysis of Negro Employment in the Building Trades," 204; Richard P. Nathan, *Jobs and Civil Rights: The Role of the Federal Government in Promoting Equal Opportunity in Employment and Training* (Washington, 1969), 139–43.
51. S. Arthur Spiegel, "Affirmative Action in Cincinnati," *Cincinnati Historical Society Bulletin*, 37 (Summer 1979), 78–88; George Lipsitz, *Life in the Struggle: Ivory Perry and the Culture of Opposition* (Philadelphia, 1988), 85; Herbert Hill, "The Racial Practices of Organized Labor: The Contemporary Record," in *The Negro and the American Labor Movement*, ed. Julius Jacobson (New York, 1968), 303–20; "36 in NAACP Picket Penn," *Philadelphia Bulletin*, Jan. 20, 1964. See also Vertical File: Building Trades Unions/NYC, Fiche 002–761, Schomburg Collection (New York Public Library, New York, N.Y.). "150 Protest Alleged Union Bias in New Rochelle," *New York Times*, Feb. 2, 1967; "NAACP Opens Drive for Jobs in Construction," ibid., June 28, 1967; Edward C. Sylvester Jr. to David Rose, memorandum, Oct. 6, 1967, in *Civil Rights during the Johnson Administration: A Collection from the Holdings of the Lyndon Baines Johnson Library, Austin, Texas*, ed. Steven F. Lawson (microfilm, 69 reels, University Publications of America, 1984–1987), part I, reel 11, frames 159–60.
52. Exec. Order No. 11,246, 30 Fed. Reg. 12319 (Sept. 24, 1965); "Memorandum to Philadelphia Federal Executive Board from Warren Phelan," Oct. 27, 1967, folder 1, box 34, Fellowship Commission Papers; James E. Jones, "The Bugaboo of Racial Quotas," *Wisconsin Law Review*, 1970, pp. 343–48.
53. Dyckman, "Analysis of Negro Employment in the Building Trades," 205; Graham, *Civil Rights Era*, 330, 540nn35–36.
54. "Negro Groups Step Up Militancy in Drive to Join Building Trade Unions," *New York Times*, Aug. 28, 1969. See also, among other articles on protests, "20 Chicago Building Projects Shut Down by Hiring Protest," ibid., Aug. 10, 1969; "Job Protest Spurs Pittsburgh Clash," ibid., Aug. 27, 1969; "Job Rights Panel Warned of Need to Check Unrest," ibid., Aug. 30, 1969; "Nationwide Black Walkout Urged to Back Job Demand," ibid., Sept. 22, 1969; Archie Robinson, *George Meany and His Times* (New York, 1981), 290; *Proceedings of the Fifty-Fifth Convention of the Building and Construction Trades Department AFL-CIO, 1969, Atlantic City, New Jersey, September 22–24, 1969* ([Washington], n.d.), 117–18; "Unions Voice 'Unalterable Opposition' to Phila. Plan," *Philadelphia Bulletin*, Sept. 22, 1969; *Proceedings of the Thirty-First General Convention of the United Brotherhood of Carpenters and Joiners of America, San Francisco, August 24–28, 1970* (n.p., n.d.), 13.

55. Clinton C. Bourdon and Raymond E. Levitt, *Union and Open Shop Construction: Compensation, Work Practices, and Labor Markets* (Lexington, Mass., 1980), 5–6; Peter B. Levy, *The New Left and Labor in the 1960s* (Urbana, 1994), 190–95; Freeman, "Hardhats"; Jefferson Cowie, "Nixon's Class Struggle: Romancing the New Right Worker, 1969–1973," *Labor History*, 43 (Aug. 2002), 257–83. On Philadelphia, see Peter Binzen, *Whitetown, U.S.A.* (New York, 1970).
56. "Shultz Defends Minority Hiring," *New York Times*, Aug. 7, 1969; "Construction Job Rights Plan Backed at Philadelphia Hearing," ibid., Aug. 27, 1969; Judith Stein, *Running Steel, Running America: Race, Economic Policy, and the Decline of Liberalism* (Chapel Hill, 1998), 148–52; William Safire, *Before the Fall: An Inside View of the Pre-Watergate White House* (Garden City, 1975); Kotlowski, "Richard Nixon and the Origins of Affirmative Action"; Joan Hoff, *Nixon Reconsidered* (New York, 1994), 90–92; *Contractors Assn. of Eastern Pennsylvania v. Shultz*, 311 F. Supp. 1002 (E.D. Pa. 1970); 442 F. 2d 159 (3d Cir. 1971); *cert* denied, 404 U.S. 854 (1971); William B. Gould, *Black Workers in White Unions: Job Discrimination in the United States* (Ithaca, 1977), 297–362; Steven M. Gillon, "*That's Not What We Meant to Do": Reform and Its Unintended Consequences in Twentieth Century America* (New York, 2000), 147.
57. Hochschild, "Affirmative Action as Culture War."

Chapter 10

The Suburban Origins of "Color-Blind" Conservatism: Middle-Class Consciousness in the Charlotte Busing Crisis

Matthew D. Lassiter

From *The Journal of Urban History*

During the winter of 1970, President Richard Nixon received a letter of protest and despair from Dr. Robert M. Diggs, a public school parent who lived in an upper-middle-class suburb of Charlotte, North Carolina. Two years earlier, the Republican president had overwhelmingly carried the suburban Charlotte vote, and Diggs began by introducing himself as a "concerned member of the silent majority which has possibly remained silent too long." The source of his confusion and anger, sentiments also conveyed in thousands of similar letters sent by his neighbors, was the court-ordered desegregation plan that called for busing throughout Charlotte-Mecklenburg's countywide school system, including the two-way exchange of students from the black neighborhoods of the central city and the white subdivisions on the metropolitan fringe. How could it be possible in America, the physician wondered, for a federal judge to punish affluent communities simply because their residents worked hard, bought homes in respectable neighborhoods, and sought to rear their children in a safe environment? Without "neighborhood schools," Diggs warned, the educational and moral standards of the middle class would rapidly deteriorate, and it seemed only reasonable that citizens showing "initiative and ambition should not be penalized for possessing these qualities." In closing, the white father from an all-white suburb pledged that his family priorities and busing anxieties had "nothing to do with race or integration." This middle-class conscious, scrupulously "color-blind" rhetoric mirrored the official stance of the Concerned Parents Association (CPA), the powerful antibusing organization supported by tens of thousands of white families who lived in the booming Sunbelt metropolis. Based in the recently developed subdivisions of southeast Charlotte, the CPA flatly rejected any shared responsibility for the official policies of residential segregation that had concentrated the majority of black students in racially isolated schools in the opposite quadrant of the city. In response to the NAACP's pursuit of comprehensive integration, the CPA launched a neighborhood-based movement of antibusing resistance that polarized a city regarded as one of the most progressive bastions of the New South and played a leading role in the explosive arrival of the "Silent Majority" in national politics.[1]

The crucible of racial busing in Charlotte produced a populist revolt of the center, as white-collar suburbanites became the architects of a potent color-blind discourse that gained national traction as an unapologetic defense of middle-class residential privileges and suburban spatial boundaries. In response to the civil rights movement's unprecedented assault on the policies of residential segregation that underpinned the politics of racial moderation in the Sunbelt South, the suburban parents who joined Charlotte's antibusing movement charted their own middle path between the caste framework of white supremacy and the egalitarian agenda of redistributive liberalism. The CPA recast a legal debate over the historical burdens of racial discrimination into an ahistorical defense of meritocratic individualism and neighborhood boundaries that normalized pervasive patterns of spatial inequality by refusing even to acknowledge the structural legacies of racial and residential segregation. This novel appropriation of color-blind ideology shaped a collective politics of white, middle-class identity that defined "freedom of choice" and "neighborhood schools" as the core privileges of homeowner rights and consumer liberties and that rejected as "reverse discrimination" any policy designed to provide collective integration remedies for past and present policies that reinforced systematic inequality of opportunity. "I couldn't believe such a thing could happen in America," the prosperous physician and Charlotte antibusing leader Don Roberson explained. "So many of us made the biggest investment of our lives—our homes—primarily on the basis of their location with regard to schools. It seemed like an absurdity that anyone could tell us where to send our children." In a way, African American plaintiff James Polk agreed with this class analysis of Charlotte's racial showdown: "We were smacking against the whole American dream. To whites, that meant pull yourself up by your bootstraps, buy a nice home and two cars, live in a nice neighborhood and go to a nice church, send your kids to the appropriate school . . . . We understood that a lot of white people would raise holy hell."[2]

As the initial testing ground for metropolitan school integration, Charlotte's experience represents a national as much as a southern story. During the 1970s, the bitter battles over court-ordered busing transcended the traditional struggle over Jim Crow to grapple with a New American Dilemma: the spatial fusion of class and racial inequality embodied in the urban/suburban divide. The antibusing revolt in Charlotte both fashioned and reflected the innovative brand of neighborhood politics spreading throughout suburban America, a middle-class mobilization based in subdivision associations, shopping malls, church congregations, PTA branches, and voting booths. Understanding the grassroots mobilization of the Silent Majority requires a consciously suburban approach to historical themes that traditionally have been folded into the framework of urban studies or submerged beneath the narrative of southern distinctiveness. Many scholars of the American South have embraced a "Southern Strategy" thesis of race-based political realignment that overemphasizes the top-down machinations of leaders such as George Wallace and Richard Nixon and fails sufficiently to incorporate the class-based and grassroots-driven dynamics produced by the postwar suburbanization of southern politics and society.[3] Historians of the Sunbelt have paid closer attention to the "suburban warriors" of the New Right, from the Goldwater partisans and tax revolts of southern California to the Religious Right activists in the sprawling megachurches, while tending to restrict analysis to a linear focus on conservative realignment rather than a broader examination of the political center.[4] In recent years, urban scholars have explored the grassroots repercussions of growth liberalism and the racial contradictions of the New Deal Order, tracing the roots of a white neighborhood-based backlash to the 1940s and mapping the currents of "reactionary populism" and the revolt of the Reagan Democrats during the 1970s and 1980s. Yet even the best of the new urban history has been written from the inside out, largely restricted to the points of direct racial friction within the city limits of the North and Midwest and lacking a metropolitan approach to the spatial landscape.[5] The antibusing movements in the suburban South, led by upper-middle-class families who lived in residentially secure neighborhoods, established powerful spatial and socioeconomic constraints on the reach of race-conscious liberalism that transcended both regional boundaries and partisan dynamics.[6]

The Charlotte story provides a revealing portrait of the dynamic interplay between the local and the national in the political culture of postwar America. The protracted busing crisis in Charlotte diverged from the broader national trends of metropolitan fragmentation because a rare combination of spatial and legal factors forced the entire community to grapple with not only racial integration but also class inequality. Because Charlotte's consolidated school system included the surrounding suburbs of Mecklenburg County, the metropolitan remedy of two-way busing meant that "white flight" from the city limits could not destroy the integration formula and that affluent white families that lived in exclusive suburban neighborhoods did not escape the burdens of social change as did most of their counterparts in the rest of the nation. Charlotte has received its share of attention as an example of how the concerted efforts of dedicated African American plaintiffs and sympathetic federal judges—in short, the supremacy of the law—attained successful school integration while keeping most white families committed to public education. But even though the antibusing revolt of the CPA failed to prevent comprehensive integration in the New South metropolis, the grassroots mobilization of the middle-class Silent Majority fundamentally shaped the national trajectory of court-ordered busing as a remedy for de jure residential segregation. By the mid-1970s, despite the Supreme Court's routine declarations that the federal judiciary would not permit popular opposition to thwart the spirit of the *Brown* decree, the populist uprising of neighborhood antibusing movements had pushed all three branches of the federal government to adopt explicit policies of suburban protection that rejected metropolitan remedies for metropolitan inequities and exempted most affluent white Americans from any collective responsibility for the past. The color-blind discourse pioneered in the Sunbelt South forged a suburban blueprint that ultimately resonated from the "conservative" subdivisions of Orange County to the "liberal" townships of New England: a bipartisan political language of private property values, taxpayer and consumer rights, children's educational privileges, family residential security, and middle-class historical innocence.[7]

The Politics of Middle-Class Respectability

More than six months before the citizens of Charlotte-Mecklenburg confronted the landmark busing order, Richard Nixon launched the southeastern swing of his 1968 campaign in North Carolina's fastest growing metropolis. The Republican presidential nominee delivered his standard stump speech to an enthusiastic crowd of seven thousand people, described by the Charlotte media as well-dressed, middle-class, and overwhelmingly white. An astute commentator observed that the candidate's populist message did not represent a strategy designed specifically for white southerners but, instead, an appeal to everyone across the nation who viewed a nice "house in the suburbs" as the prerequisite of happiness and respectability. "A new voice is being heard in America," Nixon proclaimed. "It's the forgotten Americans, . . . people who pay their taxes and go to work and support their churches, white people and black people, people [who] are not rioters." The Republican did not address civil rights until directly questioned during a local television interview, and then, he attempted to stake out a position midway between George Wallace and Hubert Humphrey by expressing support for the *Brown* decision, endorsing "freedom-of-choice" desegregation plans, and criticizing "busing for racial balance." Nixon added a personal opinion that transporting ghetto children to suburban schools would backfire because of the wide gap in academic aptitude between poor and affluent students. Through his Charlotte comments, the future president was articulating nothing less than the emerging suburban blueprint on school integration—rhetorical support for the principle of school desegregation combined with opposition to the methods necessary to overcome residential segregation. This nominally color-blind and explicitly class-conscious ideology revolved around the twin pillars of consumer freedom and residential privilege and insisted that progress in the future need not dwell on the burdens of the past. In the fall election, Nixon received about three out of every four votes cast in the sprawling outer-ring suburbs of Charlotte, a formidable margin of victory that revealed the grassroots Republican strength in the metropolitan regions of the Sunbelt South.[8]

The political and business leadership of postwar Charlotte pursued the New South synthesis of racial moderation and economic prosperity by constructing a metropolitan landscape of suburban sprawl and urban containment that reflected the strategic commitment to social peace through residential segregation. During the 1960s, while the busing crisis remained beyond the horizon, the former textile capital emerged as a magnet for white-collar professionals and cemented its reputation as one of the top banking centers in the nation, a gleaming advertisement for the Sunbelt South. A few miles southeast of the downtown district, the annexed suburb of Myers Park represented the unquestioned corridor of wealth and power in the city, its graceful and exclusive neighborhoods home to almost all leading corporate executives and almost every elected and appointed official in municipal government. Stretching farther to the south and east of Myers Park, generous federal and local government investments subsidized the rapid expansion of outer-ring suburbs where the white middle-class population doubled or tripled during the farm-to-subdivision transition of the 1960s. During the same decade, the municipal government displaced about ten thousand in-town African American residents through urban renewal and highway construction projects, and official planning policies combined with pervasive real-estate discrimination to relocate almost all of these families in the northwest quadrant of the city. Reports by the Charlotte-Mecklenburg Planning Commission revealed the intentional placement of highways and industrial zones to erect physical barriers between the affluent suburbs of southeast Charlotte and the increasingly black northwest sector. The systematic location of low-income housing in northwest Charlotte created the conditions for a horizontal ghetto and accelerated residential flight by working-class white families who lived nearby. By 1970, these developmental policies had transformed Charlotte into one of the most residentially segregated metropolitan regions in the nation, with about 96 percent of the African American population contained in the northwest quadrant, a racial geography clearly demarcated from the sprawling all-white subdivisions on the opposite side of downtown (see figure 10.1).[9]

The policies of residential segregation and the politics of racial moderation converged in a booster ethos known as the Charlotte Way, an exceptionalist ideology that represented the downtown leadership's formal response to the civil rights movement. The liberal editorial page of the *Charlotte Observer* defined the Charlotte Way as "the highest and best example in matters of racial transition . . . resolved because of the good sense and basic good will of community leaders, white and black." The Charlotte Chamber of Commerce deflected criticism of deepening metropolitan inequalities by boasting of its visionary leadership compared with other southern cities, most notably, in pushing through the desegregation of public accommodations in

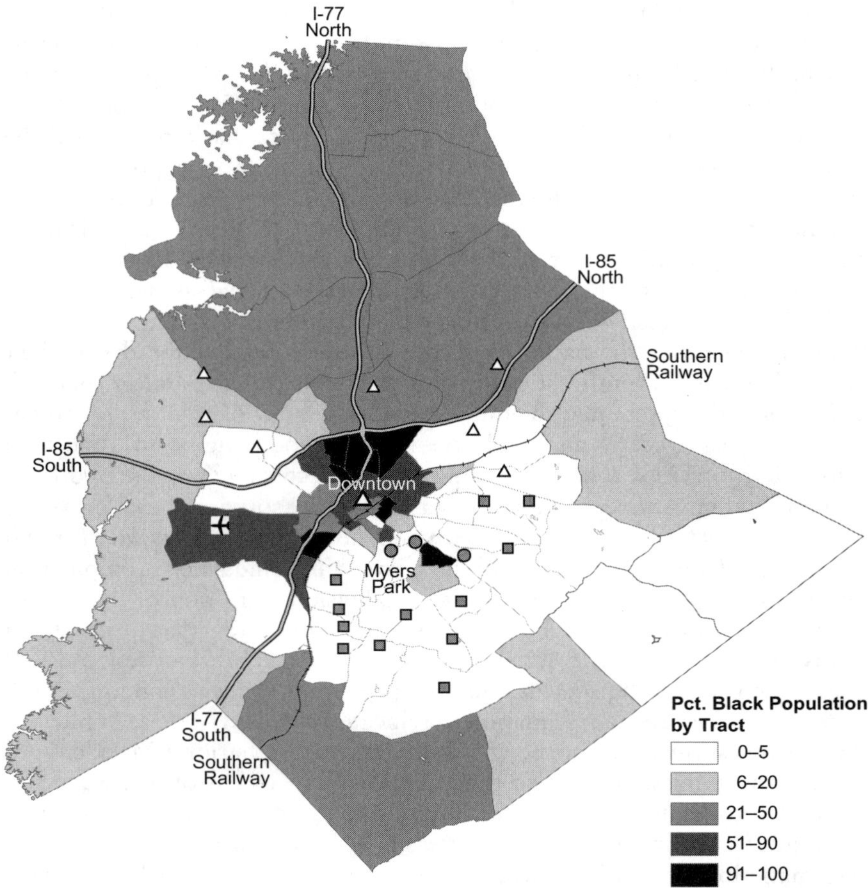

Figure 10.1 Charlotte Map 1970: Distribution of the Black Population of the City of Charlotte and Mecklenburg Country, 1970, by Census Tract. The northwest quadrant contained about 96 percent of Charlotte's black population, while ten census tracts in the southeast suburbs included no black residents at all. Municipal planners utilized transportation networks as racial barriers, especially I-85 on the northside and the Southern Railroad on the westside. The circles indicate the most affluent annexed suburbs of the Myers Park region, including older neighborhoods developed before the postwar growth boom. The squares denote the outer-ring suburbs of southeast Mecklenburg Country, constructed during the 1950s and 1960s, that formed the white-collar base of the antibusing movement of the Concerned Parents Association. The small triangles represent white subdivisions and school zones in north and west Charlotte-Mecklenburg that initially supported the CPA but later defected from the antibusing coalition and began to experience racial turnover during the battles over busing equalization.

Source: U.S. Census Bureau, 1970 Census of Population and Housing.

advance of the 1964 Civil Rights Act. The Charlotte Way operated as a discourse of power that drew black leaders into the procedural politics of racial negotiation and focused attention on civil rights issues that involved individual access to consumer spaces rather than collective remedies for structural inequality. Grassroots civil rights activists charged that "with all southern pleasantries removed," Charlotte's progressive mythology flourished by allowing affluent whites to "maintain a liberal façade . . . because of their physical and social distance from the problems of race and poverty." By the end of the 1960s, most white leaders and many white citizens in Charlotte believed with apparent sincerity that the metropolitan landscape corresponded to the northern model of "de facto" segregation and that their city had therefore complied with the constitutional requirements of the *Brown* mandate. "We all thought we were law abiding people," school board chairman William Poe later explained. After all, the educational system operated under a court-approved freedom-of-choice desegregation plan, and the Fourth Circuit Court of Appeals had recently declared that housing patterns in Charlotte constituted de facto segregation beyond any legal responsibility of the school district. The official mantra of the Community Relations Committee, the powerful biracial forum of the city's elite, reinforced the sanguine outlook of the New South metropolis: "Almost without exception, negotiation and conciliation is easier and more successful when done privately."[10]

The exception began during the spring of 1969, after Julius Chambers of the NAACP's Legal Defense Fund petitioned District Judge James McMillan to invalidate Charlotte's freedom-of-choice formula, pursuant to the Supreme Court's recent ruling that racial segregation in education must be eliminated "root and branch." In a pathbreaking approach, the plaintiffs emphasized the artificiality of the prevailing distinction between de jure and de facto segregation and argued that the Constitution required the school system to take affirmative action to overcome residential patterns shaped by government policies. Fifteen years after *Brown*, about fourteen thousand black students remained in complete racial isolation in the northwest quadrant, while the most segregated white schools dotted the newest outer-ring subdivisions in the southeastern part of Mecklenburg County. Judge McMillan's attitude evolved from initial skepticism to genuine shock as the NAACP systematically exposed the underside of the Charlotte Way, the municipal policies that had transformed the metropolitan landscape in broad daylight but remained hidden from the collective consciousness of the white suburbs. ("I lived here twenty-four years without knowing what was going on," the judge later remarked. "I really didn't know.") On April 23, 1969, McMillan issued his explosive ruling in *Swann v. Charlotte-Mecklenburg*: "The system of assigning pupils by 'neighborhoods,' with 'freedom of choice' for both pupils and faculty, superimposed on an urban population pattern where Negro residents have become concentrated almost entirely in one quadrant of a city of 270,000, is racially discriminatory." The order required the comprehensive integration of faculty and students in every school in the metropolitan system, in rough approximation of the overall 70–30 white-black ratio, an expansive remedy without precedent in any large urban district in the nation. McMillan concluded with the observation that "there is no reason except emotion" to oppose two-way busing, and he instructed the citizens of Charlotte-Mecklenburg that "the quality of public education should not depend on the economic or racial accident of the neighborhood in which a child's parents have chosen to live—or find they must live—nor on the color of his skin."[11]

Thousands of parents immediately began mobilizing throughout the white suburbs, and antibusing sentiment soon coalesced in the CPA, an ad hoc organization without formal membership that would fill a vacuum of leadership and dominate the politics of education in Charlotte-Mecklenburg for the next year and a half. The grassroots uprising began with a series of neighborhood gatherings under the direction of Thomas Harris, an insurance executive and father of three public school students. His energetic efforts proved crucial in establishing a moderate discursive framework for the antibusing movement, as the CPA rallied around a color-blind defense of middle-class respectability and insisted that opposition to busing had nothing to do with racial prejudice or segregationist preferences. The CPA arose in the outer-ring subdivisions of Mecklenburg County, where most white-collar families had settled within the previous decade, where the skyscrapers of downtown Charlotte loomed on the distant horizon, and where the black neighborhoods of the northwest quadrant became essentially invisible. Although the CPA eventually recruited supporters in the elite neighborhoods of the Myers Park area and launched chapters in the white working-class sections of north and west Charlotte, the organizational base and grassroots strength of the antibusing movement remained firmly grounded in the upwardly mobile suburbs outside the city limits. These exclusively white subdivisions consisted of young professional couples and many first-time homeowners who possessed economic means and civic energy but were much more likely to have coached their children's athletic teams or served as PTA leaders than to have participated in anything even approximating a social movement. They were not the "upper crust" of Charlotte, Tom Harris explained, but rather "essentially the middle class, and we have every intention of maintaining the proper dignity and respect." They were not right-wing ideologues either; indeed, few had been politically active at all before the government "started messing with our children." But now the parents in the CPA pledged to act within the highest traditions of American democracy, and they hoped that in the future, "our children will respect our position and, perhaps, look back upon it with pride."[12]

Ten days after the ruling, more than two thousand people attended the first major protest conducted by the CPA. A well-heeled crowd of white adults, joined by a scattering of black parents, gathered in the south Charlotte suburbs at a junior high school that enrolled a 12 percent African American population under the current desegregation program. Tom Harris opened the rally by declaring that the CPA refused to discuss either segregation or integration, as policy and on principle, but instead would defend the right of all families to freedom of choice and oppose the forced busing of any children away from neighborhood schools. The leaders of the organization also demanded that the school board appeal the court order, a position that reflected the widespread fear among white families that elected officials, with the tacit approval of the downtown business establishment, would try to avoid legal confrontation by following the consensus path of the Charlotte Way. The petitions circulated at the rally adopted a rights-based language of consumer liberty and socioeconomic privilege to insist on the autonomy of hardworking parents who had purchased their homes based on "proximity to schools and churches of their choice." In a speech drenched with class concerns, one father summed up the sentiments of most people in the overflow crowd. "I am not opposed to integration in any way," he claimed in a line that drew extensive applause. "But I was 'affluent' enough to buy a home near the school where I wanted my children to go. And I pay taxes to pay for it. They can bring in anybody they like to that school, but I don't want my children taken away from there." By May 19, when a full-page reproduction of the CPA petition appeared in the *Charlotte Observer*, more than seventeen thousand citizens had already affixed their names during neighborhood rallies and solicitation drives. The city's leading newspaper, which expressed unqualified editorial support for the integration mandate throughout the long crisis, sharply criticized the antibusing movement and warned that the political backlash threatened to destroy the entire ethos of the Charlotte Way—the "whole community's enviable record of good and humane race relations."[13]

The revolt of the center by the suburban parents in the CPA propelled public debate toward a compromise position that reluctantly accepted additional one-way desegregation but fiercely rejected comprehensive two-way integration. From the perspective of the placid and prosperous suburbs, it seemed only reasonable that the black families asking for more desegregation should assume the burdens of any transition, especially since, beginning with *Brown*, the federal courts had consistently reinforced a linear understanding of integration that almost always meant the assimilation of individual black students into identifiably white schools. Parents affiliated with the CPA flooded the local media and their elected officials with letters that carefully sought to distinguish between segregated schools and neighborhood schools, by imbedding racial anxieties within a middle-class discourse that professed tolerance for one-way meritocratic desegregation but reflected deep prejudice toward the spatial and racial construct of the "ghetto." Mrs. Charles Warren insisted that she would not complain if black parents wanted to work hard and buy a house in her subdivision to send their children to the nearby school, but "if anyone thinks they're going to bus my children across town . . . without a fight, they're dreaming." Augustus Green explained that "we have accepted integration and all of its inherent problems . . . because it was the law of the land and because we are basically good citizens," but he warned that busing would force affluent families to abandon the public school system. While this father could understand the environmental benefits of bringing underprivileged students into middle-class schools, "it is likewise very difficult to understand how the reverse can therefore be true. To expect me to put my children on buses and send them across town to a school located in a predominantly black area for the sole purpose of fulfilling a mathematical equation is both ridiculous and unreasonable."[14]

Busing opponents also spoke out as aggrieved taxpayers and as harassed members of a newly awakened swath of Middle America, claiming affiliation with the group that President Nixon had called the "forgotten Americans" during his 1968 campaign appearance in Charlotte. Identifying themselves as the essentially moderate representatives of the white middle-class mainstream, these suburban parents both embraced and reformulated the populist discourse of a center-right coalition that White House advisers would soon brilliantly designate the Silent Majority. The accidental activists and PTA populists from suburban Charlotte co-opted the rhetoric and imitated the tactics of the civil rights movement in their promises to take the political offensive to secure the defense of their homes and families and in their insistence that industrious local citizens rather than unelected federal judges should control tax-supported schools. In letters and telegrams to Washington, middle-class parents in the CPA requested relief from their congressmen and demanded action by the president. John Campbell articulated the feelings of many when he warned that the parents in the CPA represented "a majority that has been pushed around for the last five years by a militant minority and an aggressive bureaucracy, a majority whose chafing has been restrained only by its good manners, but also a majority which is reaching the end of its tether, and is going to bring forth its own revolution when pushed too far." William Westbrook requested that the Nixon administration fulfill its campaign pledge to prevent forced busing, after clarifying his credentials: "I am no crackpot, a good citizen in business for myself, paying combined taxes last year in excess of $4,000." Another father, claiming affiliation with a nonviolent "moderate majority" in the United States, wrote that "the white majority has civil rights too . . . and has tried to be very understanding, but we don't like having our feet stepped on repeatedly and we can't be expected to keep turning the other cheek forever." As William R. Overhultz, a business manager and prominent CPA leader, communicated in a clear warning to his elected representatives, "We will not continue to be pushed any farther."[15]

The one theme that never appeared in the CPA's defense of neighborhood schools was any acknowledgment of the finding at the heart of Judge McMillan's decision: that government policies had shaped the stark patterns of residential segregation that produced school segregation in Charlotte-Mecklenburg. The white parents who joined the antibusing movement thought of the location of their homes and the proximity of quality public schools as nothing more and nothing less than the individual rewards for their own willingness to work hard and make sacrifices for their children's future. This pervasive philosophy of middle-class accomplishment naturalized the glaring metropolitan inequalities in educational opportunity and finessed the internal contradictions in the meritocratic ethos through an unapologetic defense of the rights of children to enjoy the fruits of their parents' success. The spatial landscape and futuristic ethos of the white suburbs shaped a fundamental approval of the status quo, grounded in a historical narrative that emphasized the family privileges of class and consumerism rather than collective remedies for past discrimination. This suburban ideology of racial innocence underlay a predisposition to reject—or more often to fail even to consider—the abstract proposition that the government's culpability in concentrating black residents in a certain part of the city should have any personal impact on middle-class lifestyles. With few exceptions, public discourse in Charlotte simply did not address the question of whether black families systematically relocated to the northwest quadrant enjoyed the freedom of choice to live in the upscale subdivisions and attend the excellent new schools that the board diligently constructed on the suburban fringe. It should not be surprising that like the judge, most white parents in southeast Charlotte also "didn't know," in the sense that they did not reflect upon the structural roots of racial discrimination in their city or the spatial policies that subsidized the expansion of their racially homogeneous neighborhoods. The "anti-bus hysteria" of the CPA seemed "more mistaken than racist," observed liberal activist Pat Watters, in the context of fifteen years of municipal development and federal policy based on the "hypocrisy of blinding itself to the 'de jure' nature of most 'de facto' segregation." The federal courts had permitted "leaders in a place like Charlotte to convince themselves or kid themselves into thinking that, even as they continued the process of building a ghetto and a system of segregated schools, they were in compliance with the law against segregation."[16]

During the summer of 1969, the traditional business and political leadership endorsed a compromise formula of additional one-way busing that demonstrated the lingering power of the Charlotte Way but also exposed the myopic belief that an elite-imposed settlement could produce a permanent resolution of the integration crisis. Despite the political momentum of the antibusing movement, a substantial reservoir of support for full compliance had emerged, led by civil rights organizations, the League of Women Voters, the Mecklenburg Christian Ministers Association, and four of the nine members of the school board. While a narrow majority on the board intended to appeal and predicted that busing would drive white families out of the public school system, prominent civic leaders quietly urged education officials to seek a negotiated resolution. The school board responded with a one-way busing plan, explicitly modeled on the technique employed by northern cities such as Buffalo and Syracuse, which proposed the closing of seven historically black schools and the transportation of the affected students to the outlying suburbs and left eight additional inner-city schools open and completely segregated. The African American community immediately launched angry protests, including one march by more than one thousand black residents of Charlotte, along with a scattering of white supporters, in August. The fiercest resistance came from working-class neighborhood organizations instead of the black middle-class establishment. More than twenty thousand black parents signed petitions against one-way busing and rallied behind the sentiments expressed by a mother named Beverly Ford: "If it [integration] is going to come, it's going to come even-steven right down the line." Judge McMillan reluctantly approved the one-way formula as a temporary measure, but he stated unequivocally that comprehensive two-way integration would begin the following year, and he borrowed President Nixon's campaign slogan to lecture suburban parents on their responsibility to accept the principles of "law and order." For the first time in Charlotte, and indeed almost anywhere in the country, an entire metropolitan region would have to grapple with the question of how to achieve a fully and fairly integrated school system. At the crossroads of the Charlotte Way, the Silent Majority spoke loudest.[17]

Color-Blind Populism

The remobilization of the CPA during 1970 produced a powerful revolt of the center that prevented a stable resolution of Charlotte's busing crisis for the next four years and pioneered the grassroots emergence of the suburban Silent Majority onto the national political landscape. After a period of quiescence following the initial protests during the spring of 1969, when the CPA's petition drives and public rallies had shaped the climate of the one-way integration compromise, the renewed prospect of two-way busing turned a defensive movement to preserve neighborhood schools into a political offensive led by newly conscious suburban populists. "The people of Charlotte have had it with Judge McMillan and liberal federal courts," warned Don Roberson, the physician who served as vice-chairman of the CPA. "The unorganized silent majority is about ready to take to the streets with tactics that have seemed to work so effectively for the vocal minority groups." Tapping into the powerful vocabulary of populism, the CPA presented itself as "an association of, by and for the people. You can be proud to be a part." In the courts and in the streets, the CPA employed a color-blind framework that attacked "involuntary busing" as a violation of the original spirit of the *Brown* decision and the race-neutral requirement of the Constitution. Parents from previously tranquil suburbs collectively defended the residential and consumer privileges of middle-class families and all-white neighborhoods and demanded the support of elected officials at the local, state, and national levels. "A STRUGGLE FOR FREEDOM IS COMING," the CPA proclaimed. "*WHERE WILL YOU STAND?*" After only four months of grassroots agitation, the political uprising by the CPA gained control of the local school board and convinced the Nixon administration to adopt the color-blind platform of the antibusing movement as the formal policy of the executive branch. "Ultimately the will of the people governs," according to the constant refrain of the suburban populists from Charlotte. "Rulings and decrees that are overwhelmingly opposed by the general public cannot endure."[18]

The CPA launched the second round of the color-blind crusade with a series of public meetings in the outer-ring suburbs of southeast Charlotte, where several thousand white parents gathered on the weekend before the unveiling of the two-way integration blueprint. During the winter of 1969 to 1970, the school board refused to submit a proposal that would desegregate the all-black schools in northwest

Charlotte, and Judge McMillan finally appointed an outside consultant to devise a comprehensive formula. Dubbed the Finger Plan, this approach achieved a rough 70–30 white-black ratio across the district by pairing inner-city and outer-ring schools through satellite attendance zones and the cross-busing of five thousand elementary students of each race. When the judge convened hearings on the assignment formula, white opponents sang verses from the civil rights anthem "We Shall Overcome" in the hallways outside the packed courtroom. The school board tried to introduce evidence that popular opposition would make two-way busing unworkable, but the judge dismissed the line of inquiry with a brusque comment that he already had seen "ample evidence of the unpopularity of the Constitution in Mecklenburg County." On February 5, McMillan ordered the school district to implement comprehensive desegregation by April 1, based on the "integrate now, litigate later" mandate recently announced by the Supreme Court. The looming deadline prompted the *Charlotte Observer* to issue an extraordinary ultimatum to the city's civic and political elite, whose "greatest sin" involved the conspicuous public silence that had facilitated the defiance of the CPA and now risked the wholesale destruction of Charlotte's progressive reputation. School board chairman William Poe delivered the downtown establishment's response in a public statement, endorsed by Mayor John Belk and county commission chairman Charles Lowe, that called upon all citizens to "respond without open defiance and disrespect for the law" but also defended the right to appeal a judicial order of dubious constitutionality. Charting a course between calls for comprehensive integration and threats of civil disobedience, balancing the principle of peaceful compliance against the grassroots rebellion in the middle-class suburbs, this temperate antibusing stance represented the default position of moderation in a deeply polarized community.[19]

The CPA organized seven major rallies during the week following the establishment of the two-way busing deadline. For the first time, the association expanded beyond its base in the middle-class southeast suburbs and established a formal presence in every white residential section of the metropolis, from the blue-collar subdivisions of north and west Charlotte to the elite neighborhoods of Myers Park. "Our strength can be measured only in numbers and commitment," the CPA warned. "United we stand, divided we fall." Don Roberson and Tom Harris, the public leaders of the antibusing movement, proclaimed the CPA's official policy to be a mass boycott of the public schools starting April 1. "We're not against integration," Roberson insisted once again. "But to move children around from one part of the county to another to satisfy some judicial edict just doesn't make sense to me." The fliers distributed at the antibusing rallies explained that the federal courts had reversed established policy and violated constitutional principles by decreeing that race should be the determining factor in school assignment. Taking freedom of choice "away from the child solely because of his race is grievously wrong. It is morally indefensible. It puts force in the place of freedom. It creates dictatorial power and undermines the American Constitution. It destroys individual liberty in an area that is close to the hearts of us all!" Other groups of parents extended the antibusing crusade by picketing the home of Judge McMillan, demonstrating outside suburban department stores owned by the family of Mayor Belk, and convening a massive protest in downtown Charlotte on the Sunday after the judicial decision. More than 1,500 parents attended the event, where volunteers passed out telegrams demanding intervention by President Nixon, speakers called for an economic boycott of the *Charlotte Observer* and the city's largest corporations, and participants held signs with slogans such as "Don't Give Me the Finger" and "Impeach J. B. McMillan."[20]

While traditional leaders in Charlotte wanted resistance to come in the court of law, the organized uprising of the Silent Majority extended the battle into the court of public opinion and the arena of electoral politics. During the late winter and early spring of 1970, the CPA established itself as a powerful grassroots force in Charlotte, an accidental social movement of middle-class populism that embraced mass-action techniques with remarkable speed and efficiency. The foot soldiers of this energized Silent Majority included not only ideological conservatives but also many political moderates and suburban swing voters, and white-collar married couples dominated the local leadership—physicians, dentists, insurance agents, attorneys, small business owners, middle managers, and their spouses. Tom Harris and Don Roberson led the steering committee that served as the CPA's official voice and coordinated the activities of neighborhood chapters formed around churches, PTAs, and subdivisions. The gendered division of labor within the antibusing movement reflected the dominant social patterns of the postwar suburbs, as fathers represented the CPA in public meetings and media appearances and mothers performed almost all of the daytime activities such as answering queries and advertising rallies. Publicity revolved around an informal communications network that included telephone chains, distribution of fliers in carpool lines and the parking lots of churches and shopping malls, and word-of-mouth on subdivision streets and across backyard fences. For a membership contribution of one dollar, the central office sent supporters "No Forced Busing" bumper stickers, lapel pins, and yard signs. CPA literature promised that "continuing expression of public opinion is the answer" and called for the tireless lobbying of elected officials, local newspapers, and television stations. With not even two months remaining before the busing deadline, the CPA's flexible and multifaceted approach sought above all else to forge a united community front through an antibusing consensus that would stiffen the resolve of their elected representatives. "Politicians—We Parents VOTE" read a sign at one rally, and despite the warnings of sympathetic leaders that the legal appeal represented the only viable option, Charlotte's no-longer-silent majority insisted that surely something more could be done.[21]

The developments during the volatile winter of 1970 demonstrated that from the local to the national level, political leaders were following rather than directing their organized and outraged middle-class constituents. In late February, the school board voted to make a formal appeal of the Finger

Plan, with the swing vote provided by racial moderates who expressed support for compliance but explained that white parents would accept only a ruling affirmed by the Supreme Court. In a coordinated action, the Charlotte Chamber of Commerce released its first official pronouncement since the beginning of the ten-month crisis, a vague resolution that expressed support for the judicial appeal and urged the legislative and executive branches of the federal government to formulate a national desegregation standard (which in current political parlance meant an official doctrine of neighborhood schools). In Washington, Democratic Senator Sam Ervin and Republican Representative Charles Jonas introduced bills to ban forced busing and establish freedom of choice as the national education policy. The two politicians also escorted a group of CPA leaders who flew to the nation's capital for private conferences with Vice President Spiro Agnew and Harry Dent, the powerful southern affairs adviser in the Nixon administration. The delegation reported that the White House was "eager to help," especially because more than seven hundred thousand students in eight southern states faced midyear desegregation deadlines, and similar antibusing movements had emerged in Denver and Los Angeles. A few days later, HEW secretary Robert Finch released a blistering statement that labeled Judge McMillan's decision constitutionally misguided and "totally unrealistic." One of the NAACP attorneys in the *Swann* litigation protested the "cruel irony that when an able and conscientious Southern federal judge has the courage to apply the Constitution to his home town, federal officials encourage defiance." The antibusing populists in the Silent Majority believed that, on the contrary, elected officials finally were beginning to respond to their pleas and demands.[22]

The suburban parents in Charlotte's antibusing movement sent a deluge of letters and telegrams to the White House, following the CPA's directive to "write the President every day." During the first two weeks of February alone, Richard Nixon received more than five thousand pieces of correspondence from residents of metropolitan Charlotte, many of whom directed the Silent Majority trope back at the politician they had voted for two years earlier. These white parents combined racial and class anxieties into a volatile outpouring of frustration, anger, confusion, and despair. "Mr. President, I need your leadership," wrote Reverend Edwin Byrd of the Third Presbyterian Church, which hosted one of the recent CPA rallies. "I love my country and I do not want to be a party of participating in a movement that would show disrespect to the principles of our great country, but . . . [the court order] is not fair and I do not believe that it is morally right." A physician from southeast Charlotte argued that busing would destroy the middle-class ambition to create an "environment in which children may be reared so that they may . . . [achieve] their maximum attainment of intellectual and moral development . . . . The thought that this course is un-American is simply untenable." A married couple from the southeast suburbs informed the president that they supported integration and believed that high-achieving black students deserved to attend the best white schools but warned that two-way busing would drive away affluent families and "bankrupt school system." Another southeast Charlotte resident demanded that the White House "come to the rescue of the silent majority who . . . has been pushed about as far as it will tolerate." "As a member of the silent majority," yet another white father wrote, "I have never asked what anyone in government or this country could do for me; but rather have kept my mouth shut, paid my taxes and basically asked to be left alone . . . . I think it is time the law abiding, tax paying white middle class started looking to the federal government for something besides oppression." Finally, a telegram from one CPA supporter contained a pithy warning: "We don't like a president that speaks out of both sides of his mouth at the same time."[23]

The White House responded with a major policy address on school desegregation, issued under Richard Nixon's signature on March 24, 1970. Although he reaffirmed the administration's commitment to the *Brown* decision, Nixon advanced a constitutional vision that embraced an inviolable principle of neighborhood schools, even when they reflected segregated housing patterns. In short, the president endorsed the viewpoint that most remaining school segregation in the metropolitan South, as in the urban North, resulted from de facto residential forces beyond the proper jurisdiction of the federal courts. Like the suburban antibusing movement, the Republican administration refused to accept the legal finding that the artificial distinction between de jure and de facto segregation obscured the official policies that produced educational and residential segregation and the logical remedy that a fully integrated school district should contain no single-race facilities. In addition to declaring that racial busing in urban districts exceeded the Constitution and would severely damage the institution of public education, Nixon adopted the conservative mantra that public schools should not be used for liberal social experimentation. He charged that certain federal judges had launched a "tragically futile effort to achieve in the schools the kind of multiracial society which the adult community has failed to achieve for itself." The White House policy statement, a political agenda presented in constitutional wrapping, closely echoed the color-blind stance of the CPA and clearly represented a direct response to the mobilized members of the Silent Majority. While civil rights groups responded with outrage, the administration promised to intervene in the *Swann* litigation on the side of the Charlotte-Mecklenburg school board. Chairman William Poe called the address a "fine, comprehensive statement that ought to get the nation back on the road to a workable integration policy." The *Charlotte Observer* accused the president of improperly pressuring the federal judiciary and formulating a cynical policy designed to shift the political heat for desegregation enforcement from the executive branch to the federal courts.[24]

One day after the White House announcement, Judge McMillan abruptly postponed implementation of the two-way busing order until the start of the next academic year in September. The conservative majority on the Fourth

Circuit Court of Appeals had already issued a temporary stay of the Finger Plan, and although the judge denied that external pressure had influenced his decision, the CPA responded with cautious optimism based on the belief that two months of grassroots protest by the Silent Majority had resounded all the way to the White House and the Supreme Court. "The order itself has not been changed one word," Don Roberson observed. "But it does show public opinion of the masses does make a difference, politically and judicially." Encouraged by the preliminary success at the national level, the CPA moved to secure formal power at the local level by challenging three liberal incumbents during the school board election held in the spring of 1970. Tom Harris led a CPA slate that employed extensive media advertising and mobilized a large network of volunteers behind a campaign for quality education achieved through color-blind assignment policies in a system of neighborhood schools. The antibusing candidates won the election with overwhelming support in the white working-class precincts of north and west Charlotte, but they failed to carry the affluent neighborhoods of Myers Park and secured only narrow margins of victory in the outer-ring suburbs that formed the CPA's organizational base. While the outcome ensured legal resistance by the school board, the voting returns also revealed substantial opposition in the middle-class suburbs of southeast Charlotte toward the politics of defiance. Future events would illustrate the difficulty for the CPA to maintain the allegiance of two disparate groups: (1) blue-collar families from north and west Charlotte that had placed their hopes in an organization dominated by white-collar professionals from the southeast suburbs and (2) upper-middle-class moderates from southeast Charlotte who disapproved of busing but also refused to endanger the public school system. As legal developments during the summer of 1970 brought the crisis to a climax, the suburban parents in the broad but loose antibusing majority found that they could no longer avoid the choice between maintaining their traditionally deep commitment to public education and resisting through a self-destructive boycott or a self-interested retreat to private schools.[25]

Class Fairness and Racial Stability

At the national level, the mobilization of the Silent Majority depended upon a populist discourse that obscured the divisions between working-class and middle-class white voters and defined Middle America through an identity politics based on taxpayer status, consumer rights, and meritocratic individualism. In both the political and judicial arenas, the busing battles of the 1970s appeared to represent a clear confrontation between "color-blind" conservatism and "race-based" liberalism. But at the metropolitan level, the links between social class and residential geography shaped not only the initial emergence of color-blind populism but also the ultimate outcome of race-conscious legal mandates. In many urban districts across the nation, the concentration of social change in struggling working-class and lower-middle-class white neighborhoods created a debilitating chain reaction: the defense of the integrity of white neighborhoods, the destabilization of school desegregation through residential flight, and finally, a national political consensus on the general failure of busing. In Charlotte, the leverage provided by the metropolitan school district and Judge McMillan's refusal to permit resegregation eventually transformed the populist ethos of the blue-collar white neighborhoods from a reactionary defense of residential segregation into a progressive demand for racial stability through equalization of the busing burden. Beginning in the fall of 1970, the actual implementation of two-way desegregation shattered the antibusing coalition established by the CPA and created bitter resentment in the white neighborhoods of north and west Charlotte toward the privileged status of the southeast suburbs. The legal mandate to maintain comprehensive school integration produced five years of turmoil in the New South metropolis, resolved only by a political compromise designed to achieve stable racial desegregation through policies of class integration and geographic fairness.[26]

Everyone in Charlotte assumed that the Supreme Court ultimately would decide the constitutionality of two-way busing, but the political strategy of the CPA depended on a judicial resolution before the September deadline. In May 1970, the Fourth Circuit Court of Appeals issued a ruling that Charlotte-Mecklenburg faced no legal obligation to address "an intractable remnant of segregation" in the inner-city ghetto and held that "busing is a permissible tool for achieving integration, but it is not a panacea." The appellate court vacated the Finger Plan and ordered Judge McMillan to balance the goal of racial desegregation against a "test of reasonableness" that included factors such as the cost, distance, and traffic involved in crosstown busing. All sides in the litigation immediately asked the Supreme Court to clarify the situation, and the CPA sent another delegation to Washington to lobby administration officials to request an emergency session. The climate of uncertainty, combined with the CPA's continued preparations for a school boycott, produced an emotional debate about the responsibilities of leadership in a community faced with the likely implementation of an unpopular integration plan. In July, the *Charlotte Observer* rebuked the city's leading politicians and businessmen by name and demanded an elite commitment to prepare citizens to meet the crisis "calmly and constructively" in the time-honored tradition of the Charlotte Way. A few days later, the school board, city council, and county commission responded with an extraordinary joint resolution: "Once the Supreme Court speaks out loud and clear and the community is told what is required of it, uncertainties will be dispelled and its leadership can effectively assert itself by uniting the people in support of our public schools." The Chamber of Commerce released a similar statement explaining that "no leadership, regardless of strength or good intentions," could prevent the civic chaos and racial conflict that would result from the forced transition to a busing plan of suspect constitutionality. Defiance was not in the nature or the twenty-year economic blueprints of the city's political and business elite, but they had never faced a populist uprising led by the middle-class white families who embodied the future in their vision of metropolitan prosperity. If not a supreme irony, it was at the least a notable turnabout for white southerners to be placing their last-chance hopes in the highest court in the land.[27]

On August 3, Judge James McMillan ruled that the two-way busing plan in Charlotte was "expressly found to be reasonable." In a stubborn and principled message to all of his critics, the judge declared, "If a constitutional right has been denied, this court believes that it is the constitutional right that should prevail against the cry of 'unreasonableness'. . . . Constitutional rights of people should not be swept away by temporary local or national public opinion or political manipulation." With the busing deadline only one month away, the CPA mounted an intense campaign to persuade the Supreme Court to intervene. More than one hundred thousand citizens signed a petition, headlined "FREEDOM IS ABOUT TO BE LOST," demanding that the White House rescue the Silent Majority. After the Supreme Court declined to issue a stay, stunned CPA leaders blamed the president personally for the betrayal of the "hard-core, solid bedrock Americans" who had placed him in office. During late August and early September, the CPA held nightly rallies throughout the white suburbs and urged all parents to boycott the schools in a nonviolent protest that would demonstrate the unworkability of busing to the Supreme Court. Neighborhood groups also assembled several new private schools for the white students reassigned to the traditionally black institutions, a maneuver that threatened the stability of the integration plan but also exposed serious socioeconomic and ideological divisions within the antibusing movement. After both Tom Harris and Don Roberson placed their children in private academies, white moderates denounced the boycott leaders for abandoning public education, and working-class members of the CPA bitterly complained about the sanctuaries available only "on the rich side of town." On the night before schools opened, ten thousand people attended a huge antibusing rally, the last major event that the CPA would ever organize. Protest leaders urged all white families to observe the boycott out of respect for the color-blind principle of the Constitution and the higher moral law of parental protection of innocent children. "We didn't come this far to look at D-day and turn chicken," Tom Harris promised. "We will . . . win this battle—maybe not tomorrow, but we hope to gain the attention of the United States on this tyrannical act perpetuated upon us."[28]

Beneath the surface of the antibusing revolt, Charlotte's longstanding commitment to legal compliance and public education came to the fore during September 1970. The League of Women Voters and the Interested Citizens Association (an interracial group of one thousand members formed to support full integration) mobilized to assist in the massive transition, and more than four thousand parents and students also volunteered their services. Ministers and religious groups in both the black and the white communities issued appeals for peaceful desegregation, and for the first time, the leaders of the downtown establishment abandoned the stance of neutrality and called for the acceptance of Judge McMillan's decision. On September 9, after more than a year and a half of legal maneuvering and political drama, the buses finally rolled both ways in Charlotte, from the suburbs to the inner city and back again. The integration formula involved substantial dislocations, with more than thirty thousand students assigned to new facilities, and the heaviest burdens falling on the paired elementary schools that exchanged black children in grades 1 to 4 and white children in grades 5 to 6. Although ineffective or shortlived in most parts of town, the CPA boycott achieved partial success in the schools located in black neighborhoods, after more than two thousand white students transferred to private schools to escape two-way integration. The consequent "tipping" process in a number of historically black facilities threatened gradually to undermine the stability of the entire desegregation plan because Judge McMillan had ordered the school board to take affirmative action to maintain a white majority in every facility. Overall, however, school attendance averaged more than 90 percent of projected enrollment, and white flight proved to be minimal in the suburban schools, now fully integrated along the 70–30 districtwide ratio. "The war's not over yet," Don Roberson promised, and many families in Charlotte continued to hope that the Supreme Court would overturn the busing mandate. Although continued hostility toward two-way integration remained at the crux of the legal impasse, and Charlotte's saga was still far from finished, the center had held after all.[29]

The trajectory of the busing crisis in Charlotte from 1969 to 1970 reveals a dynamic portrait of the evolving attitudes toward racial integration in the middle-class suburbs of the Sunbelt South. The dire predictions that busing would shatter the moderate consensus for public education proved to be false, and almost all white students in the metropolitan district now attended facilities where the black population represented between one-fifth and one-third of the total enrollment. Sixteen years after the *Brown* decision, white liberals in the New South metropolis openly championed the principle of comprehensive racial integration and sharply criticized the antibusing movement without fear of social retribution. The most progressive activists in Charlotte endorsed the social benefits of pluralism and the moral imperative of redistributive racial policies with a confidence that would have been impossible a decade earlier. The much larger number of white moderates strongly preferred neighborhood schools and supported the appeal of the court order, but they also refused to countenance defiance of the law and chose compliance after the tactics of delay failed. The nearly complete marginalization of open segregationist sentiment owed much to the public sphere constructed by the *Charlotte Observer* but also to the politics of color-blind respectability embraced by white-collar CPA leaders who banished racial extremists to the fringes of the antibusing movement. The local and national critics who charged that all antibusing families were simply segregationists misunderstood the spatial interplay between race and class among the many white parents who accepted one-way desegregation of suburban neighborhood schools but remained unapologetically hostile toward two-way integration into black residential areas. But ideological conservatives also had learned to couch their distaste for integration in a color-blind interpretation of *Brown* and started to mobilize against what they considered a full-scale assault by federal judges and liberal bureaucrats to turn local schools into laboratories for social experimentation. The first stage of Charlotte's busing crisis demonstrated that the era of political consensus for legal segregation had definitely ended but that the debate over the meaning of racial integration had only just begun.

The CPA sincerely believed that local sentiment could influence desegregation case law, which represented a reasonable interpretation of the haphazard and decentralized enforcement of the *Brown* decree throughout the previous decade and a half. During 1970, CPA leaders helped found the National Coalition of Concerned Citizens, a confederation of local antibusing groups that claimed one million members and designated the Supreme Court's *Swann* hearings as national days of prayer. The CPA also intervened in the *Swann* litigation to guarantee that its color-blind constitutional interpretation would receive full appellate consideration. The group's legal brief argued that busing innocent children for racial balance violated the 1964 Civil Rights Act and constituted a "complete and amazing reversal of *Brown v. Board of Education*." With flowery language, the suburban antibusing movement insisted that the "true and essential meaning" of the landmark 1954 decision guaranteed that "children shall be free to attend public schools without regard to their race or color . . . . Does not this case present a clear and appropriate context in which to lift high again that guiding light?" In April 1971, ruling in *Swann v. Charlotte-Mecklenburg*, the Supreme Court rejected this argument and unanimously upheld the discretionary authority of Judge McMillan. The decision approved busing as a legitimate remedy of affirmative action for state-sponsored racial discrimination, but the justices also explicitly embraced the Fourth Circuit's "reasonableness" doctrine, a philosophical retreat from their own recent mandate to eliminate the dual school system "root and branch." Along with many other observers, the *New York Times* concluded erroneously that *Swann* applied only to the South, based on the misguided but still prevalent notion that racial segregation in the rest of the nation resulted only from de facto housing patterns. Although the NAACP celebrated *Swann* as a milestone in the battle against residential segregation, the Supreme Court's affirmation of the reasonableness standard guaranteed that *Brown* would have different meanings in different school districts throughout the nation. Judicial and political opposition to expansive integration remedies lurked between the lines of the vague opinion authored by Chief Justice Burger, who would soon lead a reconstituted Court to a formal policy of suburban protection in almost all metropolitan regions except the already consolidated school districts of the Sunbelt South.[30]

The *Swann* mandate, although elusive as a national standard, unambiguously validated Judge McMillan's discretionary authority to supervise comprehensive integration in Charlotte. After 1971, the CPA faded from the scene as a political force, but it would take three more arduous years and a new grassroots movement by ordinary white and black citizens to overcome the legacies of the antibusing uprising and break the impasse between the district court and the municipal leadership. In the wake of the Supreme Court defeat, the Charlotte-Mecklenburg school board adopted a new formula that concentrated the busing burden in the black and white neighborhoods on the north side and west side and that effectively exempted the affluent families in the southeast suburbs from two-way integration. Judge McMillan observed that the "class discrimination" in the busing plan created neighborhood schooling "protectorates" in Myers Park and other politically connected and economically powerful areas, but he suspended judgment on the question of whether obvious socioeconomic inequality would produce unconstitutional racial resegregation. In 1971, former CPA members from north and west Charlotte organized a new organization called Citizens United For Fairness and filed a class-action lawsuit against the school board to demand equalization of the busing burden across the metropolis. Wilson Bryan, the leader of the coalition of neighborhoods, explained that "we have been told by some black people that this is a similar type of discrimination to what they experienced over a period of years." During the next two years, the class and geographic discrimination in the busing formula destabilized the entire desegregation climate by accelerating white flight from the schools and neighborhoods of north and west Charlotte. Ultimately, a group of blue-collar neighborhood activists and sympathetic white liberals forged an informal but extremely symbolic alliance with African American parents to demand busing equalization through the abolition of class favoritism toward southeast Charlotte.[31]

In 1973, Judge McMillan ordered the school board to combat the tipping phenomenon in the historically black schools of northwest Charlotte by reassigning white students from the most affluent sections of the southeast suburbs. The judge dismissed predictions of massive white flight to private schools as an "apparent assumption that the people who live in south and east Mecklenburg are more self-centered or racially intolerant than the people who are already experiencing 'bussing.' " Chairman William Poe responded that "originally, the judge was talking about racial integration. Now he is talking about socioeconomic integration, and the law says nothing about that . . . . It's just the judge's idea of how society ought to be." The school board filed another appeal, with the three CPA members providing the deciding votes, but by this time, many leaders and citizens alike had decided that the long crisis must come to an end. In the fall of 1973, the League of Women Voters and the Chamber of Commerce collaborated in the formation of a coalition of procompliance organizations called the Citizens Advisory Group (CAG), which forged a rough consensus for a new integration plan that revolved around the twin pillars of class fairness and racial stability. In the winter of 1974, the judge declared the school board to be in default and empowered CAG to devise a busing formula that would produce a permanent resolution. In the school board elections that spring, three supporters of CAG defeated a slate of antibusing challengers, providing conclusive evidence that an exhausted majority of the community now supported the policy of full compliance through equitable desegregation. In the summer, the reconstituted board of education worked with CAG to submit a good-faith proposal that distributed the busing burden more evenly throughout the metropolis and pledged to take active steps to safeguard against resegregation. "We have frankly sought stability by consciously giving to every neighborhood some reason to be unhappy," William Poe remarked. "It's an odd way to gain stability, but it does show some promise."[32]

Charlotte's busing crisis culminated in a genuine political settlement, proving not only the power of the law to reshape the educational patterns of a large metropolitan district but also the myriad ways in which local people could influence the implementation of a judicial decree. Judge McMillan deactivated the *Swann* litigation in the summer of 1975, after warning the school system that it remained under an affirmative action mandate to ensure stable racial integration throughout the county. "I really think this is a more fair plan, but I don't like it," one mother from a wealthy Myers Park neighborhood remarked. "I didn't think it was fair that the young black children got most of the busing in the past, while ours haven't been bused . . . . My son, I guess, has accepted it more than I have." "Fair-minded people will not abandon the school system just because everything isn't favorable to their special interests," a liberal white father from north Charlotte promised. "I believe most people are fair if given the chance, and that our leaders have failed in their responsibility to encourage the best of our instincts and have sometimes inflamed the worst." Although around ten thousand students, representing about 20 percent of the total white enrollment, departed from the public schools during the five-year period of busing turmoil, Charlotte-Mecklenburg still combined a greater degree of racial desegregation with a higher degree of popular support than most other urban districts in the nation. After 1974, when the Supreme Court decision in *Milliken v. Bradley* halted the NAACP drive for metropolitan school desegregation plans, black and white liberals in Charlotte's countywide system maintained control of the school board and continued to champion comprehensive integration. Not surprisingly, the achievement forged during the divisive busing battles soon became incorporated into the booster vision of Charlotte as the prosperous, progressive embodiment of the latest New South. In 1984, a Republican crowd even responded with awkward silence after Ronald Reagan denounced court-ordered busing as a failed liberal program that "takes innocent children out of the neighborhood school and makes them pawns in a social experiment that nobody wants." The *Charlotte Observer* rebuked the president: "Charlotte-Mecklenburg's proudest achievement of the past 20 years is not the city's impressive new skyline or its strong, growing economy. Its proudest achievement is its fully integrated public school system, . . . shaped by caring citizens who refused to see their schools and their community torn apart by racial conflict."[33]

DÉJÀ VU

During the 1990s, a new antibusing movement called Citizens for a Neighborhood School System emerged in the sprawling suburbs of Charlotte-Mecklenburg, where many upper-middle-class residents had relocated from outside the South, drawn by the dynamic economic growth of the Sunbelt metropolis. White parents once again began denouncing two-way busing, demanding color-blind assignment policies, and defending the residential privileges of neighborhood schools. A leader of the resurgent antibusing movement even insisted that the one-way busing of low-income students into affluent neighborhoods damaged the self-confidence of poor pupils and hampered the educational opportunities of their high-scoring suburban classmates, an unabashed defense of class exclusivity and socioeconomic segregation that extends far beyond the original rhetoric of the CPA. A liberal white activist responded that "as a long-time resident who remembers what life was like in this part of the world before desegregation, I have no patience with the current crop of carpetbaggers seeking to undo thirty years of progress for their own convenience." In 1997, a white parent named Bill Capacchione filed a federal lawsuit challenging the race-conscious admissions formula in Charlotte-Mecklenburg's magnet schools, after his daughter failed to gain entrance to a facility established specifically for the purpose of achieving integration without mandatory busing. The case came before District Judge Robert Potter, appointed as James McMillan's successor by President Reagan, at the behest of Republican Senator Jesse Helms. As a local school parent three decades earlier, Potter had participated in the antibusing movement of the CPA. Now, on his own initiative, the judge expanded the litigation to include a wide-ranging review of whether Charlotte's race-conscious assignment policies violated the equal protection clause of the Fourteenth Amendment. On September 9, 1999, Potter rejected arguments by the NAACP and the school board that the historical burdens of residential segregation remained relevant in the present, and he ordered the district to undertake a comprehensive reconfiguration based on the color-blind mandate of the Constitution.[34]

The dominant ethos of American suburbia has always idealized the present and celebrated the future at the expense of any critical reflection on the past. During the 1970s, metropolitan Charlotte grudgingly acquiesced in the two-way busing order but never implemented a collective housing remedy that addressed the causes instead of the symptoms of residential segregation: the public policies that simultaneously constructed the southeast suburbs and contained the northwest ghetto. Throughout the next quarter century, the unswerving embrace of the Sunbelt growth ideology and the centrifugal consequences of subsidized sprawl exacerbated the spatial gulf between the central city and the exurban fringe, while the mobility

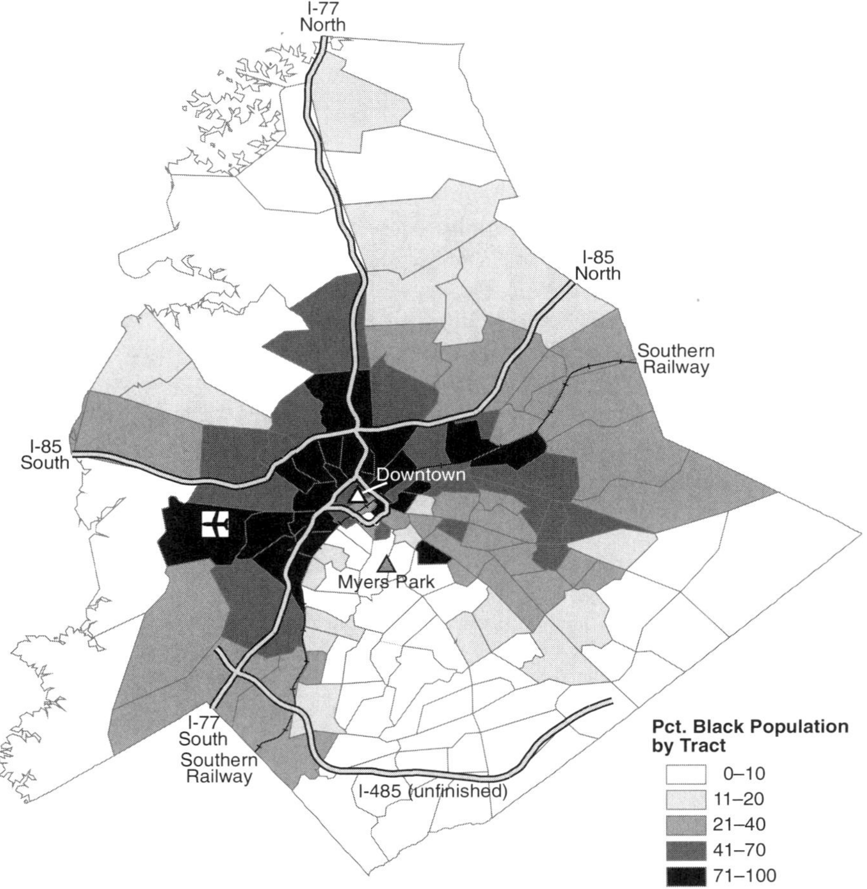

Figure 10.2 Charlotte Map 2000: Distribution of the Black Population of the City of Charlotte and Mecklenburg Country, 2000, by Census Tract. Thirty years after the busing crisis began, the northwest Charlotte ghetto displayed high levels of residential segregation by race and family income, while suburban migration by middle-class black families had produced a substantial degree of housing integration in the northern, eastern, and western section of Mecklenburg Country. The older annexed suburbs and newer upper-middle-class developments of southeast Charlotte-Mecklenburg remain overwhelmingly white. The I-485 beltway, scheduled to encircle the city by 2010, symbolizes the public policies that have subsidized the spread of suburban sprawl throughout Mecklenburg Country and into the metropolitan region beyond.

Source: U.S. Census Bureau, 2000 Census of Population and Housing.

of an expanding black middle class sharply increased the hypersegregation by race and income in Charlotte's poorest neighborhoods (see figure 10.2). On the national stage, the forces set in motion by the original uprising of the Silent Majority undermined the spatial and socioeconomic remedies necessary to confront widespread patterns of metropolitan inequality. Ultimately, the reliance on the NAACP and the judicial branch to devise, implement, and enforce the nation's desegregation policies illustrated the absence of a political coalition willing to address the suburban fusion of racial and class segregation or even to acknowledge that this represented a New American Dilemma at all. The CPA failed to prevent court-ordered busing in Charlotte, but the campaign of middle-class warfare launched in the subdivisions of Mecklenburg County played a central role in the realignment of national politics and the consequent judicial evolution toward a color-blind ideology that embraced the dual doctrines of suburban neighborhood autonomy and white racial innocence. Judge Potter's 1999 decision represents less an ironic example of desegregation case law coming full circle and more an illustration of the persistent politicization of the law itself. "Forced busing . . . is doomed to failure," CPA leader Tom Harris promised in 1970, "because people in a democracy will, in the end, have the final word." The events in Charlotte during that turbulent year sparked the legal drive for metropolitan school desegregation and propelled the grassroots backlash of the Silent Majority onto the national stage. Thirty years later, the waves that had once rippled outward came crashing back.[35]

Notes

Matthew D. Lassiter is an assistant professor in the history department at the University of Michigan. This article is excerpted in part from *The Silent Majority: Suburban Politics in the Sunbelt South* (Princeton University Press, 2006; used with permission). His research interests include metropolitan, political, and social history.

1. Dr. Robert M. Diggs to President Richard Nixon, January 31, 1970, series 1.1, folder 494, Charles Raper Jonas Papers, Southern History Collection, University of North Carolina at Chapel Hill (hereinafter Jonas Papers).
2. *Charlotte Observer*, July 12, 1975. On the busing literature, see Gary Orfield, *Must We Bus?:* Segregated Schools and National Policy (Washington, DC: Brookings Institution, 1978); J. Harvie Wilkinson III, *From Brown to Bakke: The Supreme Court and School Integration, 1954–1978* (New York: Oxford University Press, 1979); Robert A. Pratt, *The Color of Their Skin: Education and Race in Richmond, Virginia, 1954–89* (Charlottesville: University Press of Virginia, 1992); Richard A. Pride and J. David Woodard, *The Burden of Busing: The Politics of Desegregation in Nashville, Tennessee* (Knoxville: University of Tennessee Press, 1985); Jeffrey A. Raffel, *The Politics of School Desegregation: The Metropolitan Remedy in Delaware* (Philadelphia: Temple University Press, 1980); Eleanor P. Wolf, *Trial and Error: The Detroit School Segregation Case* (Detroit, MI: Wayne State University, 1981); David J. Armor, *Forced Justice: School Desegregation and the Law* (New York: Oxford University Press, 1995); James Bolner and Robert Shanley, *Busing: The Political and Judicial Process* (New York: Praeger, 1974); Nicolaus Mills, ed., *Busing U.S.A.* (New York: Teachers College Press, 1979); Paul R. Dimond, *Beyond Busing: Inside the Challenge to Urban Segregation* (Ann Arbor: University of Michigan Press, 1985); Raymond Wolters, *The Burden of Brown: Thirty Years of School Desegregation* (Knoxville: University of Tennessee Press, 1984); Lino A. Graglia, *Disaster by Decree: The Supreme Court Decisions on Race and the Schools* (Ithaca, NY: Cornell University Press, 1976); R. Stephen Browning, ed., *From Brown to Bradley: School Desegregation, 1954–1974* (Cincinnati, OH: Jefferson Law Book Company, 1975); Gary Orfield, Susan E. Eaton, and the Harvard Project on School Desegregation, eds., *Dismantling Desegregation: The Quiet Reversal of Brown*

v. Board of Education (New York: New Press, 1996). A sampling of contemporary opinion on the busing controversy can be found in Davison M. Douglas, ed., *School Busing: Constitutional and Political Developments*, vols. 1–2 (New York: Garland, 1994).

3. Dan T. Carter, *The Politics of Rage: George Wallace, the Origins of the New Conservatism, and the Transformation of American Politics* (New York: Simon and Schuster, 1995); Carter, *From George Wallace to Newt Gingrich: Race in the Conservative Counterrevolution, 1963–1994* (Baton Rouge: Louisiana State University Press, 1996). The historical literature on Sunbelt economic development and the political science scholarship on regional electoral realignment have paid more attention to the suburban South; see, for example, Bruce J. Schulman, *From Cotton Belt to Sunbelt: Federal Policy, Economic Development, and the Transformation of the South, 1938–1980* (New York: Oxford University Press, 1991); Schulman, *The Seventies: The Great Shift in American Culture, Society, and Politics* (New York: Free Press, 2001); Carl Abbott, *The New Urban America: Growth and Politics in Sunbelt Cities* (Chapel Hill: University of North Carolina Press, 1981); David R. Goldfield, *Cotton Fields and Skyscrapers: Southern City and Region, 1607–1980* (Baton Rouge: Louisiana State University Press, 1982); Numan V. Bartley, *The New South: 1945–1980* (Baton Rouge: Louisiana State University Press, 1995); Earl Black and Merle Black, *Politics and Society in the South* (Cambridge, MA: Harvard University Press, 1987); Black and Black, *The Rise of Southern Republicans* (Cambridge, MA: Harvard University Press, 2002).
4. Lisa McGirr, *Suburban Warriors: The Origins of the New American Right* (Princeton, NJ: Princeton University Press, 2001).
5. Arnold R. Hirsch, "Massive Resistance in the Urban North: Trumbull Park, Chicago, 1953–66," *Journal of American History* 82 (September 1995): 522–50; Thomas J. Sugrue, "Crabgrass-roots Politics: Race, Rights, and the Reaction Against Liberalism in the Urban North, 1940–1964," *Journal of American History* 82 (September 1995): 551–86; Gary Gerstle, "Race and the Myth of the Liberal Consensus," *Journal of American History* 82 (September 1995): 579–86; Ronald P. Formisano, *Boston against Busing: Race, Class, and Ethnicity in the 1960s and 1970s* (Chapel Hill: University of North Carolina Press, 1991). Also see Hirsch, *Making the Second Ghetto: Race and Housing in Chicago, 1940–1960* (Cambridge, UK: Cambridge University Press, 1983); Sugrue, *The Origins of the Urban Crisis: Race and Inequality in Postwar Detroit* (Princeton, NJ: Princeton University Press, 1996); Jonathan Rieder, *Canarsie: The Jews and Italians of Brooklyn against Liberalism* (Cambridge, MA: Harvard University Press, 1985); J. Anthony Lukas, *Common Ground: A Turbulent Decade in the Lives of Three American Families* (New York: Knopf, 1985). In his study of Macomb County, Michigan, Stanley B. Greenberg maintains the focus on Reagan Democrats while adopting an explicitly suburban perspective; *Middle-Class Dreams: The Politics and Power of the New American Majority* (New Haven, CT: Yale University Press, 1996), revised and updated edition.
6. My central historiographical point is that much of the new grassroots political history focuses too narrowly on blue-collar Reagan Democrats or white-collar conservative ideologues. The "color-blind" ideology that percolated in the Charlotte suburbs overlapped with Republican conservatism but expanded far beyond a right-wing base, and it ought to be understood as part of an emerging bipartisan defense of suburban autonomy and middle-class residential privilege not simply from within a teleological narrative of the New Right. For an example of this kind of class-based, postpartisan analysis of the ethos of the suburban Sunbelt, see Mike Davis, *City of Quartz: Excavating the Future in Los Angeles* (London: Verso, 1990), esp. chap. 3.

The class-conscious, color-blind uprising in Charlotte also previewed the suburban battles over court-ordered housing integration and school-funding equalization in states such as New Jersey and Connecticut; see David L. Kirp, John P. Dwyer, and Larry A. Rosenthal, *Our Town: Race, Housing, and the Soul of Suburbia* (New Brunswick, NJ: Rutgers University Press, 1995).

7. For community studies of the Charlotte busing crisis, see Davison M. Douglas, *Reading, Writing, and Race: The Desegregation of the Charlotte Schools* (Chapel Hill: University of North Carolina Press, 1995); Frye Gaillard, *The Dream Long Deferred* (Chapel Hill: University of North Carolina Press, 1988).
8. *Charlotte Observer*, September 12–13, November 6, 1968.
9. Paul Leonard, "Research Report," March 1970, folder 5, box 9, Leonard, "A Working Paper: Charlotte, An Equalization of Power Through Unified Action," April 22, 1970, folder 19, box 3; Julius L. Chambers Papers, University of North Carolina at Charlotte Library (hereinafter Chambers Papers), "Transcript of Hearing," March 10, 1969, pp. 29a–64a, "Transcript of Hearing," March 13, 1969, pp. 173a–219a, U.S. Supreme Court Records and Briefs, *Swann v. Charlotte-Mecklenburg*, 402 U.S. 1, No. 281 (hereinafter *Swann* Records). Also see *Charlotte Observer*, June 26, 1968, July 7, 1970, June 10, July 6, 1971; Thomas W. Hanchett, *Sorting Out the New South City: Race, Class, and Urban Development in Charlotte, 1875–1975* (Chapel Hill: University of North Carolina Press, 1998); Kenneth T. Jackson, *Crabgrass Frontier: The Suburbanization of the United States* (New York: Oxford University Press, 1985).
10. Pat Watters, *Charlotte* (Atlanta, GA: Southern Regional Council, May 1964); *Charlotte Observer*, January 30, 1970, July 17, 1974; Leonard, "A Working Paper: Charlotte, An Equalization of Power Through Unified Action," April 22, 1970, folder 19, box 3, "Memorandum of Decision" (District Court), July 14, 1965, folder 3, "Order" (Fourth Circuit), October 24, 1966, folder 4, box 1, Chambers Papers; "Mayor's Community Relations Committee Report to the Mayor and City Council," undated (ca. 1968), folder 12, box 1, Community Relations Committee Papers, University of North Carolina at Charlotte Library.
11. "Opinion and Order," April 23, 1969, 285a–323a, *Swann* Records; "Motion for Further Relief," September 6, 1968, folder 15, box 4, Chambers Papers. Statistics in "Desegregation of Charlotte-Mecklenburg Schools (1957–1970)," folder 13, box 2, series II, Frye Gaillard Papers, Southern History Collection, University of North Carolina at Chapel Hill (hereinafter Gaillard Papers); "Supplemental Findings of Fact in Connection With the Order of June 20, 1969," June 24, 1969, p. 459a, *Swann* Records. Quotations in James B. McMillan to Mordecai C. Johnson, April 2, 1970, folder 19, box 3, Chambers Papers; Pat Watters, "Charlotte, North Carolina: 'A Little Child Shall Lead Them,' " *The South and Her Children: School Desegregation 1970–1971* (Atlanta, GA: Southern Regional Council, 1971), pp. 29–30.
12. *Charlotte Observer*, May 6, 1969, March 7, 1970; *Charlotte News*, May 3, 10, 1969. Also see interview with William Overhultz, August 20, 1997, Charlotte, North Carolina; interview with Sharon McGinn, August 20, 1997, Charlotte, North Carolina.
13. *Charlotte News*, May 3, 1969; *Charlotte Observer*, April 25, May 1–3, 6, 19, 1969; "Defendants' Response to Motion for Further Relief," October 11, 1969, pp. 609a–615a, *Swann* Records.
14. *Charlotte Observer*, May 14, 1969; Augustus E. Green to Charles R. Jonas, May 12, 1969, series 2, folder 827, Jonas Papers.
15. *Charlotte Observer*, May 6–8, 10, 13, July 2, 8, 1969;William C. Westbrook to Charles Jonas, May 7, 1969, folder 827, William R. Overhultz to Jonas, May 14, 1969, folder 828, series 2, Jonas Papers; Senator B. Everett Jordan to Overhultz, May 15, 1969, and Senator Sam J. Ervin Jr. to Overhultz, May 15, 1969, in William R.

Overhultz Papers, Charlotte, North Carolina, copies from private collection in possession of the author.

16. Watters, *South and Her Children*, pp. 29–33.
17. *Charlotte Observer*, May 14, 20, 28, July 10, 24, 28, August 2–4, 1969; *League of Women Voters Bulletin* (August 1969), League of Women Voters of Charlotte, North Carolina Papers, Public Library of Charlotte and Mecklenburg County (hereinafter Charlotte LWV Papers); NAACP Statement to the School Board, July 31, 1969, folder 18, box 30, Kelly Alexander Papers, University of North Carolina at Charlotte Library; "Amendment to Plan for Further Desegregation of Schools," July 29, 1969, pp. 480a–490a, "Report in Connection with Amendment to Plan for Further Desegregation," August 4, 1969, pp. 491a–524a, "Order," August 15, 1969, pp. 579a–592a, *Swann* Records.
18. Concerned Parents Association (CPA), "A Struggle for Freedom Is Coming," n.d. (ca. 1970), "Concerned Parents Association, Beverly Woods, Bulletin," February 26, 1970, folder 20, box 14, Fred Alexander Papers, University of North Carolina at Charlotte Library; *Charlotte Observer*, December 10, 1969; Don Roberson to Charles R. Jonas, December 5, 1969, Jonas to Roberson, December 15, 1969, folder 827, series 2, Jonas Papers.
19. "Amendment to Plan for Further Desegregation of Schools," November 17, 1969, pp. 670a–679a, "Report Submitted in Connection with the November 13, 1969 Amendment to Plan for Further Desegregation," pp. 680a–690a, "Opinion and Order," December 1, 1969, pp. 698a–716a, "Order," December 2, 1969, p. 717a, "Transcripts of February 2 and 5, 1970, Proceedings," pp. 749a–804a; "Order," February 5, 1970, pp. 819a–839a, *Swann* Records; *Charlotte Observer*, January 28–30, February 1–4, 6, 1970.
20. *Charlotte Observer*, February 6–9, 13, 1970; CPA, "A Struggle for Freedom Is Coming," n.d. (ca. 1970), folder 20, box 14, Fred Alexander Papers; CPA Flier, n.d. (ca. 1970), Overhultz Papers, copy from private collection in possession of the author.
21. "Concerned Parents Association, Beverly Woods, Bulletin," February 26, 1970, folder 20, box 14, Fred Alexander Papers; *Charlotte Observer*, February 9–10, 13, 1970; Overhultz interview; McGinn interview.
22. "Notice of Appeal," February 25, 1970, pp. 904a–905a, *Swann* Records; Adam Stein to Robert Finch, February 25, 1970, folder 17, box 3, Chambers Papers; *Charlotte Observer*, February 20, 25; March 2, 1970. External developments in *Charlotte Observer*, February 2, 7, 13, 1970.
23. Rev. Edwin O. Byrd to Richard Nixon, February 2, 1970, Dr. Robert M. Diggs to Nixon, January 31, 1970, Mr. and Mrs. Isaac L. Falkner to Nixon, February 2, 1970, Thomas E. Conder to Nixon, February 5, 1970, Charles Jonas to Conder, February 10, 1970, James E. McDavid Jr. to Jonas, February 5, 1970, A. D. Prentiss to Jonas, February 13, 1970, folder 494, series 1.1, Jonas Papers. Also see *Charlotte Observer*, February 2, 1970; CPA flier, n.d. (ca. 1970), Overhultz Papers.
24. *New York Times*, March 25–26, 1970; *Charlotte Observer*, March 25, 31, 1970.
25. "Order," March 25, 1970, pp. 1255a–1258a, "Court of Appeals Granting Stay Order," March 5, 1970, pp. 922a–924a, *Swann* Records; *Charlotte Observer*, May 3, June 1, 1970; *Washington Post*, March 30, 1970.
26. On populism and class, see Michael Kazin, *The Populist Persuasion: An American History* (New York: Basic Books, 1995). On the general failure of busing plans to address class inequality and residential stability, see Orfield, *Must We Bus?*, pp. 279–360; Formisano, *Boston against Busing*, pp. 222–39; Jennifer L. Hochschild, *The New American Dilemma: Liberal Democracy and School Desegregation* (New Haven, CT: Yale University Press, 1984).

27. "Opinion of Court of Appeals," May 26, 1970, pp. 1262a–1304a, *Swann* Records; Joint Governing Bodies of Charlotte-Mecklenburg, "Statement and Resolution," July 13, 1970, folder 22, box 17, Fred Alexander Papers; *Charlotte Observer*, June 9–10, July 5, 14–15, August 22, 1970.
28. "Memorandum of Decision and Order," August 3, 1970, pp. Br. A1–Br. A38, *Swann* Records; *Charlotte Observer*, August 9, 16, 18, 26, 28, September 4, 6, 9, 13, 18, 22, 1970; *New York Times*, September 10, 1970.
29. "Interim Report on Desegregation," September 23, 1970, *Swann* Records; *League of Women Voters Bulletin*, September 1970, folder 3, box 5, Charlotte LWV Papers; *Charlotte Observer*, August 4, 10, 16, 18– 19, 23, October 15, November 6, 1970; September 3, 1971; *New York Times*, October 7, 1970.
30. *Swann v. Charlotte-Mecklenburg Board of Education*, 402 U.S. 1 (1971); "Motion for Expediting of Case," July 28, 1970, and other CPA legal documents in folders 14–15, box 1, Benjamin S. Horack Papers, University of North Carolina at Charlotte Library; *New York Times*, April 21–22, 1971. National Coalition of Concerned Citizens in *Charlotte Observer*, August 31, 1970; *Norfolk Virginian-Pilot*, September 12–13, 1970. Also see Bernard Schwartz, *Swann's Way: The School Busing Case and the Supreme Court* (New York: Oxford University Press, 1986); Wilkinson, *From Brown to Bakke*, pp. 134–50.
31. "Pupil Assignment Plan, 1971–1972," June 25, 1971, folders 23–24, box 5, William Waggoner Papers, University of North Carolina at Charlotte Library (hereinafter Waggoner Papers); *Swann v. Charlotte-Mecklenburg Board of Education*, 328 F. Supp. 1346 (1971). On the Citizens United For Fairness, see CUFF Petition, August 1971, folder 8, box 9, Chambers Papers; *Swann v. Charlotte-Mecklenburg*, 334 F. Supp. 623 (1971); *Charlotte Observer*, July 15, August 3–6, 26, 1971. On the interracial alliance, see "Northeast Concerned Parents" Flier, May 21, 1973, personal papers of Julian Mason, copy in author's possession; Frye Gaillard, "Charlotte's Road to Busing," *Christianity and Crisis* (October 29, 1973), pp. 216–19; *Charlotte Observer*, May 23, 31, June 2, 4, 1973; interview with Julian and Elsie Mason, April 29, 1998, Charlotte, North Carolina.
32. *Swann v. Charlotte-Mecklenburg Board of Education*, 362 F. Supp. 1223 (1973); "Notice of Appeal," July 16, 1973, folder 29, box 4, Waggoner Papers; *Charlotte Observer*, June 16, 20, 1973. On Citizens Advisory Group, see Minutes of the Charlotte-Mecklenburg League of Women Voters, January 6, September 7, 1972, folder 1, box 8, Charlotte LWV Papers; interview with Marylyn Huff, April 27, 1998, Black Mountain, North Carolina; Citizens Advisory Group, "Report to Court," April 22, 1974, folder 11, box 3, Chambers Papers; *Charlotte Observer*, November 13, 21, December 1, 5, 1973; "Order," April 3, 1974, folder 7, "Charlotte-Mecklenburg Schools: A Joint Proposal for School Assignment of Students," July 9, 1974, folder 6, box 1, Margaret Whitton Ray Papers, University of North Carolina at Charlotte Library. School board election in *Charlotte Observer*, May 8, 1974. Stability comment in William Poe speech to the Louisville Chamber of Commerce, "Five Years of Busing in Charlotte," September 25, 1974, folder 12, box 2, series II, Gaillard Papers.
33. *Charlotte Observer*, July 10–11, 1974, July 12, 1975, October 9, 1984. Statistics and aftermath in "Desegregation of Charlotte-Mecklenburg Schools (1957–1970)," folder 13, box 2, series II, Gaillard Papers; *Charlotte Observer*, February 7, June 9, 1974; Douglas, *Reading, Writing, and Race*, pp. 245–54; Gaillard, *Dream Long Deferred*, pp. 155–71. Also see *Milliken v. Bradley*, 41 L Ed 2d 1069–131; *Milliken v. Bradley: The Implications for Metropolitan Desegregation*, a Conference before the U.S. Commission on Civil Rights, November 9, 1974 (Washington: Government Printing Office, 1974).

34. "Beyond Busing" series, *Charlotte Observer*, posted April 5, 1997, at http://www.charlotte.com; Alison Morantz, "Desegregation at Risk: Threat and Reaffirmation in Charlotte," in *Dismantling Desegregation*, eds. Orfield and Eaton, pp. 179–206; *Charlotte Observer*, January 14, 1998; *New York Times*, September 11, 1999; comment by "Linda" posted January 11, 1999, at http://www.charlotte.com/observer/special/deseg/guestbook/.
35. "Deciding Desegregation" series, *Charlotte Observer*, January 13–17, 1999. Harris quoted in *Charlotte Observer*, February 6, 1970.

Other Articles Nominated for the 2006 Competition

Juliana Barr, "From Captives to Slaves: Commodifying Indian Women in the Borderlands," *The Journal of American History*, 92 (June 2005): 19–46.

Heather D. Curtis, "Visions of Self, Success, and Society among Young Men in Antebellum Boston," *Church History*, 73 (September 2004): 613–634.

Drew Gilpin Faust, " 'We Should Grow Too Fond of It': Why We Love the Civil War," *Civil War History*, 50 (December 2004): 368–383.

Mark Fiege, "The Weedy West: Mobile Nature, Boundaries and Common Space in the Montana Landscape," *Western Historical Quarterly* (Spring 2005): 22–48.

Wayne Flynt, "Religion for the Blues: Evangelicalism, Poor Whites, and the Great Depression," *The Journal of Southern History*, 71 (February 2005): 3–38.

Sarah A. Gordon, " 'Boundless Possibilities': Home Sewing and the Meanings of Women's Domestic Work in the United States, 1890–1930," *Journal of Women's History*, 16 (June 2004): 68–91.

Julia Grant, "A 'Real Boy' and not a Sissy: Gender, Childhood and Masculinity, 1890–1940," *Journal of Social History*, 37 (Summer 2004): 829–851.

Edward G. Gray, "Visions of Another Empire: John Ledyard, an American Traveler Across the Russian Empire, 1787–1788," *Journal of the Early Republic*, 24 (Fall 2004): 347–380.

Masumi Izumi, "Prohibiting 'American Concentration Camps,' " *Pacific Historical Review*, 74 (May 2005): 165–194.

Russell A. Kazal, "The Interwar Origins of the White Ethnic: Race, Residence, and German Philadelphia, 1917–1939," *Journal of American Ethnic History*, 23 (Summer 2004): 78–131.

Robert W.T. Martin, "Reforming Republicanism: Alexander Hamilton's Theory of Republican Citizenship and Press Liberty," *Journal of the Early Republic*, 25 (Spring 2005): 21–46.

Eric W. Plaag, " 'Let the Constitution Perish': *Prigg v. Pennsylvania*, Joseph Story, and the Flawed Doctrine of Historical Necessity," *Slavery and Abolition*, 25 (December 2004): 76–101.

Louis Pollack, "Race, Law and History: The Supreme Court from 'Dred Scott' to '*Grutter v. Bollinger*,' " *Daedalus* 134 (Winter 2005): 29–41.

Martha Robinson, "New Worlds, New Medicines: Indian Remedies and English Medicine in Early America," *Early American Studies*, 3 (Spring 2005): 94–110.

Sarah N. Roth, "The Mind of a Child: Images of African Americans in Early Juvenile Fiction," *Journal of the Early Republic*, 25 (Spring 2005): 79–109.

Lucy E. Salyer, "Baptism by Fire: Race, Military Service, and U.S. Citizenship Policy, 1918–1935," *The Journal of American History*, 91 (December 2004): 847–876.

Gunja SenGupta, "Elites, Subalterns, and American Identities: A Case Study of African-American Benevolence," *American Historical Review*, 109 (October 2004): 1104–1139.

Thomas Weiss, "Tourism in America before World War II," *Journal of Economic History*, 64 (June 2004): 289–327.

Meghan K. Winchell, " 'To Make the Boys Feel at Home': USO Senior Hostesses and Gendered Citizenship," *Frontiers*, 25:1 (2004): 190–212.

Chiou-Ling Yeh, " 'In the Traditions of China and in the Freedom of America': The Making of San Francisco's Chinese New Year Festivals," *American Quarterly* 56 (June 2004): 395–420.

Index